"Dee Molenaar never has made any secret of his lifelong love affair with Mount Rainier and, as a geologist, an artist and a mountaineer of international repute, he knows 'The Mountain' as few men could."
—*Seattle Post-Intelligencer*

"(Dee Molenaar) beautifully describes the mountain he knows so well."
—*Seattle Times*

"Considered the definitive book on Mount Rainier's climbing history."
—*Bellingham Herald*

"For climbers or those who like to read about their exploits, this detailed history of Rainier mountaineering is a must."
—*Sunset* magazine

"The definitive history of mountaineering on Rainier, and an interesting read for climbers and non-climbers alike."
—*San Francisco Examiner*

"The seminal work on climbing Rainier, featuring history, pioneering ascents and lore. The grim section on tragedies provides a sobering education on mistakes to avoid."
—*The Denver Post*

"Anyone who loves the mountains—climbers, hikers, just gazers, or readers who thrill to the adventure of the more virile and venturesome—should enjoy *The Challenge of Rainier*."
—*Eugene Register-Guard*

"(Mount Rainier) has cast its spell over many people . . . The magnitude of that spell is aptly conveyed by Dee Molenaar."
—*The Oregonian*

D0210662

THE
CHALLENGE
OF
RAINIER

A record of the explorations and ascents,
triumphs and tragedies,
on the Northwest's greatest mountain

DEE MOLENAAR

THE
MOUNTAINEERS
BOOKS

THE MOUNTAINEERS BOOKS
*is the nonprofit publishing arm of The Mountaineers Club,
an organization founded in 1906 and dedicated to the exploration,
preservation, and enjoyment of outdoor and wilderness areas.*

1001 SW Klickitat Way, Suite 201, Seattle, WA 98134

First edition 1971
Second edition 1973
Third edition: first printing 1979, second printing 1984, third printing 1987, fourth
printing 1991, fifth printing 1993, sixth printing 1995, seventh printing 1997, eighth
printing 2000, ninth printing 2005

Published simultaneously in Great Britain by Cordee, 3a DeMontfort Street,
Leicester, England, LE1 7HD

Manufactured in the United States of America

Design by Audrey Meyer
Sketches by the author
Cover Design: Mayumi Thompson

Cover photograph: *Mount Rainier, small tarn on the Tatoosh Range.* Photo by Dee
Molenaar
Frontispiece: *Rainier from north, showing relatively simple route up Emmons-
Winthrop Glaciers on left, more challenging "Nordwand" of Willis Wall in center,
and Ptarmigan Ridge on right. Winthrop Glacier in foreground.* Photo by Austin
Post.

Library of Congress Cataloging in Publication Data
Molenaar, Dee.
    The challenge of Rainier.
    Bibliography: p.
    Includes index.
    1. Mountaineering—Washington (State)—Rainier, Mount—History. 2. Rainier,
Mount—Description. I. The Mountaineers, Seattle. II. Title.
GV 199.42. W22R345   1979   917.97'78   79-14923
ISBN 0-916890-70-8

 Printed on recycled paper

To BILL BUTLER
Who for over 30 years was
wherever help was needed on the
mountain . . . a legend in his time . . .

And to the many others—
Comrades of the Snows

GREETINGS

Across the width of the continent I stretch out my hand in greeting to
you, Mountaineers, who are privileged to dwell within sight of the
snow-crowned monarch of Puget Sound, and to feel daily the ennobling
influence of his sublime presence. As I roam through the breadth of this
land of ours and behold so many good people living their lives amid
uninspiring surroundings, in cities of man-made sordidness, I feel
impelled to tell them of that glorious vision upon which ever and anon
you rest your eyes. More than once in the past few months has it been
my pleasure to bid my friends in imagination to the flowering parks and
crevassed ice fields and the mist-wrapped heights of Mount Rainier.
More than once have I felt the revelation of it dawn upon them and
awaken the desire to behold once, just once, though it take the savings of
a life-time, that which you see every day. To be envied indeed you are for
your wonderful source of inspiration: were it possible for all other people
to share it with you! No doubt the time will come when a pilgrimage to
Mount Rainier shall be esteemed among the most precious joys, the most
coveted privileges which a citizen of this country may hope to realize for
himself or his fellows.

Francois E. Matthes
The Mountaineer, 1915

Contents

Foreword

One of the strongest impressions I have about people in the Northwest is the deep feeling they have for "the mountain." For most, Mount Rainier forms a backdrop to the daily activities of city life. Less frequently it is a place to bring guests to picnic; to look for marmots, goats, elk, and bear, or to glory in the spectacular displays of alpine wildflowers.

For hardier souls, this mountain is a place to walk. Some tramp the lowland trails seeking solitude. Others trudge under heavy packs determined to complete the Wonderland Trail which encircles the mountain. A smaller number move ever upward and fewer still reach the summit.

For some, however, Mount Rainier has held fascination of almost magnetic quality. Dee Molenaar, who has for 30 years returned again and again to the mountain, exemplifies this bond formed between man and the mountain. In part, this bond exists because he has given so freely of himself that others could experience the joy of knowing this grand mountain. As climber, mountain guide, and Park Ranger, he acquired the physical skills and emotional stamina to travel the breadth and height of the mountain. Over the years a close and lasting relationship, which binds men who have shared danger, developed between the author and dozens of other Northwest climbers. He knows intimately many of the men whose names fill these pages. He is scientist, artist, and writer. His knowledge of the mountain and his sensitivity to its beauty, its moods, and its character have given him a unique capacity to write this book.

This history of climbing on Mount Rainier is important in several ways. It is first and most importantly an accurate and detailed record of the many men who challenged a great mountain. It is a history of success, failures, joys, and despair. It also provides a chronology of the evolution of snow and ice mountaineering during the past three decades. It is interesting to trace the development of climbing techniques and the improvement in equipment. Since the span of this history is brief and includes current as well as early efforts on Mount Rainier, readers of all ages will see familiarity both of climbers and of routes. These things deepen one's insight into the forces that influence and motivate the climbers of today.

As I have listened to the mountaineers of Dee Molenaar's generation, I have sensed the camaraderie that is peculiar to a small group who have shared common purpose. Today several thousand people make a summit attempt each season. For those of us in this larger but less cohesive group, Dee Molenaar's book is a rich supplement. Through its pages we can know better the men who pioneered the routes we follow today. Few of us will attempt a winter climb or try a north-side route. However, the accounts of those who have undertaken these more arduous and hazardous adventures will have added meaning as we relate them to our own climbing experiences.

I hope this book will be read and studied by many novice climbers with the realization that it can be a valuable tool as well as an enjoyable experience. From its pages one's judgment can be sharpened. Sound judgment before and during a climb is the climber's most valuable resource. Recently the National Park Service relaxed the climbing regulations on the mountain. This was done in the belief that the primary responsibility for an individual's well-being lies with the person himself. The park staff can assist the climber with accurate and up-to-date route information, weather forecasts, and other specific data. They can assess the climber's capacity and counsel with him to the best of their ability. However, after he has set forth, his training, skill, physical condition, equipment, companions, and personal judgment are the assets on which he must rely. To this end the author has provided a distinct contribution to mountaineering safety.

This book recounts the mountain as being both hospitable and hostile, both savage and gentle, both inviting and foreboding. Dee Molenaar has created a most intriguing and readable account of men who have challenged Mount Rainier. For all those who wish to know the mountain better, *The Challenge of Rainier* will be a rewarding experience.

JOHN A. TOWNSLEY
Superintendent, Mount Rainier National Park,
1967–1972

January 6, 1970

Preface

. . . In various travels and expeditions in the territory, I had viewed the snow-peaks of this range from all points of the compass, and since that time having visited the mountain regions of Europe, and most of those of North America, I assert that Washington Territory contains mountain scenery in quantity and quality sufficient to make half a dozen Switzerlands, while there is on the continent none more grand and imposing than is presented in the Cascade Range north of the Columbia River.

LIEUTENANT A. V. KAUTZ
Overland Monthly, May 1875

As the dominant landmark of the Pacific Northwest, Mount Rainier (Tacoma, Takhoma, or simply, The Mountain) early became a magnet to those desiring to grapple with snow and ice at high altitude. Rising to 14,410 feet above the marine waters of Puget Sound less than 45 miles distant, the massive, glacier-covered volcano is without rivals. The surrounding foothills have only a few minor rock peaks rising to slightly more than 6000 feet and other volcanic cones on far horizons are little competition for the rugged alpine grandeur and great height of Rainier.

Compared to mountaineering in the Alps, which may be said to have begun with the ascent of Mont Blanc in 1786, climbing for its own sake started much later in America. The initial explorations of our mountains came in the line of duty as settlers migrated westward, generally preceded by Army units. Following the establishment of military posts on the lower Columbia River and on Puget Sound at Forts Nisqually and Steilacoom came the first probes into the Cascade foothills. In 1833 the earliest recorded visit to the area now included in Mount Rainier National Park was made by Dr. William Fraser Tolmie, who sought herbs for medicinal use at Fort Nisqually.

Following the first widely reported ascent to the highest point of Rainier by Stevens and Van Trump in 1870, the summit became the goal of many adventurers. Most of the early ascents were from Paradise Valley, following the Stevens-Van Trump route along the ledges of Gibraltar Rock. After the formal establishment of a professional guide staff at Paradise Valley in about 1905, hundreds of tourist-climbers were led to the top via the "Gib Route." Miraculously, few serious accidents marred the opening decades of the 20th century; oldtimers recall ascents to the crater, often 20–30 people on one rope, in the years before and immediately following World War I.

Not until the catastrophe of 1929, when a guide and client met their deaths during the slide of a five-man party into a crevasse high on the Gibraltar route, was official action taken recognizing the climbing hazards on Rainier. The slip on the steep and icy upper slopes of the mountain and subsequent evaluation of the tragedy by Park authorities and the guide service resulted in the initial requirement that all guides have their boots fitted with crampons and be equipped with ice axes; however, the use of alpenstocks by guide clientele was permitted until after World War II.

Eventually Northwest climbers sought new slopes to conquer on Mount Rainier. In the 1930s a few hardy mountaineers began exploring steeper, more challenging ridges on the seldom-visited northern and western flanks. The Depression-era completion by the WPA and CCC of graded roads to Mowich Lake and the Puyallup River also allowed easier access to these sides of the Park.

Few other areas of the 48 states within weekend distance of a large population center offered such opportunities for development of climbing techniques for snow and glacier travel. The Mountaineers of Seattle and Mazamas of Portland grew in membership as they sponsored group climbs on Northwest volcanoes. In 1935 The Mountaineers became the first club in the United States to offer classes in mountain-climbing techniques. Through the experience gained by local climbers on Northwest peaks, the club was able to introduce neophytes quickly to the technical concepts and philosophy of safe mountaineering. The Climbing Course idea gained rapid popularity, as did the formation of small local climbing clubs. Today, nearly every city and college in the country near a mountain range or rock cliff has a climbing club and offers a course in mountaineering patterned after that started by The Mountaineers.

The proximity of Mount Rainier to Fort Lewis gave many soldiers and officers a chance to ski and climb in the Park during the early months of World War II. When military authorities envisioned battles being fought in the mountains of Europe, an Army unit was assigned to develop techniques for mass movement and action in alpine terrain. In 1942 a small detachment from Fort Lewis, composed primarily of well-known Northwest skiers, was temporarily stationed at Paradise Valley. Eventually the 87th Mountain Infantry Regiment was organized and later the 86th and 85th MIRs; the three regiments became the 10th Mountain Division. First on the slopes of Rainier and then at Camp Hale, Colorado, soldiers received training in techniques of mountain and cold-weather warfare which later was put to use in the Aleutian and Italian campaigns.

Immediately following World War II, and paralleling the technical growth of climbing, came an awareness of the need for a general indoctrination in mountaineering safety, and in the techniques of search and rescue. In 1948 the Seattle Mountain Rescue Council was formally organized among local climbers under the dedicated leadership of Mountaineers Wolf Bauer, Ome Daiber, and Dr. Otto Trott. Similar rescue groups later evolved in climbing areas in all parts of the United States and today they are nationally organized as the Mountain Rescue Association.

As climbing techniques advanced and as mountaineers looked farther afield for greater challenges in the higher and more remote ranges of the world, Rainier provided an ideal, easily accessible training ground. Many American expeditions to major Alaskan, Yukon, Andean, and Himalayan peaks in the past 20 years have included members who gained experience there. It was only logical that in September 1962 the American Mount Everest Expedition should select Rainier for its "shake-down cruise." All five Americans who reached the top of Everest in May 1963 had previously served as guides or had climbed on the mountain.

In view of the century-long influence of Mount Rainier on American mountaineering, it seems fitting that this compilation of the climbing record be made. This is not a treatise on mountaineering techniques, however, nor an attempt to "grade" the difficulty of routes on the mountain by the modern system applied to rock climbs. Rainier is primarily a snow-and-ice mountain; its rock is generally described as unstable and rotten "crud." It is not practical, therefore, to grade the ascents and routes by the number and types of pitons placed, or by the steepness, shape, and length of pitches scaled. Yet, Rainier is not a "simple mountain, without guile"—those who have climbed it the most are also those who have the greatest respect for its many moods.

At many times in the past 15 years this has been a sorely tested labor of love, as my typewriter scrambled to keep pace with the accelerated rate of exploration and, sadly, of an increasing accident rate. Occasionally, to keep abreast of The Action and each new decade-generation of climbers, I have joined in mopping-up operations on the peak and hopefully have continued to learn something new about the mountain and of the men and women who climb.

But it also has been a rewarding project. The research into musty club annuals and albums, and contacts with libraries and historical societies have brought to life the people of bygone days who in their time similarly were absorbed by the challenge of Rainier. The yellowing pages of the past have carried me vividly across terrain that is still much the same today. On several happy occasions I have interviewed old-timers all but forgotten or, unfortunately, never known by the present generation. My visits with Len Longmire and Miss Ella McBride linked me with the 1890 era as they clearly recalled details of their ascents with such personages as Miss Fay Fuller and Professor Edgar McClure.

Some of my early climbing companions have long since hung up their heavy iron crampons and nailed boots and now utilize their axes for garden work. Perhaps the pace was too wearying or the spread of middle years encouraged more sedentary pursuits. But it also has been good to meet old companions still on the trail. Some have found the elixir of youth and are doing climbs today they wouldn't have considered years ago. Perhaps, after a person has worried about age through his forties and finds nothing has changed, in his fifties, when the competitive parameters of the sport no longer mean so much, he finally learns the full enjoyment of mountaineering.

DEE MOLENAAR
Port Orchard, Washington
September, 1970

Postscript, 1997:

The continuing saga of "Mount Rainiering" has called for periodic updates of the climbing history and related tabulated statistics and graphs, through subsequent editions of the book. Updated information has been included in pertinent footnotes and in the Addendum (beginning on page 317), including tabulations (pages 324 and 346) and graph (page 325).

—D. M.

Acknowledgments

The compilation and interpretation of information covering both significant historical events known to many and personal experiences shared by a few necessarily requires both a borrowing from existing publications and records and a solicitous probing into the memories of countless individuals. This documentation of the mountaineering highlights of more than 100 years could not have been completed without the ready response by innumerable climbers, rangers, and guides to the questionnaires I circulated over the past 12 years. Not only were my inquiries answered in full but many people stepped forward to provide additional material and moral support.

Many oldtimers generously offered personal anecdotes, both verbal and written, and photographs that "tell it like it was" in the early days. Of particular help, starting with those farthest in the past, were Miss Ella McBride (age 100 when interviewed in 1963) and Len Longmire (age 93 in 1962); both are now gone. Next came George V. Caesar, climber of the early 1900s who still submits photos and anecdotes of his many explorations—he has sufficient data for a book of his own; Joseph T. Hazard, early chief guide at Paradise and author of several mountaineering books; Jean Landry, with valuable details and photos of his 1922 winter ascent; Miss Lulie Nettleton, for her gift of back numbers of *The Mountaineer* and *Sierra Club Bulletin* which provided information on early climbing history of the mountain; and the guides and climbers of the 1920–40 era—Ray Atkeson, Hans Fuhrer, Wesley Langlow, Harry B. Cunningham, Leon H. Brigham, Frank "Swede" Willard, Bill Butler, J. Wendell Trosper, Arnie Campbell, Ome Daiber, Wolf Bauer, Jack Hossack, Gene Jack, Val Comstock, Paul Shorrock, and Don Woods—some of these men are still active in the hills.

Those of more recent vintage who contributed information are Fred Beckey, Charles Bell, Bill Boulton, Dean Caldwell, Ed Cooper, Chuck Crenchaw, Dan Davis, Hal Foss, Gary Frederickson, Mrs. George Gilbert, Don Gordon, Dusan Jagersky, Glenn Kelsey, Eugene Kiver, Dave Mahre, Dick McGowan, Maynard Miller, Cornelius "K" Molenaar, Paul Myhre, Lee Nelson, Bill Prater, Gene Prater, Barry Prather, George Senner, Ray Smutek, Herb Staley, Fred Stanley, Tom Stewart, Joe Vance, Mrs. Len (Judy) Waller, Chuck Welsh, Jim and Louie Whittaker, Jim Wickwire, and Del Young.

I was given access to historical files in the National Park library and the office of the Chief Ranger. Park personnel over many years cooperated fully in annually supplying statistics on summit climbs and reports of accidents. Especially helpful were Norman Bishop, Dwight Hamilton, Clyde Lockwood, and George Peters.

Annual journals published by mountaineering clubs provided the substance of various ascents and the details of routes. Notably valuable were the *American Alpine Journal, The Mountaineer,* and *Sierra Club Bulletin. Summit,* the internationally distributed monthly mountaineering magazine, provided much of current interest on the mountain. Mimeographed club annuals of the Cascadians (Yakima) and Alpine Roamers (Wenatchee) supplied stories of first ascents by some of their more energetic members, most of whom also are members of the Sherpa Climbing Club.

In particular I acknowledge the detailed information given by Aubrey L. Haines in *Mountain Fever,* published by the Oregon Historical Society. This fine book I recommend without reservation to those desiring a meticulously researched and fascinatingly documented narrative of pre-1900 climbs and explorations. The 255-page volume covers both the mountaineering exploits and political events which led to the 1899 establishment of Mount Rainier National Park. Haines' encouragement in my task of extending the record to the present was greatly appreciated.

I am grateful for the permission granted for use of material from books published by the following companies: E. P. Dutton and Company, Inc., for passages from *Starlight and Storm* by Gaston Rebuffat, as translated by Wilfrid Noyce and Sir John Hunt; and Superior Publishing Company and Josef Scaylea for a passage from Scaylea's book, *Moods of the Mountain.*

Besides those from my personal file, the photos came from many sources: the National Park Service museum at Longmire, Rainier National Park Company in Tacoma, and personal collections of climbers and guides—many of the latter's photos were given them by unidentified companions and clients and in such cases it has been impossible to provide proper credit. The excellent aerial photographs are by Austin S. Post of the U.S. Geological Survey.

Line drawings and watercolors made in 1895 by C. C. Maring were supplied by Maring's daughter, Edith Maring Willey of Bremerton, an outstanding artist in her own right.

Critical reviews of the manuscript helped shape the final product. For these I am grateful to Dwight R. "Rocky" Crandell, Mark F. Meier, Donal Mullineaux, and Donald Richardson of the U.S. Geological Survey; Norman Bishop, Park Naturalist of Mount Rainier National Park; John M. Davis, Mike Layton, Tom Miller, and Harvey Manning of The Mountaineers; and Jim Wickwire of the Sherpa Climbing Club. Thanks also are due Marion Helmer for her patience in deciphering my scribblings on the first rough draft during many hours of manuscript typing, and to Peggy Ferber for her typing—and her critique—of the final draft.

Certainly the greatest acknowledgment must go to the moral support and patience of my wife Colleen and my children during the final 2 years of this project. Only a family with a mad two-fingered hunt-and-peck typist at the helm can fully appreciate the countless sacrifices required to see completion of the manuscript, sketches, and photographic work.

PART ONE *THE CLIMBING
ENVIRONMENT*

1 Park Approaches
and Trail Viewpoints

As long as I live, I'll hear waterfalls and birds sing.
I'll interpret the rocks, learn the language of flood, storm, and
avalanche.
I'll acquaint myself with the glaciers and wild gardens,
and get as near the heart of the world as I can.

JOHN MUIR

The entrance stations at the four corners of Mount Rainier National
Park are easily reached on asphalt-surfaced highways. Approximate
mileages to the Park entrances, visitor centers, and campgrounds from
major cities are given below:

	Seattle	Tacoma	Olympia	Portland	Yakima	Season
Nisqually Entrance	80	55	65	150	120	Year around
Longmire	86	61	71	156	114	" "
Paradise	98	73	83	168	100	" "
Carbon River Entrance	65	40	67	174	128	May–Nov. 1
Ipsut Creek Campground	70	45	72	179	133	June 15–Nov. 1
White River Entrance	75	64	108	172	70	Year around
White River Campground	82	71	115	179	77	June 15–Nov. 1
Sunrise	89	78	123	186	84	June 15–Oct. 1
Stevens Canyon Entrance (near Ohanapecosh)	88	77	83	156	77	May 30–Nov. 15

The required registration for hikes on glaciers and for summit ascents during
the summer season may be made at the following ranger stations: Nisqually
Entrance, Paradise, White River Campground, and Ipsut Creek Campground.
Information on winter ascents may be secured by writing the Park Superintendent. Viewpoints of Mount Rainier's around-the-mountain, continually changing panorama can be had from numerous points along the Park's excellent trail
system. For those desiring easy hikes of 1.5 to 5 miles in 1 to 2 hours, the following trail viewpoints are recommended. But be aware that flood damage in 1996
has caused closure of the road beyond the Carbon River entrance.

South side: Pinnacle Peak (6562), or trail enroute. In the Tatoosh Range south of Paradise Valley, reached by 1.5-mile trail from parking area at Reflection Lakes (4900) on Stevens Canyon Road and a .5-mile scramble to the top of peak from end of trail. Excellent views of Rainier from trail.

West side: Gobblers Knob fire lookout (5500). Reached by 2.5-mile trail from Round Pass (4000) on West Side Road. Starts in deep forest, passes Lake George, then climbs woods and open meadows to lookout on rocky crest of ridge.

North side: Tolmie Peak fire lookout (5939), reached by 3.1-mile trail from Mowich Lake (4929).

East side: Dege Peak (7006). Via easy 1-mile trail from Sunrise road, halfway between Sunshine Point and Sunrise parking area. Excellent views of Emmons-Winthrop Glaciers.

2   The Volcano

*Of all the fire mountains which, like beacons, once blazed
along the Pacific Coast, Mount Rainier is the noblest.*

JOHN MUIR

*All the evidence available tends to show that Rainier is an extinct
volcano. It belongs, however, to the explosive type of volcanoes, of
which Vesuvius is the best-known example, and there is no assurance
that its energies may not be reawakened.*

ISRAEL C. RUSSELL, 1898

THE GEOLOGIC SETTING

Mount Rainier is among the highest and topographically most impressive of the world's volcanoes. Rising to an altitude of 14,410 feet a few
miles west of the crest of the Cascade Range and with the visible height
of the mountain 9000 feet above surrounding foothills, the peak can
be seen from over 100 miles in any direction.

The geologic story of Rainier probably began between 500,000 and
1,000,000 years ago in the Pleistocene Epoch of the Quaternary Period.

Before birth of the volcanic cone of Rainier, the Cascade Range in the area that is now in the National Park was characterized by mountains rising to 6000–7000 feet above sea level. The ridges and valleys descended toward the west from the crest of the range, which was probably at about its present location along the eastern boundary of the Park. The peaks were much more rounded than now, however, as they had not yet undergone the deep cutting of Pleistocene "Ice Age" glaciers.

The rocks of the pre-Rainier mountains are comprised of andesitic lavas and related volcanic debris, mudflows, siltstones, and sandstones. Intruded into these from deep below the surface during the uplift of the range in late Pliocene time were crystalline rocks—the light grayish granodiorite that today is exposed in the walls of deep valleys and along lower slopes of peaks at several places in the Park.

The growth of the Rainier volcano began with voluminous extrusions of andesite from a centrally located vent. The lava flowed down and partially filled the ancestral Mowich and Puyallup valleys and completely buried other depressions. As the valleys gradually were filled the topography of the range became smoothed over. Then the lava from the vent, alternating with explosive eruptions of ash, pumice, and other volcanic ejecta, slowly built a cone. The generally steady construction of the cone was locally modified by the destructive forces of streams cutting into the soft ash and volcanic debris, and the slopes were not symmetrically mantled by smooth flows of lava or falls of ash, as is the case with Fujiyama or Mount St. Helens. The main vent probably shifted its location slightly during the extrusions—evidence for this is seen by the varying angles and directions of the interbedded lavas, ash, breccias, and mudflows high on the flanks of the peak.

Erosion of the volcano by streams was accompanied by the considerably more effective cutting by glaciers that mantled the peak during the Pleistocene Epoch. Products of the snow that accumulated to great thickness during the Ice Age, the thick glaciers were intermittently destroyed wholly or in part during episodes of volcanic activity.

The present rugged configuration of the summit area of Rainier is a product of both glacial erosion and volcanic activity. At one time perhaps 1000 feet higher than at present, the summit was eventually destroyed by volcanic activity about 5800 years ago, resulting in a gigantic avalanche of the upper part of the mountain down the northeast flank (Crandell, 1969, p. 40), to form the Osceola Mudflow. Inside the great breach left at the top, 1½ to 2 miles across, the present cone with a new crater was formed about 2000 years ago, with a secondary crater soon after superimposed on the eastern rim of the first. During the building of the cone, coarse pumice was blown outward for many miles, settling in a thin layer across foothills beyond the base of the volcano. This activity, which occurred about 2000 years ago (Crandell and Mullineaux, 1967) marked the last significant eruption of Mount Rainier.

ASHFALLS

Mount Rainier must be considered a dormant volcano, with a potential for someday again coming to very active life. According to a study by the U.S. Geological Survey (Crandell and Mullineaux, 1967), radiocarbon dating of ages of various ash beds and mudflows on the lower flanks of the peak suggests volcanic activity has occurred intermittently over the past 10,000 years.

Eruptions of ash from the volcano have been less frequent than mudflows, but ash beds found in the Park indicate large explosive eruptions have occurred at irregular intervals of 1000 to 2000 years and lesser blowoffs of pumice have taken place more frequently. A recent study (Mullineaux, Sigafoos, and Hendricks, 1968) revealed the existence of pumice fragments scattered across moraines below the terminus of Emmons Glacier. The age of trees on the moraines older and younger than the pumice indicates the eruption occurred between 1820 and 1854. Perhaps this evidence provides greater credibility to Indian legends of earthquakes, fire, smoke and a "lake of fire" at the summit, and to eyewitness reports by white men of ash eruptions from the volcano during the 1800s (Hopson, Waters, Bender, and Ruben, 1962).

MUDFLOWS

Mudflows or debris flows have occurred on Mount Rainier with some regularity over the past several thousand years. Individually also known by the term *lahar*, which is defined as a rapid mass flowage of rock debris mobilized by water, and originating on the slopes of a volcano, mudflows have been the most devastating of natural phenomena emanating from the flanks of the mountain in Recent time. Evidence of at least 55 definable mudflows has been found on Mount Rainier in a recent study by the U.S. Geological Survey (Crandell, 1971).

The mudflows which continue to occur and are witnessed through the present day result from one or more of the following causes: (1) volcanic heating beneath or adjacent to glaciers, which melts the ice to form water in large quantities which then rushes down the valley floors, incorporating with it loose morainal and stream-laid material; (2) disintegration of volcanic rock, pumice, and ash—by the action of chemical solvents in the steam fumaroles high on the volcano—to form large masses of clay and other weakened materials which subsequently are shaken loose to avalanche down the peak; and (3) release of large volumes of water trapped in streams within or beneath a glacier—a disruption of the glacier's internal "plumbing." Such flows of water and rock debris generally are accompanied by deep erosion of the stream channels directly downstream from the glacier and a resulting deposition of a thick slurry of mud and boulders in the lower valleys.

The largest mudflow to originate on Mount Rainier, named the Osceola Mudflow (Crandell and Waldron, 1961), occurred about 5800 years ago. The geologists believe that the gigantic flow of mud and rock down the peak started as a result of rocks near the summit becoming weakened by hot volcanic fumes and solutions and being partly converted to clay. The mass of soft rock then was shaken by volcanic activity from its position high on the mountain above the present Emmons Glacier. It rapidly gained momentum and additional moisture through the incorporation of glacier ice as it slid down the northeast side of the mountain. The mass of mud, estimated to have a total volume of half a cubic mile, ran 45 miles down the valleys of both forks of the White River, then fanned out across the lowland beyond the present site of Enumclaw in a broad sheet 20 miles long and 3 to 10 miles across.

Evidence of another large mudflow (Crandell, 1969), probably of an age similar to, or slightly older than, the Osceola Mudflow, has been found in the area of Paradise Valley. The mudflow originated similar to the Osceola, as an avalanche near the summit, then shot down the south side of the peak in a mass thick enough to cross the area now occupied by the lower Nisqually Glacier and shoot up and over the ridge beyond. Deposits of this avalanche blanketed Paradise Valley with a yellowish-orange mixture of clay and rock; this material is found today in shallow cuts along trails and roads in the Paradise area. The huge rocks scattered on the meadows between the Visitor Center and Panorama Point came down with the mudflow; some remnants of the flow are found across Paradise Valley on top of Mazama Ridge.

Mudflows of significant magnitude have occurred over the time that white man has visited the mountain, and have affected different valleys at different times (Richardson, 1968). Several large mudflows originating at the terminus of the Nisqually Glacier have occurred within the memory of man, and most have resulted in heavy damage or destruction of the highway bridges that have been replaced after each large flood. After several such occurrences, the Park Service finally constructed the present concrete bridge in 1960. With its tremendous steel girder, the bridge has a span of 300 feet between piers and clears the river channel by 85 feet. Hopefully, this impressive structure will not be damaged by outburst floods in the foreseeable future.

The most spectacular mudflow witnessed by man in the Park is that which occurred in the Kautz Creek valley on October 2, 1947. An unusually heavy rainfall and snowmelt resulted in destruction of nearly a mile of the lower part of the Kautz Glacier. Fragments of the ice, combined with slurry flows of morainal debris in the terminal parts of the glacier, were temporarily blocked in the narrow box canyon downstream from the glacier. According to the report by the Geological Survey (Richardson, 1968), "Damming the box canyon compounded the destructiveness of the flood, for great masses of mud and debris were swept downstream in repeated surges that destroyed a large area of forest, as well as the Kautz Creek bridge, and covered part of the highway. The volume of material removed by the flood was estimated by the Park Service to be about 50 million cubic yards . . ." The old road that crossed Kautz Creek valley now lies buried beneath about 20 feet of mudflow debris. The Park Service has since placed a small exhibit at the site, which is surrounded by a large area of dead trees, killed through abrasion of their cambium layers by the passing mud and boulders, and by suffocation of their root systems by the fine-textured slurry.

Kautz Creek Mudflow, showing path of dead trees along Kautz Creek above confluence with Nisqually River.

Within recent years two outburst floods in the Tahoma Creek valley have been observed by man. Both originated in the terminal parts of South Tahoma Glacier and during long dry spells of mid-summer. On August 31, 1967, an outburst flood from the glacier extended down-valley several miles and cut a deep trough in the upper mile of the stream channel, causing the resulting thick slurry and debris to pile up downstream and inundate parts of the Tahoma Creek Campground. The mudflow is believed to have resulted from a disruption of the hydraulic system within or beneath the glacier, causing a sudden release of water held under pressure—it has been postulated that subglacial thermal activity melted the ice and provided the large volume of water (Crandell, 1971). Fortunately, the campground was not occupied at the time, having been temporarily closed by the Park Service on account of the dry weather and extreme fire hazard. Owing to concern over future recurrence of such floods, the campground was subsequently designated for picnic use only. It was therefore virtually empty when a second outburst flood came down the valley on August 21, 1970, about 3 years after the first flood. The initial flush of water from the glacier terminus was heard and observed by the fire lookout atop Gobblers Knob, but the only witness to the phenomenon in the valley below was Denny Cline of the U.S. Geological Survey. Cline, who ironically was conducting a water-supply study of the picnic area for the National Park Service, relates his experience as follows:

I had just finished eating lunch and was getting ready to head up the trail at about 1:05 p.m. when suddenly I became aware of a roaring sound that was increasing from up the valley. Having become particularly aware of the previous mudflow while studying its deposits in the former campground area, I immediately decided it was time to remove myself from the area with due haste. About 100 yards from my position at the car I saw trees, some a foot or more in diameter, beginning to fall toward me. I hopped into the car and got away fast. About 1½ miles below, on the West Side Road, I stopped to listen. By then the sound of the mudflow was very faint. A Park Service patrol vehicle carrying three young women—summer employees—came by and I advised them of the situation. The rangerettes made radio contact with Park Headquarters, then we headed our cars back up the road cautiously to check on other cars in the area. The mud covered the lower part of the picnic area to a depth of about 6 inches. Although my escape route was still clear, the area was covered by mud nearly to the exit road. Tahoma Creek was chocolate brown and was rolling boulders 2 feet in diameter down its new, much-braided channel. As the main flood apparently had passed its peak, I hiked up the trail beside the creek to the junction with the Wonderland Trail about 2½ miles upstream. There, the high water had taken out the footbridge over Tahoma Creek. The bridge was at the top of a bank of boulders about 10 feet above the stream, dangling there by the cable still tied to one end.

The combined effects of these readily observed mudflows, the periodic reports of steam issuing from various points on the flanks of the mountain, and the measurable microseismic activity beneath and around the peak, have both the scientists and the laymen gaining new interest—and some apprehension—in the future of the mountain. To date, however, there has evolved no method of accurately determining whether such phenomena indicate anything unusual in the sleeping habits of the old volcano.

LITTLE TAHOMA ROCKFALL

The ultimate destruction of Mount Rainier's Little Tahoma Peak by undercutting from both sides may be presaged by a series of massive rockfalls on its north face during the winter of 1963–64. On December 14, 1963 U.S. Forest Service rangers at the Crystal Mountain Ski Area reported hearing "a very loud, sharp boom" in the direction of Mount Rainier (Crandell and Fahnestock, 1965). Though the mountain was partially obscured by clouds at the time, gradual clearing in the afternoon provided views that showed a vast sweep of the Emmons Glacier below Little Tahoma covered by dark rock debris. A large section of the north face of Little Tahoma displayed a huge triangular pink scar where the avalanche originated. Formerly a series of lava cliffs alternating with strata of softer breccia, the scar today presents a nearly vertical wall 1500 feet high.

A study of the avalanche debris was made the following summer by members of the U.S. Geological Survey (Crandell and Fahnestock, 1965) and some startling facts were brought to light. At least seven separate rockfalls and avalanches distributed debris across the lower 3 miles of the Emmons Glacier and beyond its terminus. Attesting to the great energy expended, the material covering the ice was over 50 feet thick in places, and several boulders of tremendous size (the largest: 60 by 130 by 160 feet) were carried a distance of 3 miles. Apparently, as thick sheets of rock debris hurtled off the end of Emmons Glacier and began settling toward the valley floor, they compressed air beneath them which then created an "air cushion" on which the debris was transported down the valley at speeds estimated at 100–300 miles per hour. The volume of the avalanche deposits was estimated to be about 14 million cubic yards. Whether the rockfalls were triggered by volcanic activity in the flanks of the peak is not known; possibly a small steam explosion was all that was required to bring down masses of the weak rock.

Little Tahoma Rockfall, showing path of debris down Emmons Glacier and beyond terminus. Photographed in summer 1964, after avalanches of previous winter.

The combination of volcanic activity, glacial erosion, and rock slides has provided the rugged configuration which presents the major challenges of routes to the summit. The mountain probably is more rugged in form today than at any time in the past, and as erosion incessantly continues, the ridges will become sharper and the cirque walls steeper.

One of the most prominent erosional features of the volcano is Little Tahoma, the 11,117-foot spire rising between the Emmons and Ingraham Glaciers on the mountain's east flank. The slope of the beds of lava, ash, and mudflows on the peak gives a clue to a former surface of the volcanic cone at this point. "Little T" perhaps owes its survival to being strengthened somewhat by a resistant dike of lava that may be seen running vertically up its western (uphill) face. Other sharp spines on the flanks of Rainier that are remnants of dike systems radiating from the summit are Puyallup Cleaver (with its Tokaloo Spire near Tokaloo Rock) and the ridge crest separating Inter Glacier (below Steamboat Prow) from the Winthrop Glacier. The massive buttress of Gibraltar Rock also is a more resistant remnant of the earlier greater bulk of the mountain. Conversely, the parts of the volcano that were more easily eroded, or that were not later covered by ash and lava flows, are today displayed by the deep, high-walled cirques, the more spectacular of which are Willis Wall, Sunset Amphitheater, and the headwall of South Tahoma Glacier.

Characterizing the ridges, spires, and cirque walls is the distinctive feature of alternating layers of hard, resistant lava flows and soft, relatively unconsolidated layers of ash and breccia. In combination, these strata of differing strengths have produced a climbing terrain of vertical and overhanging walls of tougher rock separated by alcoves of softer materials. The continuing undercutting of the mountain's flanks by glacial ice and disintegration of the crumbling layers of volcanic debris have produced walls unsuitable for the techniques of rock climbing appropriate to firm granite, gneiss, and schist. On Rainier, the safest and most popular summit routes follow the glaciers or the crests of rock ridges—and these ridges are best climbed in early summer when the rock is more firmly welded together by the previous winter's snowpack.

The only flank of the peak now displaying a constructional rather than erosional form is that mantled by the broad ice streams of the Emmons and Winthrop Glaciers, where the slightly convex slopes descending from the youngest of the summit craters show the results of relatively recent lava flows. The glaciers have only begun their job of cutting into this slope—here and there minor indentations separated by low, isolated rock ribs show the start of future cirque and canyon features.

Immediately beyond the volcanic cone, the scouring of the mountain's flanks by the glaciers has developed a radiating topographic pattern of broad ridges separated by deeply trenched valleys. Below 4500 feet the valleys are in the humid transition zone, contrasting sharply with flowered meadows on the ridge crests between. The fairyland of meadows and parklands near timberline provides open views of the world of ice and rock high above, while from deep in the heavily forested valleys views of the dazzling, snow-clad mountain usually are picturesquely framed between the somber dark trunks and boughs of Douglas fir and western hemlock.

3 The Glacier System

Much of the heavy winter snowfall on Mount Rainier becomes part of the glacier mass of the peak; hundreds of years of snowfall have accumulated to form the largest single-peak glacier system in the 48 conterminous states. Over 35 square miles of ice, including 26 officially named glaciers and numerous unnamed permanent icefields, are distributed across the mountain's flanks and upper summit dome. Six major glaciers flow down the peak directly from the crater rim to well below timberline; eight others originate in vast cirques where they are nourished by the heavy snowfall at these mid-altitudes and by ice avalanching from steep slopes above and from overhanging fringes of the summit icecap.

Dr. Mark F. Meier, head of the U.S. Geological Survey's glacier-study program, and his colleague Austin S. Post have been engaged for many years in a study of the annual and long-term mass changes in the glacier systems of North America, including that on Rainier. Post's yearly flights over the flanks of the volcano, and resulting photographic coverage of the glaciers at the end of each summer season, together with other measurements by Geological Survey personnel on the Nisqually, Emmons, and Carbon Glaciers, have provided observations of the "health" of the mountain's ice mass (Meier, 1966). The accompanying map shows the location of the glaciers and the extent of ice recession since they were mapped in about 1913. Summarized below are a few interesting observations of the major glaciers.

The Nisqually Glacier and its contributary neighbor to the west, Wilson Glacier, together cover an area of 2.2 square miles. Although the bottom of the ice has not been mapped, the average thickness has been estimated to be about 330 feet. The volume of ice in this glacier system is therefore on the order of 750 million cubic yards, or about four times the capacity of Alder Reservoir downstream on the Nisqually River. The position of the terminus of the Nisqually Glacier, measured annually since 1918, was observed to recede nearly half a mile in a period of 34 years. By 1952 the glacier tongue was reduced to residual, stagnant ice. In 1953, however, an active ice front began to override the stagnant ice; advance of this front continued in recent years but at a diminishing rate. In 1966–67 the advance was about 80 feet; in 1967–68 it was only 40 feet.

The most-visited icefield on Rainier is the combined Paradise and Stevens Glaciers. Actually one ice mass with two stream outlets, the glacier originates on steep slopes below 9584-foot Anvil Rock and flows

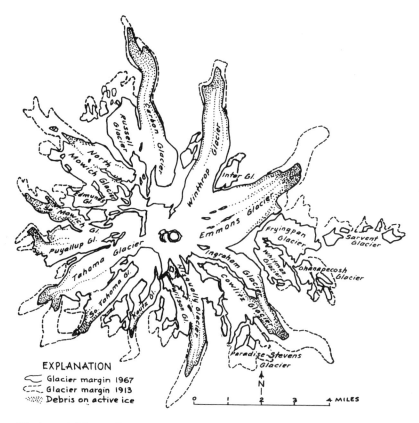

EXPLANATION
⌒ Glacier margin 1967
⌒ Glacier margin 1913
⋯ Debris on active ice

N

0   1   2   3   4 MILES

Glaciers of Mount Rainier, showing extent of recession between 1913 and 1967. Data for 1913 from F.E. Matthes; data for 1967 from M.F. Meier.

Terminus of Nisqually Glacier, 1967.

southeasterly to a shallow basin. This lower part of the glacier, relatively flat and inactive, has wasted away considerably since Stevens and Van Trump crossed it enroute to their successful climb of Rainier in 1870. Ice caves, a major tourist attraction on the mountain for many decades, are formed at the outlets of the two or three small streams that emerge from the stagnating glacier terminus. As of 1973, adventurous members of the Cascade Grotto of the National Speleological Society have mapped over 4 miles of tunnels beneath this lower stagnating reach of the disconnected glacier. Today the 3-mile trail from Paradise over Mazama Ridge and up the dusty ancient moraines to the caves is the most heavily traveled in the Park.

The Kautz Glacier terminus has retreated over a mile since first mapped in 1913. A major part of the retreat occurred in October 1947, when the terminal section was destroyed during several days of intense rainfall. Since 1959 the glacier has shown signs of readvance.

Until the early 1900s the termini of the Tahoma and South Tahoma Glaciers joined around Glacier Island. They since have retreated considerably, leaving a broad valley floor filled by morainal debris. The glaciers have advanced in recent years, particularly the South Tahoma Glacier which has come under scrutiny as a result of the mudflows of August 1967, '70, and '71. Since the 1967 mudflow the glacier has exhibited some "decay" in its lower portions and the advance has slowed considerably or come to a standstill.

The upper South Mowich Glacier, between 9500 and 11,000 feet, has been very active in recent years. In 1960 ice descending from Sunset Amphitheater was heavily crevassed and shattered from ice movement; in 1962 this zone of extreme crevassing was observed to have moved to the lower part of the glacier. As recently as 1968 new evidence of activity high on the glacier was observed in several large crevasses which extended all the way to upper St. Andrews Rock, completely cutting off the climbing route across the normally smooth slopes here.

The terminus of North Mowich Glacier retreated nearly 2 miles since the 1913 map was compiled.

The Carbon Glacier is heavily covered by morainal debris for most of its length; this protective mantle may account for the terminus retreating only about 1300 feet since 1913. Between 1959 and 1968 small advances have been recorded.

The Winthrop Glacier has undergone very little change during the period of aerial observations; its terminus is broad and marked by several moraines and areas of stagnant ice.

The Emmons Glacier, the largest on the mountain and in the 48 conterminous states, is as much as 1¾ miles in width and about 4 miles long. The glacier has retreated over a mile since 1913 due to stagnation and collapse of its terminal area; much of the stagnant ice remains along the northerly side, which has some large ice caves. Some minor activity at the terminus, first noticed in 1953, continues, but at a reduced rate. In December 1963 the spectacular rockfall from Little Tahoma Peak deposited enormous quantities of broken rock across the lower part of the Emmons Glacier. The debris buried the terminus so deeply it was impossible to map the edge of the active ice for some time afterward. In 1965 wrinkles were developing in the debris cover on the active terminus; by 1966 the terminus could again be clearly defined along most of its width. The terminus had advanced an average of 30 feet over its width during the year ending September 1967.

A most spectacular change in the Emmons Glacier occurred high on the mountain during the summer of 1969. The normally smooth and unbroken, slightly concave, part of the glacier from 13,000 feet down to 10,000 feet, left of the main climbing route, became severely broken into a mass of seracs and huge crevasses—in places the rocky bed of the glacier was exposed. The cause of the sudden activity has not been determined, but some conjecture attributes it to a warming of the glacier by subsurface volcanic heating. However, during the following winter, the heavy snowfall partially covered the massive breakup and this part of the glacier was again relatively smooth during the summer of 1970.

The only prominent *ogives* (dirt bands, Forbes Bands) on Rainier's glaciers are those on the Cowlitz Glacier below its confluence with the Ingraham Glacier. Ogives are a subject of considerable interest to glaciologists, and those on the Cowlitz Glacier are the only good examples noted in the United States south of Alaska. They have been found only on those reaches of glaciers immediately below icefalls, and are believed to result from differential ablation (downward melting) of ice as it passes through a steep icefall during summer and winter conditions. Other factors, such as differential pressure within the icefall, and winter snow versus summer dust, may also account for these alternating light and dark arcuate bands.

During the 1800s the ice on Mount Rainier covered about 55 square miles. By 1913 the area had shrunk to about 40 square miles and by 1950 was down to about 34 square miles. Since 1950 the glaciers have shown some advances and only minor retreats.

4 Snowfall and Weather

*If I wished to see a mountain or other scenery under the most
favorable auspices, I would go to see it in foul weather, so as to be
there when it cleared up; we are then in the most suitable mood, and
Nature is most fresh and inspiring. There is no serenity so fair as that
which is just established in a tearful eye.*

HENRY DAVID THOREAU

Located in the path of moisture-laden air moving from the Pacific
Ocean 120 miles to the west, Rainier receives most of its precipitation
as winter snows, which often reach depths of 15 to 20 feet at 5400-foot
Paradise Valley. The greatest snowfall is between 8000 and 11,000 feet;
above this altitude, decreasing precipitation and high winds result in
less total accumulation. The winter snowpack usually remains on the
ground until mid-July near timberline (about 6500 feet); however, variations occur from summer to summer and flower-covered meadows
sometimes dominate the alpine scene in late June. Above 9000 feet
much of the snow becomes part of the glacier mass; lower down, the
snow on glaciers generally melts to small patches, exposing the dusty
surface of the previous years' accumulations. Alpine trails are usually
open to foot travel by late July and free of snow until about mid-
October.

Summer temperatures at timberline range from 30° to over 70°F
(snowstorms are not uncommon) and higher on the peak may drop
well below freezing, but even at the summit seldom go below 0°F.

Paradise Inn in winter.

Winter temperatures at timberline range from 0° to 35°F; at the summit they can drop to −30°F or colder.

Cool, clear weather generally prevails from late July through September, with only an occasional storm of 1–2 days duration; high winds are rare at timberline in summer months. Periods of settled weather are frequently accompanied by morning fog that fills the lower valleys and covers the foothills up to 4000 or 5000 feet. The fog normally burns off through the day, then returns in evening. Summit climbers are often high above the surrounding "cloud-sea" in bright sunshine while hikers are walking meadow and forest trails in mist or drizzle. During late August and September there may be thunderstorms, particularly along the Cascade Crest and in the eastern section of the Park.

Cloud cap.

A phenomenon observed on all Northwest volcanoes, but attaining its greatest development on Mount Rainier, is the cloud cap, a lenticular cloud that settles on the upper part of the peak. Although sometimes a forerunner and indicator of an approaching storm, the cloud cap often occurs during periods of otherwise fair weather.

The cap is formed by an intimate rendezvous between warm, moisture-laden air from the Pacific Ocean and cold air over the mountain. Upon sweeping up and over the mass of Rainier, the air condenses to a characteristic mushroom-shaped cloud of fog, snow, or small ice particles. Although apparently static and "setting" on the upper 1000–3000 feet of the summit dome, in reality the cloud cap is dissipating on the leeward side as rapidly as it forms on the windward slope. Viewed through binoculars, the "innocent" cloud banner often may be noted flowing across the dome at speeds of 40 to more than 60 miles an hour.

Frequently the mushroom cloud forms in tandem, with as many as three or four separate and distinct lenticulars one above the other, or *en echelon* leeward of the summit.

Cloud caps en echelon.

To the climbing party, the presence or gradual formation of a cap can be taken as a signal to prepare for a possible descent, depending on the rate of growth of the cap and on weather and cloud conditions around the peak. Many parties have continued upward into a cap and experienced only minor discomfort and lack of visibility. The cloud cap may dissipate and re-form several times in a day; many mountaineers have turned around prematurely and returned to base camp, then looked back with frustration at cloudless upper slopes.

But the caps should never be taken lightly; often they have been factors in tragedies and near-tragedies on Rainier's upper slopes. Numerous parties have doggedly continued into a white-out of driving snow and sleet, hoping to gain protection in the crater, only to find the wind swirling from all directions and the landscape completely obliterated. Climbers frequently have been forced to retreat in a cap that descended with them; the unfortunates then pass downward through zones of snow, sleet, and driving rain before finding shelter well below timberline.

5 Mount Rainier Climbing Regulations

The regulations for climbing and backcountry travel in Mount Rainier National Park have undergone several changes in recent years, owing to increases in these activities and their effects on the Park landscape. For management purposes, in 1973 the Park was divided into three zones: trail zone, cross-country zone, and climbing zone. Backcountry use permits are now required for overnight travel and camping in these zones and are obtained at the nearest ranger station or by writing to the Park Superintendent.

The trail zone includes all trails in the Park, and camping is restricted to designated sites only, with their use being limited in the number and size of parties. The cross-country zone includes all areas which are below 7000 feet elevation and at least one-half mile from trails, roads, or other development. No open fires are permitted in the cross-country zone and only a small number of permits are issued for such use. The climbing zone, in general, includes all areas above 7000 feet elevation. Camp Muir and Camp Schurman are the only established camp areas in this zone. These and other high campsites—and climbing routes on the mountain—are also limited by permit in the number and size of parties. The restrictions on number and size of parties permitted in these zones has in some cases required advance reservations to insure permission for such travel and climbing during the busy summer season. For current information on regulations governing backcountry-use permits, the Park Superintendent or nearest ranger station should be contacted.

As of 1973, the climbing regulations in the Park are as follows:

1. Registration with the Superintendent is required prior to and upon return from climbing or hiking on glaciers or above normal high camps such as Camp Muir and Camp Schurman.
2. A person under 18 years of age must have permission of his parent or legal guardian before climbing above the normal high camps.
3. A party traveling above the high camps must consist of a minimum of two persons unless prior permission for a solo climb has been obtained from the Superintendent. Generally, the Park Superintendent recommends that parties consist of two rope teams of two persons each, or one rope team of three persons.

Due to the possible severity of weather conditions from October through April, climbers should plan trips during that period with an eye on 5-day weather forecasts. Special daily forecasts are available at all ranger stations, giving expected temperatures and winds at 5000, 10,000, and 15,000 feet and predictions of precipitation and clouds.

Over many years climbers familiar with conditions on Mount Rainier have developed a firm respect for the peak and for the necessity of being adequately clothed and equipped for any emergency that might arise. Listed below are the items of clothing and equipment recommended for both summer and winter climbs:

Summer Climbs:

    Full-frame steel crampons

    Lug-soled leather boots

    Clothing: wool for warmth in wet weather, down for cold weather, and wind-rain proof outer garments for outside protection

    Sleeping bag comfortable to 10°F

    Mittens and gloves

    Three prussik slings per person, or two ascenders (or rope clamps) plus one rope sling

    Ice axe

    First-aid kit

    Sunglasses or goggles, extra dark

    Sunburn-prevention material

    Food

    Hard hat

    Carabiners, two per person

    Rope, equal in strength to 7/16-inch synthetic fiber rope, with 120-foot length for each three people

    Team Equipment to Include:

        Flashlights or headlamps

        Map and compass

        Hardware, pitons, screws, pulleys

        Stove and fuel

        Wands

        Tent or tarp shelter

Additional Equipment for Winter Climbs:

    Down sleeping bag comfortable to −30°F

    Down parka, pants, and mitts

    Boots, double or insulated

    Snowshoes, depending on current or expected snow conditions

    Tents, expedition type to withstand high winds and provide shelter for all members of climbing team

    Snow shovel

    Wands, minimum 100

    Food and fuel supply for 2 extra days

    Radio, two-way

    Altimeter

    Avalanche cords

    Additional rope

PART TWO

THE EARLY YEARS
PRE-1900

Mount Rainier from Puget Sound.

6 Discovery and
First Explorations

Tuesday, May 8, 1792:

The weather was serene and pleasant, and the country continued to
exhibit, between us and the eastern snowy range, the same luxuriant
appearance. At its northern extremity, mount Baker bore by compass
N. 22 E.; the round snowy mountain, now forming its southern
extremity, and which, after my friend Rear Admiral Rainier, I
distinguished by the name of MOUNT RAINIER, bore N. [S.] 42 E.

Saturday, May 26, 1792:

Toward noon we landed on a point on the eastern shore, whose
latitude I observed to be 47° 21′, round which we flattered ourselves
we should find the inlet take an extensive eastwardly course . . .
We here dined, and although our repast was soon concluded, the delay
was irksome, as we were excessively anxious to ascertain the truth,
of which we were not long held in suspense. For having passed round
the point, we found the inlet to terminate here in an excessively
circular compact bay, whose waters washed the base of mount Rainier,
though its elevated summit was yet at a very considerable distance
from the shore, with which it was connected by several ridges of hills
rising towards it with gradual ascent and much regularity. The forest
trees, and the several shades of verdure that covered the hills, gradually
decreased in point of beauty, until they became invisible; when the
perpetual clothing of snow commenced, which seemed to form a
horizontal line from north to south along this range of rugged
mountains, from whose summit mount Rainier rose conspicuously, and
seemed as much elevated above them as they were above the level of
the sea; the whole producing a most grand, picturesque effect.

CAPTAIN GEORGE VANCOUVER

Whether viewed from near or far, this grand sentinel of the ages is a
source of admiration and awe to the beholder. The Indian refers to it
as TA-HO-MA, the great snow-covered peak. Vancouver, the first
Englishman to see it, called it RAINIER, after his admiral. Fremont,
in 1842 saw it for the first time and called it REGNIER, a name said
to have been given to it by an early Spanish explorer. Fremont
described it as smoking grandly.

MAJOR E. S. INGRAHAM, 1895

The first white man to visit the area that is now Mount Rainier National Park was Dr. William Fraser Tolmie. Born in Scotland in 1812 and educated at Glasgow University, at age 20 Dr. Tolmie joined Hudson's Bay Company. In 1833, while temporarily stationed at Fort Nisqually on Puget Sound, a few miles south of the later (1849) site of Fort Steilacoom, Tolmie made plans to visit the foothills of Mount Rainier to study the botanical species of the area and to gather herbs for medicinal use at the fort.

On August 29, with five Indians who brought three horses, Tolmie hiked from the fort toward the Puyallup valley. The first day they covered 8 miles, crossing the relatively flat upland of open prairies and some forest south of the present city of Tacoma. On August 30, they reached somewhere between the future sites of McMillan and Orting. The party made good progress up the valley and by September 1 was camped in the upper part of the Mowich valley below Paul Peak, now within the Park. From this point on, earlier reports had the party ascending a peak to the north, later named Tolmie Peak in honor of the intrepid doctor. However, research into Tolmie's diary by Aubrey L. Haines (1962) and Eugene Fauré (*The Mountaineer*, 1967)—coupled with the retracing of the route by these two in the late 1950s and in 1960—strongly indicates Tolmie climbed to the head of Lee Creek, then to the ridge crest between Hessong Rock and Mt. Pleasant. The views described by Tolmie and a compass bearing taken by him toward the highest visible point of Rainier (Liberty Cap) closely match those observed by Haines and Fauré from this point. Tolmie attained the ridge on September 2 with two Indians, Lachalet and Nuckalkut, and again the following day with an Indian named Quilniash. The party then returned to Fort Nisqually on the 5th, only 2 days' travel from the mountain.

Dr. Tolmie's account grossly underestimates the size of Rainier. He stated "A few small glaciers were seen on the conical portion; below that the mountain is composed of bare rock for a distance of about fifty feet down to the valley beneath. The Poyallip was fenced in to the eastward by a wall or dyke which seemed four feet high and four hundred feet in length." Despite his obvious shortcomings in estimating the scale of mountain features, Tolmie's mention of glaciers probably marks him as the first white man to make note of their existence in the conterminous United States.

The next notable "exploration" of the mighty peak was made from a long distance and through the eyepiece of a triangulation instrument. In 1842, Lieutenant Charles Wilkes, in charge of the United States Exploring Expedition of 1838-42, more commonly called the Wilkes Expedition, led a squadron of naval vessels into Puget Sound

Tolmie's view of Rainier in 1833, from ridge west of Mount Pleasant.

to map the coastline and triangulate the altitudes of various landmarks. Although he very much wanted to attempt an ascent of the great mountain on the eastern skyline, Lieutenant Wilkes was able only to make a survey of its altitude. By measuring from a baseline established on the prairies near Fort Nisqually, his triangulation credited the peak with an altitude of 12,330 feet. Failure to correct for earth curvature, atmospheric refraction, and height of his instrument above sea level probably accounts for his erroneous calculations (Haines, 1962). However, Wilkes' figure was accepted for many years, until an 1856 survey by the U.S. Coast and Geodetic Survey recalculated the height to be 14,444 feet, very close to the presently recognized altitude of 14,410 feet.

7 · Mountaineering

*When the locomotive is heard in the region some day, when American
enterprize has established an ice cream salon at the foot of the
glacier, and sherry cobblers may be had at twenty-five cents halfway
up to the top of the mountain, attempts to ascend that magnificent
peak will be quite frequent. But many a long year will pass away before
roads are sufficiently good to induce any one to do what we did in
the summer of 1857.*

LIEUTENANT AUGUST VALENTINE KAUTZ

LIEUTENANT KAUTZ' CLIMB, 1857

On July 15, 1857, Lieutenant August Valentine Kautz stood wearily
gazing about him at the rolling expanse of a glacier high on Mount
Rainier. His reddened eyes smarted under long exposure to the glaring
white world and his sunburned and bearded face showed deep lines of
fatigue and hunger. Some distance below, two companions gasped for
breath and struggled with an occasional step upward. It was 5 o'clock
in the afternoon and shadows were creeping across the ridges, outlining
windswept undulations of the snow surface. The strong breeze that had
been blowing most of the day, with accompanying freezing temperatures, was forming ice crystals in the canteens. The weather was giving
signs of deterioration as clouds began to sweep the ridges. From one of
the figures below, Private Nicholas Dogue, came the strongly German-
accented, "I guess, Lieutenant, ve petter go pack."

Kautz took another deep breath and looked about him, then down
to the gradually darkening forests and ridges which lay below the vast
sweep of the mountain's south flanks. A chill breeze suddenly took his
cap from his head and carried it beyond reach; soon the numbing sensation in his toes and fingers worked into his consciousness as he realized the hopelessness of proceeding farther under present conditions at
such a late hour. In 10 hours the party had climbed about 8000 feet
from the last camp, far below in the green meadow above the west
moraine of the Nisqually Glacier. Two members of the party, Private
William Carroll and the Indian guide Wapowety, had already given
up because of fatigue and snowblindness and returned to camp. Private
Dogue and Dr. Robert Orr Craig were some distance below the lieutenant, who had arrived at a point where, according to his own words,
". . . although there were points higher yet, the mountain spread out
comparatively flat."

With one last glance toward the snow dome that rose beyond a broad plateau, Kautz rejoined his companions and at 6 o'clock they began the descent down pinnacles and terraces of a roughly broken part of the glacier, below and over steep snowfields and rocky ridges, to the timberline camp. Weary to the point of exhaustion and weak from an inadequate diet the past few days, scratched and battered by a week of fighting heavy underbrush, dense forests, and stream crossings of the 80-mile approach from Fort Steilacoom on Puget Sound, Lieutenant Kautz and his four companions had accomplished the first clearly recorded ascent to the upper snow dome of Rainier. To them must go the credit for disproving the belief so prevalent in those days that such an ascent was impossible.

As an aftermath of the expedition, which ended when the climbers returned to Fort Steilacoom emaciated and hardly recognizable to post personnel, Wapowety nearly died, Dr. Craig was ill for many days, and the two soldiers spent several months under medical care, after which Private Carroll applied for a discharge pension on grounds of permanent injuries. Lieutenant Kautz suffered his first experience with a bad case of piles but otherwise had no permanent damage (Kautz, 1875; Meany, 1916).

August Valentine Kautz was born in Germany in 1828 and the same year came to America with his parents. While a young man he entered the army and served as a private in the Mexican War, after which he was appointed to the Military Academy at West Point. Graduating in 1852, he was assigned to the Fourth Infantry and soon found himself in the Pacific Northwest. It was while stationed at Fort Steilacoom that he attempted to ascend Mount Rainier. After the pioneering climb he went through Indian wars in the Northwest and then fought in the Civil War with a brilliant record. He attained the rank of brigadier general before he died in Seattle in 1895.

Of his planning for the ascent of Rainier, Lieutenant Kautz wrote:

I made preparations after the best authorities I could find, from reading accounts of the ascent of Mont Blanc and other snow mountains. We made for each member of the party an *alpenstock* of dry ash with an iron point. We sewed upon our shoes an extra sole, through which were driven fourpenny nails with the points broken off and the heads inside. We took with us a rope about fifty feet long, a hatchet, a thermometer, plenty of hard biscuit, and dried beef such as the Indians prepare.

Information relating to the mountain was exceedingly meager; no white man had ever been near it, and Indians were very superstitious and afraid of it. The southern slope seemed the least abrupt, and in that direction I proposed to reach the mountain; but whether to keep the high ground, or follow some stream to its source, was a question. Leshi, the chief of the Nesquallies, was at that time in the guardhouse, awaiting his execution, and as I had greatly interested myself to save him from his fate, he volunteered the information that the valley of the Nesqually River was the best approach after getting above the falls. He had some hope that I would take him as a guide; but finding that out of the question he suggested Wah-pow-e-ty, an old Indian of the Nesqually tribe, as knowing more about the Nesqually than any other of his people.

Some conjecture later arose about the highest point attained by Kautz. His words indicate he was at about the 14,000-foot altitude on the snow crest just east of Point Success and was looking across the intervening saddle to the crater rim and Columbia Crest, a little over half a mile away. It should be noted that Kautz' estimate of his altitude, "about 12,000 feet," was based on his belief that Rainier was 12,330 in height, as determined by Lieutenant Wilkes in 1842. It is therefore probable he was only about 330 feet lower than the absolute summit.

As an historical footnote, almost a century after Kautz' pioneer ascent, his granddaughter Jean, member of a Mountaineer party, became the first Kautz to complete the "Kautz Route" on Rainier all the way to Columbia Crest.

PRE-KAUTZ ASCENTS

Kautz' nearly successful effort to attain the highest point of Rainier was the first one widely reported. However, subsequent research by Haines (1962) revealed that at least two earlier attempts probably were made on the mountain. The first was an ascent of the south side about August 21, 1852 by Sidney S. Ford, Jr., Robert S. Bailey, John Edgar, and probably Benjamin F. Shaw. This group reached an altitude of 14,000 feet via an approach up the Nisqually valley, with at least one overnight camp on the upper slopes. Unfortunately the principal account suffers

Early explorers and climbers, W.F. Tolmie, A.V. Kautz.

from being presented by the editor of a frontier newspaper, but other scattered references lend credibility and detail to the story.

Also brought to light by Haines is an ascent, probably in 1855, by two white men, names unknown, via the Winthrop Glacier. The men, who were engaged in the survey of the treaty boundary of the Yakima Indian Reservation, approached the mountain from the Tieton drainage and the Cascade Crest near Fish Lake, then traveled north to the vicinity of Sunrise (Yakima Park) and camped beyond the Winthrop Glacier at Mystic Lake. They were guided by a young Yakima Indian named Saluskin (not to be confused with Sluiskin, who later guided Stevens and Van Trump). The ascent—by the white men alone—was up the Winthrop-Emmons Glaciers to the crater, where they left a cairn. Their accurate description of the crater and of steam vents inside the rim leaves little doubt they reached the top; none of these features is observable from below.

THE STEVENS-VAN TRUMP CLIMB, 1870

In early August of 1870, 13 years after Lieutenant Kautz' valiant effort, three men, General Hazard Stevens, Philemon (erroneously spelled "Philomen" for many years) Beecher Van Trump, and Edmund T. Coleman, met in Olympia, capital of Washington Territory, to plan an attempt to be the first to stand on the mountain's highest point. These were uncommon men of great accomplishment and determination. General Stevens was the son of Isaac Stevens, first governor of Washington Territory. Born in Newport, Rhode Island, in 1842, young Stevens moved with his family to Olympia in 1854 when his father was appointed to the governorship. Both father and son volunteered for

Hazard Stevens, P.B. Van Trump.

service with the Union army during the Civil War. In September 1862 Major General Isaac Stevens was killed and young Stevens was badly wounded at the battle of Chantilly. Hazard Stevens recovered from his injuries and became the youngest brigadier general of the volunteers in the Union army; at the end of the war he received the Congressional Medal of Honor. Returning to Washington Territory, he cared for his widowed mother by serving as federal revenue collector. During this time of travel across the Territory he became enamored of the great mountain and made plans to climb it, after seeking and finding a suitable companion—Philemon Beecher Van Trump.

Van Trump was born in Lancaster, Ohio, December 18, 1839. Following an education at Kenyon College and the University of New York, Van Trump traveled across the United States, prospecting unsuccessfully for gold in Montana and Idaho, then returned home in 1867 by way of California and the Isthmus of Panama. In the summer of 1867 he came to Washington Territory as private secretary of the seventh governor, Marshall F. Moore. He then became enraptured by the massive peak that was to play a large part in his life. He wrote (*Mazama*, October 1900):

> I obtained my first grand view of the mountain in August, 1867, from one of the prairies southeast of Olympia. That first true vision of the mountain, revealing so much of its glorious beauty and grandeur, its mighty and sublime form filling up nearly all of the field of direct vision, swelling up from the plain and out of the green forest till its lofty triple summit towered immeasurably above the picturesque foothills, the westerly sun flooding with golden light and softening tints its lofty summit, rugged sides and far-sweeping flanks—all this impressed me so indescribably, enthused me so thoroughly, that I then and there vowed, almost with fervency, that I would some day stand upon its glorious summit, if that feat were possible to human effort and endurance.

The mountain from near Olympia.

Edmund T. Coleman was an unusual man of many interests. A member of the Alpine Club and an artist who had exhibited in the Royal Academy on several occasions, he had an adventurous nature and a curiosity about new lands far distant from his native England. In 1862, at the age of 39, Coleman arrived in Victoria, on Vancouver Island, and began exploring the wild mountains of Washington Territory, voyaging up the Skagit and Nooksack Rivers; after several determined attempts, in 1868, at the age of 45, he succeeded in making the first ascent of Mount Baker. Coleman was an early advocate of the sport of mountaineering in a rugged new country where such pursuit was generally considered pointless and foolhardy. In fact, Sluiskin, the Indian guide who accompanied the trio to timberline on Rainier, joked of Coleman: "White men in Victoria have good sense—everybody look out of window while King George man talk mountain top!"

Ironically, Coleman's experience in the Alps indirectly resulted in his failure to keep pace with the two younger men on the Rainier ascent; aside from being older than his companions, he carried far too much equipment he considered essential to success. In the end his heavy load held him back before the ascent had fairly begun.

On August 8 the three men began their march from Olympia, arriving that evening at the Yelm Prairie ranch of James Longmire. A gay entourage of young men and women accompanied them this far to bid them good luck on the undertaking. Next morning the trio enlisted the help of Longmire and his pack horses for the journey to the base of the mountain via a crude trail constructed by Longmire in 1861. After traveling through heavy forests and across rivers, they reached Bear Prairie, on the swampy divide between the Nisqually and Cowlitz Rivers and about a mile south of the present Park headquarters at Longmire. Here Longmire's duties were ended as he procured for the climbers the services of the Yakima Indian, Sluiskin, who was to lead the party to timberline.

From Bear Prairie it would have been fairly simple to ascend the Nisqually canyon to timberline, following the Kautz route of 1857. However, the climbers were either unaware of this alternative or were dissuaded by Sluiskin's arguments for an approach along the crest of the Tatoosh Range, which rose above camp. Sluiskin may have been trying to keep the whites away from a favored hunting ground, or perhaps he wanted to prolong his paid service. In any event, next day the party started the climb up the steep cliffs leading to Lookout Mountain, just south of the present Park boundary. Coleman began falling behind and soon found a cliff he had surmounted would permit neither further ascent nor descent with his cumbersome load. He took the pack from his shoulders, attempted to drop it to a lower ledge—and in dismay watched it bound into brushy depths. He carefully lowered himself and sought in vain for the lost pack. With the others now beyond shouting distance, Coleman returned to camp to decide what to do next.

Sluiskin meanwhile led his eager young companions to the ridge crest, where they waited for Coleman, who was carrying all the bacon. Sluiskin's unsuccessful efforts to locate the Englishman convinced Stevens and Van Trump that Coleman had given up the ascent. Evening found the climbers camped in a sheltered meadow 2 miles farther along the ridge. At dawn they continued the traverse northward from Lookout Mountain, the Indian leading the white men on a winding course, in an apparent attempt to tire them out and discourage their aims for the mountain, of which he held a native dread. Finally the party reached the crest of the Tatoosh Range near Wahpenayo Peak and the first close-up view of the mountain rising high above the intervening valley. The two whites were awe-stricken by the panorama; as their ardor increased, so did Sluiskin's dejection.

Evening—from Tatoosh Range.

Descending to the vicinity of Reflection Lakes and then ascending parks of Mazama Ridge, the party made camp in a small grove of firs. After a supper of grouse felled by Sluiskin's rifle, the men reclined in fire light and discussed plans for morning. Finally realizing the white men were serious in their plans to ascend the mountain, the Indian began a solemn exhortation in broken English and Chinook, warning against so rash a venture. He described the evil spirit that inhabited

"Takhoma" and dwelled in "a lake of fire" on its summit, and the many certain dangers of the cliffs of crumbling rock and ice; many years ago, he said, his grandfather, a great chief and warrior, had ascended partway up the mountain and encountered some of these dangers, but fortunately had turned back in time to escape the vengeance of the demons of the mountaintop; no other Indian had ever gone that far before.

Finding his words had no effect, Sluiskin pleaded with his companions to give him a note declaring they had made the climb against his wishes; he would wait 3 days and then show the note to their friends in Olympia as evidence of their fate. The night ended with a long and dismal chant by the Indian.

Next morning the climbers moved camp up the ridge to a knoll overlooking a turbulent waterfall which they named for their guide. Here they attached snow spikes to their boots and with alpine staffs in hand went up the ridge to reconnoiter the route. After 4 hours climbing easy snow and rock they reached the approximate location of present-day Camp Muir at 10,000 feet, scanned the steep slopes above and decided on a long rocky spur as the best line of ascent, and returned to camp.

Early on the morning of August 17, 1870, Stevens and Van Trump started the final ascent. Beside alpine staffs and ice creepers, they carried a long rope, an ice axe belonging to Coleman, a brass plate inscribed with their names, flags, a large canteen and some luncheon, gloves and green goggles. Certain they would reach the summit and return in one day, they left blankets and coats behind.

Climbing more rapidly than on the reconnaissance, they reached the foot of the rock ridge in 3 hours and began the ascent along the jagged crest. Toiling up this irregular backbone, first on one side and then the other, keeping on the crest as much as possible to avoid crumbling rock, they gained the notch at the base of Gibraltar Rock in 2 hours.

Here they found a narrow ledge along the south face of the huge rock and crept along it, hugging the cliff, which fell nearly sheer on their left in a series of ledges to the glacier 2000 feet below. The looseness of ledge and wall demanded great care; several times they knocked off rocks which bounded into the abyss. Moreover, rocks fell from above; fortunately none found a human target. Some 500 nervewracking feet brought them to the upper end of the ledge, where it joined the snowfield descending from the summit dome. Using the ice axe to chop steps up the steep lower parts of the chute between cliff and glacier, the climbers emerged onto the upper glacier.

The snow surface was pitted and corrugated, deep hollows alternating with sharp pinnacles 2 and 3 feet tall—"suncups," as they are now called. The climbers rapidly ascended the "staircase," the slopes steadily becoming gentler. Assuming the highest point of the mountain to be on the left (west) they traversed gradually in that direction. Several large crevasses barred the way; one was crossed by lassoing a pinnacle on the upper side and climbing the rope. As the two men moved upward, the rarified air forced them to pause frequently, every 70 or 80 steps, to catch their breath. At 5 o'clock in the afternoon, 11 hours from the timberline camp, they reached the crest of the ridge, which they named Peak Success (later renamed Point Success), and planted the flag against the furious blast of wind. Looking about, they noticed a higher summit to the northeast.

Although feeling the full force of the wind and realizing the late hour would not allow a descent that day, they nevertheless crossed the intervening depression toward the highest point. Climbing over a low rocky ridge they entered a small circular crater about 200 yards in diameter. Detecting the odor of sulphur and noting numerous jets of steam, they were overjoyed to find warmth so high on the peak. A deep cavern extending down under the snow on the inner slope of the crater gave the tired and cold climbers relief from the wind. An uncomfortable night was spent here—steam heat warming one side and frigid air chilling the other side of their inadequately covered bodies.

Dawn broke slowly, dull and gray; howling wind and blowing mist greeted Stevens and Van Trump as they emerged from their refuge. Noting a brief rift in scurrying clouds, they made preparations for the descent. First, however, Stevens deposited the brass plate inscribed with their names in a cleft of a large boulder near the highest summit and left alongside it their empty canteens, covered by a big stone. The climbers then passed over the summit, which they named Crater Peak, and discovered a larger, more perfectly formed crater to the east. After briefly examining this depression and observing—through driving mist —another peak to the northwest which they named Peak Takhoma (later called North Peak, then Liberty Cap), the two miserable and benumbed men began the descent the way they had come.

Four hours from the crater they came to the lower end of the rocky spur, the end of climbing difficulties, and struck out joyfully for camp. When nearly there Van Trump slipped and plunged down a snowbank, striking loose rocks below, receiving abrasions of face and hands and a deep gash in his thigh. Camp was close, however, and the two reached it shortly thereafter. A few minutes later they saw Sluiskin slowly approaching camp, head down. He raised his head and gazed long and fixedly at the men he had by then given up for lost, and gradually decided they were alive and not spirits come to haunt him. He ran to em-

brace them with cries of "Skookum tillicum! Skookum tumtum!"
("Strong men! Brave hearts!")

Next morning the three descended to Reflection Lakes, where Van
Trump's injuries required he remain while Stevens and Sluiskin returned to Bear Prairie, this time via the shorter route of the Paradise
and Nisqually valleys, which they covered in 6 hours. Although Sluiskin
still showed an aversion to the route, his skillful guiding indicated to
Stevens that the Indian was familiar with the terrain. Upon arriving at
Bear Prairie they found Coleman glad to see them and rejoiceful of
their success. He, in the meantime, had been busy carrying two loads of
supplies to the top of Eagle Peak and was at the moment preparing
some cricketer's spikes for an attempt to make the ascent himself. The
following day Sluiskin returned partway up the valley with a pony and
succeeded in bringing Van Trump back to camp that evening.

A few days later, according to Stevens:

> As the last rays of the sun, one warm, drowsy summer afternoon, were
> falling aslant the shady streets of Olympia, Mr. Longmire's well-worn family
> carry-all, drawn by two fat, grass-fed horses, came rattling down the main
> street at a most unusual pace for them; two bright flags attached to Alpine
> staffs, one projecting from each door, fluttered gayly overhead, while the oc-
> cupants of the carriage looked eagerly forth to catch the first glimpse of
> welcoming friends. We returned after our tramp of two hundred and forty
> miles with visages tanned and sun-scorched, and with forms as lean and
> gaunt as greyhounds, and were received and lionized to the full, like veterans
> returning from an arduous and glorious campaign. For days afterward, in
> walking along the smooth and level pavements, we felt the strong impulse to
> step high, as though still striding over innumerable fallen logs or boughs of
> the forest, and for weeks our appetites were the source of astonishment to
> our friends and somewhat mortifying to ourselves. More than two months
> had elapsed before Mr. Van Trump fully recovered from his hurts. We pub-
> lished at the time short newspaper accounts of the ascent, and, although an
> occasional old Puget Sounder will still growl, "They say they went on top of
> Mount Rainier, but I'd like to see them prove it," we were justly regarded
> as the first, and I believe the only ones up to the present time, who have
> ever achieved the summit of Takhoma.

About 45 years later, General Stevens offered the following remi-
niscings on his historic climb and later visit to the Park (*The Mountaineer*, 1915):

> On a recent visit to Mount Takhoma I was astonished to find such a
> magnificent road clear up to Camp of the Clouds and to learn that over
> 30,000 persons had visited that sublime monarch of mountains this season.
> When I made the ascent in 1870 it was a vast solitude. The sensations of
> exploring new fields were most exhilarating and when Van Trump and my-
> self reached the summit and waved our flags and gave three cheers we felt

we had accomplished a great and gratifying success and so named the southernmost peak, Peak Success.

I made the ascent again in 1905 and then, as likewise on my recent trip, I observed that the snow and glaciers had receded to a considerable degree since I first visited them. At the time Stevens Glacier came close up to Sluiskin Falls. Now it is several hundred feet farther from them. The small crater on the summit in which we slept in 1870 was filled with solid ice but in 1905 it had nearly all melted out. It may be that a succession of wet seasons will restore these glaciers to their former limits.

SUBSEQUENT EARLY CLIMBS ON THE GIBRALTAR ROUTE

On October 17, 1870, 2 months after the pioneer climb, Samuel Franklin Emmons and A. D. Wilson, world-renowned geologists working on the Geological Survey of the Fortieth Parallel, made the second ascent of the mountain by the same route along the Gibraltar ledge. After obtaining helpful information from General Stevens in Olympia they headed toward the mountain, with James Longmire again leading the way to Bear Prairie. Heavily burdened with scientific equipment with which they hoped to lay out a baseline for future topographic mapping of the peak, they were unable to use the approach by Sluiskin Falls. Instead they circled the foothills to the east and went up the Cowlitz Divide.

From a base camp at Cowlitz Park, Emmons and Wilson spent several days surveying the proposed baseline. This task completed, they crossed the Cowlitz Glacier for the summit attempt. Joining the Stevens-Van Trump route somewhat below the present site of Camp Muir, the two geologists continued to the top. During the ascent of the ice chute above the Gibraltar ledge they found the rope left by Stevens

Early explorers and climbers. John Muir, James Longmire, E.S. Ingraham.

and Van Trump. While hacking steps in the chute Emmons dropped his pack, which fell out of sight to the glacier below; the lost pack carried with it their brandy, coffee, firewood, and Emmons' overcoat and ice creepers (Haines, 1962).

The geologists reached the summit shortly after noon, October 17, 1870. Owing to the loss of his overcoat, Emmons was forced to retreat into a steam cave while Wilson attempted to set up the theodolite on the summit snow dome. Heavy winds prevented operation of the instrument and he joined Emmons for a short rest before the descent. Leaving the summit at 3 o'clock, the two men descended all the way back to their camp, arriving there long after dark, having been gone 17 hours. This was the first one-day round-trip climb of the Gibraltar route, and also one of the few October ascents of Rainier. Emmons and Wilson returned to civilization by a circuitous crossing of the Cascades eastward to Fort Simcoe; from there they journeyed to The Dalles on the Columbia River.

Present information indicates that well over 100 people, in more than 30 parties, climbed the peak before 1900. So many ascents of the Gibraltar route were made between the time of the Stevens-Van Trump climb and the turn of the century that only those of particular interest are listed below.

1883, Aug. 16–17: P. B. Van Trump, George B. Bayley (well-known Sierra Club climber), and James Longmire. On the journey to the mountain the party discovered the warm mineral springs near which in the following year Longmire constructed the first permanent settlement in the area now included in the Park (Haines, 1962).

1888, Aug. 11: P. B. Van Trump, E. S. Ingraham, John Muir, A. C. Warner (who took the first photographs on the summit), Charles

Miss Fay Fuller, Len Longmire.

V. Piper, D. W. Bass, Norman O. Booth. (William Keith, artist, and Henry Loomis did not complete the ascent.) During this trip the name Gibraltar Rock was suggested by Major Ingraham. High camp, originally called "Cloud Camp," was renamed "Camp Muir" by Ingraham: "Upon reaching that point in the ascent, Mr. Muir suggested it was a good place to spend the night, saying that the presence of pumice in large quantities indicated the absence of wind." (Ingraham, in *The Mountaineer*, 1909; John Muir, *Steep Trails*; Meany, 1916).

1890, Aug. 10–11: First ascent by a woman. Party included Reverend E. C. Smith, Len Longmire, W. O. Amsden, R. R. Parrish, and Miss Fay Fuller. In correspondence with Mrs. Fritz von Brieson (Fay Fuller) in 1933, Park Naturalist C. Frank Brockman received the following description of the climb: "The costume . . . will amuse present-day climbers. I had it made at the time when bloomers were unknown and it was considered quite immodest. How anyone could have scrambled over the rocks thus attired is now inconceivable. There were no boots or heavy shoes available for women at the time and I bought the strongest shoes that were sold to boys. I believe the stock [alpenstock] was made by a blacksmith at Yelm from a curved shovel handle." According to Len Longmire's account of the climb, Miss Fuller refused assistance from the men at difficult spots and stated that if she could not achieve the goal without their help she would not deserve to reach it (Brockman, 1940). It also is worth noting that this climb marked the beginning of 20 years of guiding on the mountain by Len Longmire.

1890, Aug. 11–13: Solomon C. Hitchcock, Arthur F. Knight, F. S. "Van" Watson, and Will Hitchcock. These four men, totally inexperienced with mountains, accomplished the feat on the day following the climb by the above-mentioned party. While at the crater they inscribed their names on the face of a large rock, then later wondered if this was ever found by other climbers. It was, 64 years later; in August 1954, guide Jim Whittaker found the inscription on the west face of a rock just inside the crater rim, about 200 feet west of the lowest point of the rim.

1891, July 29–31: Second ascent by women. Susan Longmire (13), Edith Corbet (Yelm schoolteacher), with Len Longmire and others (Brockman, 1940).

1894, July 18–19: Major E. S. Ingraham led a party of 14, including three women. The party was stormed in at the summit for 26 hours. The name "Columbia Crest" (originally "Columbia's Crest") was given the highest point on the crater rim. According to their barometric readings it was 15,550 feet above sea level, "the highest point in the United States, exclusive of Alaska."

1895, August 4: Albert D. Durham and Roger S. Greene, Jr. made the ascent to Columbia Crest and return to Paradise in the round-trip time of 10 hours.

1897, July 27: The largest party to assemble on the mountain to that date was a group of over 200 members of the Mazamas club of Portland. Among the party was Professor Edgar McClure of the Department of Chemistry at the University of Oregon. With a yard-long mercurial barometer he obtained measurements at the summit which later were computed by a colleague to give an altitude of 14,528 feet. Details of the Mazamas' ascent are presented below.

On July 19 the party of Mazamas traveled by train from Portland to Tacoma, where they were honored by a reception at city hall. The next morning the group left with horse-drawn stages (most of the climbers walking beside the horses) for Eatonville, the first night's stop. Two days later they were at the end of the road at Longmire, where most spent the night, a few pushing ahead on the trail to Paradise. On July 23 the main party arrived at Paradise, where 45 tents were set up and the 4 tons of supplies assembled. Two beef steers, seven milk cows, and many horses were tethered to graze on nearby slopes. On July 26, after 2 days of rain, during which several members climbed Pinnacle Peak as a conditioner, a dozen climbers started for the summit from Paradise, with five making the round trip to the top and back that day. The main party stopped at Muir to prepare for the summit assault next day.

On the 27th, led by guide Ed Curtis, 58 Mazamas reached the crater, the first group arriving about 3:30 p.m. Eight members of the party (including Miss Fay Fuller, who was on her second ascent of the peak) decided to spend the night on the summit, a common practice in those early days. The others returned to Camp Muir by 9:30 in the evening, nearly losing two men in a fall on the ledges. Since it was a clear, moonlit night, about half the party, including Professor McClure, started down from Muir in several small groups. During the descent McClure slipped and fell to his death from the rock that now bears his name. The tragic loss, and the near death of two other men in a fall into a crevasse next day, caused the Mazamas to shorten their intended 2-week outing and return to Portland on August 4 (Haines, 1962; Ella McBride, oral communication, 1963).

In July 1905, during the outing sponsored jointly by the Sierra Club and Mazamas and with members of the Appalachian Mountain Club participating, 112 people attained the summit. General Hazard Stevens, then 63 years old, made his second ascent of the route he had pioneered with Van Trump in 1870. Among others who took part in the climb or evening campfire programs were such distinguished scientists and mountaineers as Henry Landes, State Geologist of Washington; W. D. Lyman, Whitman College; Stephen T. Mather, later to become Director of the National Park Service; Professor Charles E. Fay, President of The American Alpine Club; Professor Joseph N. Le-Conte, geologist; Claude E. Rusk, author of the classic *Tales of A Western Mountaineer*; Asahel Curtis, photographer; and other notable members of the three outdoor organizations (*Mazamas*, 1905; *Sierra Club Bulletin*, 1906; *Appalachia*, May 1906).

EARLY ASCENTS OF THE EMMONS-WINTHROP GLACIERS

Southward, 9,000 feet above you, so near you must throw your head back to see its summit, is grand Mount Tacoma; its graceful northern peak piercing the sky, it soars single and alone. Whether touched by the glow of early morning or gleaming in bright noonday, whether rosy with sunset light or glimmering, ghost-like, in the full moon, whether standing out clear and cloudless or veiled among the mists it weaves from the warm south winds, it is always majestic and inspiring, always attractive and lovely. It is the symbol of an awful power clad in beauty.

BAILEY WILLIS, 1883

The inspiration gathered in these early days of exploration about the great snow fields and glaciers, and beneath the towering peaks that crown the superb scenery of the Cascades has never left me and is still a source of joy as I recall the wonderful beauty of the virgin forest and the fascination of the ice-world. I have seen the glories of Switzerland, the grandeur of the Andes, and the grace of the beautiful cone of Fujiyama, but among the most renowned scenery of the world, I know of nothing more majestic or more inspiring than the grandeur of my own old camping ground, Mount Rainier.

BAILEY WILLIS
The Mountaineer, 1915

As noted earlier, a climb of the mountain by the Winthrop Glacier probably was made in 1855 by two surveyor-engineers, names unknown. These men approached the peak from the southeast, from their area of work along the boundary of the newly-designated Yakima Indian Reservation. The ascent apparently was never recorded by the men and the first knowledge of it came years later from an old Indian who had accompanied the explorers to their timberline camp near Mystic Lake (Haines, 1962).

All subsequent pre-1900 ascents of this side of the peak were made by a circuitous approach from the coal-mining communities of Wilkeson and Carbonado in the foothills northwest of the present Park. By 1881 partial access to the northern flanks of Rainier was given by completion of a trail between Wilkeson and Spray Park; the upper part of the trail followed much the same route as the present road to Mowich Lake and trail to Spray Park. Constructed under the direction of Bailey Willis, brilliant young geologist in the employ of Northern Pacific Railroad Company, the trail was initially designed to promote land-buying and coal-mining ventures along the lower valleys, but Willis' foresight encouraged extension of the trail to timberline for purposes of attracting tourists.

The first well-substantiated ascent of the Winthrop Glacier to the crater was in 1884 by three men from the town of Snohomish: the Reverend J. Warner Fobes, George James, and Richard O. Wells (Haines, 1962). Following the Bailey Willis Trail to Spray Park, the trio established a base camp in the alpine meadow and from there made several sorties in the surrounding area. On August 16 they attempted to scale the mountain by way of Ptarmigan Ridge. At an altitude of 11,000 feet (according to their barometer) they found the mountain "unsurmountable from this side." They returned to camp and the following day each man took off on a separate exploration, returning in the evening with tales of the day's adventures. Fobes told of his crossing the Carbon Glacier; James described his encounter with a large black bear; and Wells felt fortunate in being alive to recount his experiences after falling into a crevasse high on the Carbon Glacier.

On August 18, after shooting a large, old goat for what succulence might be derived from the tough meat, they crossed the Carbon Glacier to the alpine meadows beyond. From a camp pitched at about 6000 feet they had impressive views of ice avalanches pouring down 4000-foot Willis Wall. The following day they attacked the mountain again, first climbing to 9000 feet on Curtis Ridge before rock walls discouraged further efforts. They descended to the Winthrop Glacier, which appeared to offer a simpler, all-snow line of ascent. Equipped with "Alpine staffs, a small axe and a rope," the men climbed around several crevasse fields and "were compelled to walk on the verge of a deep chasm" before reaching about 13,000 feet at approximately 1:30 p.m. Their difficulty with breathing and dizziness forced them to descend to the camp far below.

Depressed by two failures and running low on provisions, the trio considered giving up the attempt. However, the next morning they one by one decided to make a final effort. Following a better route discovered during the descent the day before, they traveled more rapidly and attained the crater and summit at Columbia Crest a little after 2:30 p.m. After giving three cheers, they discovered what completely surprised them: evidence they were not the first to climb the mountain. They found a stick poking from the snowy crest, and nearby, in rocks of the western crater, came across the lead plate bearing the date of

August 16th, 1883 and the signatures of G. B. Bayley, P. B. Van Trump, James Longmire, and W. C. Ewing (who had turned back below Gibraltar Rock). The three Snohomish men added their names on the back of the plate and replaced it in the rocks. For an hour they admired the clear views in all directions, recognizing other high points of the Cascades to the north and south and the Olympic Mountains far beyond Puget Sound. On the Sound they could discern, by a trace of black smoke, the movement of a steamer. After briefly examining several steam fumaroles near the summit, the men began the descent at 3:30 p.m. Using their staffs for balance and brakes, they made rapid progress, sliding down parts of the glacier slope, and reached camp at 6 p.m. Elation over the ascent was only slightly dampened by bad cases of sunburn and snowblindness (Haines, *The Mountaineer*, 1954; Haines, 1962).

In 1896 a Geological Survey party composed of Bailey Willis, geologist-in-charge, geologists Israel C. Russell and George Otis Smith, and camp hands F. H. Ainsworth and William B. Williams ascended the Winthrop-Emmons Glaciers. The geologists were all to achieve greater distinction in years to come. Willis was born in 1857 in New York and by the age of 24 had attained the position of Assistant Chief Geologist of the Northern Transcontinental Survey. He later joined the U.S. Geological Survey, and also worked for some time in China, before becoming professor of geology at Stanford University. Russell was born in 1852 in New York and became one of America's most distinguished scientists. He traveled widely in geological explorations, spending time in New Zealand and Alaska and also in the West Indies during the eruption of Mount Pelee on the island of Martinique. In 1892 he was appointed professor of geology at the University of Michi-

Bailey Willis, I.C. Russell.

From Eagle Cliff.

gan. He spent many summers in geological work in the Pacific Northwest. Smith was born in Maine in 1871 and graduated from Johns Hopkins University in 1896, at which time he joined the Geological Survey, of which he became Director in 1907.

Primarily dedicated to exploration and examination of the glaciers and rocks of Mount Rainier, the expedition in its early stages also included Professor Henry Landes of the University of Washington, Willis' 10-year-old daughter Hope, the camp cook Michael Autier, and the packer Fred Koch. The party traveled up the Carbon River valley to the terminus of the Carbon Glacier and pitched camp on the slopes above the west wall of the glacier. From there, Russell and Smith made an exploratory trip into Spray Park followed by a circuit to the north, around the head of Mist Park and over Knapsack Pass to Mowich Lake (then called Crater Lake). Although previously considered the remnant of an ancient volcanic crater, the men's observations led them to believe the lake was a feature of glacial erosion. From the outlet they struck the trail built by Willis to Spray Park; this they followed to the impressive viewpoint at Eagle Cliff and on past Spray Falls back to the park, from which they returned to their camp above the edge of the Carbon Glacier.

The climb to the summit was begun on July 22 from a camp pitched at 8000 feet, above the west edge of the Winthrop Glacier. Taking blankets, a small supply of rations, an alcohol lamp, alpenstocks, a rope 100 feet long, and a few other articles, the five men worked their way up and across the glacier to the upper part of the rock ridge which they named The Wedge (today better known as Steamboat Prow). According to Russell (1898):

On reaching The Wedge we found it an utterly desolate rocky cape in a sea of snow. We were at an altitude of about 10,000 feet, and far above timber. Water was obtained by spreading snow on smooth rocks or on rubber sheets, and allowing it to melt by the heat of the afternoon sun. Coffee was prepared over the alcohol lamp, sheltered from the wind by a bed sheet supported by alpenstocks. After a frugal lunch, we made shelf-like ledges in a steep slope of earth and stones and laid down our blankets for the night. From sheltered nooks amid the rocks, exposed to the full warmth of the reclining sun, we had the icy slopes of the main central dome of the mountain in full view and chose what seemed the most favorable route for the morrow's climb.

Surrounded as we were by the desolation and solitude of barren rocks, on which not even a lichen had taken root, and pure white fields, we were much surprized to receive passing visits from several humming birds, which shot past us like winged jewels. They came up the valley occupied by the Emmons Glacier, turned sharply at The Wedge, and went down the way of the Winthrop Glacier. What tempts these children of the sunlight and the flowers into the frozen regions seems a mystery. That the humming birds are bold explorers was not new to me, for the reason that on several occasions in previous years, while on the snow-covered slopes of Mount St. Elias, far above all vestiges of vegetation, my heart had been gladdened by glimpses of their brilliant plumage.

When the sun declined beyond the great snow-covered dome that towered above us, and the blue shadows crept down the previously dazzling cliffs, the air became cold and a strong wind made our perch on the rocks uncomfortable. Wrapping ourselves in our blankets we slept until the eastern sky began to glow with sunrise tints.

Early on the morning of July 24 the men began the ascent of the snow dome above the bivouac site. Leaving blankets cached in the rocks, they roped together and slowly worked their way upward. Numerous large crevasses necessitated detours to right and left and some members of the party felt effects of the altitude. At one point Ainsworth lost his footing and slipped down the slope, pulling Williams off his feet and causing him to fall over the lip of a crevasse. Fortunately the others held and Williams was able to haul himself up without assistance from those anchored above. Continuing on, the men at last gained the rocks of the crater rim, which they had observed from time to time from the undulating surface below. It was 4 o'clock as they descended into the crater to gain protection from icy winds. Russell writes:

Descending into the crater, I discovered crevices from which steam was escaping, and on placing my hands on the rocks was rejoiced to find them hot. My companions soon joined me, and we began the exploration of the crater, our aim being to find the least uncomfortable place in which to take refuge from the freezing blast rather than to make scientific discoveries.

The crater that we had entered is one of the smaller and more recent ones in the truncated summit of the peak, and is deeply filled with snow, but the rim is bare and well defined. The steam and heat from the rocks have melted out many caverns beneath the snow. In one of these we found shelter.

The cavern we chose in which to pass the night, although irregular, was about 60 feet long by 40 feet wide, and had an arched ceiling some 20 feet high. The snow had been melted out from beneath, leaving a roof so thin that a diffused blue light penetrated the chamber. The floor sloped steeply, and on the side toward the center of the crater there was a narrow space between the rocks and the descending roof which led to unexplored depths. As a slide into this forbidding gulf would have been exceedingly uncomfortable, if not serious, our life line was stretched from crag to crag so as to furnish a support and allow us to walk back and forth during the night without danger of slipping. Three arched openings or doorways communicated with other chambers, and through these drafts of cold air were continually blowing. The icy air chilled the vapor rising from the warm rocks and filled the chamber with steam which took on grotesque forms in the uncertain, fading light. In the central part of the icy chamber was a pinnacle of rock, from the crevices of which steam was issuing with a low hissing sound. Some of the steam jets were too hot to be comfortable to the ungloved hand. In this uninviting chamber we passed the night. The muffled roar of the gale as it swept over the mountain could be heard in our retreat and made us thankful for the shelter the cavern afforded.

The floor of our cell was too uneven and too steeply inclined to admit of lying down. Throughout the night we leaned against the hot rocks or tramped wearily up and down holding the life line. Cold blasts from the branching ice chambers swept over us. Our clothes were saturated with condensed steam. While one side of the body resting against the rocks would be hot, the strong drafts of air with a freezing temperature chilled the other side. After long hours of intense darkness the dome of snow above us became faintly illuminated, telling that the sun was again shining. After a light breakfast and a cup of tea, prepared over our alcohol lamp, we resumed our exploration, none the worse for the exposures of the night.

The following morning, July 25, the men descended the mountain by the Gibraltar route, arriving at Paradise Valley at 2 o'clock in the afternoon. There they were met and extended warm hospitality by a party that included Major E. S. Ingraham. A restful evening was spent admiring the comparative luxuries of the alpine setting. For the Major's part in making their brief stay comfortable, the geologists later named the Ingraham Glacier in his honor.

From Paradise the party returned to the north side of the mountain by crossing the Cowlitz Glacier, then the Ingraham Glacier above Little Tahoma, descending alongside that peak for about a mile, then crossing the Emmons Glacier back to The Wedge, where they recovered the blankets left days before. They made rapid progress in traversing the Winthrop Glacier and descending back to their camp above

On Cowlitz Glacier—Little Tahoma on right.

Mystic Lake, where they were warmly greeted by the little girl, the old geologist, and the cook (Russell, 1898; Haines, 1962).

ASCENT OF THE INGRAHAM GLACIER, 1885 OR 1886

The Ingraham Glacier is a long, narrow ice stream flowing down the east slope of Mount Rainier between Gibraltar and Cathedral Rocks on the southwest and Disappointment Cleaver and Little Tahoma on the northeast. An interesting account of the presumed first ascent of this glacier is described by Allison L. Brown (*The Mountaineer*, 1920).

In 1885 or 1886, Brown was apparently the only white man in a party of Yakima Indians engaged in a hunting excursion along the Cowlitz Divide. The party of about 30 Indians and their white companion crossed the Cascades at Packwood Pass and traveled up the Ohanapecosh valley to the Cowlitz Divide. Finding no game in an area that generally had been their best hunting ground, they climbed higher toward snowline, where a party of about seven or eight Indians and Brown decided to climb toward the summit of Rainier. The party crossed the lower Whitman Glacier and dropped onto the Ingraham Glacier at about the 8500-foot altitude (probably at the point where present-day climbers attain the Whitman Glacier in ascending Little Tahoma from the Paradise approach). The horses apparently were left at the near side of the Whitman Glacier, according to Brown's account. The party crossed the Ingraham and climbed along the west slope of Cathedral Rocks, then back onto the Ingraham, which they followed upward to an undetermined point. Brown states they "did not reach the highest pinnacle." Most of the party wore Indian moccasins and some had alpenstocks cut from mountain ash and other bushes in the forest below. They also carried one or two "lariats to use in case of emergency, but never found it necessary to use them." During the descent of the mountain they spent a night at the base of a rock that, according to Brown's description, fits Gibraltar Rock (*The Mountaineer*, 1920; Haines, 1962).

ASCENTS OF THE TAHOMA GLACIER

The first recorded ascent of the Tahoma Glacier, which was also the first climb of Rainier from its western flank, was made August 11–12, 1891 by P. B. Van Trump, Dr. Warren Riley, and Alfred Drewry. Accompanying the party on the entire trip was Dr. Riley's deerhound. The climb began from Indian Henrys Hunting Ground, a meadowland on the mountain's southwestern slope. The men ascended the lower part of Success Cleaver and crossed the South Tahoma Glacier at about the 9000-foot altitude to the base of Tahoma Cleaver, where high camp was pitched. Early next morning they moved onto the Tahoma Glacier and ascended its center to the summit crater. There they added their names to a lead plate which Van Trump had placed during his 1883 ascent of the Gibraltar route. After spending the night in the crater, the party descended via Gibraltar, thus making the first summit traverse of the mountain (Haines, 1962).

The second ascent of the Tahoma Glacier followed the first by a week. On August 20 Frank Taggert, Grant Lowe, and Frank Lowe, of Orting, Washington, reached the summit via a climb of the entire length of the Tahoma Glacier from its lower terminus (Haines, 1962).

In 1892, on July 30–31, two separate parties were for the first time together on the summit of Rainier, both by way of the Tahoma Glacier. Dr. Warren Riley of Olympia and George Jones were joined on the upper part of the glacier by Frank Taggert and Frank Lowe (both on the previous year's ascent of the route). The four men spent the night in the crater and the following morning all accomplished the first ascent of North Peak, later renamed Liberty Cap (*Sierra Club Bulletin*, May 1894; *Tacoma Ledger*, August 8 or 9, 1892; Haines, 1962).

On August 21–22, 1892, P. B. Van Trump and George B. Bayley climbed the Tahoma Glacier to the summit and reached North Peak (Liberty Cap) the following morning, only to be disappointed in their hopes of being the first on this point. During the descent of the Tahoma Glacier, Bayley was badly injured by a slip into a crevasse. He was able to climb out, fortunately, when Van Trump lowered a rope to him, but the long journey back to civilization with cracked ribs was painful. Bayley, a charter member of the Sierra Club and an early-day conservationist, had climbed widely in California's Sierras, making numerous explorations and ascents of the higher summits of the range. He had been on several previous ascents of the peak with Van Trump, including that with James Longmire in 1883, when the trio first made note of the mineral springs later developed by Longmire. Bayley's life came to an early and tragic end in 1894 when he was accidentally killed in a San Francisco elevator (*Sierra Club Bulletin*, May 1894; Haines, 1962).

In the late 1890s and early 1900s a guide service was operated by Van Trump from a tent camp at Indian Henrys Hunting Ground. The camp was reached by foot or horseback from Longmire Hot Springs, where the stables were located. From Longmire a trail ascended and crossed Rampart Ridge, then dropped down to cross the Kautz Creek valley before climbing to Indian Henrys. During the period before establishment of Mount Rainier National Park in 1899, the area was administered as the Pacific Forest Reserve, and Van Trump had the distinction of being the first government ranger to serve within the present Park area.

Liberty Cap ("North Peak") from near summit.

8 Early Tourism
and Accommodations

The growing interest in the mountain and its surrounding parks and forests before the turn of the century is noted in a small publication by E. S. Ingraham (1895). The booklet describes the transportation facilities and journey into the Longmire and Paradise areas from Tacoma.

The Pacific Forest Reserve is destined to become one of the great resorts of America, having attractions for the pleasure-seeker and health-seeker possessed by no other. Apart from its great scenic beauty, its elevation, cool climate, clear atmosphere and pure water combine to make it a paradise. One visit is sure to be followed by another. It is a place for recreation and rest. While at present it takes two days of staging and one-half day's travel over a rugged mountain trail to get to Paradise Park from Seattle or Tacoma, yet no one seems to mind the fatigue. Good meals at some of the farm houses along the route and occasional draughts from crystal mountain streams, restore the lost energies as often as necessary.

It is un-American to visit other shores when our own country contains so many places of interest. Alaska with its glaciers, the Yellowstone with its geysers, lakes and waterfalls, the Pacific Forest Reserve combining all in a greater or less degree, offer to the American tourist unsurpassed opportunities for travel and sight-seeing.

Leaving the Northern Pacific railroad at Tacoma, a short ride on the Jefferson Avenue street car line takes the tourist to Center. There he takes a steam motor line to Lake Park about eleven miles away. This ride is a delightful one affording one of the best views of the mountain to be had from any point. By the time the park is reached his appetite has begun to assert itself and an early noon meal at the hotel will be in order. He then boards the stage for Eatonville, the distance being twenty-four miles. This ride is not without interest. Several beautiful lakes are passed, Ohop and Clear being among the prettiest. A hospitable welcome is accorded the tourist by the good people of Eatonville and if he is not in a hurry a day may be well spent in fishing in the numerous streams near by. If in a hurry, he will order an early breakfast and take stage for Longmire's mineral springs, a distance of thirty-one miles, arriving there in time for a late supper. Of course he has not been without his noon meal—a bountiful one having been eaten at one of the farm houses in Succotash Valley. Once at the Springs he is advised to take life easy. If he be an invalid, the water of some one of the mineral springs—all different—will suit his particular case. And the baths—delightful! To stand in those baths and feel the warm water bubbling up from the earth's interior, heated by its subterranean fires, is a novelty and a luxury not to be missed. The hotel may be wanting in modern convenience, but it possesses a charm in being in keeping with the surroundings. Carved out of the cedars of the forest and painted with ochre from a mine near by, it is typical of pioneer life in the far west. The host and hostess, Mr. and Mrs. Longmire, are unbounded in their hospitality and provide well for their guests. The "springs," some twenty in number, occupy an amphitheater of about twenty acres, flanked by a high battlement of basaltic cliffs and the Nisqually river. Some of them pour forth a genuine soda water, while the waters of others possess an agreeable acidity due to the presence of iron compounds. The number of visitors to the Springs increases each year, many taking a camping outfit with them and spending weeks in this healthful region.

The wagon road ends at the Springs. For the next four miles a mountain trail leads up the Nisqually canyon, now skirting its walls, now taking middle ground and in turn following the banks of the river for a short distance. This trail covered, on horse-back or a-foot, as the tourist may choose, the crossing of the Nisqually is reached. About one-third of a mile above the bridge, the river issues from a great cavern in the glacier. It repays the tourist to visit the glacier at this point as it is among the few having terminal moraines. By ascending the right bank of this glacier, left looking up, for about one-half mile, then crossing diagonally to the left bank, a point may be found about one mile above its mouth from which an ascent may be made into Paradise Park a little below Camp of the Clouds.

After crossing the bridge the trail ascends by means of a switch-back to the summit of a spur about 2,000 feet above the river. Crossing a small meadow, the trail leads to the right and takes a broad curve around a high knob and then leads directly into the park. Camp of the Clouds is generally the objective point in Paradise Park, although numerous good camping places among the flowers, beside crystal streams and within sight and sound of dashing waterfalls may be selected. One, two or three weeks' sojourn in this enchanted region would prove delightful and profitable, for, be it remembered, this is practically an unexplored region. The novelty of being the first to climb yonder peak, to discover a new lake or waterfall will be the lot of the ambitious tourist for years to come. A mountainous region thirty-six by forty-two miles cannot be explored in a day.

Should the objective point of the tourist be Columbia's Crest, the services of some one who has made the ascent, for a guide, should be secured.

The south side of the mountain will probably claim the attention of tourists for some time to come, on account of its accessibility. The north and east sides, however, contain attractions unsurpassed by any other part of the Reserve. Seattle Park, on the north side, can be reached by the old Bailey Willis trail and Elysian Fields, on the northeast side, by the Carbon River trail, which is the most direct route to the glaciers.

PART THREE

MOUNTAINEERING AFTER 1900

Longmire in 1895.

Horses crossing footbridge over Nisqually River.

9 *Mountaineering on the South Side*

Paradise Park presents many and varied charms. It is a somewhat rugged land, with a deep picturesque valley winding through it. The trees grow in isolated groves. Each bunch of dark-green firs and balsams is a cluster of gracefully tapering spires. The undulating meadows between the shady groves are brilliant in summer with a veritable carpet of gorgeous blossoms. In contrast to the exquisite charms of the groves and flower-decked rolling meadows are desolate ice fields and rugged glaciers which vary, through many tints and shades, from silvery whiteness to intense blue. Added to these minor charms, and towering far above them, is the massive summit of Rainier. At times the sublime mountain appears steel-blue in the unclouded sky, or rosy with the afterglow at sunset, or all aflame with the glories of the new-born day. Clouds gather about the lofty summit and transform it into a storm king. Avalanches rushing down its side awaken the echoes in the neighboring forest. The appearance of the mountain is never the same on different days; indeed, it changes its mood and exerts a varying influence on the beholder from hour to hour.

ISRAEL C. RUSSELL, 1898

Besides the trails, the various routes to the summit of the mountain should be described, with their advantages and disadvantages . . . Another important feature that should be included is a description of the various "high-line" routes connecting the camping places on the slopes of the mountain.

ROGER W. TOLL
Superintendent
Mount Rainier National Park
1919

DEVELOPMENT OF PUBLIC FACILITIES

By 1900 Paradise (Paradise Valley, Paradise Park) had become established as the hub of climbing activity within the National Park. The initial explorations from the west, which followed the Nisqually valley to the mountain's base, and the subsequent development of trails and roads into the south side of the Park, made Paradise not only the center of Northwest mountaineering but the mecca for climbers from Europe who sought glacier-crowned peaks in America.

Initially, trails and then roads were constructed up the Nisqually valley to Longmire; from here early-day climbers hiked to Paradise. In 1891 James Longmire and his sons completed construction of the road to Longmire, where a log hotel (built the previous year) accommodated the traveler. In 1895 the trail to Paradise Valley was built along the Nisqually River to near the glacier terminus, then crossed the river on a log bridge before climbing steeply up the east side of the canyon to Paradise. In 1904 the Tacoma Eastern Railroad Company completed the railroad to Ashford, 6 miles outside the Nisqually Entrance. In 1908 the first automobile arrived at Longmire. The road was extended toward Paradise and in 1910 the first car reached the bridge below the Nisqually Glacier; the following year a car made it to Paradise—where it was reportedly chained to a tree. The horse and wagon were still the principal mode of transportation to that point until 1915, when the Longmire-Paradise road was opened for public use. The journey from Tacoma to Longmire generally required 2 days, with an overnight stop at Eatonville.

The first public accommodations at Paradise were at "Camp of the Clouds," a tent camp established in 1895 by Henry C. Comstock on the east shoulder of Alta Vista, the wooded knoll above the present parking area. According to Val Comstock (written communication, 1962), "I have an old-time, perfectly restored print and film of my father's tourist camp . . . taken during the summer of 1895. He told me . . . that he was absolutely sure that his was the first tourist camp ever established at Paradise . . . The camp consisted of tents for cooking, serving meals and for lodging accommodations. The price for meals was 50 cents each, and for lodging, 50 cents per night . . . At the beginning of the next summer season, a Mr. Reese . . . took over and ran the famous Reese's Camp for about thirty [actually more like 20] years."

In 1897 John Reese set up another tent camp on Theosophy Ridge at the south base of Alta Vista. This camp was in operation until 1915 and served as a headquarters for the professional guide service managed by Reese and others. Until recently, evidence of this old tent camp was still noted in the form of squared-off platforms cut into the ridge crest; much of the evidence is now covered by wide asphalt-topped trails that ascend from the parking area.

During that period, as now, the prices charged by the concessioner for various facilities and services offered at Longmire and Paradise were approved by the National Park Service. Rates for rooms and tents at Longmire ranged from $1.50 per day for one person in a tent to $3 per day for two in a room; weekly rates ran from $8.75 to $17.50 for the same facilities. At Reese's Camp at Paradise, tent rentals ranged from $3 per day for one to $4 for two; weekly rates were from $14 to $24 for comparable facilities. For George B. Hall's tent camp at Indian Henrys Hunting Ground, beds and meals were each 75¢. Meals at Longmire were a la carte, and at Paradise were 50¢ each for breakfast and dinner and 75¢ for lunch. The authorized saddle horse and stage rates from Longmire to Paradise were $3 round trip; saddle horse trips to Indian Henrys were $3 round trip.

The opening of the public road to Paradise in 1915 brought a demand for more sophisticated overnight accommodations and facilities. In 1916 the Rainier National Park Company was formed and construction began on Paradise Inn. The Inn, of rustic western style, was completed in 1917 and, with the later addition of an annex still provides the principal hotel and dining facilities in the Park. In 1930 Paradise Lodge was completed half a mile to the west to serve the rapidly increasing

Road and trail approaches to climbs on Mount Rainier. (Mudflows have caused closure of West Side Road above Fish Creek. See NPS for road information.)

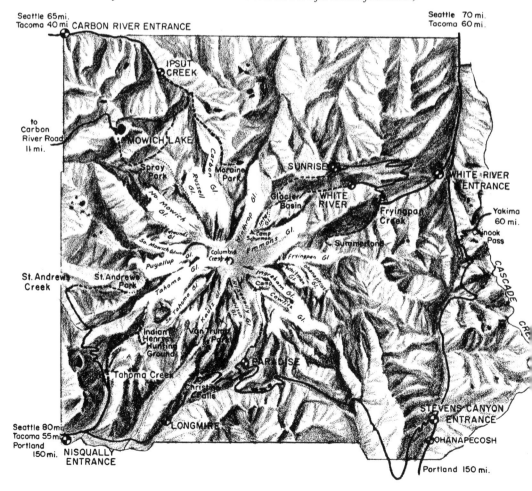

Reese's Camp on Theosophy Ridge at Paradise, 1910.

tourism. Later, about 275 wooden cabins were built below the Lodge to handle overflow crowds and offer housekeeping facilities. During World War II the cabins were removed from the Park and sold for emergency housing in the Puget Sound area.

Several buildings at Paradise were removed in later years. The Community Building, which for many years was the center of Park naturalist activities and stood adjacent to Paradise Lodge, was torn down in 1948; Paradise Lodge was removed in 1964 and replaced by the Visitor Center of contemporary design. Opened to the public in September 1966, this circular structure is today the center for naturalist exhibits and programs, headquarters for the Park rangers; it also has a lunch counter and souvenir shop. Other buildings at Paradise that passed out of the picture in recent years were the old Tatoosh Club and Park Company warehouse, now replaced by a much-needed enlargement of the parking area. The "Ski Dorm," constructed in the early 1940s, now provides quarters for summer employees of the Park Service and concessioner. Nearby, another building of alpine design also serves as a dormitory for summer employees.

FACILITIES FOR THE MOUNTAINEER

Paradise Valley

During the period 1915–20, in the early days of "See America First" tourism, it became apparent the tent headquarters for the guide concession was inadequate to handle the growing mountaineering business in the Park. In 1920 the steep-roofed Guide House was built across the parking area from Paradise Inn. The rustic structure has served since as the beginning point for the tourist-climber and as a dormitory for summer employees of the Rainier National Park Company.

Camp Muir

At 10,000-foot Camp Muir, takeoff point for most climbs on the southeast side of Rainier, two stone shelter cabins have been situated for years on either end of the low rock saddle separating the "Muir Snowfield" from upper Cowlitz Glacier. The smaller of the two cabins was built in 1916; the large shelter was completed in 1921. The two buildings have served nearly 50 years as a relief from mountain storms and as a base of operations during numerous search and rescue activities higher on the peak.

The smaller cabin, the "guide hut", had been used for many years by the professional guides as their base for summit ascents and mountaineering seminars, and as a cache for search and rescue equipment and supplies. The history of the cabin's varying occupancies is reflected

Paradise Inn in the 1920s.

Guide House.

in the numerous names and initials of past guides and clients which have been carved by knife or smoked by candle in the cedar beams overhead. The hut is permeated with the smells and memories of bygone days which made it a part of the climbing legend.

In 1970, owing to the growing demand for space and updated facilities, the interior of the guide hut was completely remodelled, which included addition of side windows and a ceiling skylight. The covering of the rough stone interior by brightly painted plywood panels, and replacement of the crude tables by formica counters, have given the place a fresh look. It now serves solely as a kitchen and living quarters for the attractive young women who cook for the guide service. Downslope from the hut, a larger prefab plywood cabin was installed to serve as a dormitory for the guides and their clients. This spacious building, about 15 feet by 25 feet, has three tiers of bunks and sleeps about 40 climbers comfortably, and more under emergency conditions.

The large stone shelter at the east end of the rocky saddle was designed for public use. It was remodelled in 1968: the old steel-frame bunks and the moldy horsehair-filled mattresses were finally replaced by two full-length wood tiers covered by thick sponge pads. The cabin now accommodates 18–20 persons reclining crosswise to the length of the room. On busy weekends, however, space rapidly becomes filled and most climbers must pitch tents on the adjacent glacier and scree slopes or spread sleeping bags in the numerous rock-encircled windbreaks dug out along the ridge and around the cabins.

The years and erosive agents have taken their toll, however, particularly of the small guide hut perched on a continually narrowing crest. Repairs are required annually—recementing loosened stones and shoring up the slabs around the cabin's base, where the Cowlitz Glacier persistently eats away at the ridge. The doorway of the larger cabin was moved from the south side to the west several years ago; there it is better located and less subject to the drifting of winter snows. Two stone privies near the large cabin were the only such facilities available until 1969. They usually were filled with snow and ice until early July and even after being cleared for action the seats were not entirely protected against chilly updrafts from the glacier. In 1970 the situation was improved slightly by the addition of two one-holer chemical toilets. The main problem with these has been their rapid filling by garbage other than that intended—and their demand on busy weekends.

The 1969 climbing season also saw the installation of a new ranger facility. To maintain a closer liaison with mountaineers making use of

Panorama of Camp Muir, 1970.

The Beehive   Gibraltar Rock   Cadaver Gap   Cathedral Rocks

Butler Shelter A-frame)   Guide cabin (dorm)   Guide hut (Kitchen)   Public shelter

From Anvil Rock, below Camp Muir.

Camp Muir and heading for higher regions, and to serve as an emergency shelter for sick and injured climbers, the Park Service constructed a small ranger patrol cabin on the ridge above the guide hut. Built with a 9-by-10-foot base of pumice blocks and with wood A-frame sides, the cabin is now manned by experienced climbing rangers during the summer. The cabin was most appropriately named the Butler Shelter in honor of retired ex-Assistant Chief Ranger William J. "Bill" Butler, whose search and rescue missions on the mountain are legendary.

Each September, following the Labor Day weekend, Park rangers and guides face the monumental task of cleaning out the facilities at Camp Muir and making repairs necessary for protection of the cabins against the coming winter. The door of the large public shelter is secured by three screw-down flanges that effectively seal the building from drifting snow, yet still make it easily available to winter climbing parties. The garbage cleanup detail has been the major bugaboo. The trash not carried down the mountain by hikers and climbers must be raked up, packaged, and then lifted out in cargo nets by a helicopter—a costly "collection service." The job of the rangers was considerably eased late in the summer of 1969 by volunteer help from Tacoma's Summit Alpine Club. Members of the club made a round-trip hike between Paradise and Camp Muir, picking up trash along the well-beaten trail—bottles, cans, paper cartons, candy wrappers, etc. discarded by thoughtless hikers. It is hoped the example set by the climbing club will be followed by others. In 1970, a trash burner was installed at the camp to partially alleviate the local garbage situation.

Camp Muir is reached by hundreds of hikers each summer, many shod in only street shoes or sneakers and clad in shorts. The 3-6 hour, 4-mile climb from Paradise provides the Sunday hiker with an intimate view of Rainier's upper icefalls and rugged ridges, and perhaps a brief association with those who struggle upward under heavy packs and higher ambitions. Frequently during the summer Camp Muir is in clear weather high above a cloud-sea that is dismal fog at Paradise, and the hike takes the neophyte into an arctic-alpine region he will seldom find so accessible elsewhere.

Certain hazards lurk to trap the uninitiated, however. Every year hikers become lost in sudden, thick fogs. The snowfields leading to Muir, in many years apparently harmless, and well-marked by tracks of countless hikers, also occasionally have large crevasses hidden beneath a few inches of snow. More than one hiker has experienced the shuddering step through thin snow that covers a dark hole along the beaten path. The list of near-fatal experiences, and tragic loss of life, continues to grow each year as poorly-clad, ill-equipped individuals hike to Camp Muir.

Cloud-sea from Camp Muir.

GIBRALTAR ROUTE

Early accounting of numbers is vague, but doubtless several thousand climbers reached the crater rim via the "Gib Route" between 1870 and 1936, the last year the original ledge trail was intact.

These people all share similar memories: the 4-6 hour trudge to Camp Muir from Paradise; the crowded, dimly-lit interior of the Muir cabins, or if these were already filled, the night outside under the stars, protected from the wind only by a low rock wall; the early rise near midnight with a hasty breakfast of tea and cereal or perhaps just a chocolate bar; the numb-fingered fumbling with knots and ropes; the climb by headlamp or flashlight to the crest of Cowlitz Cleaver beyond the Beehive, through the high windy notch at Camp Misery; the breathtaking traverse along the narrow rock ledge high on the icicle-festooned west face of Gibraltar Rock, followed by the steep ice chute above Gib; the morning sunlight at the top of Gibraltar and a brief rest before the long, seemingly endless struggle to the crater rocks—those with more ambition sharing memories of the slow trudge across the saucer-shaped, snow-filled crater to the highest point at Columbia Crest. During the descent, all recall the wary traverse across the Gib ledge during the heat of day, when falling icicles and rocks continually threaten instant destruction.

In 1936, following several summers when ever-increasing quantities of dripping water and icicles were a feature of the overhanging section of the Gibraltar trail, and a few days after the final climb of the summer, a large section of the ledge tumbled away in a rock avalanche, leaving only a vertical scar at the site of the trail. According to guide Gene Jack (oral communication, March 1969), during his descent along the trail just prior to Labor Day of 1936 he noted in the ledge next to the wall a crack forming which was large enough for him to

The Beehive.

Old Gibraltar trail before ledge avalanched away in late summer 1936.

shove in his gloved hand. A few days later Jack observed from below at Paradise that debris from a large slide lay across the surface of the Nisqually Glacier below the face of the vast wall.

For the next 11 years numerous attempts were made to find a way across the Gibraltar face but all were thwarted by discouraging rockfall and loose footing. Finally, on July 13, 1948 my brother K Molenaar and George Senner, seasonal Park rangers, found a way by dropping to a lower ledge system, following this around several points and alcoves in the face of Gibraltar, and climbing to rejoin the upper end of the original trail. This exploratory effort re-opened Gib and in subsequent years it again provided the most direct route to the summit snows from Camp Muir. Even then, however, spasmodic barrages of rockfall tended to relegate the Gib route to a secondary choice among mountaineers. The route now is recommended only with caution for small parties of fast-moving climbers. Hard hats are strongly recommended.

A statistical study of rockfall hazards during climbs since 1950 on the Gibraltar ledges was made by Tom Miller (*The Mountaineer*, 1954). Miller's compilation, based on response to questionnaires mailed to leading Northwest climbers, is summarized:

Of 172 reported morning crossings of the ledges, 80% experienced rockfall. These included 12 near-misses and 3 personal direct hits—an

Nisqually ice cliff and chute from Gibraltar trail.

Rainier from south, showing routes climbed from Paradise Valley and Van Trump Park.

average of about one hit per 46 individuals crossing the ledges in the morning hours. Of 88 personal crossings of the ledges in the afternoon, after the sun had melted icicles and loosened ice-held rocks, 97% experienced rockfall, 21 had near-misses, and 2 were hit—an average of about 1 hit per 44 crossings. Those reporting afternoon rockfall conditions state the rocks and icicles were falling continuously (or at least 10 times) during their time on the ledge system. Probably of greater impact are excerpts from testimonies volunteered by those questioned:

I don't like the "Gib" route. It is going to kill someone some day . . . B. H. was hit on the head by a rock the size of a building brick—a glancing blow, just above the roping-down place . . . About three truck loads of large size rocks fell about three seconds later but we had gotten under the overhang just in time . . . no more "Gib" route for me . . . The impressive and frightening thing was they [the rocks] came without sound or warning—

Gibraltar ledge trail and overhang in 1928.

due to steep and overhanging nature of cliffs much stuff falls free, without any bounces . . . Without warning the rocks started shedding extremely large pieces, most of which fell between two rope teams. The rope teams in the rear returned to Muir . . . At a vantage point halfway across the ledge (descending 2 p.m.) we held up our trip for an hour counting the rocks. For the first half hour a rock that could have been fatal fell on the average of one every five minutes. Then the sun went behind a cloud and for the next half hour nothing fell and we made a hasty crossing . . . [when] the sun reappeared . . . a tremendous rock fall occurred . . . that lasted over five minutes. Had we been caught under this fall we could have done nothing to save ourselves . . . I would avoid this route in the future—too nerve racking.

Yet, to some, the route gave no particular problems, as suggested by the following comments:

The Gibraltar route hasn't produced any casualties in the past [not true!], so not having any other convenient route that could make use of the Camp Muir facilities it probably serves as the route for guided parties . . . Our accident report file indicates only an occasional minor injury from small falling rocks . . . injuries average 2 to 3 per season, none serious . . . Myself, in three trips over, have yet to see a rock come down . . . The danger in Gibraltar depends on whether the weather is hot or cold the day of the climb. Last year a party turned back on account of rock the day before our climb. It was very cold [during our climb] . . . and we experienced no rock fall either a.m. or p.m. . . I see no need to discourage the use of Gib by competent parties . . . As a guide using this route for two years and having totally inexperienced clients I've found it to be the most rapid route to the summit and as safe as the leader wishes to make it.

My personal experiences on the Gibraltar route during both summer and winter ascents have indicated that no formula revolving around time of day, weather, or season should be followed to evaluate the feasibility of a safe climb. During a climb on February 8, 1968 our party of 12 found conditions extremely hazardous. It had been a relatively mild winter, however, and snow depths along the ledges were considerably less than those during the winter ascent of 1922. Also, the day of our climb was warm and the snow was quite mushy. We experienced fall of both rock and large icicles during our passage of the ledge system.

Although the nature of the climbing conditions on the Gibraltar route, and on Rainier generally, has never encouraged its slopes to be used for footraces, two unusually fast round-trip climbs were made in July 1959. The Gibraltar route was climbed to the crater rim from Paradise and descended in a round-trip time of 7 hours and 20 minutes by John Day, 48-year-old Oregon rancher-sportsman, and the twins Jim and Lou Whittaker. Not to be outdone, 2 weeks later guides Dick McGowan and Gil Blinn left the Paradise Ranger Station at midnight and, via the Cadaver Gap-Ingraham Glacier route, reached the crater rim

Party on ladder ascent of crevasse wall at 13,000 feet, about 1928.

and returned to Paradise in time for breakfast at 6:40 a.m. According to McGowan (written communication, January 1969), "Our so-called speed record was timed by Park Ranger James Mink and Federal Trade Commissioner Lowell Mason. The time was 6 hours and 40 minutes, but Mink thought it would be better to go to 6 hours 41 minutes so it would not sound rounded off, and we had quite a discussion as to whether it should be 6 hours 39 minutes or 6 hours 41 minutes. The Trade Commissioner arbitrated the discussion and since the climbers were in no condition to argue much or to chase Mink around the parking lot, the time was finally arranged at 6 hours 41 minutes."

The normal climbing times on the Gibraltar route are 4-7 hours Paradise to Camp Muir, 5-8 hours Muir to crater, and 6-8 hours descent from crater to Paradise.

INGRAHAM-DISAPPOINTMENT CLEAVER

Since the late 1950s the most popular route to the summit from Paradise and Camp Muir has been by way of either the Ingraham Glacier or Disappointment Cleaver, depending on crevasse conditions. The Ingraham Glacier is reached from Camp Muir by contouring across the upper Cowlitz Glacier and climbing a steep scree slope to the 10,700-foot crest of Cathedral Rocks. Sometimes early-season snow conditions allow a shortcut to the upper Ingraham through 11,300-foot Cadaver Gap, the deep notch in the ridge crest between Cathedral Rocks and Gibraltar Rock.

The Ingraham is ascended (as crevasses allow) either directly up the glacier to opposite the top of Gibraltar Rock at about 12,700 feet, or by a traverse across the glacier from Cadaver Gap to near the base of Disappointment Cleaver, the long rock island separating the Ingraham and Emmons Glaciers. A ledge system of loose rock on the left (south) side of the cleaver above its base affords access to steep snowfields. Usually a staircase of suncups by July, the snow is followed along the crest of the cleaver to its top at about 12,300 feet. The merging upper parts of the Ingraham and Emmons Glaciers are then ascended to the crater rim. In some years the Ingraham is so badly crevassed that even the base of Disappointment Cleaver cannot be reached; under these conditions a long traverse must be made below the cleaver to the Emmons. On these routes, on the sides of the mountain facing the sun, suncups generally are well developed between 11,000 and 13,000 feet and by early July offer good footing during the ascent. However, during the descent on clear, warm days the sun-softened snow staircase provides sloppy footing and memorable frustrations to the tired climber.

Above 11,000 feet the Ingraham Glacier changes from year to year;

Sunrise on the Ingraham.

it is either a relatively smooth "highway" to the top of Gibraltar or is a chaos of crevasses and broken ice blocks that can provide the most challenging ice climb on the mountain. Also, any ascent of the upper Ingraham that approaches Gibraltar requires constant observation for rockfall from the cliffs.

An ascent of the Ingraham Glacier by an Army unit was made in late spring of 1942, following the entry of America into the conflicts in the Pacific and Europe. The 87th Mountain Infantry Regiment was formed in early 1942 at Fort Lewis, Washington. A detachment of 350 officers and men from the 87th was temporarily assigned to training exercises at Paradise Valley from mid-February to late May 1942. There the group tested equipment and rations and practiced winter troop movements and survival. As a windup to the maneuvers, a party of eight officers and men spent 2 weeks high on the mountain, with a base camp established at Camp Muir on May 8. Foul weather most of the period held the soldiers close to camp, with 1-6 inches of snow falling nearly every day. After several scouting trips, a high camp was established at 12,300 feet at the top of Disappointment Cleaver. From there the summit was reached on May 16.

Normal summer climbing time: Camp Muir to crater rim 6-8 hours; descent to Muir about 3-4 hours.

KAUTZ GLACIER

When first climbed by Kautz and his companions in 1857, the approach to the upper Kautz Glacier was made from below the terminus of the Nisqually Glacier and up through Van Trump Park and the steep snowfields above. With development of Paradise Valley and subsequent use of the Gibraltar ledge trail as the main route to the summit, little interest was shown in repeating Kautz' trek until 56 years later.

Although never previously reported, an ascent of the Kautz route in 1913 was brought to my attention by Harry B. Cunningham (chief guide 1925–32). Cunningham wrote (December 1968): "In 1913, a group of seven men and three women started up from the Nisqually bridge for a climb via the Kautz route. Dr. Meany was an old man then [Meany was 51 at the time], and with two of the women, he stopped at the 6500- or 7000-foot elevation and returned to the Reese camp in Paradise Valley. Joe Hazard was the guide. As I recall . . . we named the rock cliff below the Kautz Ice Fall 'Camp Hazard' where we stopped for 3 or 4 hours prior to continuing the climb to the summit." Because Joe Hazard never mentioned his participating in this climb of 1913, and wrote only of his 1921 and 1924 ascents of the Kautz route, I questioned Cunningham further. He advised that he was certain of the year but was not entirely sure about Hazard's part in the ascent.

A more clearly recorded ascent of the Kautz Glacier was made on July 26–28, 1920 by a party composed of Swiss guides-brothers Hans and Heinie Fuhrer, Park Superintendent Roger W. Toll, and Mountaineer Harry M. Myers. The group began the climb from Christine Falls on the Longmire-Paradise Highway and ascended by way of Van Trump Park to the upper snowfields followed by Lieutenant Kautz 63 years earlier. The party had little difficulty climbing directly over the Kautz Glacier icefall and from there continued to the summit. The descent was via the Gibraltar route (Brockman, 1946; Hans Fuhrer, oral communication, 1956).

Since 1934 the Kautz route has been ascended at least once each summer. During the period 1939–50, following closure of the Gibraltar route when the well-traveled ledge avalanched away late in the summer of 1936, the Kautz route was used almost exclusively as the line of ascent from Paradise, by both guided and independent parties. The route of the earlier approaches by way of Christine Falls and Van Trump Park was replaced by that now taken from Paradise. From the trail at Glacier Vista (6400), a descent and crossing of Nisqually Glacier are made to the steep snow gully cutting the opposite wall. From the top of the gully the route ascends the upper west edge of the Wilson Glacier and rock ridges to "The Turtle," the large snowfield rising from 9800 to 11,000 feet. This is climbed to a high camp usually at Camp Hazard on the rock ridge at about 11,300 feet, below the Kautz ice cliff. Owing to the loss of elevation in crossing the Nisqually Glacier and the location of camp at such high altitude, the first day of the climb requires 8-10 hours from Paradise. At Camp Hazard the only protection from

Edge of Wilson Glacier on lower Kautz route.

winds that sweep the pumice-covered ridge is provided by low rock walls laboriously constructed by climbing parties.

I spent my first summer of guiding on Mount Rainier in 1940 and nostalgically recall a typical evening at Camp Hazard (*The Mountaineer*, 1944):

This high camp is reached at five o'clock in the evening and soon all packs are cast off. The climbers step around drunkenly under the effects produced on the suddenly unweighted shoulders. This wears off, however, and the preparations for the night are made by building of rock-ringed windbreaks. Sleeping bags are found in a small canvas tent. This is left here throughout the summer to protect the bags and primus stoves that are not necessarily brought from below on each climb . . . Meanwhile, the guide brings water from the small stream flowing from the cliff, before the now-increasing cold freezes the water over for the night. The primus stove is finally started up and hissing, after the usual amount of oral persuasion, and hot tea and soup are soon warming the body. Meat sandwiches and chocolate bars fill the menu and the climbers relax after supper to enjoy the scene spread out below . . .

The sun has nearly completed its arc in the sky and is turning to a ball of red in the west. The sharp, black silhouette of Success Cleaver forces itself boldly and obliquely into the right edge of the colorful picture. Upon closer scrutiny into the darkness of the ridge, cold névé patches are barely discernible. Long icicles hang from rocky ledges in the gathering darkness and add to the frigidity of the scene. The Kautz Glacier, comparatively narrow at this point, possibly a quarter mile across, flows steeply from the icefall and, in its narrow channel, disappears in the distance over another cataract of ice. As the sun sinks lower, a few scattered clouds in the west, golden-lined, present an unforgetable picture that brings to mind here the short poem by Chief Guide Clark Schurman:

"Into the cloud-sea far below,
I, lonely, watched the red sun go,
Then turning, miracle of glad surprise,
Enchanted, saw a full moon rise.

The night is drawing near and the still coldness of the upper regions settles in as the men, after having their packs made ready to go, prepare to catch a few hours of sleep and to rest weary muscles. An early start at 2:30 a.m. is anticipated and the guide lays out the ropes, knots ready, to avoid a later unnecessary fumbling and seeking ends in the frigid morning air. The individual shelters and sleeping bags now resemble so many cocoons. Darkness comes slowly and with this the snow domes of Adams and St. Helens, no longer rosy in the afterglow of sunset, turn purple, then only the gray summits are visible through the dusk and distance. Stars come out slowly and give one a vague feeling of intimate nearness to Heaven, while far below in contrast the lights of the valley indicate the presence of the human element.

Suddenly a bright light is flashed up from the valley. It is 9 o'clock and time for the pre-arranged signal back to the Guide House. The link with friends below is momentarily connected as the guide flashes back that all is well and going according to schedule. Soon all is again silence about, save for an occasional snap and tinkle of a frozen fragment of ice breaking and falling somewhere in the cliff above. A faint rustle of wind whips up the pumice dust about the shelters and the sleeping bags are drawn closer about the shoulders. The constellations in the vast firmament above blink down over all, and a small, big-eyed mouse, proprietor of Hotel Hazard, scampers among metal pots in his watch to see that all guests are resting well.

Today the principal attraction of the Kautz route is the ice cliff, which offers 300-500 feet of technical challenge. The character of the cliff between 11,300 and 12,000 feet changes from year to year. It may

Routes over Kautz ice cliff and up chute.

Descending Kautz ice chute.

offer a direct climb above camp, through an intricate maze of ice pinnacles and narrow terraces, or it may start with a vertical wall 25-100 feet high, requiring the less spectacular, though more assured, line of ascent up the snow chute to the west. By mid-July in most years, however, the steep upper part of this chute loses its snow cover and requires some step-chopping or a traverse into ice pinnacles and terraces on the margins. During descents of the Kautz route, highly exposed rappels of 50 feet or more often may be made from the ice cliff. As described later, the party making the first ascent of Sunset Ridge in 1938 had considerable trouble descending the mountain by way of the Kautz ice cliff.

Although some ice can be expected to break away anytime from the towering wall, there have been few avalanches of major proportions. In July 1946, though, a large party of Mountaineers had barely regained Camp Hazard when the gully they had just left was swept by blocks of

Rappel from Kautz ice cliff.

ice "as big as freight cars." Had the fall come several minutes sooner, the result might well have been disastrous for the entire party. For safety, camp should be located near the ridge crest or in a protected position free from potential ice fall. On more than one occasion, during my numerous canteen-filling sorties to trickles of water melting from the slopes near camp, fragments of ice from above have come uncomfortably close.

Among my memories of the pre-war era on this route is that of an immensely enjoyable climb with a party of seven energetic young Navy ensigns from Bremerton in late August of 1941. Less than 4 months later, on December 7th, five of the seven officers lost their lives during the bombing of Pearl Harbor.

Normal climbing time: 8-10 hours to Camp Hazard; 5-8 hours to summit; 6-8 hours return to Paradise.

FUHRER FINGER (1920)

On July 2, 1920 another route was pioneered to the summit from Paradise Valley. A party of guides including Hans and Heinie Fuhrer, Pey-
ton Farrer, Thomas Hermans, and Chief Guide Joseph T. Hazard, took
"the shortest distance between two points" and headed directly up the
mountain from the valley. They crossed the Nisqually Glacier and
climbed through crevasse fields to near the head of the Wilson Glacier.
From there they followed a long and steep snow-filled couloir which
gave direct access to the summit snow dome at about 11,500 feet on
the upper west edge of the Nisqually Glacier. Although originally called
"a climb of the Nisqually Glacier," the party was on the Nisqually only
in its lower and upper reaches. The snow couloir is known today as
Fuhrer Finger in honor of the two popular Swiss brothers.

Among the interesting subsequent ascents of Fuhrer Finger is that
by Ranger William J. Butler, whose previous and later exploits in search
and rescue operations on the mountain provide enough material for a
book in itself. As the story goes, Butler left Paradise Inn in a huff one
evening after his girl friend Marthie (later to become his wife) decided
to dance with another fellow. To relieve frustrations, Butler headed up
Rainier during the night, taking the shortest route, Fuhrer Finger. He
was back from the summit 11 hours 20 minutes later; to his dismay,
Marthie hadn't missed him.

A further demonstration of the practicality of the Fuhrer Finger
as a fast route occurred April 13, 1951 when a Park ranger party, of
which I was a member, made a 14-hour non-stop ascent in an effort to
help Lieutenant John Hodgkins, who had just made an unprecedented
(and unauthorized) plane landing on the summit snows of Rainier.

Since 1951 Fuhrer Finger has become increasingly popular and is
now climbed by several parties each summer and usually at least once
in the winter season. High camp is best located at about 9500 feet,
either on the rock ridge on the west edge of the Wilson Glacier, or on
the ridge east of the bottom of the finger. Some rockfall down the long
couloir must be anticipated in late summer, as snow melts downward
and more rock is exposed. Up higher, where the finger joins the upper
Nisqually Glacier, long crevasses open in late July and some problems
are then encountered in climbing rapidly above this point.

Normal climbing time: 5-7 hours to high camp; 5-8 hours to summit; 4-5 hours return to Paradise.

NISQUALLY-GIBRALTAR CHUTE (1946)

Rising steeply from the Nisqually Glacier cirque at 11,000 feet to the upper north end of Gibraltar Rock at 12,000 feet is a long couloir which early in the summer is filled with snow. Later it becomes a dirt- and ice-scoured chute down which drains the debris breaking loose from Gibraltar Rock. A complete ascent of the chute from the Nisqually Glacier, via a traverse around from Camp Muir, was reported to the writer by Paul Gilbreath (written communication, 1956). According to Gilbreath's memory, he made the climb with Stan DeBruler and "a man named Hewitt" during the summer of 1946. They descended the same way. A second ascent of the route was done by guide Gary Rose and two clients on July 1, 1956. This is not a popular climb; it involves a long traverse from Camp Muir and considerable hazard of rockfall and icefall from both Gibraltar and the hanging cliff of the upper Nisqually Glacier. Midwinter ascents of the chute were made by two parties on February 22, 1969.

NISQUALLY ICEFALL (1948)

The Nisqually Glacier, largest on the south side of Rainier, extends from the crater rim and summit dome in a long and tortuous descent of 4½ miles into the deep, timber-lined canyon opposite Paradise Valley. At 13,000 feet the glacier is split into two ice streams by a rock buttress, Nisqually Cleaver. The eastern half of the glacier descends toward Gibraltar Rock and at about 12,000 feet forms an abrupt 200-foot ice cliff completely detached from its continuation far below. The western part of the Nisqually Glacier flows in a jumbled cascade through the narrow constriction between Wapowety Cleaver on the west and Nisqually Cleaver on the east. This is the Nisqually Icefall, often the steepest and most heavily broken glacier area on the mountain. Although in clear view of Paradise during the many years of exploration and development on the south side of the mountain, not until 1948 was this line of ascent successfully attempted. It was my good fortune to be a member of the two-man party.

On the afternoon of July 14, 1948 Bob Craig and I, both employed at the time as seasonal Park rangers, climbed to Camp Muir. After a few sleepless hours filled with apprehensions, we arose about midnight, eager to get the anticipated ordeal underway. Our departure from Camp Muir was premature, however, and it was still too dark to find a way across the badly crevassed cirque of the Nisqually. To keep warm and pass the next hour until dawn we huddled together in rocks at the edge of the ice. At first hint of light we headed diagonally upward across the glacier, passing around long crevasses and isolated towers of ice—debris of avalanches from the icefall high above. Once we had arrived at the base of the icefall we proceeded immediately "into the fray,"

In the Nisqually Icefall, 1948.

gaining elevation rapidly up a steep 500-foot slope that extended into the frozen cascade above. Sighs of relief accompanied our attaining the inner sanctum of the icefall, where we no longer felt so exposed to the funneling of falling ice. The next 8 hours were spent in working a route through a great mass of fallen seracs and debris-filled crevasses; at several places we were forced to jump downward to cross the holes, thus cutting off our retreat. The biggest problem besides a cotton-mouthed thirst lay above the jumble of the main cascade, where we found many huge cracks extending nearly the entire width of the glacier, with upper lips overhanging the steep lower approaches. Once about the 12,500-foot level, however, the glacier assumed a more gradual slope to the crater rim, which we reached at 2:30 in the afternoon. Our descent was by a long glissade down Fuhrer Finger (*American Alpine Journal*, 1949; *The Mountaineer*, 1948).

Several attempts were made in subsequent years to repeat the ascent but not until July 10, 1959 was the icefall again climbed—by guides Dick McGowan and Gary Rose (*The Mountaineer*, 1960). Several ice screws were required to negotiate a nearly vertical 200-foot ice wall at the 11,500-foot level. The ever-changing character of the icefall is reflected in the subsequent pattern of successes and failures. From 1962 to 1967 ascents were made annually, 1964 being the banner year with 32 climbers negotiating the steep glacier. Among the parties completing the ascent in 1964 was one composed of four conquerors of Mount Everest: Tenzing Norgay, Jim Whittaker, Dr. Tom Hornbein, and Lute Jerstad. Tenzing's petite 90-pound wife Dhaku accompanied the men and was the first woman to scale the icefall (*Summit*, November 1965).

A winter ascent of the Nisqually Icefall was made February 11, 1968 by a nine-man party led by Gary Frederickson. The climb was relatively direct and no crevasse or serac problems were encountered. The descent was by the same route. During the summer of 1968, however, all attempts on the icefall ended in failure and during the following winter (1969) none of the five parties trying the route was successful.

WILSON GLACIER HEADWALL (1957)

The weekend of July 20–21, 1957 saw simultaneous climbs on two challenging "rotten" areas of Rainier—Curtis Ridge on the north side of the mountain and the Wilson Glacier headwall on the south side. The setting for the ascents was provided by a period of fresh snowfall followed by a period of thaw and melting and then a cold snap which firmly froze together the loose rocks.

Wilson Glacier headwall and Fuhrer Finger and Thumb routes.

Kautz ice cliff from Wilson Glacier headwall.

The Wilson Glacier heads in a steep-walled cirque at about 10,000 feet. Above the bergschrund several ice-filled couloirs rise to join a broad icefield pocketed within the apex of converging ridges that culminate at the 13,000-foot top of Wapowety Cleaver. Although now an inactive and ablated ice slope, prior to the mid-1940s it was a steep hanging lobe of thick ice fed from the west by the upper Kautz Glacier; the lobe formed a continuation to the east of the Kautz ice cliff. Today, only slides of loose rock and fresh snow down the couloirs attest to the past glories of large ice avalanches that once nourished the Wilson Glacier.

The climbing conditions and weather were perfect as Pete Schoening and I left Paradise at about 2:45 in the afternoon of July 20, 1957. Ascending rapidly on relatively unbroken slopes on the edge of the Wilson Glacier, we reached the bergschrund in late afternoon, crossed it on the right, then worked directly up the left (west) edge of the main central couloir in the headwall. Without removing crampons we gingerly ascended a 15-foot rock ledge across the avalanche-scarred constriction in the center of the gully. From here we climbed along the left side of the couloir to where it opens out at about 11,000 feet. A small rock ledge beneath a protecting overhang was leveled off and we were in our sleeping bags by 8 o'clock, restlessly wary of the 200-foot Kautz ice cliff above and out of sight beyond the overhang. Pete and I recalled that exactly 4 years earlier, on K2 in the Himalayas, we shared similarly small campsites on narrow platforms, but there we were not menaced by such an ice cliff.

After a typically sleepless night, but one that was nonetheless beautiful and clear, we arose at the first hint of dawn at 2:30 a.m. and continued upward. A steep diagonal traverse was made on the frozen snow covering the upper ice slope, and no rockfall was noted. We reached the apex of Wapowety Cleaver (13,000) with the first pink rays of the rising sun. After a brief pause for a cold breakfast we continued upward to the crater rim, arriving at 6:15 a.m. with hardly a crevasse detour on the upper Nisqually Glacier. We descended via the Gibraltar route, arriving at Paradise at 10 a.m. (*American Alpine Journal*, 1958; *The Mountaineer*, 1958).

The second ascent of the headwall was made 10 years later by Dan Davis, Tom Stewart, and Bruce Loughlin, who climbed the couloir to the west of the one followed by Schoening and me. The Wilson headwall can provide a relatively straightforward climb during ideal conditions of early summer and when snow covers the rocks, but it can be extremely hazardous at other times and hard hats are strongly recommended. High camp is best situated at about 9500 feet on rocks above the west edge of the Wilson Glacier.

NISQUALLY ICE CLIFF (1962)

The Nisqually ice cliff, between the Nisqually Cleaver and Gibraltar Rock, was first climbed by two men who were to gain wider fame by standing together on the summit of Mount Everest less than a year later. On August 13, 1962 Barry Bishop, National Geographic Society photographer-writer-mountaineer, and Rainier guide Lute Jerstad made the ascent of the ice cliff during the evening "off hours" of a Camp Muir climbing seminar. After noting favorable snow conditions on the mountain, they left Muir about 7:30 in the evening of a moonlit night and traversed around the corner and upward to the head of the Nisqually cirque below the left end of the ice cliff. They climbed to the base of the rock below the ice wall and worked up this to the ice. An ice screw was used for belaying around the left end of the 200-foot wall. The top of the cliff was reached at 10:30, after which a diagonal climb was made to the top of Gibraltar Rock. They descended to Camp Muir along the ledge trail by moonlight (*National Geographic Magazine*, May 1963).

NISQUALLY CLEAVER (1967)

The cleaver which separates the Nisqually Icefall and ice cliff was first climbed on June 19, 1967 by Jim Wickwire and Fred Dunham. Finding the lower two prominent buttresses and the rock band above offered no feasible route, they were forced to follow the route taken in 1962 by Bishop and Jerstad to gain the top of the ice cliff. While trying to climb an overhanging rock cliff below the ice wall, Wickwire "peeled off" twice, so they decided to attain the crest of the cleaver higher up. The climb to the head of the Nisqually Cleaver (13,000) involved considerable route-finding problems on snow ledges and over alternating rock bands. From Camp Muir the ascent required 6½ hours (Wickwire, written communication, 1967).

Routes above Camp Muir. From left: Nisqually Cleaver, Nisqually ice cliff, Nisqually-Gibraltar chute, Gibraltar.

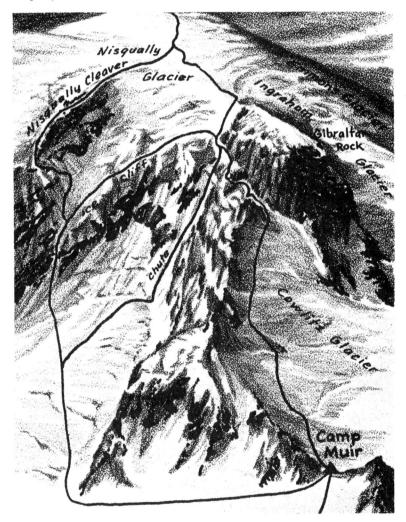

KAUTZ CLEAVER (1957)

Rising from its base at 8800 feet to about 13,000 feet, where it merges into the upper part of Success Cleaver, the Kautz Cleaver forms the divide between the Kautz and Success Glaciers. The ridge is composed of vertical rock bands alternating with loose, steep slopes of pumice and scree, and offered a climbing terrain that was attractive only until the first ascent had been pioneered.

On August 31, 1957 George Senner and Charles "Bud" Robinson left Christine Falls and climbed through Van Trump Park to the 8000-foot level on Wapowety Cleaver, overlooking the lower Kautz Glacier. Here they dropped to the Kautz and followed its right margin to about 9000 feet before crossing a heavily-crevassed area above a prominent icefall. (A week earlier George Sainsbury suffered a broken ankle in a fall into a crevasse in the icefall.) The crest of the cleaver was gained at about 9300 feet. A climb to 10,000 feet brought them to a narrow ledge protected by an overhang of firm rock on the otherwise-crumbling ridge. After leveling the pumice and troughing a narrow platform wide enough to hold two sleeping bags securely, Senner and Robinson bivouacked for the night on this airy perch overlooking the Kautz Glacier.

It was a relatively warm night, and the late summer sky was filled with stars, a promise of excellent, though hot, weather for the next day's climb. But, as later described, the mountain was to levy one of its rare tolls on one of several parties heading for the summit the next morning.

Rising early, Senner and Robinson started up the cleaver. The ridge crest widened as they gained altitude and the route alternated between several snow gullies and rock ribs for 1500 feet. The cleaver merged into the area where a number of ridges and couloirs formed a broader aspect of the face. The upper 2500 feet of the climb to Point Success was on the upper part of Success Cleaver. The face here is banded by numerous short rock cliffs separated by snow and scree slopes; several snow gullies provide passage at various points. The top of Point Success (14,150) was surmounted at 3 p.m. As they rested they noted several military aircraft passing above slopes on the opposite side of the summit dome, but they were unaware of the tragic drama being played that day on the upper slopes of the Ingraham Glacier.

The lateness of the hour discouraged them from crossing the low saddle to the crater rim and Columbia Crest. They returned the way they had climbed, reaching the bivouac at 6 o'clock and the upper meadows of Van Trump Park as darkness arrived.

According to Senner, the climb is devoid of technical difficulties and the upper part of the cleaver is broad and offers a number of variations. However, suitable campsites are rare and their selection seemed to be the best (*American Alpine Journal*, 1958). A second ascent of the cleaver was made May 28–30, 1966 by Ray Smutek, Len and Judy Waller, and Bob Forgie.

KAUTZ GLACIER HEADWALL (1963)

The Kautz Glacier headwall is the steep finger of snow and rock that rises toward Point Success on the right (east) side of Kautz Cleaver. It is bounded on the east by the upper part of the Kautz Glacier, which comes into the lower part of this steep couloir at about 11,000 feet in the form of a detached narrow tongue of ice below the Kautz ice chute.

The headwall was first climbed July 8, 1963 by Pat Callis, Dan Davis, and Don Gordon (Claunch). The trio climbed from Christine Falls and Van Trump Park to the lower part of Wapowety Cleaver, where they made high camp at about 10,000 feet. From here the descent was easy to the glacier, which was then climbed to the left of the ice breakups below the hanging upper part of the Kautz Glacier. Several crevasses were skirted as they ascended the snow couloir and entered the upper slopes. The climb to Point Success was completed in a whiteout and involved working around and over several rock bands. Due to blizzard conditions at the top they were forced to spend a miserable night in a snow cave, continuing to Columbia Crest next morning (*American Alpine Journal*, 1964).

Because the climb was made in early summer, the upper slopes were well covered by snow; later in the season considerable rockfall must be anticipated.

FUHRER THUMB (1972)

The mopping-up exercises on minor gullies not sought earlier on the mountain included two early season climbs made a day apart in the 1500-ft snow gully designated as Fuhrer Thumb, immediately west of Fuhrer Finger. The two parties diverged their ascents in the middle part of the gully. The first climb was made May 27, 1972, by Jim Wickwire, Charlie Raymond, and Tom Stewart, who stayed to the right side of a rock island partway up. The second party, Niels Andersen and several members of his climbing class, climbed around the left side of the rocks on May 28. Wickwire reported sustained rockfall down the 40-degree slope; they climbed unroped to allow freer dodging ability. The ascent took 2 hrs. from the bergschrund to the top of the gully where it joins the snow slope above Fuhrer Finger. There the party bivouacked in a snow cave, to the tune of Stewart's harmonica and Scottish ballads. The summit was reached in 4 hrs. the following morning, with the descent to the cave taking only an hour. For Wickwire, Raymond, and Stewart, this ascent provided a good conditioner for their rugged climb a short time later on the south face of Mount McKinley.

A winter ascent of Fuhrer Thumb on February 27, 1973, by Lee Nelson and Jerry Hasfjord, involved a week's storm and snow-cave bivouac. Repeated days of heavy snowfall and high winds prevented attainment of the summit after the gully was climbed in waistdeep snow.

10 Ascents from Tahoma Creek

The best approach to climbs on the southwest flanks of Mount Rainier is from the Tahoma Creek Picnic Area (3100) 4.3 miles up the West Side Road. (The picnic area until 1967 was a campground but was closed following partial inundation by a mudflow from the terminus of the South Tahoma Glacier.) A trail along Tahoma Creek is followed 2.2 miles to the bridge, where a side trail of 1.4 miles leads to Indian Henrys Hunting Ground (5300), a base for guiding operations before 1900 by P. B. Van Trump and in the early 1900s by guide Joe Stampfler. This beautifully situated alpine area is the starting point for ascents on Success Cleaver, the South Tahoma Glacier headwall, and the Success Glacier couloir. Registration for the climbs can be made at the Nisqually Entrance. There one also can obtain information on the condition of the West Side Road, which may be snow covered during early summer.

SUCCESS CLEAVER (1905)

Success Cleaver, the long ridge that dominates the left skyline of Rainier as viewed from Paradise, is in late summer the only all-rock route to the 14,000-foot level on the mountain. The cleaver rises from above the base of 6937-foot Pyramid Peak to Point Success in a series of scree and pumice slopes, rock ledges, and knife-edged cockscombs.

Point Success from near Pyramid Peak.

Columbia Crest

Pt. Success

Liberty Cap

Camp Hazard

Sunset Ridge

1965

1937

1965

Kautz Cleaver

Kautz Glacier

Sunset Amphitheater

1958

1939

1958

St. Andrews Rock

1959

1805 or 1905

Success Cleaver

Success Glacier

1960

Today's routes

1963

South Tahoma Glacier

Pyramid Glacier

Cleaver

Camp site

Tahoma Glacier

1891

Tahoma Cleaver

puyallup

1934

St. Andrews Park

Tahoma Glacier

Success Cleaver

To Indian Henrys Hunting Ground

Glacier   Island

To Tahoma Creek

Rainier from southwest, showing routes climbed from Tahoma Creek and St. Andrews Creek on West Side Road.

The lengthy ridge has never been a popular route. Until 1969, the year when 10 of 12 climbers starting reached the top, few parties have attained the characteristic for which the ridge was named. The climb is best in early summer, when snow still covers the sloping ledges of loose rock.

The first ascent of Success Cleaver was made by two young men of the joint Sierra Club-Mazamas Outing of 1905, Ernest Dudley and John R. Glascock. On July 27, 1905, upon hearing that another group was planning an attempt on the ridge from Indian Henrys Hunting Ground, Dudley and Glascock quickly took off from their party's large encampment at Paradise Valley and crossed the Nisqually, Van Trump, and Kautz Glaciers to attain the Cleaver beyond. The precise route taken by the two is somewhat unclear from their description, particularly the point at which they began the climb of the ridge proper, but there is no doubt they reached the summit by traversing Point Success from the rocky ridges below. Their descent of the mountain was made with other members of the outing who had come up the Gibraltar route the same day (*Sunset Magazine*, November 1905; Seattle *Post Intelligencer*, July 27, 1905).

Joe Stampfler, from his guide-tent headquarters at Indian Henrys Hunting Ground in the early 1900s, led two parties up Success Cleaver in 1914; one of these both ascended and descended the cleaver. The

Guide Joe Stampfler and party at Indian Henrys Hunting Ground, August 2, 1912, before making an ascent of Success Cleaver. From left: Phil Barrett, Stampfler, Frank Kandle.

group included Margaret Hargrave (Wunderling), the first woman to complete the ascent of the ridge (*The Mountaineer*, 1920; Mrs. Wunderling, written communication, 1949).

Five subsequent ascents were made of Success Cleaver prior to World War II.

From 1935 through 1969 the ridge has been attempted during only 21 of the 34 summers and success on Success Cleaver was achieved in only 8 of these years.

An early-day description of the cleaver route is provided by the following excerpts from an article by J. H. Weer (*The Mountaineer*, 1918). The article covers the 1918 climb in which he took part with R. S. Wainwright and Harry M. Myers:

. . . Success Cleaver entices those fond of rock-work in mountain climbing. Untraversed by any glacier it is one of the only two all-rock formations connecting timber-line and Rainier's snow cap, the other unsurmountable. Extending downward, southwesterly, from Peak Success, Success Cleaver has been ground by glaciers to a remarkably narrow and sharp ridge. At its right [left] the cirque of South Tahoma Glacier impressively displays the destructiveness of Rainier's glaciers.

This article is based chiefly on observations and experiences of three Mountaineers, R. S. Wainwright, H. McL. Myers [H. M. Myers], and the writer during an ascent on August 23, 1918, the descent, on the following day, having been via Gibraltar route. Previous ascents via Success Cleaver are reported to have been three in number, by small parties under leadership of guide Joe Stampfler, from the last of which the descent was accomplished via the same route.

Five days of heavy rain . . . were followed by several remarkably clear days and nights. Camp (6500) at north base of Pyramid Peak was left at 2:15 a.m. and climbing was easy for a few hours, but after passing the 10,000-foot level difficulties were ever present.

At intervals every form and variety of rock entering into the structure of Mount Rainier was repeatedly encountered, ranging from fine sand to enormous upstanding projections at whose base it sometimes was necessary to crawl under outjutting ledges. The route at no place affords breadth of more than fifty feet in width to pick a course. Sometimes progress was along the very comb of the jagged cleaver, pulling and crawling up onto a huge rock and dropping down beyond. Again upstanding masses were skirted to right or left, though usually to right where the glaciers have not produced a sheer wall as has the South Tahoma.

That which seemingly makes this route impracticable for general use or for any other than experienced mountain climbers is the succession of treacherous chutes of rock, snow and ice, extending sharply downward to the main bodies of Kautz, Success, and Pyramid glaciers. These chutes must be traversed at varying angles at their very tips. During the climbing season their surfaces are mostly loose fine rock or sand, affording very insecure footing. On this occasion two inches of soft new snow increased the difficulties. A descent via Success Cleaver holds vastly greater hazards than an ascent.

This party found to their surprise, and gladly used, ropes in position for scaling at elevations of about 10,500 feet and 13,000 feet. These appeared so new it was assumed they had been recently placed. Later it was learned that Joe Stampfler had placed them in 1914 when making his last ascent, and only descent, via this route. This party included Margaret Hargrave, Mountaineer, the only woman to climb via this route and one of the only two people, according to report, to have ascended Rainier over three of the four known routes.

Nearing the top of Cleaver, and under Peak Success, the course swings to right up onto a snow slope leading by easy grade to the saddle between Peak Success and the crater.

Views of surpassing splendor by moonlight and at early dawn in the first stages of the ascent occasioned slow progress. Later, difficulties of the climb made speed impossible. Thus, over fifteen hours were consumed in reaching the saddle. Another hour was required to reach and cross the smaller (west) crater to its north rim, making a total time of sixteen and one-half hours. Hot lemonade and tea were made over steam jets at crater rim, then sleeping quarters were selected in one of the nearby steam-heated ice caves.

In late August of 1949 Chuck Welsh and I made a cross-mountain traverse by way of Success Cleaver and the Ingraham Glacier. We left the Tahoma Creek Campground at 1:30 on a hot summer afternoon, the coolness in the woods along Tahoma Creek being the only comfort experienced all weekend. Although we gained altitude rapidly once past Pyramid Peak, the climb for the next 5500 feet was a combination of scrambling up a steep incline of sand, racing breathlessly across sidehills of sliding scree and rubble, and cautiously straddling knife-edged cockscombs of crumbling lava. A bivouac at 11,000 feet involved the dig-

On Success Cleaver at about 10,000 feet.

ging of two small platforms in the pumice. Little water was to be found and we had a thirsty night. By the first light we continued up, swinging into the large alcove on the right side of the ridge at about 12,000 feet. A short scramble over several rock bands brought us onto the broad crest that combines the upper part of Success and Kautz Cleavers. For several hundred feet more we each selected our individual routes over and around low rock bands and reached Point Success unroped—to have been tied together below would have invited the rope to join us in tearing apart the rocks of the ridge. Our experience convinced us that Success Cleaver is best done early in the season—a staircase of sun-cupped snow generally simplifies the climb until late July in most years.

Normal climbing time: 11-13 hours to summit from road.

TAHOMA CLEAVER (1959)

The last major ridge on Rainier to be climbed was Tahoma Cleaver, the sharply eroded crest that separates the Tahoma and South Tahoma Glaciers. The cleaver is best reached from Tahoma Creek and the Emerald Ridge trail to the confluence of the moraines of the Tahoma and South Tahoma Glaciers below Glacier Island. A broad snow couloir up the center (west side) of Glacier Island is then ascended to the north edge of South Tahoma Glacier, which is followed to the base of the main cleaver at about 9000 feet. Camp can be made here or at about 10,000 feet. At that point is the highest suitable campsite, a small alcove at the base of a reddish rock tower.

The upper ridge was explored first in 1950 by seasonal Park Rangers Bob Johnson, K Molenaar, and George Senner. The ridge rises steeply from the 8400-foot altitude to a prominent rock spire at 11,700 feet which provided the vantage point for the reconnaissance. Beyond here a knife-crested gap separates the spire from a large rock buttress, the major obstacle to reaching the upper part of the cleaver. The 1950 exploration was halted below this point by a discouraging combination of steady rockfall and extreme heat.

A second attempt on the cleaver was made early in the summer of 1958 by George Senner, Willi Unsoeld, Klindt Vielbig, and me. Our climb began in beautiful weather but by the time we had retired into our four-man tent at 9000 feet on the cleaver we had strong misgivings about the clouds beginning to boil up around camp. Dawn found several inches of fresh snow covering the ground and the upper part of the mountain hidden in a swirling mist. However, we left camp for some exercise and continued nearly to the saddle below the base of the buttress before turning back.

On June 6, 1959 Vielbig returned to the attack with Paul Bellamy,

Tony Hovey, Don Keller, and Herb Steiner. The sharp spire on the ridge was bypassed on the right (south) side of the cleaver by a traverse on steep snow slopes about 200 feet below the crest. The ridge was regained at the base of the large buttress. About 40 feet to the left of the rock wall a 20-foot vertical pitch on firm rock was led by Vielbig. Another 200 feet of steep and touchy climbing brought the party to the top of the buttress. Rockfall was a constant hazard during the scramble. The ascent was continued on a broad, steeply sloping snow ledge to its upper end at about 13,700 feet, north of Point Success, with the Tahoma Glacier far below on the left. The climbers entered a cloud cap, working their way around a corner to the right for 300 feet. A serac field was then crossed to the summit icecap. The ascent from high camp to the top of the ridge required 11 hours (*The Mountaineer*, 1960).

A second ascent of the Tahoma Cleaver was made June 16, 1968 by Dan Davis, Steve Marts, Gene Prater, and Tom Stewart. A variation of the 1959 route was taken when the climbers found the rock pitch on the buttress had been completely eroded away to form a vertical wall. They were forced to traverse below the buttress for about half a mile on steep ice ledges on the north side of the ridge. Where the ledges petered out they ascended two long pitches of loose rock to regain the top of the main crest, which was followed to the upper part of the Tahoma Glacier below Point Success (Dan Davis, written communication, 1968).

120–degree panorama of upper Tahoma Glacier and Sunset Amphitheater, from 11,700 feet on Tahoma Cleaver.

The climb of the Tahoma Cleaver is another of the many rock routes on Rainier that should be done in early summer or late spring, when snow covers ledges and steep slopes that are later formed of loose scree and talus.

SUCCESS GLACIER COULOIR (1960)

The Success Glacier couloir is between Success Cleaver and Kautz Cleaver at the head of the Success Glacier. The long, steep, snow-filled gully was descended in 1947 by Park Rangers George Senner and "Forrey" Johnson after an ascent of Success Cleaver. Senner's interest in the various ridges and gully systems on this side of the mountain brought him back for an ascent of the long couloir in 1960 with Dick Wahlstrom.

On July 16, Senner and Wahlstrom approached the couloir via the lower Success Cleaver and an upward traverse of Pyramid Glacier to its head at about 9000 feet. There a low rock ridge was crossed to the Success Glacier, which was ascended to its head and to the base of the finger at about 10,500 feet. Near the top of the glacier a sleeping bag detached itself from Wahlstrom's pack and rolled down the long slope and into a crevasse far below. But the two continued upward, crossed the bergschrund, and climbed the lower part of the couloir to about 11,500, where they dug a campsite on the adjoining rock ridge.

The next morning, July 17, the climbers worked their way up the steep snow couloir to about 12,500 feet, where they zig-zagged on short, steep snow fingers around outcrops of loose rock toward the top of Kautz Cleaver. The Success Cleaver route was gained at about 13,800 feet and followed to Point Success. Following a brief pause, they descended by the same route, noting a fresh slide of snow had taken out their tracks for about 1000 feet in the lower reaches of the couloir. After jumping downward about 10 feet to cross the bergschrund, they descended the Success Glacier to the crevasse that contained the errant sleeping bag, which was retrieved.

Owing to the steepness of Success Finger and its exposure to the sun on this southwest slope of Rainier, considerable danger of snow avalanches exists in early summer; the route probably is best climbed in about mid- or late July when a suncupped snow surface offers better footing. After that the gully becomes nearly bare of snow and then is a long, tiring ascent up loose scree and rubble, with accompanying rockfall hazards. The confining nature of such a chute for snow avalanches and rockfall should restrict the use to small, fast-moving parties. Also, like all routes that have their approaches from Tahoma Creek (3100), the ascent involves a great gain in altitude (*American Alpine Journal*, 1961; *The Mountaineer*, 1961).

SOUTH TAHOMA HEADWALL (1963)

Between the Tahoma Cleaver and Success Cleaver is the deeply cut cirque of the upper South Tahoma Glacier. Rising from the bergschrund at the head of the glacier (about 10,300) to Point Success (14,150), the South Tahoma Glacier headwall is a towering incline of steep snow cut horizontally by bands of crumbling volcanic rock and vertically at several places by deep avalanche troughs.

The South Tahoma Glacier received national attention following the crash of a C-46 Marine Corps plane into the mountain in December of 1946. Winter snowfall covered all trace of the plane and its 32 occupants, mostly young Marine recruits. In July 1947, following several months of futile efforts to determine the site of the crash, Assistant Chief Ranger Bill Butler sighted wreckage at about 8500 feet on the glacier. A month later I was with a party led by Butler which located the victims and other parts of the plane at about 10,000 feet, over a mile farther up the glacier. Owing to extreme hazard of rock avalanches from adjacent Tahoma Cleaver during the attempted evacuation of the remains, the bodies were left to be covered by subsequent winter snows, Point Success towering as an appropriate headstone. For many subsequent years, in deference to parents and other survivors of the victims, most of the South Tahoma Glacier was off-limits to travel and exploration; in memory of the Marines, a stone memorial was placed at Round Pass on the West Side Road, within sight of the glacier.

On July 12, 1963 Fred Beckey and Steve Marts made the first ascent of the headwall. From Indian Henrys Hunting Ground they

South Tahoma headwall, showing route climbed.

followed the lower part of Success Cleaver to a campsite at about 8000 feet. A cold wind blowing across the ridge assured them conditions on the face would be favorable, with the snow firmly frozen.

Early in the morning Beckey and Marts descended to the ice and climbed to the base of the headwall. Once across the large bergschrund they scrambled directly up the face, finding ideal snow conditions, with only negligible rockfall channeling down gullies to the north of them. Their early start allowed them to complete the ascent in morning shadows, their crampons biting firmly into the frozen surface. Point Success was attained about noon, after 7 hours on the face. The climbers descended via Success Cleaver. Beckey (oral communication, 1963) stated that late in the summer the route would be hazardous due to rockfall (*American Alpine Journal*, 1964).

11 Ascents from
St. Andrews Creek

After the winter snowpack has been cleared from the West Side Road, in late June or early July, the parking area at St. Andrews Creek (3800) is the logical starting point for the numerous routes on Rainier's vast western slope. A 2½-mile trail leads through the picturesque transition from deep dark forests to open meadows of Klapatche Park (5500), where a small lake provides the foreground for a vista of the rugged west side of the peak; a campsite in the trees below offers a stopover for those desiring to hike partway in the evening before the long treks to higher camps. From Klapatche Park the Wonderland Trail connects with St. Andrews Park (6000), a mile farther, and also with a picturesque alpine tarn. From Klapatche or St. Andrews Parks ascents are easily made in 4-8 hours to high-camp locations for climbs on Tahoma Glacier, Sunset Amphitheater, Sunset Ridge, and Mowich Face.

The best high camp for ascents of the Tahoma Glacier and Sunset Amphitheater is on the snowfield adjacent to, or in the rocks near, the

Rainier from northwest, showing routes climbed from St. Andrews Creek on West Side Road.

crest of Puyallup Cleaver at about 9200 feet, about a 5- to 7-hour climb from the road. Ascents of Sunset Ridge also can be made from here, or from a camp at the head of Colonnade ridge (8300), or on the 9200-foot divide between the South Mowich and Edmunds Glaciers. This latter location, however, requires that all gear (tents and sleeping bags) be carried over the summit to avoid the inconvenience of a return. For ascents of the Mowich Face the most suitable high camp is on a rock island (9600) near the head of the Edmunds Glacier, about an 8- to 9-hour climb from the road. This site also requires carrying all gear over the summit for an easier descent by the Tahoma Glacier.

For a more leisurely pace, one can do the 1½-hour hike into Klapatche or St. Andrews Park in the evening and camp there in a beautiful alpine setting, then do the next day's climb to high camp in the cool morning hours.

Registration for ascents from the West Side Road can be made at the Nisqually Entrance, where a ranger generally is on duty into the evening hours.

TAHOMA GLACIER

The view of Rainier from the west most clearly shows the truncated structure of the summit area; only from this direction are all three of the mountain's prominent high points seen: Liberty Cap (14,112) on the north, Columbia Crest (14,410) in the middle, and Point Success (14,150) on the south. Bounded on the south by Success Cleaver and on the north by Ptarmigan Ridge, the west side of the mountain presents a much-dissected and extensive array of ridges, glaciers, cirques, and steep ice and rock slopes, all virtually unexplored until the late 1930s.

Tumbling steeply from Columbia Crest, and bordered on each side in its upper course by the north and south summits, Tahoma Glacier flows through a narrow gap in the summit dome and descends in a direct course for 4½ miles—the most impressive ice stream on the west flank. More than a mile wide in places, the glacier has a surface broken into numerous small icefalls which alternate with comparatively smooth and open expanses. In its lower reach the glacier separates, one narrow lobe of ice moving southward around the edge of Glacier Island toward the terminus of the South Tahoma Glacier and the main lobe continuing to about the 5000-foot level, below timberline.

After the development of Paradise Valley the tent camp at Indian Henrys Hunting Ground lost some of its advantages as a base for guided climbs of the mountain and for many years the Tahoma Glacier had few visitors. After a climb of the Tahoma Glacier from Indian

Henrys on July 17, 1914 by Joseph Stampfler, Winthrop T. Hovey, Roy Young, and Roscoe Young (*The Mountaineer*, 1920), 20 years followed before the route was climbed again.

The opening of the West Side Road in the mid-1930s brought new attention to Rainier's western flanks. In early July 1934 guide Hans Fuhrer and a young client-friend from New York, Alfred E. Roovers, both on a summer-long climbing trip through the mountains of the American and Canadian West, made one of the first trips up the new trail to Klapatche Park. On July 5, after camping at about 6600 feet above St. Andrews Park, they arose at 1:35 a.m., climbed the crest of Puyallup Cleaver to about 8000 feet, then dropped to the Tahoma Glacier, which they ascended directly, reaching the summit at 3:45 p.m. They descended via the Gibraltar route and reached Paradise at 8:30 p.m. (*American Alpine Journal*, 1935).

Since World War II the Tahoma Glacier route has become increasingly popular. Today it generally is ascended by several parties each year, nearly all taking the trail approach from St. Andrews Creek. From St. Andrews Park, the most direct access to the steep upper part of the glacier is by way of Puyallup Cleaver and the near margin of the Puyallup Glacier. From a notch in the Cleaver at about 8000 feet, half a mile beyond Tokaloo Spire (7630), the glacier is followed around

Sunset Ridge   Sunset Amphitheater   St. Andrews Rock   Tahoma Glacier   Point Success

From lower Puyallup Glacier.

the north side of the massive high buttress that forms the cleaver. An excellent high camp overlooking the Tahoma Glacier can be placed at about 9200 feet near the crest of the ridge beyond the prominent buttress. From there the glacier can be reached best by continuing up the snowfield to a deep notch at about 9500 feet, which early in the summer usually offers an easy snow-filled ramp down to the glacier. Otherwise the glacier can be reached higher up by a descent of a steep snow slope off the cleaver at about 10,000 feet. Early in the summer the glacier can be followed directly to the summit from these points of access with only minor deviations around crevasses. In some years, and generally after mid-July in most years, the lower reaches of the glacier below 11,000 feet are badly crevassed and the steep reach above must be attained by climbing over St. Andrews Rock. Lower St. Andrews Rock generally is easily climbed (though composed of very rotten rock) and a traverse is then made around upper St. Andrews Rock on the edge of the upper South Mowich Glacier. If crevasses bar this traverse, one can climb directly over the crest of upper St. Andrews. Because of extremely rotten rock, great care should be taken in any climbs on St. Andrews—do not rope up.

Normal climbing time: 6-8 hours from road to high camp; 7-9 hours to summit; 7-9 hours return to car.

SOUTH MOWICH ICEFALL-TAHOMA SICKLE (1958)

An interesting variation of the Tahoma Glacier route was taken on June 8, 1958 by a group of Mountaineers from Tacoma: Leroy Ritchie (leader), Edward Drues, Mark Haun, Monte Haun, Larry Heggerness, Allan Van Buskirk, and Bob Watson. They climbed around the north side of St. Andrews Rock, making a first ascent of the South Mowich Glacier icefall between 9500 and 11,000 feet (this early in the season the ice cascade was well covered by snow and the crevasse problems were reduced considerably). From above St. Andrews Rock the climbers ascended the steep, curving, ice-and-snow trough along the north edge of the upper Tahoma Glacier (*American Alpine Journal*, 1959). This chute, named the "Tahoma Sickle" by the party, has since provided a more direct access to the summit dome when crevasses bar the route up the center of the Tahoma Glacier. However, because the chute is lined along its right (south) wall by small ice cliffs, it requires constant observation for falling debris, particularly during afternoon descents.

Because of the relative directness of the routes up the Tahoma Glacier and its Sickle trough, particularly early in the summer, they are used frequently as routes of descent after climbs of adjacent Sunset Amphitheater, Sunset Ridge, and Mowich Face. Conditions are generally favorable for afternoon glissades down the Sickle, but falling ice from the upper margin of the narrow chute must be anticipated. Furthermore, extremely mushy snow conditions can be expected in the Tahoma Glacier-Sunset Amphitheater area during the afternoons of warm, clear days.

SUNSET AMPHITHEATER-TAHOMA GLACIER ICECAP (1937)

Sunset Amphitheater, the high, many-hued cirque wall rising above the head of the South Mowich Glacier between Sunset Ridge and the Tahoma Glacier, attracted the interest of two Park Company guides who sought diversion from too-frequent ascents from the Paradise side. On July 12, 1937 J. Wendell Trosper and Fred Thieme (later to become vice-president of the University of Washington and then president of the University of Colorado) left the new West Side Road at St. Andrews Creek in hopes of doing a new route on this side of the mountain, followed by a traverse across the summit back to Paradise.

The weather was extremely cold and high winds hampered the two as they climbed into a thick fog. By evening they decided to camp on the crest of Puyallup Cleaver at about 9200 feet. During the night the wind tore at their small tent and eventually snapped a ½-inch dural tent pole and ripped the canvas, forcing them to break camp and head up the mountain, their clothing damp from mist. They climbed over the crest of lower St. Andrews Rock and around the north side of upper St. Andrews Rock, probably the first persons ever to do so. By noon they were on the upper South Mowich Glacier, at the base of the high amphitheater wall. There they were offered two choices of new routes: up the long rock ridge (Sunset Ridge) on the north rim of the huge cirque, or directly up the cirque wall to the ice cap of the summit snowfield. Owing to the lateness of the hour, and to the freezing temperatures which they felt would firmly weld together the loose rock of the wall, they elected to pursue the latter course; they also felt this would shorten the summit traverse by a day.

A delicate scramble was made across an ice block bridging the huge bergschrund at the base of the wall. The wall itself featured numerous small steep chimneys and gullies filled with ice—evidence of the flow of meltwater down the face on warm days. However, the cold temperatures during their ascent permitted a safe climb of the steep wall to the ice above. Only an occasional falling rock reminded them of the precariousness of the slope.

About half way up the ice cliff they were able to enter a crack leading to the glacier surface. Chopping deep steps in each side of the crevasse, and using ice pitons and crampons (which they donned while in the crack), they stemmed upward with backs against one side and feet against the other. After a while the sun hit the side against which they braced their backs and soon they were soaking wet. By mid-afternoon their maneuvers brought them out atop the glacier and by 5:30 they completed the trek to Columbia Crest. A cold wind at the summit discouraged lingering; almost immediately they headed down the Fuhrer Finger. A quarter-moon provided a little light as they descended in fog to Paradise, arriving at 3 a.m. (*The Mountaineer*, 1937).

SUNSET RIDGE (1938)

The next route to be explored on the west side was Sunset Ridge. Rising above the South Mowich Glacier at about the 8500-foot level, this long ridge climbs in a series of steep ice slopes and crumbling rock crests to Liberty Cap. On the north the ridge is flanked by the broad sweep of the Mowich Face; on the south it serves as a rim to Sunset Amphitheater. Because of its proximity to the amphitheater, the name Sunset Ridge was given it by Ome Daiber, who had made plans to reconnoiter this corner of the mountain after his 1935 ascent of Liberty Ridge. At the last minute Daiber was unable to make the proposed trip, but he suggested to fellow-aspirant Don M. Woods, widely-traveled climber of the Sierra Club, that he join in the attempt with Seattleites Lyman Boyer and Ezra A. "Arnie" Campbell, both highly cognizant of the problems of steep ice and crumbling rock on Rainier.

(It is interesting to note that at the time of the climb Woods considered this ridge and Curtis Ridge as the two remaining routes yet to be climbed on Rainier—in the years since 1938 over 30 distinct new routes have been completed.)

After a late start from Seattle on August 26, 1938 the trio arrived at Longmire, where they were checked out by Paradise District Ranger Bill Butler. It was significant of the wary attitude toward exploratory ascents in those days that, according to Woods, they were given permission for the climb only with the understanding they would not under any conditions establish high camp if a cloud cap then on the peak persisted into the next day.

At 9 p.m. they left the end of the West Side Road at the North Puyallup River Bridge and hiked the switchback trail to Klapatche Park. There they camped in a grove of fir trees beside the small lake, huddled around a fire since they were not carrying sleeping bags—the extra weight was undesirable for the proposed summit traverse.

At dawn the mountain was clear of the cloud cap, a happy greeting to the climbers. They continued upward through St. Andrews Park and onto the crest of Puyallup Cleaver. The ridge was followed past Tokaloo Spire to about 7500 feet, where they donned crampons and roped up. After crossing the South Mowich Glacier above the upper end of Colonnade ridge they ascended the steep tributary ice lobe at the base of Sunset Ridge. About halfway up this slope Boyer's right crampon broke under the ball of his foot, leaving the front section nearly detached. This was repaired with a piece of wire, but there were grave doubts it would hold together on the steep ice above. At about 9000 feet the slope lessened somewhat and the climbers rested on the rock ridge dividing the Edmunds and South Mowich Glaciers.

After a short lunch the trio returned to the glacier and continued upward, crossing the bergschrund without difficulty. Above this they were faced with a long and steep ice gully which at places attained an angle of 50°. By 5 o'clock in the afternoon, at about 11,000 feet, they decided to bivouac, chopping a platform in the ice and lining it with flat rocks and newspapers for insulation. A chilly night was endured as they huddled together in a bivouac tent held up with pitons, their backs directly against the ice, a howling wind tearing at them from above.

At 6 a.m. they were again on their way up the gradually steepening and narrowing ice finger to a saddle in the ridge at 11,900 feet. From there they enjoyed—very briefly—the view over the Sunset Amphitheater, from whose depths blew a high wind. A few hundred feet of scrambling along the ridge crest brought them to about 12,500 feet, where a nasty bit of climbing involved a rappel from a rotten rock cliff and a delicate traverse along the crumbling knife-edged crest. According to Don Woods (written communication, August 1969):

The rocky pillar around which we placed our belay sling was really not too secure, believe me. When the two guides [sic—Rangers K Molenaar and George Senner] repeated this route some years later on the second ascent,

Across Sunset Amphitheater from 12,000 feet on Sunset Ridge.

they cut this sling rope we had left and . . . the rocky pillar fell to pieces and tumbled down the slope on either side! Some belay pillar! From this spot I belayed one at a time Campbell and Boyer about 80 feet directly down the rocky ridge and about another 30 feet across a very rotten and dusty lava slope . . . I then rappelled down to their position.

Beyond this stretch the trio encountered a 45-50° slope of névé, up which they scrambled 1000 feet on their crampons—to have cut steps up the long slope at this late hour would have been out of the question. Another 1000 feet of heavily suncupped snow brought them to Liberty Cap at 1 p.m. Woods describes the deeply scalloped surface:

I also remember to my dying day those sun cups. They were hideous! From Liberty Cap, which I believe ordinarily takes an hour to Columbia Crest, it took us THREE hours of the most exhausting work. The cups . . . were 4 and 5 feet across and deep. We had to climb down into nearly every one, and crawl out and then came the next one. When we reached the Crest at 4 P.M. we were completely corked. We flopped and rested an hour of our very valuable time.

After signing the summit register they began the descent toward Paradise by way of the Kautz Glacier. The exertions of moving downward through more suncups brought them to the Kautz ice cliff as darkness was settling over the slopes. As the climbers began their descent of the cliff late in the evening of August 28, 1938 they found some of the toughest work of their 4 days on the mountain still awaiting them. According to Don Woods:

The descent of the icy slope above the Kautz ice cliffs was very interesting. We had just one 10-inch aluminum ice piton with a big ring in the top. We drove this in at the top of the steep slope as an anchor, then I

lowered each fellow one at a time down about 110 feet to the snow hummock nearest this descent point. The first 55' rappel that I made was from
the piton halfway to their position. Here there was an ice hummock that
I could use as the second belay point. It was rounded on all sides, but I cut
a deep groove in the upper side as low down as I could, so the doubled rappel
rope wouldn't slip out and let me go down. From here I must have had 5
or 6 more icy hummocks as rappel points, all grooved on the upper side just
as the first. One of the boys slid the last 100' of icy slope to a level platform
below, and made it safely, but the other two of us climbed down much
more cautiously. The couple of hours that we spent in the ice cliffs after
dark with only one headlamp flashlight working was most thrilling, but we
were not able to see below us due to the darkness, and perhaps this was
good.

When we finally stopped about 11,000 feet, and near Camp Hazard (we
never did know when we were there or were never sure we saw it) we were
exhausted. We simply made a flop on the rocks, pulled our tent around us,
ate some cold food, and tried to snooze. We were so tired that we really
did sleep, even though fitful.

The next morning (Monday) our descent showed how dry the slopes of
Rainier were. I believe this was one of the driest years in many, many years
for Rainier. The usual snow gullies and snow fingers present in late August
were entirely gone, all rock. The Wilson and Nisqually Glaciers were just
bare ice. The Nisqually was far more bare than usual, making it much more
difficult to cross. When we were finally across the Nisqually, and we looked
down a thousand feet or so to the grassy slopes above Paradise, there
running toward me was my six-year-old boy, and soon he was in my arms.

The climbers arrived at Paradise 24 hours overdue (*American Alpine Journal*, 1939; *The Mountaineer*, 1938).

Suncups between Liberty Cap and Columbia Crest, late August 1938.

The second ascent of Sunset Ridge was made August 10, 1949 by Rangers George Senner and K Molenaar. From a high camp at 8300 feet on Colonnade ridge they accomplished the long climb of the ridge and descent to the terminus of the West Side Road in the rapid time of 15½ hours. During the ascent they found the rappel sling left by the 1938 party (*The Mountaineer*, 1949; *American Alpine Journal*, 1950).

Normal climbing time: 5-7 hours to high camp at head of Colonnade ridge; 10-12 hours to Liberty Cap; 1½-2 hours to summit.

SUNSET AMPHITHEATER-SUNSET RIDGE (1939)

A variation of the Sunset Ridge route was pioneered in the first week of August 1939 by J. Wendell Trosper and Hans Grage. After an ascent to the head of South Mowich Glacier via St. Andrews Rock, similar to the Sunset Amphitheater-Tahoma Glacier Icecap route of 1937, a traverse was made to the north below the amphitheater cliffs, followed by a climb of the steep ice slope which joins the cirque with Sunset Ridge at about 12,000 feet. The upper part of Sunset Ridge was ascended to Liberty Cap (J. Wendell Trosper, written communication, 1957). This variation was climbed again on July 8, 1961 by Gene Prater, Barry Prather, Fred Dunham, and Jim Wickwire. The rope sling left by the 1938 party was still in place, contrary to Don Woods' statement that it had been cut by the second-ascent party. According to Prater, 10–12 goats were observed crossing the Amphitheater from lower St. Andrews Rock to Sunset Ridge, over which they disappeared.

The ice breakups encountered by the 1938 party on the lower part of the ridge in August generally are well covered by snow until about mid-July and no particular routefinding problems occur on this upper part of the South Mowich Glacier early in summer. The traverse across the high-angle ice on the upper ridge and upper Mowich Face also is considerably easier in early summer.

SUNSET RIDGE-MOWICH FACE VARIATION (1963)

A climb of lower Sunset Ridge, with a traverse onto and up the steep ice gullies on the right (south) edge of the Mowich Face was made on May 31, 1963, by Fred Dunham, Dave Mahre, Gene Prater, and Jim Wickwire (Prater, *Cascadians*, 1963). Although planning a climb of the Mowich Face, the group approached the slope during the early morning darkness and began the assault by climbing the lower part of Sunset Ridge before working out onto the face itself. The climbers then became involved in a series of poorly defined rock ribs and snow gullies on the south edge of the face. These led them back to a point midway up Sunset Ridge, which was then resumed to Liberty Cap. For Prater and Wickwire the frustration laid the groundwork for an effort on the central part of the face 3 years later.

SUNSET AMPHITHEATER DIRECT (1965)

As viewed from the air and from near St. Andrews Rock, the deeply gullied cirque headwall of Sunset Amphitheater appears nearly vertical, colorfully combining hues of red, black, and yellow in alternating strata of volcanic lava, breccia, ash, and pumice. As noted earlier, in 1937 the right side of the wall was scaled to the top of the Tahoma Glacier ice-cap by Trosper and Thieme, but it was not until nearly 30 years later that the highest part of the amphitheater wall, immediately below Liberty Cap, was climbed in its entirety.

On July 24, 1965 Dave Mahre, Don McPherson, Gene Prater, Fred Stanley, and Jim Wickwire left the West Side Road at St. Andrews Creek and hiked to a camp at about 9200 feet on Puyallup Cleaver. During their approach they noted that conditions on the amphitheater wall appeared favorable for an attempt. The snow perched on the face was clean, indicating very little rockfall, and at one point it formed a cap along the crest of a steeply inclined crest of rock, delineating a possible "ramp" up which to ascend diagonally to Liberty Cap at the apex of the wall.

A cloud cap over the mountain held them in their tent until about 5 o'clock in the morning. The cap then dissipating, the party left camp at 6 a.m. and quickly climbed over lower St. Andrews Rock and around upper St. Andrews Rock to the large glacial bowl below the cirque wall. The ascent to the head of the glacier and the crossing of the right end

Routes on Sunset Amphitheater.

of the bergschrund required a long detour below the foreboding ice cliff capping the wall high above. Once above the crevasse they traversed back toward the main face by crossing several rock buttresses. The traverse proved to be the crux of the climb, their only belays of the day being required here.

The snow patches leading higher up the face were deeply sun-cupped and provided an excellent staircase that was rapidly ascended. Several narrow rockfall trenches were crossed quickly, but the cold, shadowed slopes were inactive at this time of morning. Scree slopes between the snow patches offered no problems and the route generally was simpler than anticipated. Once they were on the steep snow ramp, suncups provided excellent footing, and as the ramp was atop a small ridge crest, the climbers were safe from small trickles of rock that began falling about mid-morning. An exit from the ramp was made up a deep gully that brought them above the next cliff band. A stream of melt-water in the gully gave unexpected refreshment, an abnormal luxury on the cold, windy upper slopes of the mountain. The slope then eased off to the snow dome of Liberty Cap, which they reached shortly after noon.

The party descended the upper Tahoma Glacier via the Sickle route. Carefully controlled glissades brought them to the crevassed area below, which was crossed to just above St. Andrews Rock, where they rested and noted water and rocks coming down gullies that only 4 hours earlier had been frozen and silent. The car was reached at St. Andrews Creek at 8 p.m.; a cloud cap lowering on the mountain behind them was accompanied by considerable thunderstorm activity (Gene Prater, *Summit*, July–August, 1966).

THE MOWICH FACE

By 1957, a century after Kautz' memorable achievement on the south slope of Rainier, over 20 routes had been climbed on the mountain, including the major glaciers descending from the summit snow dome and nearly all the prominent rock ridges. It was then that attention focused on the steep walls rising between the ridges and above the glacial cirques. Among the more attractive of the new challenges was the Mowich Face.

Bordered on the north by Ptarmigan Ridge and on the south by Sunset Ridge and rising in a vast sweep above the Edmunds and North Mowich Glaciers, the Mowich Face forms a broad triangle 2 miles across the base and nearly a mile high. As viewed head-on or from the air, the face presents an impressive aspect of sheer steepness, broken only by incipient rock ridges and several ice cliffs. Two of the cliffs cling precariously halfway down each side of the main face while the northern half of the face is topped by a 200-foot-thick icecap. This wall of ice overlooks a system of rock bands which angles upward to the snow dome at the apex of the wall at 13,500 feet. Liberty Cap (14,112) lies half a mile beyond the dome.

The impression of near-verticality is deceptive. Although the angle of the slope generally would be estimated to be 55-60°, in the reality it probably averages between 40-45°. Nonetheless, the length of the incline offers a challenge and an opportunity to test crampons and ice-climbing techniques and from 1957 through 1970 five parties pioneered routes up the face (not including the 1963 variation of the Sunset Ridge route).

The most favorable conditions for climbing the Mowich Face probably occur between June 15 and July 15. Before June 15 the West Side Road may be closed by snow, involving a long hike, or a snow-mobile ride, on the road to the approach from St. Andrews Creek. After mid-July blue ice appears in places and in August rockfall hazards and hard black ice prevail for much of the climb. Also, the descent route down the Tahoma Glacier generally is badly crevassed later in the summer. During the hike to camp it is wise to observe route possibilities on the Tahoma, which even in early summer is generally softened by afternoon sun to the consistency of mush—with hidden crevasses always to be anticipated. Once down the steep upper part of the Tahoma Glacier, a party usually can find a route on the snow slopes on the north side of upper St. Andrews Rock, then traverse over the top of lower St. Andrews. However, in some years, as in 1968, crevasses on the upper South Mowich Glacier extend all the way to upper St. Andrews Rock and make the snow-slope traverse around the rock impossible. At such times, the crumbling crest of the rock must be tackled directly to bypass this glacier descent route.

Edmunds Headwall (1957)

On June 22–23, 1957 Fred Beckey, Don Gordon (then Claunch), Tom Hornbein, John Rupley, and Herb Staley made the first ascent of the Mowich Face via the headwall above the Edmunds Glacier (Beckey and Claunch, written communication, 1957). Leaving the West Side Road at St. Andrews Creek (4000) the party hiked in 5 hours to St. Andrews Park, up Puyallup Cleaver and across the Puyallup Glacier to the head of the Colonnade ridge at 8200 feet, where camp was made about sunset. At 5 a.m., after debating about deteriorating weather and soft snow, the party left camp and crossed the South Mowich Glacier and the lower ice lobe of Sunset Ridge to the rocky saddle at the edge of the Edmunds Glacier. A long traverse across the upper Edmunds was required below the bergschrund at the head of the glacier before they could find a suitable bridge to the slope above. The climb for some distance above the bergschrund was relatively direct and the group made rapid progress kicking steps in the soft snow. The ice cliffs which break off from the left edge of the main slope were passed about mid-face; from here the slope steepened to about 50°. A hard surface made difficult progress and steps had to be chopped as their route merged with the final steep pitches of upper Sunset Ridge. Gathering clouds rising up the slope obscured visibility and the party struggled through a white-out to Liberty Cap, reached about 2:30 p.m. Due to poor visibility the group decided to retrace their steps. After carefully belaying each other down the steeper stretches of ice with the picks of their axes the climbers were able to plunge-step the lower slopes. The car was regained about 10 p.m.

Central Face: Route One (1966)

For many years following my first examination of the great face, from near Sunset Park in 1948, I contained my tantalizing ambitions to make an attempt on it. Finally, on July 23–24, 1966, I joined with Gene Prater, Jim Wickwire, and Dick Pargeter in a climb directly up the central ice slope and through the rock bands at the top. Our high camp was pitched on a flat-topped rock island at 9500 feet at the base of the face—in full but safe view of one of the most spectacular ice avalanches any of us had ever seen on Rainier.

It started out as a loud boom on the peak high above our four-man tent, arousing us from mid-afternoon dozing and mixing of package after package of Gene's vast store of instant breakfasts. Grabbing for the tent exit, we hurtled into the bright glare of the afternoon sun and quickly looked up. From the upper right side of the face came plummeting a wall of ice blocks which were turning in the air and be-

Avalanche on Mowich Face.

coming engulfed in a growing white cloud of snow and ice dust. The cloud moved rapidly down the steep incline, so gaining in momentum and size that soon the entire mountain above was hidden from view. Quickly noting that our camp was out of the line of fire atop the crest of the nunatak, we relaxed to enjoy the display. The cloud swept down to the break in slope below the face, then across the north edge of the Edmunds Glacier. At the base of the billowing mass we watched the ice blocks sliding and rolling across the surface of the glacier opposite camp. Gradually the movement slowed to a stop, the cloud settled, and again the upper mountain returned to view. The path of the avalanche down the slope was marked by a chaos of clean white snow and ice above which floated a few wisps of the cloud still in suspension.

Although we had planned for a midnight start up the face, a short storm moved in and covered the peak in a cap, the lower part spitting a few snowflakes against the flapping tent. By 4:00 a.m., however, the wind died down and the sky above cleared; somewhat reluctantly we arose to our commitment for the day. By 5:30 we packed the tent, roped up, and started the traverse across the jumbled wake of the avalanche. The going was straightforward and snow conditions excellent—crampons biting easily into the slightly corrugated surface, the steep angle seeming to level off as we ascended directly up the face. In what seemed to be considerably less than the actual 4 hours required, we reached the steep ice—blue water ice in places—leading up to the lowermost of the rock bands. The key to the route was negotiation of a 15-foot rock cliff at the waist of an hourglass of ice. Once above the rock cliff and on a narrow snow-covered ledge we held a discussion on the merits of working to the right on the ledge and joining the upper part of the 1957 route or dropping slightly around a narrow corner to the left and "doing our own thing" by completing an entirely virgin path up the face. The others were temporarily inclined to favor heading for the previous route, but I had hoped for something entirely new by exploring the icecap and chute north of the prominent cliff bands. At this point I exercised my prerogative as party leader—being the oldest, I was given this distinction by the others at the time of our checkout for the climb—and soon we headed off to the left on the steeply sloping snow ledge. Inwardly, I enjoyed the satisfaction that comes so infrequently to an older climber: revealing to the younger generation a small spark of initiative in route selection and follow-through.

Around the exposed corner at the end of the snow traverse we found the ice chute to head directly up, between the fluted bulge of the icecap on the north and the rock wall on the south. A coathanger ice screw placed in the chute was the only hardware used during the entire ascent. A switchback course up the 50-degree ice, now directly into the late morning sun, brought us to the rounded crest of upper Ptarmigan

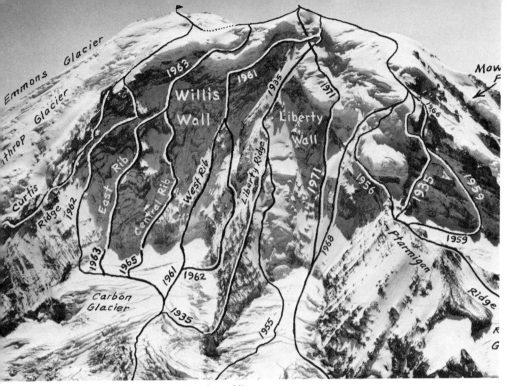

Routes on Rainier's "Nordwand."

Ridge. Once on the broad upper slopes we sat down to rest, and to observe the weary movements of a party of four far below, emerging from the critical portions of the Ptarmigan Ridge route.

The sun beat down impassively as we arose and completed the long slog to Liberty Cap, arriving there at 12:30 p.m. Our route down was made by the Tahoma Sickle. The glacier surface had become soft in the sun and the descent was filled with frustration as we floundered to our knees, feeling each step to be a plunge into a hidden crevasse. We finally rounded the north slopes of upper St. Andrews Rock and found the deep goat-worn trail along the snow crest of lower St. Andrews Rock. There, lowering clouds brought a short sleet storm upon us, but eventually we broke below the clouds and descended rapidly down Puyallup Glacier to Tokaloo Spire and beyond to the welcome greenery of St. Andrews and Klapatche Parks. The cars were reached at 7:30 p.m.

During this July 1966 climb the snow on the lower part of the route was firmly frozen and the corrugated surface provided excellent footing. Higher, a smoother surface and considerable blue ice required step-chopping alternating with short bursts of scrambling directly upslope on the forward-projecting crampon points. In another week considerably more blue ice would have required increased caution and greater use of ice screws for belay positions.

On July 15–16, 1967, a second ascent of our route through the rock bands was made by Chuck Crenchaw, Chuck Patzer, Chuck Schaeffer, and Tom Stewart. (This marked Stewart's 11th ascent of the peak, by his 11th different route. By 1969, he had added three more routes to his "collection.") According to Crenchaw (written commun., 1967), "the hourglass was a 40-foot rock pitch—we removed crampons and climbed. Finding the exact chute was a bit tricky but when we found it we popped over like jumping beans . . . This was the nicest route I've ever done on Rainier. It was clean and really classic."

Central Face: Route Two (1967)

Conditions on the Mowich Face vary greatly from year to year and throughout the summer, as shown by the ascents made in 1967. On July 4th, a party of young climbers including Bill Cockerham(17), Ed Marquart(16), Bill Sumner(24), and Del Young(19) made a variation of the upper part of our 1966 route. Due to the conditions of blue ice and loose rock below the rock cliff climbed by our party in the previous year, this group found the route impractical and traversed diagonally upward below the system of rock bands, then directly up the steep open ice slope at the apex of the face. Numerous ice-screw belays were required during the laborious and ticklish 8-hour traverse. Liberty Cap was reached at 8:30 p.m. and a bivouac was made there for the night. According to Del Young (written commun., 1967), although "not as pure a route as either of the other two,—it is somewhat more difficult than the 1957 route, and could be considered as an alternate means of 'escaping' the face under late summer conditions which would make the 1966 route too dangerous."

North Mowich Headwall: Route One (1968)

A third major route up the Mowich Face was completed July 22, 1968 by Dan Davis, Mike Heath, Mead Hargiss, and Bill Cockerham.

Routes on upper central Mowich Face.

According to Davis (written communication, 1968), they ascended the northern of the three major ice slopes on the face and climbed around and over the right end of the ice cliff at the top of the rock bands. From a high camp at 9200 feet on the rock ridge that divides the Edmunds and North Mowich Glaciers, they ascended left to the bergschrund at the base of the wall, crossed the schrund, then climbed directly up the ice slope. Just above the bergschrund a narrow hourglass of rock and ice gave them some trouble and required use of one ice screw for belay. Above that constriction the slope of 40–45° was rapidly climbed to the rock bands at about 12,000 feet, below the dominant ice cliff at the top of the face. Here a traverse was made to below the right end of the ice wall. Sloping ledges of ice alternating with rock bands provided the route. A 50-foot vertical rock cliff, of class 5–6 difficulty, was climbed with the aid of piton belays and gave access to the ice slope on the right end of the ice cliff. At one point they had to pull themselves up on an icicle. The 60° bulge of ice was ascended with ice-screw belays to above the ice cliff, from where the slope gradually rounded off for the long trudge to Liberty Cap. The climb from high camp took 12 hours.

This was Davis' 14th ascent of Rainier, each by a different route. He reports this as one of his most difficult climbs on the mountain, requiring four rock pitons and six ice screws. (By 1970 Davis had climbed a total of 17 routes.)

North Mowich Headwall: Route Two (1970)

A variation of the 1968 route up the north side of the Mowich Face was made on June 26, 1970, by Jim Wickwire and Rob Schaller. As the chief source of my frustrations in attempting to keep this record apace with the most recent new ascents on Rainier, Wickwire describes his seventh "first" on the mountain:

. . . . In the face of your threats to us for doing anymore new routes on the mountain, Rob and I were able to do that route at the extreme left-hand side of the Mowich Face on June 26 . . . we bivouacked Thursday night on the same rock ridge used by Davis in 1968. At 5:00 a.m. . . we traversed to the start of the route, which must be below 9,000'. The first problem was a traverse left two leads on black ice above the bergschrund. We were then in the narrow gully which parallels the lowest section of the icefall. Here, we encountered severe rockfall and were forced to do some fairly adroit scrambling to avoid being hit. Although the weather threatened throughout the day, it was very warm and thus the reason for the rockfall. We climbed several leads to the broad snowslope up which Davis climbed in 1968. As a result of a shift in the icefall or for some other inexplicable reason, the gully was not there and we were forced to climb a vertical section about 35-40 feet high which Rob led. The rock was excellent and pins were not required. Another short rock pitch led higher to a point where we were able to move out on to the left-hand edge of the ice slope described above. This was at a point about 200' above Davis' "hourglass".

For about 500', we paralleled Davis' route. We stayed at the extreme left-hand edge of the slope while Davis apparently went up the middle of it.

As soon as we reached a point near the top of the highest section of the icefall on the left, we angled diagonally left, heading for the exit gully through the rock wall which forms the upper part of Ptarmigan Ridge. On this section, we encountered one difficult snow lead above a gaping bergschrund. The problem was porous snow lying on hard ice at an angle in excess of 45°. The exit gully itself involved the hardest rock pitch of the climb. It was a steep slab, covered with verglas. I led it with crampons on and used two pins for protection. The pitch itself was only about 25', but was very exposed.

We exited from the face at about 1:45 p.m., and then climbed into a cloudcap at Liberty Cap. It was not snowing, but visibility was virtually nil and the winds were probably in excess of 50-60 miles per hour. Taking a compass reading from Liberty Cap, we headed off toward the southeast to reach the saddle between Liberty Cap and Columbia Crest. Rob's compass must have been acting up, because it soon became apparent that we were going down the right-hand side of Liberty Cap as you face Columbia Crest. The upper rocks of Sunset Amphitheater indicated we were headed in the wrong direction. We then got a brief glimpse downward and were able to pick our way down to the saddle. The wind continued to rage and it was only when we got near the top of the Tahoma Sickle that it cleared up. It was quite clear farther to the west, although there were two or three cloud layers, one of which was some distance above the mountain. The descent of the Sickle was quite laborious, as we sank into the snow above our knees most of the way down. We finally reached the standard Tahoma Glacier high camp at about 9500' at 9:45 p.m. We bivouacked there for the night, and came out the rest of the way the next morning in three hours.

12 The Nordwand

Viewing Mount Rainier from the north, one is impressed by the tremendous double-cirqued wall rising above the head of the Carbon Glacier. The eastern and larger cirque of Rainier's "Nordwand" is named Willis Wall in honor of Bailey Willis, the distinguished geologist whose early explorations contributed much to the knowledge of this side of the mountain. The westerly of the two glacier headwalls more recently has been given the name "Liberty Wall" by those who in 1968 pioneered a route up its steep ice.

Willis Wall rises 4000 feet in a long sweep of crumbling, downward-sloping ledges of lava, ash, consolidated breccias and mudflows, and dirty, rock-impregnated ice. Resting atop the vast 45° incline is the summit icecap, which here exposes a 300-foot thick wall of blue ice overhanging the face—the source of the largest avalanches on Rainier. On many a warm day in early summer one can watch parts of the ice cliff calve off and, gathering speed swiftly down the huge cirque wall, shoot out onto the Carbon Glacier in huge clouds of ice and dust.

Willis Wall is bounded on the east by Curtis Ridge, a steep-sided arete that separates the Wall from the Winthrop Glacier. On the west,

Rainier from north, showing routes climbed on the "Nordwand."

Avalanche on Willis Wall.

Willis Wall is separated from Liberty Wall by Liberty Ridge, the most consistently steep cleaver on the mountain. Rising from the Carbon Glacier at the 8500-foot level, Liberty Ridge ascends directly to 14,112-foot Liberty Cap. To the west of upper Liberty Ridge, the hanging ice-falls of the "Liberty Cap Glacier" form the upper part of Liberty Wall. Beyond, and forming the western edge of the Nordwand, is the ice-and-rock crest of Ptarmigan Ridge.

As on most high peaks in the Northern Hemisphere, where the greatest snow depths have accumulated on the northern slopes to form the largest glaciers which in turn have carved the deepest cirques, the Nordwand of Rainier provides the greatest challenges on the peak. Here, the combination of the thick icecap dominating the upper sky-line, the steep ice, and the crumbling volcanic rock, has set the stage for the most rugged ascents of Rainier.

PTARMIGAN RIDGE (1935)

In 1932 the completion of the gravel road to Mowich Lake opened the way for exploration and attempts on Ptarmigan Ridge. The ridge rises from Observation and Echo Rocks above the meadows of Spray Park in a series of sharp rocky crests which separate the deep canyon of the North Mowich Glacier on the west from the broad undulating snow-field of Russell Glacier on the east. The Ptarmigan Ridge route begins above 10,500 feet, where the ridge makes an abrupt rise and becomes an intricate combination of steep ice gullies and rock cliffs flanked on the east by the 300-foot ice cliff of the Liberty Cap Glacier. Above 12,000 feet the ridge again smooths out and rises toward Liberty Cap as a broad snow ridge "of interminable length."

From edge of Russell Glacier and lower Ptarmigan Ridge.

Although Ptarmigan Ridge was reportedly climbed May 18, 1905 or 1906 by Lee Pickett "and another man" (*The Mountaineer*, 1920), this ascent has never been substantiated. It is doubtful that at so early a date such a climb reached much above 10,000 feet, where the technical difficulties begin. As noted earlier, in 1884 the three men from Snohomish gave up the attempt at about 11,000 feet. In 1912, Dora Keen (later Mrs. Handy), the famous woman mountaineer who had just done the first ascent of Mount Blackburn in Alaska, made two brief reconnaissances of the ridge, but these were halted below 10,000 feet by poor weather conditions. Miss Keen suggested (*The Mountaineer*, 1912): "If the start is at 2 a.m., with wind-proof Alpine lanterns, this interesting first ascent by the northwest side might safely be accomplished in a day."

The next serious attempt was by J. Wendell Trosper, Hans Grage, and Jarvis Wallen on the Labor Day weekend of 1933. This party was able to ascend the steep rock-and-ice couloir to the west of the prominent ice cliff of the hanging glacier which guards approaches to the ridge. At about 11,000 feet the lateness of the hour dictated a retreat by several rappels down the icy slope (*The Mountaineer*, 1933). The following year Hans Grage returned to the attack with Wolf Bauer. An early-summer attempt was rebuffed by blizzard conditions but they were back again on September 2. Taking the 1933 route, Bauer and Grage chopped their way up the ice-covered rock to about 12,500 feet, well above most of the major climbing difficulties. Only one steep ice pitch and a long, gentle snow slope led toward Liberty Cap, but the many hours on the steep slopes below had used up most of the day and they were forced to descend. Not desiring to retrace their route down the treacherous couloir, Bauer and Grage worked their way across to the north edge of the Mowich Face, which they descended to a point where they were able to traverse back to their high camp via the North Mowich Glacier (*The Mountaineer*, 1934).

Smitten by the challenge of Ptarmigan Ridge and frustrated by failure to complete the ascent to the summit, Wolf Bauer was back on the mountain September 7 and 8, 1935, this time with Jack Hossack, another outstanding rock and ice climber from Seattle. Although they first considered avoiding the rock-strewn chutes on the west side of the ridge by traversing below the 300-foot ice wall to the ice slopes of Liberty Wall on the east side of the ridge, they were discouraged by the unstable aspect of the ice cliff. With some deviation from the previous year's route in the chutes they were still obliged to expend 12 hours in tediously cutting steps up the verglas-covered slope and it was not

Routes on upper Ptarmigan Ridge, from 10,000 feet.

until 9 p.m. that the two exhausted climbers attained Liberty Cap. Using sleeping-bag covers for shelter, they established a hasty bivouac there on a rocky slope, a welcome relief from the long hours of danger and tension on the cliffs below. This was the first time Liberty Cap acted as host for benighted climbers (*The Mountaineer*, 1935). Their descent to Paradise was via Gibraltar.

Following the Bauer-Hossack ascent, 20 years passed before the next attempts. In the early summer of 1955, and again in 1956, two or three parties were frustrated by deep snow and dangerous avalanche conditions, the ice wall frequently spewing large fragments onto steep slopes below.

Finally, on July 17–18, 1959 Gene and Bill Prater completed the second ascent of the steep ridge. With a two-man support party, the Praters left Mowich Lake at 5 a.m. At 1 p.m. they arrived at the 10,300-foot col below the prominent ice cliff, rested while awaiting the stabilizing cold of evening, and at 10:30 p.m. began the climb. Good snow conditions on the steep initial slope permitted easy step-kicking a considerable distance upward before hard ice was encountered. Continuous belaying and the use of ice pitons at belay points (four pitons per 100-foot lead) were required to the base of a sheer rock cliff. From there snow slopes were ascended and traversed toward the Liberty Cap Glacier. At about 12,000 feet broken rock was climbed to its top, where a traverse to the right (west) brought them to the summit snowcap (12,000) at 6 a.m. After an hour's stop for breakfast, the Praters completed the long trudge to Liberty Cap (*Cascadians*, 1959).

A variation in the route on the upper part of the ridge is climbed today by some parties. On July 24, 1966, a party composed of Arnold Bloomer, Glenn Kelsey, Harold Pinsch, and Paul Williams, after climbing the steep ice slopes and gullies of the central part of the route, ascended through a notch to the right, which brought them out on the upper north edge of Mowich Face. From there they climbed up a steep gully in the rock cliff and on to the lower end of the snow slope leading to Liberty Cap.

Ptarmigan Ridge, one of the most interesting climbs on the mountain, now is ascended by one or more groups each summer (in 1969, 13 climbers in three parties climbed the ridge) and has been successfully challenged by the fair sex—on the Fourth of July weekend of 1965 Mrs. Len (Judy) Waller made the ascent with her husband Len and several others.

Normal climbing time: 8-10 hours to high camp from Mowich Lake; 9-12 hours to Liberty Cap.

LIBERTY RIDGE (1935)

The first ascent of Liberty Ridge on September 29–30, 1935 was, like the ascent of Ptarmigan Ridge 3 weeks earlier, a classic. At the time of the climb the north side of Rainier between Ptarmigan Ridge and Curtis Ridge was considered in its entirety as Willis Wall—an ascent of Liberty Ridge would be an "ascent of the Wall." By today's definition the adventures on that early fall weekend of 1935 would not be rated as a wall climb, but it would be considered a "winter-season" ascent. Mountaineers of today often wonder why the trip was made so late in the season. According to Arnie Campbell (written communication, 1969):

Never considered our climb to have been a winter season ascent. At the time it just seemed to be the proper time to do it when all the rotten rock would be in shadow and remain frozen . . . It never entered my mind that the climb would mean anything to anyone but the three of us. As a consequence, I made no reference to maps . . . elevations were strictly guesses. The same applies to temperatures, since we had no means of measuring them. It was just the most fun climb of my life and I didn't want to forget its minor details. To think now that today's climbers cut their baby teeth on that same climb, I almost feel ashamed to have made any record of the event.

Descriptions of the ascent are well covered in the *American Alpine Journal* (1936) and *The Mountaineer* (1935), but for a more personalized account of the "classic route" on Mount Rainier, giving an intimate feel of climbing in the years of the Depression, here are presented excerpts from the diary of Arnie Campbell:

Members of party—leader Ome Daiber, Jim Borrow, and myself. Sunday Sept. 23rd we went to Carbon Glacier for the day to look over the situation, myself not knowing that was the object. I had a slight touch of ptomaine poisoning and did not enjoy the outing very much. While there I commented that I thought the wall could be climbed . . . Ome has been thinking of the climb for several years. So much for preliminaries.

Friday night [September 27] at 6 p.m. Jim phoned saying Joe [Halwax] could not go and asked if I could go . . . We were to leave at 6:45 a.m. Saturday Sept. 28th. Got my equipment together . . .

Saturday morning dawned bright and clear . . . Ome and Jim arrived at 9 a.m. and we made our start. Jim's car persisted in overheating. At Kent car doing fine, but Jim feels in fixing mood so we stop. After fussing with the timer . . . It wouldn't run at all. Finally call in some experts and they replace a few parts and she runs like a top. At 11 a.m. we left Kent . . . Ome and Jim decided we needed apples to eat. We watched for old abandoned orchards, but they all seemed to be in someone's front yard and the house was too close . . . we had no apples.

After due time, stopped at Carbon River Ranger Station and was informed by the Ranger that they did not encourage climbing on the North side of the mountain at any time, and particularly at this time of the year. He would not let us go, by his permission. Ome called Major Tomlinson, the Park Supt., who knew of the plans and had been definitely convinced the climb was safe if done right. He gave his o.k. to the Ranger. Ome told him of my replacing one of the members of the party as submitted to him previously.

The first "Nordwanders," pioneers on Ptarmigan and Liberty Ridges. Wolf Bauer, Jack Hossack.

Tomlinson said if I was satisfactory to Ome, that was the only recommendation he needed.

Ome made out the official report and we all filled out the necessary papers. We set Monday night at 10 p.m. as the deadline of our return. We were almost certain we would be back early that day.

In the car again and on to the end of the road . . . Lunch at that point consisted of Buttermilk, sandwiches, and apricots. At 2:15 p.m. we picked up our ice axes and hit the trail.

Packs were not very heavy, probably 50 to 55 pounds . . . About 2 miles up we rested in the shade at Moraine cabin. Continued on into Moraine Park . . . About 6,000 feet up [above sea level] we spotted what appeared to be, and was, our last water. Camped a few hundred yards above it. I was elected to sharpen Jim's and my crampons while he and Ome got the water, made camp, and cooked the meal. Decided for the 150th time to have some "moth balls." These are sugared hazel nuts and happened to be stale. My front teeth were all out and grooves had been ground out preparatory to replacing a bridge, the snow created a not too pleasant sensation in them.

At 10:30 p.m. I finished the crampons and sleep seemed to be in order. I rolled in first. Ome got in Jim's bag, Jim followed as best he could. At last they got their breathing synchronized and we dropped off to sleep. About the middle of the night Jim couldn't wait but dreamed that we were climbing the wall and he was holding up the party. He gathered all his strength and started to go. He did, right out of the sleeping bag, then the tent and a few yards down the ridge before waking up. On coming back he could not get into the sleeping bag again so sat up and froze the rest of the night. Ome did quite well.

Sunday Sept. 29th 1935. Up with the crack of dawn at 5:30 a.m. Following the meal we rolled up toothbrushes, etc. in our sleeping bags and left them. We distributed the load again, and our packs consisted of extra wool shirts, sox, parka, hat, gloves, glasses, crampons, carbide and light, primus

Ome Daiber, Arnie Campbell, Jim Borrow.

stove, knife, kettle, spoons, dirty cups, quart and pint of gasoline, one candle, box of matches, one pipe, can of tobacco, 100 feet of rope, 3 ice axes, 2 slickers, camera and films, extra laces, blizzard tent, few gasoline sandwiches, 6 apples (found deep in one of the packs, left over from the previous week's trip), 3 oranges, chocolate, can of powdered milk, shredded wheat, corn meal, sugar, salt, assorted nuts, dates, mothballs, 100 trail markers, first-aid kit, sun-ex, etc.

Ready to leave. At 7:30 a.m. take an orange apiece and start up the ridge . . . and dropped down to the edge of the ice.

Campbell's diary then goes into several pages of description of the difficulties in finding a route across the Carbon Glacier to the base of Liberty Ridge. By midsummer in most years the Carbon is badly crevassed; this party was there in early fall.

We finally got onto Liberty Ridge. 3 p.m. and our start had been made. We were on the wall.

. . . We were glad to be on rock for a change . . . We had hoped for solid rock, but found the wall to consist of bits of pumice held together by coarse dirt and in some places by frost. At this time of the year the sun is on the opposite side of the mountain and we were now in continual shade . . . At last we came to a steep ice slope with two inches of fresh snow on it. At the top of this was a col and gave promise of being the only place to stay overnight. This point 11,000 feet we reached at 6:30 p.m. Below it had looked flat, but it was just less steep, about 40° for a distance of 100 feet.

We turned to with the ice axes to level out a place in the pumice to stay. After two hours we had a platform about 6 feet by 4 feet 6 inches. We took off the packs, set them down, and got out the blizzard tent . . . a silk affair folded and sewed on two ends forming an envelope. We crawled in with the packs and sat down to stay for the night. The edge of the tent draped over the edge of the platform and in this part we put the packs. Jim went down with the kettle just below and got some snow. We were plenty thirsty, nothing to drink all day. Ome lit the primus and we made tea. Then more corn meal and canned beef. Mothballs for dessert. Then more tea. About 10:30 and 6 long hours of darkness ahead. Removed our boots and put on more clothes. The primus gave off too much heat and more fumes. Lit the candle about 12 p.m. for light and found it gave off just the right amount of heat. However, it burned out.

. . . To our right the ridge dropped off straight, to the left nearly so. We found a can of condensed milk . . . on finishing, Jim took the can, tossed it through the rip in the top of the tent—no sound. Then what appeared to be five minutes later a faint clatter as the can hit the bottom. That was a sensation; so close to the edge and so far to the bottom.

Our spot being on a cleaver in the middle of the wall we had tons of ice dropping off the top of the mountain every half hour . . . Down one side or the other. First a loud explosion, then a small clatter; silence; to be followed by a roll of thunder as our ridge shook beneath us . . . Thank God we were not in the way and we had nothing to fear. . . .

Toward morning the stars began to fade. Five a.m., and it became time to stir. On with the cold and stiff, frozen boots. More snow to melt in which Ome put some shredded wheat, ¼ pound of butter, salt, and sugar. This cooked for twenty minutes makes an excellent paste and Ome could make money selling it to the boys for kites.

However, on finishing my cupfull I found Jim and Ome putting it on their spoon and with a deft twist of the wrist sending it out over the edge. This seemed to be sort of a novelty and was indulged in by all until the kettle was empty. So the stuff was not wasted, yet we didn't have to eat it . . .

Monday Sept. 30th, 1935— 8 a.m. Shouldered the packs and started out. Ome in the lead, myself next, and Jim being heavier and the photographer on the end of the rope as the day before.

At this point we went out on the ice on which was a covering of 2″ of fresh snow. Very tricky stuff and demanding utmost care. Steps had to be cut all the way. We would have liked to help Ome with his cutting, but it was impossible to move out of line to change positions.

The climb continued slowly up the ridge on steep pitches "varying from 70 degrees to straight up." Step cutting in the ice alternated with climbing loose rock. Several narrow steep chimneys were ascended. At one point a piece of the ridge gave way under Ome as he leaped to the side and safety. At 4 p.m. they got into deep fresh snow on a 50° slope and bogged upward to the top of the rocks and the snow below the final bergschrund. By now it had become obvious they would never make it down to Paradise that night as scheduled. Campbell continues:

. . . A few more hundred feet elevation and we topped our rise only to see a huge overhanging crevasse where we had hoped to go through the ice cliff just below Liberty Cap . . . it seemed too wide to cross in any manner. However, a narrow spot was found and an attempt was made to cut steps in the opposite side but we could not reach it. The opposite side was above our heads and about eight feet across at our feet but slightly less at our heads . . .

Anchoring our axes on the rope Jim and I each took one of Ome's feet and lifted him nearly to arms' length above our heads. At the arranged signal Ome leaned out and jumped as we shoved, stuck his axe in the easy slope above, and hung on. On getting up, he anchored while we again went up on the rope. A hundred yards farther and there was Liberty Cap. Practically level to the top. We had won. No more trouble. We called our first halt of the day, shook hands and sat down.

. . . We rose again, dropped down the other side of the cap and thence across the top of the mountain to the crater rim.

As we stepped into the ice-filled crater we experienced the most extreme cold any of us had ever felt. At least 40° below zero (Well—anyway it *felt* like it). It was dark by now and at the other side we found Register Rock. We sat down at 7:30 p.m. completely worn out. As I took my boots off with much trouble, Jim and Ome slept for about ten minutes, but the cold awoke them. Again the packs were opened and the tent spread . . . With the carbide light we tried to signal either Paradise Lodge or Sunrise to let them know we were safe, as we were in no condition to go down . . . sleep was out of the question . . . we spent the night watching the stars, fixing the primus, thawing each others' feet, and eating mothballs . . .

After a seeming eternity, light streaks appeared on the horizon. This was our signal to get going.

. . . At 6 a.m. we started down . . . At the head of the Ingraham Glacier the sun came up. Jim exposed our last film looking directly into the sun without shading the lens. The route seemed like child's play. Detouring slightly to Anvil Rock hoping the lookout was still stationed there, but he was not, so we had to hurry on down again.

A short way further we found our first water since starting the climb . . . Went all the way down the creek to the lodge, stopping every hundred yards to drink again.

Reached Paradise at 10 a.m. On reporting, we found the Rangers had been sent out to look for us . . .

Conclusions:

The most enjoyable climb and most interesting I have ever been on.

Our blizzard tent could be improved upon as it was hard on the neck holding it up. Do not carry cans of gasoline in the same pack as the grub . . . it is not the best flavor in the world.

. . . . Jim's and my first climb of Rainier.

Liberty Ridge was not climbed again until 20 years later, on August 21, 1955, by Marcel Schuster, Dave Mahre, Mike McGuire, and Gene Prater. Instead of following the ridge crest, as was done by the 1935 party, this group stayed on the ice slopes to the west of the ridge to about the 12,000-foot level, where they cut back across the rocks to the final ice pitch leading toward Liberty Cap. They climbed with two

ropes of two men each, using the "all-fours" technique—the front crampon points, axe in one hand, ice piton in the other. Each rope team moved upward by having each man climb up to his belayer, then a rope length above, thus saving costly time on the tiring 3000-foot slope. Some rockfall from the ridge above caused the party anxious moments (*The Mountaineer*, 1955).

Liberty Ridge today is most often approached from the White River Campground and is the most popular of the Nordwand routes. Since 1958 at least one party has attempted the climb each summer; 131 individuals have made the ascent as of the end of the 1969 climbing season. The first ascent of the ridge by a woman was on the Memorial Day weekend of 1965, by Mrs. Len (Judy) Waller of Seattle with her husband and others.

During our early-season climb of Liberty Ridge on May 11–13, 1968 we found excellent conditions as firm snow covered the ice slopes and rock that late in the summer require great care in climbing and alertness for falling debris. Certainly our May ascent found the ridge in its most ideal conditions, in great contrast to those encountered during that ascent of late September 1935.

Normal climbing time: 7-8 hours to 7500-foot high camp from Ipsut Creek, or 5-6 hours from White River Campground; 2-3 hours to base of Liberty Ridge; 14-16 hours to Liberty Cap.

PTARMIGAN RIDGE-LIBERTY CAP GLACIER (1956)

Among several efforts to complete another ascent of Ptarmigan Ridge was a climb on August 4–5, 1956 by Fred Beckey, John Rupley, and Herb Staley. Instead of following the 1935 line of assault, the trio traversed easterly below the 300-foot ice cliff that forms an impressive part of the ridge at about 11,000 feet. The following account of the ascent is given by Herb Staley (*The Mountaineer*, 1956):

At approximately 4 a.m. the climb was begun. . . . Within 30 minutes we had traversed the final half mile of knife-edged moraine and reached the broad saddle directly beneath the ice where we donned rope and crampons in awkward haste.

A hurried survey confirmed the necessity of skirting the 400-foot icefall. To the right, the steep trough climbed by Wolf Bauer and Jack Hossack on the first ascent was now a bowling alley down which rock and ice fell onto the North Mowich Glacier 500 feet below. We moved very rapidly up a 200-foot névé slope onto rock slabs at the base of the ice . . . We moved upward, here traversing left across the steep glazed rock. The ledge steepened and narrowed beneath blue ice down which water began a slow trickle. We rounded a corner and climbed a 20-foot step onto a broad ice-littered ledge that fringed the bulk of the lower icefall. A rapid traverse was made, spurred by the growing factor of time. The terminus of the ledge was marked by 40 feet of steep exposed ice up which Rupley belayed Fred, while I remained at rope's length as lookout on the ledge. The wall at that point towered some 300 feet above the ledge with broken seracs commanding respect. As I moved to join Rupley I became aware of the singular sound of moving ice overhead and although it proved a false alarm, I could see my own tension mirrored in Rupley's gaze. Above the step we were once again on glazed rock, a small rock island that pointed toward the summit. We were not free of the lower icefall, since at this point it angles abruptly upslope for 1,500 feet before again turning above to form an inverted S. Route-finding now became an immediate problem.

To the left was a broad slope of steep névé extending from the upper icefall to the lip of the cliffs overlooking Russell Glacier below. A switchback-crossing of the slope might have provided a way out but at double risk. To the right and above, the wall was less thick and perhaps sufficiently broken to afford access to the glacier proper. We chose the latter course. Fifty feet of crampon rock climbing plus the traverse of a delicate ice chute provided contact with the icefall. A narrow trail threaded upward between tilted seracs, then broadened and curved, a white highway onto the glacier.

The actual time below the ice was little over an hour. A leisurely period of meditation and breakfast was spent in the shelter of a friendly crevasse. It was a beautiful day. Far below we could see the ridge and the tiny figures of our companions [support party] struggling downward under heavy loads. The remainder of the climb involved steep névé, route-finding among spectacular crevasses and the endless traverse to Liberty Cap. The summit was reached at 2:30 p.m. and the descent was made via the Gibraltar route. Our celebration consisted of a milkshake reunion [with our support party] at Paradise Inn.

A second ascent of this route was made on June 6, 1968 by Bruce Barris, Dick Bennett, Ted Carpenter, Mike Heath, and Joe Vance (written communication, February 1969).

LIBERTY WALL (1968)

A direct ascent of the Liberty Cap Glacier, from the lower bergschrund to above the upper ice cliff, was made on June 30, 1968 by Paul Myhre, Don Jones, and Roger Oborn. Instead of traversing below the ice cliff from Ptarmigan Ridge, the three climbed directly from the Carbon Glacier and up the steep ice slope which they named Liberty Wall.

According to Paul Myhre (written communication, 1968), from a camp pitched at the western edge of the Carbon Glacier, at 3 a.m. they hiked to the base of the wall, crossed the bergschrund, and began the ascent of the face rising steeply toward the ice cliff high above. They climbed directly upward, using front crampon points and keeping near the crest of a flat rib that diverted minor falls of rock or ice from above.

They found hard ice in the lower section, then ice covered by 6 inches of fresh snow. The trio ascended to the upper part of the glacier above the ice cliff via a steep ice ramp east of that pioneered in 1956. Once above the ice cliff they were able to relax; from there to Liberty Cap involves only a long trek up gentler snow slopes. However, at about 12,000 feet one of the climbers had knee trouble and the party was forced to retrace their route down the wall by several rappels, and returned to Mowich Lake. They reported considerable rockfall during the afternoon descent of the lower part of the wall.

A more complete, "diretissima" ascent to Liberty Cap was made September 20–21, 1971, by guides Dusan Jagersky and Gary Isaacs. They scaled the ice cliff to the east of the previous two routes, clawing their way up a very steep 150-foot ramp-chimney with ice hammers and short-shafted axes. About 15 ice screws were used for protection. After 12 hours of climbing from the bergschrund, they bivouacked near upper Liberty Ridge. Liberty Cap was reached in an hour the next morning, and the descent was made by the Emmons-Winthrop Glaciers back to Moraine Park and Ipsut Creek Campground (Jagersky, written communication, February 1973).

CURTIS RIDGE (1957)

By far the most sought-after route on Rainier, and the one attempted most often without success over the longest period of years, was Curtis Ridge, between the Carbon and Winthrop Glaciers. The history of explorations on the sharp-spined crest of crumbling lava and ash, ice, and nearly perpetual dust and rockfall dates back to the early 1900s. A photograph in an early publication (Williams, 1911) shows parts of the ridge and is labeled "Avalanche Camp (11,000 ft), on the high ragged chine between Carbon and Winthrop." (Webster defines "chine" as a "backbone . . . a ridge; a crest." The name fits well.)

At least seven attempts were made between 1936 and 1957 by some of the foremost climbers of the Northwest. Among those mounting serious assaults in 1936 and 1937 were Ome Daiber, Arnie Campbell, and Jim Borrow, who had made the first ascent of Liberty Ridge in 1935. These and others all returned with the same story of rotten rock cliffs and a continuous barrage. The day of the hard hat had not arrived and few Northwest climbers were yet philosophically adapted to such objective hazards. This was to be left to the postwar generation.

I vividly recall an attempt on Curtis Ridge during the Memorial Day weekend of 1948, in company with my brother K and Maynard Miller—a reunion after our climb together on Mount St. Elias in Alaska 2 years previously. Our efforts on Curtis Ridge were rather brief, due to poor weather and deep snows. Like that of most of our predecessors, our view of the ridge was from the upper end of the sharp-crested 200-foot buttress at about 10,000 feet, the rappel point for starts of the difficult climb above. Through swirling clouds we occasionally glimpsed the rugged topography beyond the knife-edged gap. Our greatest efforts of the day, however, were back at high camp: while taking down the mountain tent, Miller sank one leg into soft snow to his hip. For 5 minutes we struggled to free him from the clamp the snow held on his foot deep below the surface. In this ignominious fashion one more attempt on Curtis Ridge came to an end.

While mountaineers of the Puget Sound country were making history on Rainier during the first half of the century, little was heard from those on the eastern slope of the Cascades. Occasionally reports drifted across the mountains from hiking organizations in the Yakima, Ellensburg, and Wenatchee areas, but they left little imprint in the pre-1950 records of notable ascents on Rainier. It wasn't until a successful assault on Curtis Ridge in 1957 by two members of the Sherpa Climbing Club that the stage was set for a rapid succession of ascents by Yakima and Ellensburg climbers on the tougher routes on the north side of Rainier.

On July 20, 1957 Marcel Schuster and Gene Prater, with a three-man support party (Bob McCall, Stan Butchart, Herb Buller) left the White River Campground and hiked through Glacier Basin to St. Elmo Pass. After crossing the Winthrop Glacier they climbed onto lower Curtis Ridge and camped beside a small lake at about 8500 feet. That afternoon, while the others rested, Prater and McCall scouted the route above to determine the availability of an easy descent off the prominent buttress at 10,000 feet. McCall found a spot from which a rappel could be made off the west (Carbon Glacier) side. After marking this rappel point for the next morning's assault, the two studied conditions higher on the ridge. As similarly observed on the opposite side of the mountain by Pete Schoening and me while making our attempt on the Wilson Glacier Headwall the same weekend, a well-frozen layer of new snow had welded the loose rocks to the peak and there was little sign of fresh rockfall.

The final climb by Schuster and Prater began at 4:30 a.m. Sunday, July 21. The two wore hard hats but observed no rockfall during the ascent. The rappel went smoothly and soon they were traversing steep snow and ice to the notch at the crest of the ridge beyond the big buttress. The knife-edged ridge there had two more vertical steps, which were passed on the right by a traverse below the ridge crest, and a large gendarme which was passed on the left side. The sharp-crested ridge ended at 10,500 feet, where the major problem of the climb was faced: a high step of lava that cut across the ridge, considerably broadening its aspect. Standing on Prater's shoulder, Schuster reached the first ledge

Curtis Ridge from 10,000 feet.

on the 75-foot cliff; there he found an old piton and carabiner to remind him of earlier explorations. The piton was reset and used for the next nearly overhanging pitch. Prater found it necessary at this point to use a stirrup for footing as he led another 50 feet. He then belayed Schuster, who was carrying the two rucksacks. After a brief rest they continued up gentle slopes to the second major cliff, the source of extensive rockfall onto the Winthrop Glacier. In view of the time required to negotiate the cliff below, they decided to bypass this wall by traversing onto the marginal part of Willis Wall on the Carbon Glacier side of the ridge. There, broader slopes brought them around the end of a long rock band, then back toward the ridge crest and through a gully system partly obscured on the left side of the final massive rock cliff, about 500 feet high. The steep narrow snow gullies brought them above the final rocks and onto the snow ramp atop the upper ridge at about 12,500 feet. It was 1:30 p.m. and time to relax; they had only an easy slog to the summit dome from there.

Meanwhile, after the support party observed the two figures disappearing over the upper skyline, Bob McCall returned to 10,000 feet to retrieve the rope from the rappel point. They all then headed back across Winthrop Glacier and St. Elmo Pass to await the summit party.

After reaching the saddle between the crater and Liberty Cap, Prater rested while Schuster climbed to the summit register box, which he reached at 5:30 p.m. The two then hurried down the Emmons Glacier to Steamboat Prow and on to the foot of Inter Glacier, where they rejoined their support party only 2 hours after leaving the top. The long trudge back to White River Campground was culminated by hot tea and cinnamon rolls served by Ranger Jack Davis (*The Mountaineer*, 1958; *The American Alpine Journal*, 1958; *Cascadian Annual*, 1958).

Curtis Ridge has been climbed four times since 1957: in 1964, 1965, 1967, and 1969. For a time, until the tragic accident of June 1969, the aura af great difficulty due to extreme rockfall was dispelled, and the ascents marked a new era and outlook on the objective dangers of the mountain. On November 1–3, 1969 the ridge was conquered under conditions of heavy new snowfall, the first climb ever recorded on Rainier so late in the year.

WILLIS WALL, THE ULTIMATE CHALLENGE

By 1960, following successful ascents of most major ridges and cirque headwalls on Rainier, climbers finally turned their eyes and ambitions toward the conquest of Willis Wall proper. In the tradition of discouraging what for many years was considered suicidal, the National Park Service long turned down all requests for permission to attempt the climb, but mounting pressures and a growing public acceptance of the appeals of mountaineering eventually resulted in a more permissive attitude.

The first attempts to climb Willis Wall met with failure owing to the psychological aspects of facing the unknown under the inhibiting legal restrictions of that time, and the intimate display of the objective hazards of the face. Several parties approached the huge bergschrund at the base of the wall in early-morning darkness but retreated from the menacing sound of ice and rockfall and, for some, the thoughts of the wife and kids. Eventually, however, these early efforts were brought to fruition, but not without considerable controversy and allegations of deceit and fraud stemming from the vague reporting of surreptitious unauthorized solo climbs on the wall. However, dedicated efforts by Jim Wickwire to get the facts straight after 10 years of wondering about the "firstness" of two of his own presumed pioneering ascents on the wall eventually brought to light the story that both he and I now accept. My review of Wickwire's correspondence with Charles Bell, the principal in the story—and our meticulous critical scrutiny and comparison of photos taken by both Wickwire and Bell—led me to no other conclusion than to concur with Wickwire that Bell proved his climb of 1962, and we have no real basis for doubting his claim of an ascent in 1961. The story below provides essentially the sequence of events as interpreted from the research.

The West Rib (1961)

In early June 1961, a reconnaissance of the wall was made by a party led by Gene Prater and including Dave Mahre, Eric Bjornstad, Fred Dunham, Barry Prather, and Bob Baker. Following the party to the wall was Charles Bell, a small and bespectacled, but solidly built Easterner whose credentials were unknown to the Northwesterners at the time. The weather turned sour, however, and, with the exception of Bell, the party returned to town. Bell had no other plans and decided to remain on the mountain for a day or two longer. He was there, alone, unheralded, unauthorized to climb, and, most unfortunately, without a camera to record what transpired.

A report by Bell, prepared in the third person for obvious reasons, describes his wandering back to the base of the wall for another look-see:

The ascent was made June 11–12, 1961 of "Damocles Rib" (West Rib), westernmost of three ribs—between Liberty Ridge and Curtis Ridge. From camp in upper Moraine Park beside the Carbon Glacier, the route follows lower Curtis Ridge to the point—from which—an easy descent is made to the glacier. The Carbon Glacier proved relatively free of crevasses this early in the season and the crossing was made in about three hours directly to the base of "Agricola Rib" (Central Rib), midway between "Damocles Rib" on the west and "Prometheus Rib" (East Rib) on the east. As the bergschrund seemed impassable at this point, exploration was continued up a shelf of ice which sloped upward to the right (west). After an abortive attempt to cross the bergschrund just west of the base of "Damocles Rib" a passage to the left crossing with all deliberate speed a four-foot-deep chute in the snow caused by falling rocks brought the party to the 45-degree snow slopes of the rib. The ascent continued over excellent snow, keeping to one side (usually the left side) of the rocky crest of the rib. Most prominent feature of the lower rib is the "Colossal Cairn", a structure of piled flat boulders some 30′ high which sits on the crest at an altitude of about 10,500. Visible now and then directly above was "Damocles" itself, an enormous, apparently over-hanging serac, somewhat dubiously attached to the ice cliffs directly above the rib. It was the party's optimistic theory that if Damocles should fall dur-ing the ascent, it would shatter against the upper part of the rib and cascade neatly down the gullies on both sides without annoying the climbing party. Perhaps a sounder foundation for optimism lay in the fact that during the entire climb nothing whatever broke off from the ice cliffs above, excepting four small avalanches far to the east, in the vicinity of "Prometheus Rib". Nor was any rockfall noticed in the vicinity of the climbing route, although rocks came down fairly frequently through the gullies on both sides.

As light grew dim, the party sought a suitable bivouac spot, and finally settled for a sloping ledge of snow with a four-foot-wide rock ledge below, situated at about 12,000′. A shallow trench was scooped in the snow, all extra clothing donned, chocolate bars consumed, and, preparations thus com-pleted, the party faced what proved to be a relatively warm and comfortable night.

When the sun had risen sufficiently to turn the billows of the Carbon Glacier into spectacular pink and gold, the bivouac spot was left behind. Soon the rib ceased to crest, and the party was left with nothing between it and "Damocles" but a few hundred feet of gradually steepening slabby slopes, mostly snow-covered but with a few rocky outcrops showing through. These were soon crossed, and the party stood at the base of the great serac, at the top of the wall. The new route had been made, the ascent of the wall completed. The immediate question, however, was where to go from here. Passage directly over the ice cliff did not appear possible to either side of "Damocles", at least not to a party equipped as this one was. The most prom-ising possibility for such a passage lay east of the top of "Agricola Rib", and would require a traverse of some two thousand feet of snow-covered slab to reach. Altogether the sanest alternative seemed to lie in following the base of the ice cliffs to the right, checking one promising gap in the cliff to the right, and—if the passage would not go—continuing to the right, around the western end of the cliffs and up the slopes of Liberty Cap. This course was followed: the promising passage reneged on closer inspection; a diagonal descent of about 50′ brought the party to the uppermost part of the true Liberty Ridge, just below the point at which it intersects with the broad snowslopes of Liberty Cap. The first of two schrunds on this slope was crossed on the extreme left (east) by clambering through an odd ice structure in which the schrund seemed to lose itself completely. A diagonal up the slope to the right brought the party to the snowbridge across the second schrund. A hot, slow trudge straight up through softening snow led to the west ridge of Liberty Cap, whence the summit of this, the second of Rainier's three summits, was soon gained. On the descent into the "valley" which separates the Cap from Columbia Crest, the highest summit, a detour was made along the top of the ice cliffs, in order to determine the feasibility of forcing a passage through the cliffs above "Agricola Rib". As far as could be determined from above, this passage could be quite feasible.

After an endless hot slog to a summit which turned out to be wind-blown, snowcovered, and registerless, the party retraced its steps to Liberty Cap and proceeded to descend Liberty Ridge, keeping to the snowslopes on the western side of the ridge for the most part. A detour east of the ridge crest was necessary to avoid a dropoff at about 12,000; the ridge was again crossed to the east near its base in order to regain the Carbon Glacier at the point where the bergschrund petered out to become a mere jumpable moat. No difficulties were encountered during the descent apart from the softening of the snow through direct exposure to the sun for two straight days; as the party heeled down the 45-degree slopes (there was no glissading), the snow would frequently slough off to a depth of two inches or so. Snow also balled badly in the crampons until, about halfway down the ridge, it became necessary to remove them for the first time since the start of the ascent. Relocating its tracks of the previous day across the Carbon Glacier, the party regained camp shortly after sunset and arrived, happily but quietly, at Ipsut Creek Campground at midnight.

No record was found of any previous ascent of "Damocles Rib." Three small cairns were left along the rib, rather to authenticate the ascent than to indicate the route, which is obvious. The extent to which this route, as well as other thoroughly feasible ones on the other two ribs, depends upon proper conditions is indicated by the fact that a larger party attempting to repeat it only ten days later was defeated by incessant rockfall and huge ice avalanches. It appears, as Gene Prater of Ellensburg was first to recognize, that these ascents can be made with relative safety during the last weeks of May and early part of June, when the rock of the face is still frozen into place and before the ice cliffs begin to disintegrate and rake the face with their lethal debris. The hairline which divides relative safety from suicide may depend on such a trifle as which part of the face receives sun in the morning, which in the afternoon: on the days of the ascent, small avalanches were observed on the eastern side of the face and large ones on the Russell Glacier headwall (Liberty Wall) west of Liberty Ridge; both of these are "Afternoon sun faces." The western half of the wall, a "morning sun face", remained safe for several days.

Charlie Bell returned to Seattle and casually reported his ascent to Eric Bjornstad, whose amazement was tempered by some skepticism. As a result, Bell was invited to join a group the following week, in the first officially approved attempt on the wall. Besides Bell, the party included Bjornstad, Dave Mahre, Barry Prather, Bob Baker, and Herb Staley— with Fred Beckey joining them at high camp. Bell was obviously the subject of much quizzing regarding his line of ascent. According to Bell's letter to Wickwire (December 18, 1971):

When I returned about ten days later, after a fierce hot spell, with Bjornstad, Baker, Mahre et al—and Beckey tagging along—we found the snow in much worse shape and I allowed myself to be persuaded to bivouac in the bergschrund instead of pushing on to the safety of the rib. Our decision to abandon the climb next morning gave birth to the skepticism that engendered the second climb.

Bell's lack of photographic proof (having no camera with him on the earlier climb) and a pointing out of his route being considered by some members of the party as "vague" resulted in a general "no-credence" disposition of his alleged ascent of the West Rib. Bell left the Northwest shortly thereafter, and it wasn't until a few months later that he learned of the increasing widespread aspersion cast upon his claim; this was reflected in a refusal of prestigious mountaineering journals to accept his story. To refute what he now considered an implied discredit of his character, Bell returned to Willis Wall early the following summer, again alone and unauthorized, but this time with camera and film.

On June 21, 1962, Bell found the bergschrund impassable along the base of the wall, and he was forced to detour toward Liberty Ridge. He began his second climb along the base of the east slope of lower Liberty Ridge and states he was never on the ridge itself during the ascent. His photos clearly record his gradually ascending traverse of the steep flank of the ridge, where he experienced considerable rockfall. He crossed the prominent avalanche trough between Liberty Ridge and the West Rib and gained the crest of the rib about two-thirds of the way up from the foot of the wall. A meticulous examination of Bell's many photos— singly and in panorama mosaics—and comparing them with photos taken by Wickwire and Bertulis during their subsequent winter ascent of the rib in February 1970, proved beyond a doubt to Wickwire and me that, at least in 1962, Bell was on the upper third of the West Rib, that he climbed to the base of the upper ice cliff, and that he ascended diagonally to the west along the base of the ice cliff to upper Liberty Ridge. From there he continued on to Liberty Cap and Columbia Crest, where he duly signed the summit register before descending the mountain by way of the Emmons-Winthrop Glaciers and Moraine Park.

Only one day earlier, preceding Bell to the summit register, were Ed Cooper and Mike Swayne, who had just completed an unauthorized ascent up the west side of Willis Wall. Cooper's report to the press resulted in Park rangers checking the summit register: to their amazement, they found not only the signatures they sought but that of Charles Bell. All three climbers eventually paid fines ranging from $50 to $150 to reinstate their good names with the Park Service. Of this Bell states:

I cannot quarrel with the Rainier authorities. We all know that the park regulations at Rainier and certain other parks have been unduly strin-

gent. But unless one wishes to take the extreme position that the park authorities should make no regulations of climbing whatever, I must confess
that I cannot imagine any set of possible regulations which would legalize
solo climbs such as mine. I believe, of course, that I exercised reasonable
judgment in my ascents; I find it paradoxical that Bonatti got a medal for
his Matterhorn solo and I paid a $50 fine for my Rainier solo; but if I were
running Rainier park, I would surely prohibit myself from doing it again.

After the late-spring ascents of Willis Wall, and opening of the
mountain to year-around climbing without restrictions on routes, a
number of climbers examined the vast slope under winter conditions. On
February 10–11, 1970, during a trip that lasted 5 days, Jim Wickwire and
Alex Bertulis completed a winter ascent of the West Rib. They followed
much the same route soloed by Charles Bell in 1961, but at the time
were not sure of Bell's line of ascent and were psychologically exploring
new ground. The shortness of the winter day forced a bivouac beneath
the highest westerly arc of the ice cliff. The next morning they traversed
to Liberty Ridge, which they descended in a whiteout to the Carbon
Glacier.

From his experience gained on 19 routes on the mountain, including Ptarmigan, Liberty, and Curtis Ridges and the three major ribs on
Willis Wall, Wickwire considers the three Rib climbs his most difficult.
He states that, although Ptarmigan and Curtis Ridges have short, tech-
nically difficult sections, the three ribs on the wall involve lengthy climbs
of sustained difficulty. The ice cliff looming overhead adds an extra dimension of apprehension throughout, particularly on the West Rib, and
the margin of safety is often razor thin. This is particularly true during
winter ascents characterized by short days, long approach hikes, and prolonged periods of foul weather not conducive to cosy search and rescue
operations. At best, any climb of the wall involves taking the calculated
risk.

Willis Wall-Upper Curtis Ridge (1962)

At the same time as Bell's second effort, two other climbers, Ed
Cooper and Mike Swayne, also entered the sacred domain without first
obtaining approval of Park rangers. The two were the first to ascend
from the Carbon Glacier to the upper part of Curtis Ridge. Ed Cooper
describes the climb (written communication, June 6, 1969):

We did the climb in late June 1962 . . . the details follow: We left
the Carbon River Campground late in the morning. Our plan was to make a
leisurely walk to the base of the wall, observing it carefully for avalanches and
rock fall on the way, and to arrive there 3-4 hours before sunset, where we
could rest until after sunset, when we would start up the route I have marked
in dots on the enclosed photo.

When we arrived at the point where we could observe the wall, we saw that a good-sized avalanche had recently fallen down the very chute where we planned the lower part of our route. This, however, didn't change our plans for the route. Rather, we felt that the avalanche that was likely to occur here had "already fallen," and that it would certainly be safe when we started up it after sunset . . . Further, this chute was not exposed to the direct fall of the ice cliffs above.

As frequently happens with carefully made climbing plans, our progress was slower than we had estimated. I had done very little high-altitude climbing earlier in the year, and so felt the effects of the higher altitude. Further, the summer solstice sun had made the snow very soft on the Carbon Glacier. An ice screw broke on us going over a small snow cliff on the Carbon Glacier, and Mike fell in a hidden crevasse; all these things contributing to our general tiredness. When we did arrive at the base of the wall, the sun was setting.

Because of these delays, and the fact that we needed a little rest, we decided to postpone our start until 2-3 hours after sunset. We settled into a temporary bivouac about a ¼ mile below the avalanche cone . . . About an hour after sunset, while it was still light enough to see up high on the mountain (at a time when we had originally planned to be starting up the avalanche cone and working our way into the chute) we heard a tremendous roar, and we could make out a large avalanche making its way down this same chute. It was, in fact, larger than the previous avalanche, and we immediately realized that we were in danger at our point. We quickly ran, unroped, without our shoes on, in the semi-darkness, across the surface of the Carbon Glacier to avoid the path of the avalanche, which actually reached the level of our bivouac spot, perhaps 150-200 feet to our left.

We were absolutely astounded. It seemed to us as though the laws of nature had been contravened. Where did all the material for the avalanche come from? The one that had already fallen at that point had been a very large one, and looked as though it would have gotten rid of all the unstable snow in that chute. And to occur after sunset! By all rights the snow surface should have been more stable then. In all my mountain ramblings I have never seen an avalanche under these conditions. The only explanation I can offer is that during the process of freezing after sun had set, the contraction of the snow as it got colder broke bonds holding the snow together.

By all logic, the route we had planned would be even safer now that a second avalanche had fallen in the same place, even larger than the first. But our logic had failed us when the second one had unexpectedly taken place. We were badly shaken. It was the moment of truth where I realized that, for me, the climb was not worth the ultimate sacrifice. Not just this climb; any climb. I would much rather be enjoying the mountain from a beautiful flower-covered meadow above timberline.

But we had come to climb, and climb we must, if for no other reason than to search our own souls. I pushed aside my sane thoughts for later, when I might better contemplate them in leisure. We compromised our plans; we decided to settle for less than we had come for. We would skirt the very left edge of the wall.

Everything seemed anti-climactic after this point. About midnight we started up the route indicated. There were no exceptional difficulties. There was some rock scrambling through the first series of rock bands, on the left edge of the wall. Our only feeling of challenge and excitement came near the end of the traverse of the snow field on the upper part of the wall. The slope grew steeper, and there was a constant barrage of small rocks. One tried to pretend not to see how pitted this snow field was with rocks and rockfall paths. Sometime in the early dawn we saw a lone figure working his way up the Carbon Glacier to the base of the wall somewhere near Liberty Ridge. This must have been Charles Bell, alleged to have made one solo ascent somewhere on this North side, and evidently aiming to repeat it. We did not see him after this.

The rock band above the snow slope offered a suitably appalling prospect. It looked like a boulder field at about a 60-degree angle. (This is where I took the picture I sent you.) For safety and speed we had not roped to this point, and we saw no reason to rope here, as it would just be a potential source of rockfall. It was easy enough to climb, but exceptional care was needed. Once above this band the difficulties were over. We had done a new climb on Mt. Rainier, but the solution to Willis Wall still lay ahead.

East Rib (1963)

Dave Mahre, already familiar with several of the most rotten faces of Rainier and its satellite Little Tahoma, was probably the first to seriously consider tackling the wall directly through the upper icecap. In several reconnaissance trips he discerned two possible routes: (1) a direct route on the right side of the wall, offering little protection against hazards from the ice cliff above; and (2) a less direct route on the left (east) side of the wall, offering a great rock buttress as protection from falling debris. This latter route was eventually selected.

On June 8, 1963 Willis Wall directly through the upper icecap was conquered for the first time by Mahre, Fred Dunham, Don Anderson, and Jim Wickwire, all members of the Sherpa Climbing Club. Following the 8-mile hike from the Ipsut Creek Campground, high camp was pitched at 7300 feet on the lateral moraine of the Carbon Glacier. This is the highest point on the margin of the glacier from which an easy descent can be made to the ice. Gene and Bill Prater and Fred Stanley helped the party carry gear to the camp; the Praters had to return to their ranch but Stanley remained as support. With a walkie-talkie radio he provided moral support to the climbers as they worked up the face the next day.

The party left camp at 10:30 p.m. and ascended to the head of the Carbon Glacier at the base of the wall. The bergschrund was crossed at the east (left) end and soon they were on the lower slope of the wall proper. Immediately some rockfall was encountered, but hard hats protected them against injury from cascading pebbles. They then climbed diagonally toward the right, aiming for the crest of the ridge that held the buttress. After 2 hours of climbing ice, rock, and water they reached the base of the buttress. Don Anderson, although in poor condition relative to the others, who had climbed a new route on the Mowich Face a week earlier, led a 75-foot pitch of vertical rock and soon they all stood on top of the ridge. From there they radioed Fred Stanley, advising him they would make it to the exit ramp between the two ice cliffs in a couple of hours—but it was to be considerably longer. A small ice avalanche, the only one of the day, broke from cliffs to the right.

From the top of the buttress they worked their way to the head of the small ridge, alternately on snow and rock, and to the prominent snow band leading west to the central avalanche couloir. As Dunham led across the gully to the safety of another short ridge, he had to chop steps in extremely hard water ice to cross the couloir—always with one eye on the ice cliff looming high above. Once on this ridge, the party followed the right side of the crest upward. By this time a cloud cap had formed on the summit and was moving lower by the minute. Mahre led the last long exposed snow pitch to the final rock bands. Snow was blowing around the party as Wickwire took the lead up the last 150 feet of rock below the exit passage.

The lower part of the pitch was not too difficult, though consisting of rocks the size of bowling balls seemingly glued to the face. Then came a 15-foot traverse left on steep dirt, and a difficult vertical step on solid rock ending on a ledge between the first and second of the three major bands that support the summit icecap. Wickwire led the way up this Class 5 pitch without pitons. The narrow ledge above, which provided the last traverse to the snow ramp, was highly exposed; blowing snow added to the peril of the crossing. Once above the rock the party became lost in swirling sleet and an hour was spent locating the snow ramp. They found themselves several times directly beneath and against the overhanging base of the 300-foot ice cliff. Eventually the slope eased off but they were not certain of their whereabouts on the summit near Liberty Cap. With Don in a state of exhaustion, and possibly in an early stage of pulmonary edema, the party decided simply to head down the mountain, no matter what the direction or route.

As they descended, both the weather and Don's condition improved. Breaks appeared in the fog and eventually the climbers found themselves moving down the lower part of the Mowich Face. About 24 hours after leaving high camp, they were back at timberline along the North Mowich River, a blazing fire coaxed from wet wood serving as reward enough for the grueling ordeal. After a night spent in two sleeping bags and down parkas, they hiked out to the Mowich Lake road. It is worth noting that though Don Anderson had many years of mountain experience and had been on several expeditions, this was his first climb of Rainier (*American Alpine Journal*, 1964; *Cascadian*, 1963; *Summit*, June 1964).

Central Rib (1965)

A fourth route on Willis Wall was pioneered on June 20, 1965 when Paul Dix and Dean Caldwell climbed the central of the three major ribs or incipient "ridges" on the cirque wall. According to Caldwell (written communication, 1967), they began the climb from the bergschrund at 5:45 a.m. and scrambled onto the snow above at a point immediately east of the base of the main central buttress. Falling rock and ice with a consistency of hail was experienced but hard hats protected them. Moving diagonally up to the right, they gained the ridge crest, where the falling rock slackened. Four rock bands arching across the ridge were ascended to the left of the crest. Above the fourth arch they climbed to the right on snow slopes for several hundred feet to the top of some low cliffs. Directly overhead, about halfway up the wall, was a buttress of volcanic ash and mud capped by a lava flow.

The top of the buttress was gained by passing around the left side on steep snow. Above and slightly left of the buttress a short snow chute was then ascended, after which they traversed rightward on verglas to slabby rock At the top of these rocks an extremely steep snow and rock pitch, resembling a frost-covered cliff from below, was bypassed by a difficult rock traverse of 40 feet to the left, followed by an easy 20-foot vertical pitch. Three or four more rope-lengths of scrambling on snow brought them to the steep rock forming the base for the summit icecap.

Dix and Caldwell were now at the point where the route taken by the 1963 party merged with their route. The traverse upward on the rock bands here followed the original route of ascent to the top of the ice cliffs.

As with the previous party on the wall, a lowering cloud cap hit them with sleet as they arrived on the summit icecap about 1 p.m. Strong winds made it difficult to maintain footing and they had to resort to crawling for a while. Near Liberty Cap they sought protection in a shallow crevasse but were covered with ice and apprehensive about a bivouac; fortunately, at about 7 p.m. they were able to start down, following a wanded route marked on the Emmons Glacier by their support party, and arrived at the White River Campground at 3:30 in the morning (Caldwell, written communication, February 1967).

In retrospect, the observation can be made that the three ascents of Willis Wall were during periods of cloud-cap formation when temperatures were probably low enough to diminish rockfall hazard and ice avalanches. However, on a cirque wall as extensive as this, overhung for its entire width by a 250-300-foot wall of ice, an avalanche of tremendous proportions could occur at any time, regardless of time of day, temperature, snow cover, or season. The well-known French alpinist, Guido Magnone, after a flight around Rainier with Fred Beckey, stated that he would have strong reservations about attempting an ascent of such a wall of rotten volcanic rock topped by a forebodingly thick ice cliff.

Photos taken by Charles Bell during his second climb of West Rib on Willis Wall, June 21, 1962.

Ice avalanche, viewed from midway on West Rib.

Ice cliff from near top of West Rib.

Ice cliff from traverse to Liberty Ridge. Tracks barely visible at base of cliff.

13 Mountaineering from White River

EARLY HISTORY

White River Campground, 12 miles inside the northeast corner of the Park and 82 miles from Seattle, is the usual starting point for ascents of the Emmons-Winthrop Glaciers route and most attempts on Curtis Ridge and Liberty Ridge. Some parties have preferred to begin from Sunrise (6600), then trek over Burroughs Mountain to St. Elmo Pass. Climbers can register at the White River Entrance, White River Campground, or Sunrise.

Rainier from northeast, showing routes climbed from White River Campground.

Rainier sunrise from Sunrise.

The campground is at 4400 feet, and Camp Schurman on Steamboat Prow is at 9500 feet and about 6 miles distant, so the ascent to high camp under heavy loads generally takes most of a day. Climbers often make an evening hike into Glacier Basin (3.2 miles), then ascend leisurely to Camp Schurman the following morning, a schedule which allows plenty of time to laze about and prepare for an early start for the summit the next day.

The history of man's activities on this side of the mountain has not been widely publicized, and hikers reaching Glacier Basin, or old Storbo (sometimes spelled "Starbo") Camp, often are puzzled by rusted mining equipment and remnants of buildings amidst the beautiful alpine setting. Because the original mining claims pre-date establishment of Mount Rainier National Park in 1899, the rights of the owners maintained precedence over regulations against mining within the Park, and considerable development occurred after 1900. According to Park Service records, in 1897–98 prospectors were working claims in the basin and some ore, chiefly copper, was taken out. The creation of the National Park in 1899 did not deter subsequent filing of 41 additional claims, as this activity was permitted by federal mineral laws. In 1905 the Mount

Rainier Mining Company incorporated at Enumclaw. An act of Congress in 1908 prohibited further filings, but existing claims were not affected and between 1914 and 1930 special-use permits were granted by the Park Service to the miners for campsites, mills, tunnels, water, and flume sites in connection with working the claims. Permit fees ranged from $125 to $500 per year.

During the winter of 1906–07, while a camp was operating in Glacier Basin, an avalanche off Mount Ruth killed two men and a boy; the men were buried in the basin and the boy was brought out by horse in a log coffin. The Storbo Hotel was built in 1914–17 and a power plant was brought into the basin. In 1916 the road was extended into the National Park from Greenwater on the old Enumclaw road. The first machinery was brought into the basin, partway by truck; additional equipment was trucked in 1926–27. A sawmill and generating plant were built in the basin through 1921–27.

In 1924 patents were granted on eight claims, totalling about 165 acres. The rest of the claims were relinquished. The mining company was subject to several complaints by stockholders in the 1920s, resulting in two of the major figures in the company being convicted of using the mails to defraud. They were fined $1000 each and sentenced to 18 months in the federal penitentiary at McNeil Island.

Sporadic activity occurred through subsequent years. In 1948 a shipment of 47 tons of ore was made to the American Smelter Company in Tacoma. However, in spite of the stockholders placing a value on the holdings of from $2–2½ million, a U.S. Geological Survey study found little evidence the operation would ever be profitable; the claims

Storbo Hotel in 1921. From photo by Norman Huber.

were valued at $500 with a $6000 maximum. In 1957 the company reported doing a little improvement on the access road to the mining claims, but this has been the last indication of any work.

The small log ranger station in White River Campground was constructed in 1926. For many summers, nearly to his retirement as a school teacher in Snohomish, a familiar figure to the many mountaineers passing through the campground enroute to Glacier Basin was Paul Shorrock. Paul and his wife Gertrude have many memories of their years in the Park Service and have delighted campers with evening talks on the local history. Beside supplying some of the foregoing information, Shorrock describes an interesting account of an early-day climb of the mountain from the White River area:

Your question about "interesting and humorous anecdotes of early climbs" probably refers to a climb led by Major Ingraham on Sept. 6, 1916. This was to advertise the opening of the Renton Grange Fair by firing of rockets and flares from the summit of Mt. Rainier. A friend of ours, John Lehman of the Everett Mountaineers, who, with his brother Chris was a member of the party, typed up the account of the trip and loaned a copy to us for a time . . . I remember that the party assembled at Renton, had a long, difficult trip to Auburn, and finally reached Enumclaw. Here, they met Peter Starbo who wrote out a permit allowing them to drive over the road of the Mount Rainier Mining Company. The rest of their trip in is one long, sad tale of bad roads and cars breaking down.

Finally the climb began. Their lack of equipment was astounding . . . One man had only a "shawl" and two of the other men had a cotton blanket each; some had sleeping bags. Part of the men carried bedding and the rest carried the fireworks. The first night was spent on Ruth Mountain. Their progress the next day was very slow and finally Major Ingraham decided they must turn back. After some discussion, our friend John Lehman obtained permission to take three of the strongest of the party and attempt to complete the climb. It developed that these four spent two nights on the summit in a howling blizzard, surviving unbelievable hardships. John's account was a mastery of understatement. How they ever got back alive is a marvel. They had no ice axes, just alpenstocks, and he said they were so badly frozen that they slipped and slid most of the way back down the mountain.

Today the climb from Glacier Basin to Steamboat Prow usually is by way of Inter Glacier, the sometimes smooth, sometimes badly crevassed, icefield on the backslope of the wedge-shaped Prow. In the mid-morning glare on this northeast slope of the mountain, the glacier is an efficient reflector of the summer sun and the heat often becomes oppressive as "glacier lassitude" sets in. For this reason some climbers prefer to climb out of Glacier Basin via the crest of the ridge leading to, and over, 8700-foot Mount Ruth. There, breezes from the broad expanse of the Emmons Glacier make for more comfortable hiking. The notch beyond Ruth Mountain is the site of Camp Curtis, used as a high camp by many mountaineers in early days. From there one can either descend easily to the Emmons Glacier and hike up the snow to the upper end of the Prow at Camp Schurman, or continue up the ridge above Camp Curtis to the top of the Prow and descend to the hut by a series of steep snow or scree gullies.

Camp Schurman is the name given to the shelter cabin constructed by volunteer labor of many mountaineers and Explorer Scouts headed by veteran Mountain Rescue men John Simac, Max Eckenburg, Ome Daiber, and Bill Butler. The first two or three summers of the project involved backpacking heavy steel culvert sections, lumber, and other construction materials from White River Campground to the Prow. I will long remember the Big Carry as it started in 1958, scores of climbers and hikers of all ages and walks of life, old climbers and young Scouts, Mountain Rescue personnel, ex-Park rangers and one-time summit guides. The cabin was eventually completed after several more summers of hard work and was named in memory of Clark E. Schurman, chief guide at Paradise 1939–42 and a leading figure in Northwest mountaineering and Scouting activities.

The cabin is constructed of the tough corrugated steel used for highway culverts and is lined on the outside by cement and native stone. The interior has bunk space for 18 people and in emergency situations will shelter up to 50 persons. It contains a Park Service rescue

Camp Schurman at Steamboat Prow.

cache, emergency food and equipment, and a radio. With a Park ranger on duty here during the summer months, Camp Schurman serves on this side of the peak in the same capacity as does Camp Muir above Paradise. Its usefulness has already been well proven in several storm situations and rescue operations.

EMMONS-WINTHROP GLACIERS (1855)

The view of Mount Rainier from Sunrise (Yakima Park) and other northeastern vantage points shows more clearly than any other side the true bulk of the peak and its massive cover of glacial ice. The broad sweep of the combined Emmons and Winthrop Glaciers constitutes perhaps the only flank of the volcano which has not been eroded since the most recent eruptions and the development of the present crater.

The Emmons Glacier, the largest undivided single-named ice stream in the 48 conterminous United States, extends from the 14,000-foot crater rim to well below timberline in the White River valley, in a sweep about 4 miles long and as much as 1½ miles wide. The Winthrop Glacier, longer than the Emmons today but not as wide, flows into the valley of the West Fork White River.

The most popular route to the summit from the eastern approach, and the route on the mountain with probably the least amount of technical climbing problems, is that ascending directly toward the crater rim from Camp Schurman and Steamboat Prow. First climbed probably in 1855, this all-glacier route involves only the normal problems of routefinding through crevasses as they become exposed and lengthen later in the summer. From the Prow the route is upward for a short distance, then works leftward to the crest of a relatively gentle and smooth ramp of the glacier often called the "Corridor." This is followed to about 12,000 feet, where it fades into steeper slopes usually slashed with large crevasses. From here, the most dependable and customary choice is an ascending traverse to the right from the top of the Corridor to the final crevasse of the upper Winthrop Glacier, finding a convenient crossing into the broad saddle between Columbia Crest and Liberty Cap and then gaining a final and easy 500-700 feet of elevation on snow and rubble to the summit.

The Emmons-Winthrop Glaciers route has long been preferred by large parties and by relatively inexperienced climbers wanting to do the mountain "on their own," without professional guides. On July 30-31, 1909 a group of 62 members of The Mountaineers made the ascent from Moraine Park by about the same route of the pioneer climbs described earlier (*The Mountaineer*, 1909). In more recent years parties of 40 to 60 or more are frequent sights on this slope in early summer;

by summer's end the trail is a deep trough. The relative lack of technical difficulties, however, must not lead to an underestimation of the
potential dangers of a slip on the frequently hard-frozen surface of the
Emmons and Winthrop Glaciers.

Normal climbing time: 6-8 hours from White River Campground
to Camp Schurman; 5-8 hours to summit; 6-7 hours return to car.

RUSSELL CLIFF-UPPER CURTIS RIDGE (1960)

The upper part of Curtis Ridge drops over 1500 feet to the Winthrop
Glacier in a series of steep snow and ice slopes alternating with crumbling lava ledges. The rock-banded head of the precipice bears the name
of Russell Cliff in honor of Professor I. C. Russell, early-day geologist
and explorer who in 1896 ascended the mountain by way of the
Winthrop-Emmons Glaciers.

In July 1960 Dave Mahre, Gene Prater, Don Jones, and Jim Kurtz
made the first ascent of this hitherto-unexplored segment of the peak.
Although the face had been described as one of the more treacherous
on the mountain, the climb proved fairly simple; the only real problem
was selecting an approach to the base of the slope across the badly-
crevassed trough in the middle of the Winthrop Glacier.

The party left Steamboat Prow at 10 o'clock on a very warm night
and found the glacier surface very soft during the ascent. The traverse
was made at about 10,500 feet, between large seracs and over freshly
fallen ice blocks. Once to the opposite side of the Winthrop, at 11,500
feet, the climbers proceeded up the long snow slope. The surface was
conveniently suncupped and offered a staircase for a rapid ascent. The

Russell Cliff route, from Camp Schurman.

crest of Curtis Ridge was gained at 12,500 feet just as the rising sun cast a pink hue across the lava rock. Far below, a Mountaineer party of 30 members was observed on the Emmons Glacier, while near at hand on the ridge a squirrel was seen scampering across the snow and rock. The crater rim was reached at 9 a.m., well before the arrival of the larger party. The descent of the Emmons Glacier was enlivened by Jim Kurtz tumbling into a crevasse; he was quickly yanked out, only slightly subdued (*American Alpine Journal*, 1963; *Alpine Roamers*, 1960).

CHRONOLOGICAL SUMMARY OF FIRST ASCENTS OF DEFINABLE ROUTES ON MOUNT RAINIER, 1855–MAY 1972.

YEAR	DATE	ROUTE	MEMBERS OF PARTY (in most cases listed alphabetically)
1855	6/?	Emmons-Winthrop Glaciers, via approach from southeast	Two men, names not known, led to Mystic Lake area by Saluskin, Indian guide (climb reported years later by Saluskin)
1857	7/15	Kautz Glacier (to 14,000')	A. V. Kautz, W. Carroll, R. O. Craig, N. Dogue, Wapowety
1870	8/17–18	Gibraltar	H. Stevens, P. B. Van Trump, led to timberline by Sluiskin
1884	8/20	Emmons-Winthrop Glaciers, via approach from north	J. W. Fobes, G. Jones, R. O. Wells
1885 or '86	"Fall"	Ingraham Glacier (summit not reached)	A. L. Brown and several Yakima Indians
1891	8/12	Tahoma Glacier (from Indian Henrys Hunting Ground)	P. B. Van Trump, A. Drewry, W. Riley
1905	7/27	Success Cleaver (from Paradise Valley)	E. Dudley, J. R. Glascock
1920	7/2	Fuhrer Finger	Hans Fuhrer, Heinie Fuhrer, P. Farrer, J. T. Hazard, T. Hermans

1934	7/5	Tahoma Glacier via Puyallup Cleaver	Hans Fuhrer, A. E. Roovers
1935	9/7–8	Ptarmigan Ridge	W. Bauer, J. Hossack
1935	9/29–10/1	Liberty Ridge	J. Borrow, A. E. Campbell, O. Daiber
1937	7/12–14	Sunset Amphitheater—Tahoma Glacier Icecap	F. Thieme, J. W. Trosper
1938	8/27–30	Sunset Ridge	L. Boyer, A. E. Campbell, D. Woods
1939	8/?	Sunset Amphitheater—Sunset Ridge	H. Grage, J. W. Trosper
1946	?	Nisqually—Gibraltar Chute	S. DeBruler, P. Gilbreath, "man named Hewitt"
1948	7/13	Gibraltar (new ledge route)	C. M. "K" Molenaar, G. R. Senner
1948	7/15	Nisqually Icefall	R. W. Craig, D. Molenaar
1956	8/5	Ptarmigan Ridge—Liberty Cap Glacier	F. Beckey, J. Rupley, H. Staley
1957	6/23	Mowich Face (Edmunds Glacier Headwall)	F. Beckey, D. Claunch (Gordon), T. Hornbein, J. Rupley, H. Staley
1957	7/21	Wilson Glacier Headwall	D. Molenaar, P. Schoening
1957	7/21	Curtis Ridge	G. Prater, M. Schuster
1957	9/1	Kautz Cleaver	C. E. Robinson, G. R. Senner
1958	6/8	South Mowich Icefall—Tahoma Sickle	E. Drues, Mark Haun, Monte Haun, L. Heggerness, L. Ritchie, A. Van Buskirk, R. Walton
1959	6/7	Tahoma Cleaver	R. Bellamy, T. Hovey, D. Keller, H. Steiner, K. Vielbig
1960	7/?	Russell Cliff—upper Curtis Ridge	D. Jones, J. Kurtz, D. Mahre, G. Prater
1960	7/17	Success Glacier Couloir	G. R. Senner, R. Wahlstrom
1961	6/11–12	Willis Wall (West Rib, to ice cliff, upper Liberty Ridge and summit)	C. H. Bell
1962	6/20	Willis Wall—upper Curtis Ridge	E. Cooper, M. Swayne
1962	8/13	Nisqually Ice Cliff	B. Bishop, L. G. Jerstad
1963	5/31	Sunset Ridge—Edmunds Glacier Headwall	F. Dunham, D. Mahre, G. Prater, F. Stanley, J. Wickwire
1963	6/9	Willis Wall (East Rib, through central icecap)	D. M. Anderson, F. Dunham, D. Mahre, J. Wickwire
1963	7/8	Kautz Glacier Headwall	P. Callis, D. Davis, D. Gordon
1963	7/12	South Tahoma Headwall	F. Beckey, S. Marts
1965	6/20	Willis Wall (Central Rib, through central icecap)	D. Caldwell, P. Dix
1965	7/25	Sunset Amphitheater Direct to Liberty Cap	D. Mahre, D. McPherson, G. Prater, F. Stanley, J. Wickwire
1966	7/24	Central Mowich Face Route 1	D. Molenaar, R. Pargeter, G. Prater, J. Wickwire
1967	7/4	Central Mowich Face Route 2	W. Cockerham, E. Marquart, B. Sumner, D. Young
1967	6/19	Nisqually Cleaver	F. Dunham, J. Wickwire
1968	6/30	Liberty Wall to 12,000 ft.	D. Jones, P. Myhre, R. Oborn
1968	7/22	North Mowich Headwall Rt. 1	W. Cockerham, D. Davis, M. Hargiss, M. Heath
1970	6/26	North Mowich Headwall Rt. 2	R. Schaller, J. Wickwire
1971	9/20–21	Liberty Wall to Liberty Cap	G. Isaacs, D. Jagersky
1972	5/27	Fuhrer Thumb	C. Raymond, T. Stewart, J. Wickwire

14 Winter Ascents

Mount Rainier speaks most eloquently in the Winter, especially after it has been hiding, perhaps sulking for several weeks behind a curtain of clouds and rain. Then one cold morning we awaken and there it is, rising out of the swirling mists, its eastern profile shining in the early morning light. Ah, Mount Rainier is unveiled and will be at its conversational best. This visual communion will perhaps go on for several mornings but will never be as impressive nor show the sparkle and enthusiasm of that morning of reawakening.

> Josef Scaylea
> Moods of the Mountain

The man who climbs only in good weather, starting from huts and never bivouacking, appreciates the splendor of the mountains but not their mystery, the dark of their night, the depth of their sky above . . . some mountaineers are proud of having done all their climbs without a bivouac. How much they have missed! And the same applies to those who enjoy only rock climbing, or only the ice climbs, only the ridges or the faces. We should refuse none of the thousand and one joys the mountains offer us at every turn. We should brush nothing aside, set no restrictions. We should experience hunger and thirst, be able to go fast, but also know how to go slowly and to contemplate. Variety is the spice of life.

> Gaston Rebuffat
> Starlight and Storm

THE 1922 ASCENT OF THE GIBRALTAR ROUTE

Until 1964 climbing on Mount Rainier was with few exceptions restricted by the Park Service to the period from Memorial Day to Labor Day, the general feeling being that ascents of the mountain required a minimum of snow on approach trails, well-consolidated snow on the upper glaciers, and long daylight hours. Before World War II the limitations imposed by clothing and equipment kept mountaineers pretty much homebound during winter months. A few hardy souls ventured into the hills on snowshoes, but skiing had not yet come of age and the rare enthusiasts who enjoyed their telemarks across the wintry landscape were looked upon with some skepticism.

Considerable interest was therefore generated when in February of 1922 a party of French alpinist-skiers—Jean and Jacques Landry and Jacques Bergues—applied for and was given official endorsement from the Park Service to make a winter attempt on Rainier.

The night before the attempt the climbers were guests of Rainier

National Park Company in Paradise Inn, where an atmosphere of high excitement prevailed; until now, a winter climb of Rainier had been publicized as "impossible." News reports during the week before the climb emphasized the great amount of preparation necessary, including liaison between the Army at Camp Lewis and Park Superintendent W. H. Peters. Jean Landry tells the story, as he recalls it over 40 years later (written communication, February 1963):

We had planned, at first, to make our Rainier climb mostly a ski-tour. However, after examining pictures of the mountain and talking the matter over with local climbers, members of the Seattle Mountaineers, we decided to try the Gibraltar Route rather than the more skiable and more protected east slopes, where the overnight shelter was of the open-sky variety.

Owing to this decision, what had been planned as a modest and private mountaineering experience became a semi-official expedition with extensive publicity. The Rainier National Park Company offered its hospitality at Paradise Inn. The National Park Authority gave moral support and the use of its Fire-Lookout cabin at Anvil Rock. A detachment of the U.S. Army's Signal Corps placed a telephone line between Paradise Inn and Anvil Rock over which news of the ascent was given to reporters sent to Paradise Inn by all major newspapers of Seattle and Tacoma.

To cap all this, Charles Perryman, a news-cameraman, asked to accompany us and film the ascent. This involved the additional risks of carrying more than 60 pounds of cinematographic equipment and taking along an in-

Members of winter-ascent party of February 13, 1922. From left: Jacques Bergues, Jean Landry, Jacques Landry.

experienced person, for Perryman had never climbed a mountain before, not even in the summertime. If we had any misgivings on that subject, they were proved to be unjustifiable, as Perryman performed as if mountain climbing had always been his principal hobby.

Technical climbing difficulties were limited to the icy "chutes" after leaving the Gibraltar Ledge to gain access to the gentle upper slopes. A great deal of patience was required, however, to wait for favorable weather between storms. We waited several days at Paradise Inn and again at Anvil Rock. Taking the film consumed much time because hand cameras at that time were not good, and every scene meant setting tripod and camera, each of which weighed about 30 pounds.

The first good day (February 11) was spent taking scenes from Anvil Rock to the Gibraltar Ledge, leaving the camera there and returning to the hut, which was almost filled with snow. The following day was stormy again, but February 13 was favorable with a cloud deck varying between 9,000 and 10,000 feet. We picked up camera and tripod at Gilbraltar, completed the ascent, taking scenes as we went, and returned to Anvil Rock in the evening (about 10 or 11 p.m.).

We discarded our skis below Anvil Rock. Except for a short stretch in the wind shadow of Cowlitz Ridge, the snow was everywhere compacted to hardness by the very strong wind accompanying the winter storms.

It is probably difficult for present-day mountain-climbers to imagine the conditions and attitudes which prevailed only 40 years ago in America. It was then impossible to find skis in the Seattle stores other than the kind that had for binding just a toe-strap nailed to the wood. Crampons and ice-axes had to be forged and ski boots had to be made to order. As for the attitude toward winter climbs, it was one of disinterest or disbelief or futility. No one seemed to have discovered as they had in the Alps that mountains are even more beautiful in the winter and that trips are more enjoyable without the summer crowds.

At the time of our climb the political situation both here and abroad was relatively uneventful so that editors had difficulty in attracting the public's interest to their newspapers. This may be why they devoted so many columns to the story of our climb before, during, and after. In their articles we found much inaccuracy, exaggeration, falsehood, and fancifulness . . .

In the early twenties Seattle was still in the afterglow of the Klondike and Alaska gold-rushing adventures. Some people were advising us to use fur parkas; however, an Alaska outfitter [Filson?] wisely recommended a thin windbreaking material [silk duck] and made for us parkas and over trousers which were wonderful. The coldest temperature observed at Anvil Rock during our stay was about 10 degrees F. above zero and I am quite sure that it never declined below zero at any time during our climb . . .

If there was in some quarters a vague doubt concerning the success of the climb, it was dispelled the following summer when a party of the Seattle Mountaineers making the first ascent of the season found our names inscribed on a piece of film which we had left in a container on Columbia Crest.

Two of the clippings call the peak Mt. Tacoma; these come, naturally, from a Tacoma newspaper. In that city there was a strong proprietary feeling

Scenes during winter ascent of 1922. Clockwise from left: on Gibraltar ledge; above Gibraltar; at summit.

concerning the mountain and our climb seemed an opportune occasion to let the world know that the name Mt. Rainier was an usurper.

I read with amazement about the "6th class stuff" and other doings of the present generation of climbers. The limits of the possible have been pushed so far beyond where they were during my time that I hardly recognize myself as a climber. However, I have no regrets; the challenges are greater today but, to a great extent, this is owing to the improvements in techniques and equipment. The relation of challenge against capability has probably remained constant and so has, therefore, the moral reward of the climber's experience.

CLIMBS OF THE EMMONS GLACIER, 1928 AND 1936

From 1922 through 1965 only four ascents of Rainier were recorded for the season between October and late May. One of these, the January 1936 solo climb of the Emmons Glacier by Delmar Fadden, ended tragically. The other two, although successful, actually were made in early spring rather than the true calendar winter.

On April 7, 1928 the first of the spring ascents occurred somewhat as a consolation for failure to achieve the main object of the trip—the first ski ascent and descent of the mountain. Seattle climbers-skiers Walter Best, Hans-Otto Giese, and Dr. Otto Strizek climbed on skis to about 12,000 feet on the Emmons Glacier before icy conditions compelled them to revert to crampons for the remainder of the journey to the crater rim (*The Mountaineer*, 1928).

In 1936 Delmar Fadden made his solitary dash to the summit of Rainier via the Emmons Glacier, doing so without first notifying the Park Service. During the descent he apparently suffered a broken crampon, then slipped and fell on the upper part of the mountain. His body was spotted from a plane 5 days later, at an altitude of about 13,000 feet. A rescue party led by Ranger Bill Butler and Ome Daiber recovered the body from the ice a few days later.

CHASING LIEUTENANT HODGKIN: ASCENT OF FUHRER FINGER, 1951

In the late afternoon of April 12, 1951, Lieutenant John Hodgkin of the Army Air Force made the first landing of an aircraft on Rainier's summit dome. Flying a ski-equipped 85 hp J-3 Piper Cub from the runway near Spanaway, Hodgkin flew to the mountain and landed in the 14,000-foot saddle between Point Success and Columbia Crest. Upon landing, however, he turned off the engine and hiked to the crater rim. On his return to the plane, he was unable to restart the engine; the spark plugs had froze. Hodgkin was forced to spend the night inside the downed aircraft, literally flying the plane as it hovered on ropes tied to small sheets of plywood he had driven into the snow.

Hearing of the pilot's unauthorized landing atop Rainier, and of his inability to leave the summit, the Park Service organized a rescue effort headed by Assistant Chief Park Ranger Bill Butler. In the party also were Rangers Delmer Armstrong, Elvin R. Johnson, and me. Support parties followed a few hours after our group left Paradise at 2:30 in the morning of April 13. Following the most direct line to the summit from Paradise, we ascended Fuhrer Finger in ideal snow conditions. However, we arrived at the landing site at 4 o'clock in the afternoon, about half an hour after Hodgkin had taken off in a powerless glide down the steep slopes of the upper Tahoma Glacier. He landed on ice-covered Mowich Lake, where he was greeted by District Ranger Aubrey Haines, who had hiked up to assist him. Eventually he got his engine started and took off for the return to Spanaway.

Meanwhile, back on the summit, our "rescue team" scouted the slopes for the goodies of equipment (sleeping bags, stoves, and food) dropped to us by planes from McChord Air Force Base. We laid out our camp in the open saddle between Point Success and the crater and spent a chilly night contemplating the stars from our frost-lined co-coons. Our efforts were not without their rewards, however, and we descended the mountain next morning heavily laden with our acquisitions of new cold-weather gear. Thinking of outfitting his wife and two growing sons, Armstrong was particularly avaricious and resembled a small truck as he packed down four sleeping bags and an equal number of parkas. Once below Fuhrer Finger we reached our cache of skis left the previous morning. From there back to Paradise we enjoyed a fine run, albeit topheavy, in company with other personnel who had stood in support at a camp below the Finger—Wolf Bauer, Dr. Otto Trott, Lou Whittaker, George Senner, and my brother K.

As an aftermath to the incident Hodgkin was tried by the Park Commissioner. For his illegal landing of an aircraft inside the Park he was fined $300 and given a suspended 6-month jail sentence. The Commissioner was only slightly amused by the contention of Hodgkin's attorney that the pilot had not landed on the mountain proper, but rather on a snow surface which was only a transitory part of the Park landscape.

Hodgkin's plane near Point Success. From photo by John Hodgkin.

Following World War II an increase in the number of Alaskan and Himalayan expeditions originating among climbers of the Pacific Northwest was paralleled by an improvement in cold-weather clothing and equipment and by increased year-around mountaineering. Outdoor clubs extended their hiking programs through the winter months as greater knowledge was gained of cross-country travel and survival techniques on the snowy landscapes of the Cascade and Olympic Mountains. Eventually the National Park Service adopted a more flexible policy toward climbers who sought to develop their skills on the upper slopes of Rainier.

In 1964, after much deliberation, and formulation of regulations which evolved from several meetings with representatives of Northwest mountaineering clubs and search and rescue groups, the Park Service opened Rainier to summit climbs during the winter season. The winter season subsequently (1969) has been unofficially defined (for purpose of maintaining season records of climbs) as the period following the second weekend of September and preceding the second weekend in May.

On April 25–26, 1964 the first party to take advantage of the "new freedom" included climbers from the eastern and western sides of the Cascades: Gene and Bill Prater, Barry Prather, and Chet Marler, Jr., from Ellensburg; Glenn Kelsey, Arnold Bloomer, Gil Blinn, Paul Williams, Bill Dougall, Tony Hovey, and me from the Puget Sound area. The weather was unsettled, however, and after a stormy night at Camp Muir and a late-morning reconnaissance to about 11,000 feet on the Ingraham Glacier, we retreated in a blizzard. Our only achievement was learning that the upper snow slopes of Rainier are windpacked and firm during the winter.

Over the New Year holiday of 1965, four parties tackled Rainier from two separate approaches—White River Campground and Paradise Valley. All were highly experienced and well-equipped, but they found the snow at low elevations too soft—snowshoes sank a foot or more into the unpacked surface and most of the parties barely made it to timberline; one attained 8500 feet. An attempt in early February had the same results as a party of veteran mountaineers took several hours to climb a mile beyond Paradise to the base of Panorama Point.

Finally, on March 2, 1965, a party that had been on standby for a month awaiting a clearing of the weather headed up the mountain from Paradise. Equipped with sleds and a radio, and led by Park Ranger

Gil Blinn and Tacoma fireman Lee Nelson, the group also included John Simac, Glenn Kelsey, Everett Lasher, Chuck Gross, and Dr. Rob Schaller. Enroute to their first camp at about 8000 feet Blinn and Nelson kicked loose a slab avalanche on the steep slope below Panorama Point and most of the party below was caught in a jumble of snow blocks and equipment. Fortunately no injuries occurred and no equipment was lost. Above Panorama Point they found the snow windpacked, so snowshoes and sleds were cached for the return. They continued climbing until 5 p.m., when approaching darkness forced them to pitch camp at 8000 feet, well below their objective of Camp Muir. The next morning they continued up the mountain past Muir, across the Cowlitz Glacier, and onto the Ingraham Glacier beyond Cathedral Rocks. Their three tents were pitched at 5 p.m. on a small shelf between two seracs at about 11,600 feet.

Leaving camp at 7:40 in the morning, March 4, they found excellent conditions, with windpacked snow and solid crampon footing on the upper part of the mountain. Crevasses were well covered by firm snow and the crater rim was attained at 11:20 a.m. The temperature was 6°F. and the wind from the south had a velocity of 30 miles per hour. After an enjoyable time with cloudless views in all directions, the party descended, arriving at high camp before dark (*Summit*, November 1965).

Conditions on the Gibraltar route have proven to be more stable in winter than summer, when rockfall presents a continuous hazard. With the loose material on the face cemented by winter snow and rime, the route generally is more safely traveled. However, the winter stability of the route is only relative and may vary. On the climb of February 8, 1968 by a 12-man party led by Lee Nelson and of which I was a member, unusually high temperatures along the ledge during the afternoon descent resulted in considerable melting of icicles, softening of the snow cover on steep ice, and numerous small waterfalls. As I was traversing back down the ledge system in the afternoon a large piece of ice or rock fell from high above and buried itself in the soft snow only a foot ahead of me.

Those who made the first winter climb of the Nisqually Icefall, on February 11, 1968, were carrying the banner of the newly formed Summit Alpine Club of Tacoma. The party included Gary Frederickson (leader), Glen Frederickson, Chris Chandler, George Dockery, Ron Fear, Jim Langdon, Bill Lehman, Zac Reisner, and Pete Sandstedt. The party left Camp Muir at 2 a.m. in good weather: clear, no wind, and with a temperature of 20°F. The climbers found ideal conditions in the icefall and arrived on the summit between 9 and 10 o'clock in the morning. On top the temperature was a balmy 17° and the wind only 10 miles per hour. They were back at Muir at 2 p.m. According to Gary Frederickson (written communication, March 1968):

> . . . The snow was medium to firm windpack all the way up (our steps were no more than 2″-3″ deep); we encountered small, isolated patches of ice that had been uncovered by wind action at various points along the route; the climbing in the steepest part of the icefall was very straightforward and well protected from ice fall (the steepest pitch may have been as much as 45 degrees, but no more); our only route finding problems were encountered immediately above the icefall proper at about 11,000 feet where we were forced to thread our way amongst a considerable number of large crevasses (this feature of the route surprised me since I had expected virtually all crevasses to be filled with snow—three of us had climbed the icefall last June and found the crevasses to be smaller than we did now so the explanation must be the low snowfall we're getting this year).
> Conditions on the descent were as follows: the snow had begun to soften up but didn't become a problem until we reached the crevasses around 11,000 feet where we experienced some anxious moments on a couple of weakening snowbridges; the steep pitch was so soft that our crampons balled up badly—we overcame the soft-snow problem by using some pickets and fixed rope we had carried up to safeguard any steep, exposed pitches that we might have encountered; a few chunks of ice dropped off the ledge of the icefall and a few sounds were heard from the direction of the ice cliffs but our route was well protected at all times so we experienced no worry over the possibility of ice-fall. P.S. There was lots of activity on Gib that afternoon, too!

The first winter ascent of the Emmons-Winthrop Glacier since the tragic solo climb of Delmar Fadden was made March 1, 1968. On February 27 the party of six (Glenn Kelsey, leader, Paul Haertel, Cleve Pinnix, Gary Tate, and Dwight and Marilyn West) rode snowmobiles from the White River Entrance Station to the White River Campground, then hiked into Glacier Basin, where the first night's camp was pitched. On the 28th they climbed to Camp Schurman at Steamboat Prow. The ascent to the crater rim and summit from the Prow was in a nearly direct line, but they found either soft snow or a breakable crust into which they sank to their knees. Also, some wind was encountered during the 9-hour climb to the crater and 4½-hour descent back to the Prow (Glenn Kelsey, oral communication, March 1968).

The Liberty Ridge climb of May 11–13, 1968 showed both the practicality and the drama of early-season ascents on the north face of Rainier. In contrast to the first ascents of Ptarmigan and Liberty Ridges in September 1935, which involved considerable rockfall, touchy crampon work on steep black ice, and crevasse problems high on the face, the May ascent found the mountain in excellent shape. The winter snowpack still covered most of the rock on the ridge crest and the blue ice on its flanks and the bergschrund below Liberty Cap was crossed without the difficulty generally encountered in summer. The seven-man party, organized by Lee Nelson and me, also included Sandy Bill, Warren Bleser, Dave Mahre, Peter Renz, and Dr. Rob Schaller. We made relatively rapid time up the ridge, despite a late start (4:30 a.m.) from camp at 7500 feet at the edge of the glacier. The problems of finding a route through crevasses on the Carbon Glacier that plague climbers late in the season were nonexistent and we reached the base of the ridge in about 2½ hours. The climb of the ridge required another 13 hours to Liberty Cap, but we were slowed slightly when Bleser's crampon broke at about 12,500 feet, forcing him to "limp" up the remaining steep ice.

The main problem of climbs early in the season became evident: our arrival at Liberty Cap at 8 p.m. was followed rapidly by darkness. Visibility decreased further during our retreat from the summit plateau in a cloud cap. At the eastern edge of the plateau, where it breaks off sharply to the upper Winthrop Glacier, Sandy Bill plunged through a thin cover of snow and fell 10 feet into a crevasse. After a rapid Bilgeri retrieval of our comrade, we floundered a few hundred feet farther down the mountainside, with hesitant steps above several apparent drop-offs, and with flashlights reflecting against blowing snow inches from our faces. By 11 p.m. and at about 13,000 feet, we finally sought and found a shallow crevasse into which to huddle together until dawn. We had anticipated such a bivouac and individually were prepared with an assortment of lightweight down bags, half-bags, a bivouac sack, extra layers of down clothing (my 1953 Eddie Bauer parka, used on K2, still

served me well), and lightweight tarps ("space blankets") for protection against the drifting snow that rapidly piled over us. Daylight came none too soon, however; several in the party were experiencing numb fingers and toes. Fortunately the blowing clouds cleared below 12,000 feet and soon we were basking in the happy contrast of warm sunshine at Camp Schurman, wet garments spread on the rocks and on the cabin roof for rapid drying. The return trip across the Winthrop Glacier to our high camp above the edge of Carbon Glacier required little more than an hour.

The winter of 1968–69 brought an extremely heavy snowpack to lower elevations; extended periods of foul weather prevented any serious attempts on the mountain until late February, on the weekend of Washington's Birthday. Then three separate parties moved up the mountain from Paradise, each with different objectives. Soft, dry powder snow forced each party to use snowshoes all the way to high camp. The Lee Nelson party originally had planned to climb the Nisqually ice cliff but the unconsolidated snow and indications of avalanche conditions on the cliff discouraged attempts in that direction. Instead they followed the Jim Mitchell party up the Nisqually-Gibraltar Chute. The snow surface enroute to the summit was soft enough to allow several of the climbers to make the ascent without crampons. During the night following their return from the top (via the Ingraham Glacier) 2 feet of snow fell at their high camp (Nelson, oral communication, February 1969).

The major drawback to embarking on a winter ascent from any point other than Paradise, which is open to auto travel through the winter, is having to start from valleys well below timberline. Even though the Park Service permits use of snowmobiles on the snowbound roads (West Side Road, White River Road), their use is restricted to within ½ mile of roads. Hence, the winter climber must work his way to the open slopes above timberline by way of steep snow-covered valley sides. Under heavy packs, and on snowshoes, this can readily reconvert one to summer mountaineering.

A climb of the Tahoma Glacier was made April 25–30, 1969 by Jerry Smith (leader), Harold Pinsch, Roger Beckett, Gary Tate, Steve Wennstrom, Harvey Schmidt, and Mark Wilder. By ferrying supplies and personnel on a snowmobile operated by Don Gillam the party was able to travel the West Side Road to the South Puyallup River bridge. From there the group hiked up the valley to about 4500 feet, crossed the river, and climbed the steep slopes to 6200 feet near upper St. Andrews Park, where the first night was spent. On the 26th they ascended the right (south) side of Puyallup Cleaver, then descended to Tahoma Glacier at about 9100 feet. Camp was pitched the second night at about 10,000 feet; from there they watched a spectacular ice and snow avalanche off the upper cliffs of Tahoma Cleaver.

On April 27 the climb of the steep upper Tahoma Glacier was made, with only one crevasse problem, at 11,500 feet, encountered. The summit was attained at 3:45 p.m. and tents were pitched inside the crater. The weather was clear, wind was about 20 miles per hour, and temperature was about 7°F. The following morning, after leaving camp in an increasing overcast, they started down the mountain toward Fuhrer Finger, by compass headings. The storm increased to blizzard intensity and forced them back to the crater in 5-10-foot visibility. They took refuge in a steam cave on the southwest side of the crater. According to the report by Harold Pinsch (written communication, November 1969), "Wind had arisen with clear skies above but tremendous ground blizzard. Don't know strength of wind but could not stand up in it. Cave quite comfortable after some remodeling. Very little note of sulphur fumes." Two nights were spent in the cave.

On April 30, as reported by Pinsch, "Weather clear and calm. Descended to Fuhrer's Finger. Snow hard and crusted . . . At Paradise by 12:30."

The first ascent of Rainier in deep new snow of autumn was that on rugged Curtis Ridge November 1–3, 1969 by Jim Wickwire, Del Young, and Ed Boulton. (This was Wickwire's 14th of 19 ascents of Rainier, each by a different route; at this writing he holds the distinction of being the first person to climb three routes on Willis Wall and all three Nordwand ridges—Ptarmigan, Liberty, and Curtis.)

The party left White River Campground at 9 a.m. on Saturday, November 1. They encountered about 6 inches of fresh snow in Glacier Basin but had no trouble crossing St. Elmo Pass and Winthrop Glacier and climbing in good step-kicking snow to their first bivouac at about 10,000 feet on Curtis Ridge, which was reached at 6 p.m. They were amazed at the amount of fresh snow on the crest of the ridge, considering the relatively small amount in the 7000-9000-foot zone.

They left camp at 7 a.m., essentially without breakfast in the interest of saving the sparse daylight hours left for the climb of the upper ridge. A short time was taken preparing for the rappel off the ridge crest at 10,500 feet—once below this massive cliff they were committed to continuing the climb to the summit. The "Aid Pitch" beyond the sharp-crested ridge, which was now plastered with new snow, was reached shortly before noon. This cliff was bypassed by a traverse along the ledges to the right and a climb of easier rocks beyond. Some rockfall was experienced on the snow slope above the rock band, directly below the prominent cliff band on the upper ridge. Once above the lower cliff band they continued upward to the right to the next obstacle

—a frozen waterfall which descended steeply from the cliff band above. The ice was about 40 feet across and at an angle of about 50°. Del Young led the pitch, the most difficult of the entire climb, by placing two ice screws and an ice piton and a nylon runner for protection. He completed the pitch by a tension traverse to snow-covered rocks on the opposite side of the ice cascade. The pitch consumed an hour but allowed access to the broad snow slope, immediately above, which led to the exit gullies.

Wickwire led the 40° snow slope diagonally left to a narrow snow-filled gully; Boulton led this and continued across rock to the bottom of the final exit gully. Young led the first steep rock pitch into the gully and Wickwire then continued up steep snow to the snow ramp above the last rocks of Curtis Ridge. The climbers reached this point about dark and prepared their second bivouac by leveling a snow platform. The jello and tea consumed here were the first warm liquids they had had for 24 hours.

An extremely high wind buffeted the bivouac during the night as a storm covered the summit dome 1000 feet higher. A cloud cap descended to their level but by 3 a.m. had dissipated. Morning dawned cold and clear and the wind continued to lash them as they left camp at 8 a.m. and struggled upward. Having difficulty keeping their footing in winds estimated in excess of 60 miles per hour, they took 2 hours to attain the saddle below the crater. The Emmons Glacier was descended under ideal conditions, however, with most of the crevasses partly filled by recent snowfall. Camp Schurman was gained at 2 p.m.

Curtis Ridge ascent of November 1–3, 1969. Ridge from 10,500 feet; bivouac at 12,500 feet.

and, after quenching thirst and radioing word of their return, they continued down, reaching the White River Campground at 5:40 p.m.

In summary, Wickwire states:

> In former years, our climb of Curtis Ridge at this time of year would have been impossible in view of then prevailing restrictive regulations. We were able to take advantage of a brief spell of good weather to complete the fifth ascent of one of the mountain's hardest routes, and the first climb of the ridge done so late in the year. The previous four successful ascents of the ridge took place from late May to late July. We were all in agreement that one more snow storm could have made snow conditions on the ridge much more difficult than they were, and of necessity more days would have been required to complete the climb. We spent three full days on the mountain, utilizing every bit of daylight. Of the three north-side ridge routes, I would rank Curtis Ridge ahead of Liberty Ridge in difficulty and on a par with Ptarmigan Ridge under the conditions that we found on the route.

Wickwire's November climb of Curtis Ridge was merely a prelude to his more ambitious plan to tackle Willis Wall in midwinter. On February 10–11, 1970, he and Alex Bertulis made the first winter ascent of the wall, by way of a second complete ascent of the West Rib (first climbed in 1961 by Charles Bell).

However, for Wickwire, in his incessant search for new experiences on the mountain, the West Rib winter climb proved to be child's play compared to his 8-day epic in a mid-May ascent of the Central Rib with Ed Boulton. Below are summarized the highlights of the trip which found them battling for survival in a prolonged storm high on the peak.

With forecasts for a spell of good weather, Wickwire and Boulton left Ipsut Creek Campground on May 10 and hiked to snow-covered Moraine Park for the first night campout. The next day they worked their way up the Carbon Glacier to the base of the wall, where a second night was spent. After a difficult and tiring struggle up the steep hard ice and crest of the Central Rib, following much the same route of the 1965 party, they were still below Liberty Cap late in the afternoon of the third day. A cloud cap on the mountain all day had developed into an unpredicted raging blizzard. With new snow plastered to the steep rock below the narrow exit ledge, they had a difficult time on this section of the route. Immediately above, the soft new snow required waist-deep upslope wading for the two; at that altitude they began feeling the effects of incomplete conditioning for the climb. A third bivouac was made in a small moat beneath a rock band, with increasing cold and several avalanches off the ice cliff above making sleep impossible. On the fourth day, 5 hours were taken to reach the vicinity of Liberty Cap, where the storm's ferocity increased, forcing them to dig a small snow cave into the slope. High winds packed the cave entrance shut with snow, and, fearing suffocation, the two broke out of the cave early in the evening. They spent the remainder of the night wrapped in their wind-ripped bivouac sack near the cave entrance. Much of their gear and one pack became irretrievably buried under the compact snow. By the morning of the fifth day they were near the end of their physical resources. Without a rope, but under temporarily clearing skies, they weakly struggled arm-in-arm down the Emmons Glacier to Camp Schurman. They entered the cabin through a window and at last found shelter from the elements that continued to rage for two more days. Food in the cabin's cache brought back some strength, but they still had miles to go. Late in the afternoon of the seventh day, with the weather finally clearing, they headed down Inter Glacier to the White River Campground, for a few hours rest, then the next morning to the White River Ranger Station and to the main highway. At the nearest telephone they learned of the search underway toward Willis Wall, by their much-concerned comrades of the Sherpa Climbing Club.

In a true sense, winter climbs of Rainier logistically resemble small expeditions: greater planning and preparations are necessary than for summer ascents and a greater reliance must be placed on 5-day weather forecasts and favorable snow conditions. Except for periodic contact with the Park world by radio (if the party has one) the sense of isolation is complete once the party is well up on the mountain. The party must be equipped and mentally prepared for greater independence from outside assistance should an emergency situation arise. The rigors of winter conditions, with rapidly forming high-altitude blizzards, and the short days, would make extremely difficult any search or evacuation efforts by aircraft.

The rewards of winter mountaineering, however, are great. For those unable to participate in expeditions farther afield, a 4-5-day wintry trek up Rainier can provide an acceptable substitute. The normal 2-day climb of Rainier during the summer season generally is too rushed and madly paced to permit a leisurely contemplation of the mountain scene and a fuller enjoyment of one's companions. The thin veneer of city mannerisms is replaced by a more robust enjoyment of the simpler elements of the wintry world around us. One's activities become focused on the basic needs: reaching a certain point on the mountain, selecting a campsite and making it a home, preparing the meals, laying out the ropes, looking at the sky and weather, and enjoying the scene spread below. On a winter climb there is no need to arise at midnight and fumble through darkness to prepare for the dash to the top and back before things start softening up. The wind-packed surface is little affected by the weak, slanting rays of the winter sun. We can relax more and enjoy more the high white world of unmarked virgin snow and rime-coated rock.

15 Skis on Rainier

With the introduction of skiing to the Northwest by Scandinavians in the 1920s came explorations of the wintry slopes of Mount Rainier. At first the skiing and snowshoeing were confined to trail-breaking treks from Longmire to Paradise; on the slopes of Alta Vista, the major activity was ski jumping. Skiing packed slopes with the fancy techniques of today was unknown and most advocates of the sport were satisfied to tour the white landscape with an occasional telemark turn to lend excitement. By 1930 other areas of the Park were marked by the tracks of cross-country skiers. An article by W. J. Maxwell (*The Mountaineer*, 1930) describes those early ski jaunts:

> Entrancing trips have been made to Indian Henrys Hunting Ground; from Paradise Camp to Panorama Point, and on beyond to Cowlitz Rocks; climbs to the saddle of Pinnacle Peak in the Tatoosh Range; to Anvil Rock and Camp Muir; from Paradise Park down the Nisqually Glacier to its snout; from Storbo Cabin to St. Elmo Pass and Curtis Ridge. [Note: Maxwell probably refers to Camp Curtis, below Steamboat Prow.] A most delightful run is from Cowlitz Rocks across the Paradise, Williwakas and Stevens glaciers to the ridge above Sluiskin Falls, then down steep Mazama Ridge to the Paradise River. Here every type of snow is available to suit either beginner or expert . . .
>
> Of these trips, one of the most fascinating is the run from Steamboat Prow . . . to Storbo mining camp, a descent of thirty-six hundred feet, over slopes that vary from steep pitches to gentle grades. Chilled from the breeze which usually prevails at Curtis Ridge [Camp Curtis] you point your skis downhill. Swiftly they rush, and perforce you fight to keep up with them. Your blood warms with the struggle, and for a moment your whole effort is concentrated on the idea of balance; desperately you sink from the erect position to an extreme crouch; your eyes water; your face glows from the whipping of the wind; a spray of snow fluffs behind; your muscles relax somewhat as you grow accustomed to the swift descent; your mind blots out the idea of fear and telegraphs to every nerve the sheer joy of living; the thrill of speed exalts you and every petty worry fades away—this, indeed, is life.
>
> Soon a slope, too steep to take straight, looms ahead; a partial stop-turn to check your speed, and then a fast downhill turn and off again on the opposite traverse. Again you swing back towards Ruth Mountain. Suddenly, disaster threatens; the slope is too steep to turn on, and rocks are straight ahead. Leaning boldly away from the hill until it seems that you will surely fall, you throw the heels slightly downward and your skis sideslip safely to somewhat gentler slopes. Stretching out over the very points of your skis until at last the slippery boards skid around to change direction, you rush down in wild ecstasy of speed—down, down, past the mine tunnel of summer time, across the side of Burroughs Mountain, over the snout of the glacier to the shelter of the mining camp.

Some of the more adventurous ski tourers eventually began seeking higher runs on the mountain. Besides W. J. Maxwell were others: Hans-Otto Giese, Otto Strizek, Walter Best, A. W. Anderson, E. Lester La-Velle, Orville Borgerson, and Ben Spellar. In the early 1930s Strizek, Spellar, and Borgerson made a one-day spring ski trip from Paradise to the White River Entrance Station by way of Camp Muir, a crossing of the Emmons Glacier, and down Inter Glacier to Glacier Basin and the highway.

Several attempts were made to ski the long smooth slope of the Emmons Glacier during the 1920s and 1930s but all were forestalled by poor snow conditions or unsettled weather. The first of these trips, made April 30, 1927 by W. J. Maxwell, A. W. Anderson, and E. Lester LaVelle, ended at about 12,500 feet (*The Mountaineer*, 1927). The following year, on April 7, another partial ski ascent of the Emmons was made by Walter Best, Hans-Otto Giese, and Dr. Otto Strizek. The three continued to the summit on crampons (*The Mountaineer*, 1928).

On July 1, 1939, during an ascent to the summit via Emmons Glacier by Sigurd Hall and Andy Hennig, Hall kept his skis on during the entire climb. However, owing to icing conditions near the summit, both men cramponed back down to about 12,000 feet before donning skis for the run to Steamboat Prow and Glacier Basin (*The Mountaineer*, 1939). In 1940 Sig Hall met a tragic death when he crashed into fog-shrouded rocks during the internationally-famous Silver Skis Race, a 4-mile run from Camp Muir to Paradise Valley that was an annual event in the 1930s.

The first complete ski descent from the 14,000-foot crater to timberline was made on July 18, 1948 by Kermit Bengtson, Dave Roberts, Cliff Schmidtke, and Charles E. Welsh (*The Mountaineer*, 1948). With a support party preceding them to Steamboat Prow, the four made plans to spend the night of unsettled weather at Glacier Basin. However, at 1 a.m. they noticed a few stars and therefore quickly loaded packs and left for the summit. After a meager breakfast near Steamboat Prow they proceeded upward on skis until icy conditions forced all but Dave Roberts to remove skis and substitute crampons. The summit register was attained in a brisk breeze at 2 p.m. The descent was done with two men to a rope, each using a ski pole in one hand and an ice axe in the other. Several belays with the pick of the axe were required to safeguard passage of crevasses near the top, but once below these they were able to proceed downward without belays. Snow conditions were variable and ever-changing: they experienced ice near the top, then trap crust followed by slush before they found skiable summer snow below 9000 feet.

In the early summer of 1955 a second ski descent was made via the Emmons Glacier by Robert McCall and Marcel Schuster of the Yakima Ski Club (oral communication, 1955).

The first ski descent from the summit by way of the Ingraham Glacier was on June 18, 1961, by John Ahern, Bill Briggs, Roger Brown, Gordie Butterfield, Joe Marillac, Roger Paris, and Jim and Louie Whittaker.

On August 5, 1962, the first ski descent by a woman was that of Erline (Anderson, Schuster) Reber, via the Emmons Glacier and accompanied by Robert McCall. Of note is that Ms. Reber was born without fingers on her right hand and had previously achieved the first ski descent of Mount St. Helens by a woman. *(See photo of Ms. Reber on p. 345.)*

16 The Summit

The view we enjoyed from the summit could hardly be surpassed in sublimity and grandeur; but one feels far from home so high in the sky, so much so that one is inclined to guess that, apart from the acquisition of knowledge and the exhilaration of climbing, more pleasure is to be found at the foot of the mountains than at their frozen tops. Doubly happy, however, is the man to whom lofty mountain-tops are within reach, for the lights that shine there illumine all that lies below.

JOHN MUIR

The average climber, upon reaching Columbia Crest, finds that a quick glance around the broad summit dome satisfies his meager appetite for further explorations. It is enough to struggle to the inner slope of the crater and out of the wind, hopefully to bask in the warmth of a kind sun and recoup energy for the long return to high camp and the valleys far below.

Few remain on the summit long enough, or muster enough ambition, to hike more than the shortest line to the register box. A weary glance into shadowed hollows between rock and ice generally satisfies curiosity about steam caves.

Once the climber has dutifully signed his name in the register boxes (National Park Service, The Mountaineers, and the Mazamas), he can truly relax—his mission has been completed. He will then seek the nearest and flattest patch of sun-warmed scree and "flake out" for a bit of rest and euphoria. Companions' voices gradually fade as they, too, drift off in slumber on this high beach.

Stories by some early visitors to the summit carry undertones of mysticism—perhaps they, too, were caught in the spell of sun-warmed reverie at the top of the peak. Several tales smack of hallucinations

150–degree panorama of east crater from southeast rim. Columbia Crest across crater.

Scenes near summit. Above: along crater rim toward Columbia Crest; below: steam caves inside crater rim.

caused by altitude. One man described large hairy creatures residing in caves in the crater; others talk about feeling "watched" while on the summit. Indian legends tell of "a fiery lake" of steaming water and of rumbling noises—both quite possibly due to volcanic activity in the vicinity of fumaroles.

Of more substance, but nearly as baffling, are more fully substantiated reports. In the early days a party of Mazama climbers, upon reaching the crater rim, noted a large black bear disappearing over the crest on the opposite side of the crater. On July 17, 1948 a porcupine was observed at close hand traveling energetically along the edge of a crevasse just below 14,000 feet on the upper Nisqually Glacier. The climbers (Art Landry, Al Wilson, and George Purdy) signed an affidavit attesting to the sighting and a photograph of the animal was taken by Purdy to convince possible disbelievers. Several recent observations of wildlife at or near the summit include that of a summit guide who in 1967 reported seeing a golden-mantled ground squirrel on top with a white-footed mouse in its mouth; also in 1967, a guide party saw a white-footed mouse at 13,000 feet on the upper Ingraham Glacier. In 1969, Assistant Park Naturalist Dale Thompson saw a Douglas squirrel at the crater. Ravens have been seen at the summit, even in midwinter, as noted by Lee Nelson's party of February 9, 1968. During a spell of exceptionally warm, windless weather in mid-July 1951, a climber wearing a red stocking cap was repeatedly "buzzed" by bumblebees all the way up the Emmons Glacier to 14,000 feet. The frozen bodies of small rodents, birds, and insects are occasionally found on upper slopes of the mountain; some of these may have been carried, then dropped, by birds of prey. Other animals, like the bear and porcupine, doubtless arrived under their own power, either by some inclination to gain altitude, or

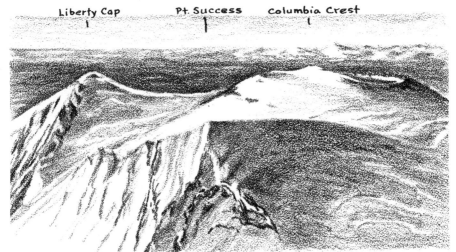

View north across summit dome.

View south across Rainier's three summits. Mt. Adams in distance.

by being caught in a snowstorm during a crossing of a snowfield, then finding it easier to keep moving uphill than to come down on steep ice and snow in the face of the wind.

Located in the center of the vast, mile-wide summit dome, and only slightly above surrounding icefields, Columbia Crest does not offer the spectacular view of rugged adjacent peaks generally associated with alpine summits. The Cascade Range to the north, east, and south and the Olympic Mountains to the northwest across Puget Sound lowland are too distant to be impressive. Only the white cones of the other volcanoes—Mount Baker and Glacier Peak to the north and Mounts St. Helens, Adams, Hood, and Jefferson to the south—and the Chimney Rock and Mount Stuart massifs to the north and northeast, stand noticeably above lower peaks.

The configuration of the summit area of Rainier is the result of geologic forces that both constructed and destroyed the mountain at various stages in its history. The three summits give evidence of at one time forming parts of the ragged rim of a much larger crater which was subsequently filled by the present cone of ash and lava. The more westerly of the two summit craters on the cone is slightly older and today is seen as a small plateau of ice rimmed on the west and north by a short arc of rock. This rock rim joins the younger, more easterly crater at a small snow dome, the summit of which is Columbia Crest.

The completely enclosed younger crater has a circular rim that cants eastward; the edge of the rim overlooking the Emmons Glacier is about 300 feet lower than Columbia Crest. The saucer-shaped crater is about ¼ mile across and is completely filled with snow and ice. Around the inner slope of the rim, fumaroles have melted small caves

Liberty Cap
and Columbia Crest
from Point Success

between the ice and rock. The steam issues at temperatures of about 186°F (boiling point of water at this altitude) and throughout the year keeps snow from clogging the caves completely. Infrared images taken in July 1969 from a Marine Corps aircraft, in cooperation with Robert M. Moxham of the U.S. Geological Survey's Geophysics Branch, show the hottest spots of the summit area to be on the northwest rim of the younger (east) crater and the north rim of the west crater (Moxham, 1970). In August 1970, I conducted a 2-day reconnaissance of temperatures of fumarole areas of both craters, as part of a Geological Survey study, and the radiometer and tele-thermometer gave readings of 50–72° C at the warmer steam vents. In September, in a unique effort to monitor day-by-day changes in the crater temperatures, Robert Moxham installed a more sophisticated instrument on the rim of the west crater, with several transducer probes extending to nearby

Columbia Crest
and Point Success
from Liberty Cap

fumaroles. However, the instrument was successful for only a few weeks in relaying, via satellite, daily temperatures data to the Washington, D.C. office.

Numerous mountaineers, faced with the prospect of a night on the summit, just as were Stevens and Van Trump in 1870, have descended for protection into the steam caves. Such cave occupancy is not conducive to exploration, however. Among the more miserable of my mountaineering experiences was a night and part of a day trapped on the summit during a storm, during which we made partial use of one of the caves, as described below:

During the "first postwar climb of Rainier" on June 1, 1946, Maynard M. Miller, my brother K, and I were granted permission by Park authorities to spend a night on the summit to test stoves and sleeping bags to be used on Mount St. Elias in Alaska a few weeks later. After reaching the summit without difficulty except for soft deep snow on the upper Ingraham Glacier, we leveled platforms on the inner slope of the crater and spread our sleeping bags. The sky was clear as we snuggled into the bags and we fell asleep. During the night, however, the weather deteriorated.

Awakening early in the morning, we found ourselves sprinkled by several inches of snow. Soon we became aware of the dampness of our bags, soaked from below by the melting of snow against the warm volcanic scree. Hastily we rolled up the wet bags, loaded packs, and prepared to head down the mountain. But at the crater rim we were knocked off balance by driving wind and sleet. Unable to leave the summit, we retreated to the crater. This early in the summer, entrances to steam caves were partially blocked by snow and we couldn't find a cave large enough to hold all three of us; we located only a small hole barely big enough for one man to enter. For the next 2 hours we took turns chopping away at the icy walls, eventually enlarging the hole to allow two of us to lie side-by-side against the slope, the third man lying atop the others. By now our wet sleeping bags and clothing were frozen and stiff. With chattering teeth and shivering bodies we managed to maintain some activity—we optimistically considered pneumonia our greatest concern.

Periodically as the morning wore on to noon we imagined sunlight through the clouds and made efforts to leave the summit, but each time were driven back into the crater and our cold and stiff bags, finally with cramponed boots still on our feet. Eventually, to gain inner warmth and nourishment, we set a stove on a ledge and after several attempts managed to get it started. Corned-beef hash was beginning to heat up in a small pot when suddenly at about 2 o'clock in the afternoon we realized the sun was shining. First making sure our imagination was not playing tricks, we struggled from the miserable hole, leaving sleeping bags and pot of half-cooked hash behind, and again climbed to the crater rim. With great relief we found we could maintain our footing and could see, far below, the dim outline of Gibraltar Rock. With hardly a pause, we headed down. Enroute one of my crampons broke but I pulled it off and hand-carried it in our rapid descent to more-sheltered slopes on the north side of Gibraltar. Scurrying downward as clouds continued to boil around the summit, we arrived at Paradise about 6 p.m. There we were met by District Ranger Gordon "Pat" Patterson with a terse remark, "So you didn't make it, eh!"

As a sequel to this climb, during the summer a guide party led by Bil Dunaway came upon the remains of our crude bivouac—they were led to it by the musty odor emanating from rotting feathers of the sleeping bags. Dunaway, a veteran of the 10th Mountain Division, described the cave as "smelling like a Kraut dugout." However, the bags were retrieved, dried and ventilated, and left at Camp Hazard for use by the guides' summit clients. The party failed to notice, or did not disturb, the pot of hash. At summer's end, upon our return from the Alaska expedition, K and I revisited Rainier's summit and found the pot and its contents of frozen hash still on the ledge.

Some individuals have been caught in severe summit storms not so much during pleasure climbs as "in line of duty." Many years earlier, during the summers of 1910 through 1913, a Geological Survey team made triangulations between Pinnacle Peak in the Tatoosh Range and the summit of Rainier to determine the altitude of the mountain. Two climbs with heavy instruments were made from Camp Muir during 1913, and on August 16 storms forced the party (C. H. Birdseye, C. B. Harmon, and Frank Krogh) to bivouac in the crater. Final measurements were taken August 20 by C. H. Birdseye, W. O. Tufta, O. G. Taylor, and S. E. Taylor. The altitude was officially determined to be 14,408 feet (Francois E. Matthes: *Sierra Club Bulletin*, 1914; *The Mountaineer*, 1915). According to Matthes:

The Geological Survey's *Bulletin* little more than hints at the fortitude and pluck of Mr. Birdseye and his party in their almost disastrous experiences on the peak. Survey men are so frequently confronted by peril in their daily work, that they are not apt to write or talk about it, and as a consequence the public seldom learns the intimate details. It is to be hoped that the history of this undertaking will some day appear in full.

It is a tribute to the skill and accuracy of the surveyors of 1913 that, when another survey was made in 1956 by the U.S. Geological Survey, only 2 feet were added to the earlier computation. On the latter occasion the surveyors, Charles R. Lloyd, Toivo J. Nelson, and William Kirschner, were carried by helicopter to the saddle between Point Success and Columbia Crest.

Miller initiated spending several summers at the summit of Rainier (*Harvard Mountaineering*, 1961). From a tent camp on the north rim of the westerly crater, about 500 feet from Columbia Crest, the group ("Project Crater") conducted glaciological, climatological, and physiological studies. Two members of the party, Barry Prather and Dave Potter, were 53 days at the summit, coming down to 11,000 feet for supplies only once. Among their experiments was the planting of a bean seed in the soft, warm, rich soil of the crater rim. Protected by a fiberglass windshield that provided a greenhouse effect, the bean grew rapidly to a small leafy plant about an inch high before it was nipped by frost; its demise was a blow to camp morale. The lowest and highest temperatures recorded were −16°F (September) and 42°F (August). Wind velocities greater than the maximum obtainable on the anemometer (60 mph) were recorded at least three times. Other observations included the growth of algae at the summit, steam temperatures of 186°F (temperature of boiling water at 14,400 feet), and ice temperatures of 10°F.

Episodes unrelated to mountaineering or science are occasionally reported to occur on Rainier's crown. A wedding ceremony took place there September 7, 1921. The wedding party of 16, including the groom

Camp of "Project Crater," 1959. Columbia Crest at upper right.

Edward L. Hamilton and the bride Lenora Allain, was led by guide Hans Fuhrer. Other summit activities have included a watermelon feast, a "football game" in the crater, driving a golf ball, and flying a kite. This latter event unfortunately occurred during a nearly windless day: Dan Davis (written communication and photographs, October 1968) was forced to jog along the crater rim to get the box kite aloft for a few seconds.

Once in a while a distinguished visitor accepts the challenge of the mountain. Among VIPs making the ascent in recent years was Tenzing Norgay, who in 1953 was the companion of Edmund Hillary on the first ascent of Mount Everest. During a visit to the United States in 1964, courtesy of the India Tea Board, Tenzing and his diminutive and pretty young wife Dhaku were invited to join an ascent of Rainier by American Everest climbers Jim Whittaker, Lute Jerstad, and Tom Hornbein—a truly exclusive group. The party ascended the Nisqually Icefall, a route never before climbed by an Everester, or by a woman (*Summit*, November 1964).

The summer of 1965 saw the first ascent of Rainier by an incumbent Chief Executive of the State of Washington. Governor Daniel J. Evans, an Eagle Scout in his youth and mountaineer-skier in his rare leisure time, reached the summit by the Ingraham Glacier in a party organized and led by George Senner. Senner invited me along to lead one of the rope teams in the nine-man party, and it was my pleasure to observe Dan's expertise in mountaincraft and his enjoyment of

Washington's Governor Daniel J. Evans at summit with State flag. From left: William Bell, Gov. Evans, George Senner, Frank Pritchard.

"Everesters" climb Rainier. From left: *Jim Whittaker, Tenzing Norgay, Tom Hornbein, Dhaku (Mrs. Tenzing Norgay), Lute Jerstad.*

Robert McNamara.

the big hill. To my knowledge, no previous Governor of the State had ever achieved the highest point in his domain.

In 1966 Robert S. McNamara, then U.S. Secretary of Defense, also an inveterate mountaineer when time allows, climbed Rainier via the Ingraham in a party led by Lou and Jim Whittaker and including Mc-Namara's daughter Kathleen (22) and son Craig (16). Upon reaching the summit, 50-year-old Secretary McNamara had sufficient energy left to circle the crater rim, a distance of nearly a mile.

The irrepressible Kennedy family, through the friendship developed between the late Senator Robert F. Kennedy and Jim Whittaker, also has become absorbed in its own discovery of Mount Rainier. In August 1969, young David Kennedy(15) accompanied Whittaker and his son Carl (14) to the summit. In 1970 Joseph P. Kennedy III, age 18 and the oldest son of Ethel Kennedy, served on Lou Whittaker's staff as an apprentice guide and made several ascents of the peak. Ethel herself hiked to Camp Muir with Jim Whittaker early in the summer and indicated a desire to make a summit attempt at a later date.

A 7-year old, 58-lb. girl, Laura Ann Johnson of Tacoma, has attained the crater rim. Probably the oldest person to gain the summit is Burr Singleton of the Cascadians club; in 1958 he climbed the mountain at age 76, in a party led by Bill Prater. Singleton had climbed many peaks in his youth but gave up the sport during about 40 years of married life; upon becoming a widower, he took up where he had left off.

Among the more interesting of those aspiring to stand atop Mount Rainier are the few individuals who also have stood atop the 66 other 14,000-foot peaks in the 48 conterminous United States. Since 53 of these peaks are in the Colorado Rockies, nearly all the climbers have come from that state. After climbing their home summits they invariably head to California to tackle the Sierra 14,000-footers and Mount Shasta before culminating their endeavors on Rainier.

Among those making the pilgrimage of the "Fourteeners" have been the five climbing members of the Smith family of Denver. After having completed the Colorado peaks in 1968, the Smiths—father George (41) and sons Flint (17), Quade (13), Cody (12), and Tyle (10)—began in 1969 a 24-day assault on the remaining 14 peaks. Their effort to achieve their objectives in the last 3 weeks of summer vacation, before school started for the boys, was replete with troubles. An accident in the Nevada desert early in the journey resulted in total loss of their late-model car. In desperation they purchased an oil-gobbling 1953 station wagon—miraculously the vehicle held up for the remainder of the trip. However, the delay in their finely timed schedule forced them to climb several peaks in the Mount Whitney area and in the Palisades with very little sleep and rest between; they arrived at Paradise Valley near the end of their tether. The Smiths persevered to Camp Muir however, only to be delayed a day by high winds. The final frustration came when they descended to Paradise to accommodate a local reporter who had requested an interview—but the reporter failed to show up. So, back to Muir they climbed. The following day the Smiths reached Columbia Crest, the last of their 67 objectives. Ten-year-old Tyle and 12-year-old Cody are the youngest two to have climbed all 14,000-foot peaks in the 48 states. George Smith himself is a remarkable person; severely injured in a childhood accident at age 4, he has accomplished his mountaineering with the handicap of a withered right arm.

George Smith and sons. From left: Tyle, Cody, George Smith, Flint, Quade.

Porcupine at 14,000 ft. on upper Nisqually Glacier, July 1948.

17 Crater Explorations

Since first visited by the early climbers, the two summit craters of Mount Rainier have been a source of scientific interest, even though most explorations have been perfunctory searches for overnight shelter and for temporary protection from storms. Stevens and Van Trump in 1870 spent a night in a cave of the west crater, and the Willis-Russell-Smith Geological Survey party of 1896 spent a night in the steam caves along the inner rim of the east crater. Many others have since experienced similar nocturnal bivouacs, but until the mid-1960s few have explored more deeply the passageways between the steep crater slope and the thick saucer-shaped ice plug filling the huge depressions.

Among the early probes into the subsurface world of the summit is that related by Major E. S. Ingraham, founder of the Washington Alpine Club and early explorer and leader of climbs on Rainier's slopes. The doughty major apparently also was a dispenser of interesting tales around evening campfires and also, as we see below, in his informal publication (Ingraham, 1895) of his meeting with "The Old Man of the Crater":

> While my companion and I were exploring the steam-caves at the time of my second visit to the crater of Mt. Rainier, I noticed peculiar marks and scratchings on the floor of the cave. In some places the ground appeared as though it had been the scene of a conflict between some maddened beasts, so extensive was the disturbance. In other places there were depressions that might have been made by some flat-footed animal pawing in the earth. My curiosity was deeply excited. The lower we descended the cave, the more frequent but less marked became those scratchings. As the sunlight from without became dim, I noticed a peculiar, soft glow in the atmosphere of the cave, hardly perceptible, that might have been produced by either light or heat, but it was probably brought about by the presence of some force more subtle than either. I also felt a peculiar sensation of the body, such as a person feels when standing upon an insulated stool with his hand holding the pole of an electrical machine slightly charged. Whether my companion noticed these startling phenomena I do not know. If he did, he like myself remained silent upon the subject. The situation was extremely interesting to one of a scientific turn of mind and invited investigation; but I suggested to my companion a return to the outer world. Within my own mind I had decided to revisit the cave alone later.
>
> Late in the night, when my three bed-fellows were sound asleep, I cautiously crawled from under my scanty covering and was soon in the cave again. While it was intensely dark within and cold without, the warmth of the steam-cave soon restored my benumbed body to an unusual degree of comfort and my sleepy senses resumed an unwonted activity. Slowly groping my way along the floor of the cave I was soon within the influence of the

mysterious glow I had noticed upon my first descent. The situation was weird and startling. Midnight in a crater! the vaulted sky above you the only familiar object, with the hot rocks and hissing steam around you suggesting what once was and what may again be; to leave my sleeping companions and the last familiar object, to descend toward the source of the heat and steam, to go down, down toward the earth's hot interior, all tended to try my nerves and fill my mind with strange forebodings. While prudence and caution would bid me return to my companions and leave the mysteries of the cave unsolved, I still cautiously groped my way onward. The sense of feeling became strangely acute. I could readily keep in the center of the cave by extending my hand to either side and noting the change of temperature caused by the adjacent ice walls. The mysterious influence of a still more mysterious force enabled me to *know* my surroundings quite distinctly. As before stated, these steam-caves seem to radiate from the center of the crater, a single passage branching into two or more as it nears the rim of the crater. I had reached a point where another passage joined, or more properly separated from the one I was following, when I was startled by a noise, followed by several stones rolling down the tributary passage. Had my companion of the first visit noticed the mysterious things that I had, and was he, like myself, seeking to discover their cause? I quickly stepped within a recess in the wall of ice on my left and awaited developments. I had not long to wait, for almost immediately there came, now rolling, now making an attempt to crawl, a figure of strange and grotesque appearance, down the passage. It stopped within a few feet of me, writhing and floundering very much as a drowning man would do, when drawn from the water as he was about to sink for the last time. Its shape was nearer that of a human being than of any other animal. The crown of its head was pointed, with bristled hair pointing in every direction. The eyeballs were pointed, too; and while they appeared dull and visionless at times, yet there was an occasional flash of light from the points, which increased in frequency and brilliancy as the owner began to revive. The nails of its fingers and toes were long and pointed and resembled polished steel more than hardened cuticle. I discovered that the palms of its hands and the soles of its feet were hard and calloused. In fact the whole body, while human in shape, except the pointedness of the parts I have mentioned, seemed very different in character from that of the human species. There was nothing about the mysterious being, however, that would make it impossible that its ancestry of long ages ago might have been human beings like ourselves. Yet by living in different surroundings and under entirely different conditions, many of its characteristics had changed.

By degrees this strange being began to revive. Gradually an electric glow covered the entire body with light-centers at the ends of those pointed nails, the eyes and the top of the head. It seemed to accomplish its revivification by rubbing its hands vigorously together. As soon as it was able to stand, it began to rub its feet rapidly upon the floor of the cave. This increased the glow of its body and caused the light-centers to shine with increased brilliancy. It seemed to receive some vital fluid from the earth that at once gave new vigor to its whole system. Involuntarily I imitated its actions and immediately found myself undergoing a very peculiar sensation. I seemed to be growing in accord with the strange being who then for the first time noticed my presence. He at once redoubled his former movements. He would rub his hands vigorously together and then quickly extend the points of his fingers in my direction when sparks of light would dart therefrom. Having become deeply interested in this strange exhibition, I went through the same manoeuvre with a similar result although apparently in a much lesser degree. The effect was magical! I was becoming *en rapport* with the Old Man of the Crater! I could see a brilliant point of light gradually forming on the crown of his head. Feeling my own hair beginning to rise I removed my knit cap and felt my hair bristling upward to a common point. The light from his crown seemed to form an arch above and between us and WE WERE IN COMMUNICATION. There, in that icy passage connecting the unknown interior of this earth with the exterior, by means of a new medium, or rather an old medium newly applied, two intelligent beings of different races were enabled to communicate, imperfectly at first of course, with each other.

For an hour I received impressions from the Old Man of the Crater. It is a strange story I got from him. While the time was comparatively short, yet what he told me, not by voice or look, but by a subtle agency not known or understood by me, would fill a volume of many pages. Finally expressing doubt at what he communicated, he commanded me to follow him. I had anticipated such a demand and was ready to resist it. So when he turned to descend, to the hot interior of the earth as I verily believe, by a superhuman effort I broke the spell and hastened upward and back to my sleeping companions.

This is no myth. The old man told me of his abode in the interior, of another race to which he belonged and the traditions of that race; of convulsions and changes on the earth long, long ago; of the gradual contraction of a belt of matter around the earth until it touched the surface hemming in many of the inhabitants and drowning the remainder, and of the survival of a single pair. All was shut out and the atmosphere became changed. Gradually this remaining pair was enabled to conform to the new order of things and became the parents of a race which for the want of a better name I will call SUB-RAINIANS. This Old Man of the Crater had wandered far away from the abode of his race in his desire to explore. Far away from my home we had met, each out of his usual sphere.

More recent and of greater substance is a description of a descent along the inner slope of the crater by Jim Whittaker (written communication, January 1957):

In August of 1954, around 10 a.m., we made our most extensive exploration. Up until that time on two previous occasions we had descended as far as we could without flashlights. Lou and I left our clients resting on the crater rim by Register Rock and descended into the first large steam cave just east of this. We were not roped nor did we have crampons—just ice axes.

The floor falls away at about 25 to 30 degrees, and consists mostly of pumice and loose rock with a few solid ridges; the roof, being ice, is convoluted from wind and melting and forms all sorts of interesting tunnels and passages. We followed the largest tunnel downward and to the right. The flashlights were our only source of light and that was limited because of the amount of water vapor in the air. As we kept going the largest tunnel seemed to be dropping to the right but we had no compass so couldn't tell for sure. Twice we came to what seemed to be dead ends but upon further search found additional tunnels that led down. Once we had to take a tunnel through the ice—that is, the floor as well as the walls and ceiling were ice, which ended on top of an eight-foot drop back down to the pumice.

Inside crater steam cave.

After jumping down to the crater floor again Louis complained of a headache and I noticed I had one too. You know this is not uncommon at the summit but this being our 12th trip that summer and not having had a headache that year we began to doubt the air we were breathing and thought it best to get out of there.

We were about 300 to 400 feet down the inner slope of the crater rim. The tunnel seemed to be opening up into a much larger room than we had ever encountered and as we rolled rocks down the slope we heard them continue for quite a while, ending in what seemed to be water.

The desire was strong to continue and there seemed to be a breeze coming up from the center of the crater but we were not sure what oxygen problem we might encounter (or sulphurous gases) and also decided our clientele might be getting impatient and worried over our return. Louie made a dash down about 15 feet while I watched, then while he watched I dashed 15 feet down. It didn't show us any more than we already knew so we began the ascent. Instead of taking the route back we tried another tunnel to the east of it and followed it to the surface, out of the warm moist air into the below-freezing atmosphere of 14,000 feet where, after catching our breath, we gathered our customers and resumed earning our bread and butter.

About 10 years later, according to John Simac (oral commun., August 1970), he and fellow Mountain Rescue veteran Max Eckenburg led a group of Explorer Scouts through a tunnel which took them across the crater beneath the ice plug. They repeated the trip several times in subsequent years but made no public record of the sub-ice explorations. It was therefore not until 1970 that the exciting breakthrough in recorded Rainier crater explorations occurred, during the Centennial year of the 1870 ascent of the mountain by Stevens and Van Trump.

On June 16, guides Lou Whittaker and Lee Nelson, after leading members of an expedition seminar to the summit and pitching camp inside the crater, proceeded to explore the depths of the great bowl. They entered at about the same steam cave on the south rim that Lou and his brother Jim had explored in 1954. Equipped with oxygen tanks

Summit craters of Mount Rainier, showing generalized tunnel system explored in 1970. Tunnel locations adapted from map by Eugene Kiver, Martin Mumma, and William Steele, Eastern Washington State College, 1970–71.

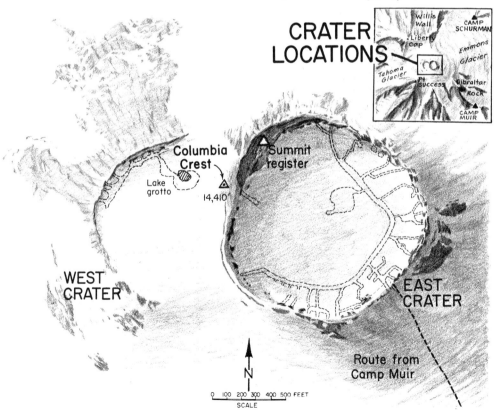

Descending steam cave toward main tunnel.

and masks and with extra flashlights and batteries, Whittaker and Nelson extended the previous discovery and followed steam-melted alcoves and tunnels across the crater. After 55 minutes below the ice, they emerged into the bright outer world at the north rim, about 250 feet east of the summit register box below Columbia Crest.

Beneath the ice Whittaker and Nelson found several chambers which were interconnected and led down the 30-35 degree slope to a major tunnel about 250-300 feet below the crater rim. They first took the east branch of the tunnel which was followed on a general contour across steep slopes of hard mud and loose gravel and boulders. The final 300 feet involved a steep climb upslope to where light once again could be seen. Enroute they found both hot steam vents and drafts of cold air. After making their exit at the north rim of the crater, they returned through the tunnel and continued through the westward extension to its point of exit in a cave on the west rim south of Columbia Crest.

According to Nelson, good flashlights and extra batteries and bulbs are imperative to one's return from the stygian blackness of the depths. In places in the west branch of the tunnel the two men were forced to crawl in mud beneath low ice ceilings and, to make their exit, they had to chop a hole in the ice. They found a small stream of water and a larger chamber with several pools of cold water, also a moraine-like embankment of rocks and gravel which probably is a remnant product of downward melting of a retaining wall of ice.

Whittaker and Nelson reported no problems with noxious gases and they had no breathing problems below the surface. As they entered the cave system they left a pot of snow over one of the vents; it was near boiling upon their return. The atmosphere inside the tunnels was generally foggy, which created some problems of throwing the flashlight beam for great distances. In places overhead meltwater dripped heavily and waterproof outer garments were found useful. The greatest hazard appears to be from loose boulders perched on the steep slopes.

Following the initial exploration, some guides led their more adventuresome clients through the main tunnels—a new attraction to the summit of Mount Rainier, though hardly for the average tourist. Several other chambers and passageways were discovered by the guides and amateur speleologists, and several map versions appeared showing the cavern system. Late in the summer a group of scientists under the lead-

In main tunnel.

ership of Drs. Eugene Kiver and Martin Mumma of Eastern Washington State College camped at the summit and spent several days in a more detailed mapping of the steaming labyrinth. Among the party's discoveries was a woolen glove found protruding from the ice ceiling above—doubtless dropped by a climber while crossing the crater snows decades earlier, and through the years gradually buried deeper beneath the surface. Dr. William Halliday, noted speleologist and founder of the Cascade Grotto of the National Speleological Society, states that his group's explorations of the crater show that the ice-tunnel system is possibly the highest of its size in the world.

Another sensitive indicator of the thermal activity at the summit also has its special attraction to a growing number of new sportsmen, the SCUBA and skin-diver set. Beneath the center of the west crater, at a depth of about 150 feet below the snow surface, is a grotto about 170 feet by 130 feet containing a lake formed from the melting of the crater ice by thermal activity. Discovered in 1971, during the summer explorations of the cavern system, the lake is about 50 feet by 20 feet and about 15 feet deep.

Bill Lokey, in charge of the Project Crater group camped for the summer near the summit, studied the lake and adjoining tunnels during the summers of 1971–72. In late August 1972, he possibly achieved the distinction of making the world's "highest" wet-suit "dive." He was preceded by rugged, shorts-clad Tacoma fireman-mountaineer Lee Nelson and fireman Damon Herd, who had just made his first climb of the peak. With the lake temperature hovering around 32 degrees, Nelson's and Herd's exits from the water were as rapid as their entries.

18 Ascents of Little Tahoma

A treatise on the climbing history of Rainier would be incomplete without a summary of the ascents of its satellite, 11,117-foot Little Tahoma, distinctive enough to be considered by some the third-highest peak in the state. The Matterhorn-like spire, the most prominent feature on the mountain's flanks, is a remnant of the earlier uneroded form of the volcanic cone. The extremely rotten pinnacle is a much more touchy climb than its massive neighbor.

The ascent of "Little T" is normally made along the steep upper snowfields of the Whitman Glacier on its eastern (back) slope, via an approach either from Summerland and Fryingpan Glacier or from Paradise and a crossing of the Cowlitz and Ingraham Glaciers. Owing to the small size and disintegrating character of the final rock tower, numerous climbers come within 8–10 feet of the summit without "completing the ascent," particularly if they are with a large group. But the view from the top is worth the extra effort.

90–degree panorama of Rainier from Little Tahoma.

From the apex of Little Tahoma one gains the most complete panoramic view of Rainier's broadly-glaciered eastern flank, from Gibraltar Rock on the south to Curtis Ridge on the north—the viewpoint is aerial in perspective and is further enhanced by being stationary. Far below, the long rock wedge of Little Tahoma's base splits the Ingraham and Emmons Glaciers, the numerous crevasses and undulations formed as the waves at the prow of a ship. Some of the largest crevasses and ice rolls on the mountain are found in this area. North are views of icefalls on the Emmons Glacier not generally seen from climbing routes. Culminating the vast sweep of the Emmons is the crater rim, easily defined by a thin line of rocks. On a cold, clear day, one may observe occasional wisps of steam rising from the rocks and fading into the deep blue sky.

The first recorded ascent of Little Tahoma was on August 29, 1895 by J. B. Flett and H. H. Garrison. In 1921 Stella Shahan became the first woman to complete the climb, which now is done by over a dozen parties each summer. In April 1933 a ski ascent and descent of the sharp peak were accomplished by Paul Gilbreath and J. Wendell Trosper. According to Trosper (oral communication, 1956), the two used skis to "within 8 feet of the top," a delicate feat considering the high angle of the upper several hundred feet of the peak. A winter ascent of Little Tahoma was made on February 11, 1968 by Tom Falley, Jerry Smith, and Gary Tate. They reached the summit at 1 a.m. on a cold and windless moonlit night (*Summit*, October 1969).

The greatest challenge offered by Little Tahoma is the north face, which rises in a steep sweep of snow and ice broken by a few bands of lava and ash. A climber's first view from the summit down this 2000-foot wall gives the airy feeling of hanging over space and sighting directly into crevasses on the Emmons Glacier. Not until the late 1950s did mountaineers consider an attempt on the face as other than suicidal.

On June 22, 1959, after 5 years of preparing psychologically, Dave Mahre and Gene Prater climbed in moonlight from the shelter at Summerland to the upper slopes of the Fryingpan Glacier to the notch above K's Spire (Peak 8849). From there they dropped to the Emmons Glacier and, after crossing the bergschrund and working around crevasses, reached the base of the north face. A little after 4 a.m. they began the ascent of the steep snowfield above the left (east) end of the bergschrund. Fortunately, fresh snowfall had melted, then refrozen, to weld the normally loose rocks; if conditions could ever be considered "ideal" for such a climb, this was the moment. The absence of dirt streaks on the snow above indicated further that no recent rockfall had occurred.

The east end of the bergschrund was overcome by a 60-foot ascent of nearly vertical rotten rock, then a traverse via a narrow snow ledge back to snow slopes on the right. This delicate pitch was crossed "on all fours"; no belay was possible for the leader. Once on the open slope beyond, the left margin of the hardened snow was ascended to a prominent rock band which crosses the face midway to the summit. After a traverse to the left, protected from rockfall by the nearly overhanging rock cliff, Mahre and Prater attained the east end of the upper snow terrace through a break in the cliff. From there they climbed a gap to the

North face of Little Tahoma, showing route climbed.

snow ledge below the summit rocks. At this point, at 8 a.m., they traversed downward on the upper Fryingpan Glacier and to the summit by the standard route on the east side of Little Tahoma. The extreme verticality and rotten condition of the upper 300 feet of the north face precluded consideration of any direct ascent there.

Mahre's narrative (*American Alpine Journal*, 1960; *The Mountaineer*, 1960) states that the melting and refreezing of recent snowfall had decreased normal rockfall hazards considerably; also, since the ascent was on a Monday, there was little chance of rockfall caused by weekend climbers. Hard hats and 12-point crampons were recommended by Mahre, along with a higher placement of camp—at the notch above K's Spire.

Another route on Little Tahoma was pioneered the same summer. On August 23 Dave Mahre returned with Bob McCall and Lex Maxwell. From the previously described approach to K's Spire they ascended the steep and heavily crevassed upper Fryingpan Glacier. The major cliff band at 9500 feet was passed on the left and the summit ridge was attained on the north (right) side of the skyline pinnacle. An 80-foot rock pitch just east of the pinnacle brought them to the ridge, which was traversed on the south side for 200 feet to a notch. Three succeeding gendarmes on the crest were climbed directly before the summit was reached. The ascent was described as Class 4 and required 9 hours from high camp (*American Alpine Journal*, 1960; *The Mountaineer*, 1960).

A variation on the normal Whitman Glacier route was made on June 28, 1964, by Jim Foster and Ron Muecke. Foster described the route (*The Mountaineer*, 1965) as follows:

"At the headwall of the Whitman Glacier, 100 feet to the right of the notch used on the usual route, we climbed the broken rock face, angling right to a large ledge. We climbed a chimney to the right of an overhang which continued to the summit ridge. We followed the ridge about 100 yards left to the summit.

"This Class 3 and 4 variation on the usual route was composed of surprizingly good rock and contributed substantially to the interest of the climb."

On July 13–14, 1965 an attempt was made to climb Little Tahoma by the long, jagged west ridge which separates the Ingraham and Emmons Glaciers at about 10,250 feet. According to Paul Myhre (written communication, 1968) he and Roger Oborn climbed onto the ridge at its "prow" and ascended on either side of the ridge crest until stopped at about 10,600 feet by vertical walls of crumbling rock. A completion of this line of ascent to the summit will doubtless involve some of Rainier's most difficult and unstable rock.

On north face of Little Tahoma.

The Mountaineers'
"Round-The-Mountain"
Outing of 1915.
From top:
at Ashford railhead;
from Ashford by auto;
on Pyramid Peak;
on summit.

19 Encircling the Mountain

The first men to traverse the lower flanks of Rainier did so only in geological explorations or to seek approaches to summit ascents, and no real effort was made to hike entirely around the mountain until after 1900. According to an article by J. H. Weer (*The Mountaineer*, 1915) J. B. Flett and C. A. Barnes, Jr. encircled the mountain in 1911 by traveling well above timberline, crossing glaciers and descending to timberline meadows to camp at night. These two men repeated the trip the next year in company with Calvin Philips, Jr., and J. H. Weer.

In the fall of 1913, Charles Albertson and H. B. Bennett made an extensive trip around the mountain. They covered not only the higher glacier route but also explored the principal timberline parks to gain information about their merits as camping sites and to determine the feasibility of people with horses traveling from park to park. Their recommendations to The Mountaineers resulted in the trustees selecting the Park as the scene of the 1915 outing. At this time the Department of Interior was nearing completion of the round-the-mountain trail; The Mountaineers' plan for the outing stimulated a speed-up of trail construction necessary to cover most of the proposed route.

The Mountaineers traveled clockwise around the mountain from Paradise in 3 weeks. A summary of the trip, interspersed with excerpts from an account of the memorable outing by Philip F. Rogers (*The Mountaineer*, 1915), is presented here to recapture the flavor of that early expedition.

A joyous crowd gathered in the depot at Seattle at seven o'clock on the morning of July 31, 1915, a big jolly, jostling, bustling, and bubbling crowd, dressed *cap-a-pie* for the mountains, boots hobbed and calked, dunnage bags stuffed fat and round—too fat in some cases, as the cold-hearted scales showed—alpenstocks in hand and spirits high in anticipation of the happy, care-free days to come. A strange and incongruous sight, was it, this Robin Hood crew, looking as though it might have been transported bodily from far-away Sherwood Forest and plumped down suddenly in a metropolitan railway station, and the few ordinary travelers abroad at that early hour rubbed their eyes and stared in mild wonderment as the tripod was erected and the dunnage weighed. It might have been thought to be some queer ceremonial performance but for the laughter and hilarity it provoked when some unlucky wight found his bag was overweight. Jests and jibs were exchanged, greetings shouted and backs were slapped with resounding whacks as friends and comrades of former hikes met for another glorious outing.

Boarding the train, the group rode to Tacoma, was joined by another contingent, and continued to Ashford. From there they traveled in buses to Longmire, where they had their last tabled dinner before proceeding another few miles to the end of the road below the terminus of the Nisqually Glacier. A hike up a steep trail brought them to the meadows at Paradise (5400) and the first camp, Saturday, July 31. After a surprisingly successful dinner highlighted by melt-in-the-mouth baking-powder biscuits and an evening campfire under cloudy skies, they retired to the "downies."

Aug. 1, Sunday: Dawned clear and cloudless. As a conditioner and for a viewpoint, a large segment of the party hiked across the valley and ascended Pinnacle Peak, with 37 reaching the top and signing the summit register ("record cylinder number 4").

Aug. 2, Monday: Up at 4 a.m. in preparation for the trek to Van Trump Park. The party hiked above Alta Vista and descended to the Nisqually Glacier. Owing to the large party and many crevasses, 3 hours were required to gain the opposite side. From there they climbed to about 7000 feet, then traversed the Van Trump Glacier in gathering clouds. The descent to Van Trump Park took them into heavy fog. The pack train (following a lower route, by trail) arrived late in the evening and Camp Two (5400) wasn't pitched until after dark.

From Van Trump Park.

From above Indian Henrys Hunting Ground.

Aug. 3, Tuesday: The continuing heavy fog changed plans for an above-snowline traverse to Indian Henrys Hunting Ground. Instead, the party followed the trail down into the timbered valley of Kautz Creek, which they crossed, then climbed to the park and Mirror Lake, where Camp Three (5400) was established in brilliant sunshine and "the most magnificent view yet seen" was spread before them.

From here one looked across to the great rock mass of Glacier Island rising high above the immense fields of ice surrounding it, which it splits into the South Tahoma and the larger Tahoma Glacier proper. To the right was Pyramid Peak and reaching up toward the summit from it the rugged rocky Success Cleaver, terminating far aloft in the snowy Peak Success, while to the left, as far as one could see, stretched the abyss. Some of the more ambitious ones climbed the Pyramid during the afternoon, and a few, Mount Ararat in addition, but most of us were content to be lazy and we slept, wrote letters, and basked in the warm sunshine while drinking in the marvelous views.

Aug. 4, Wednesday:

". . . Rising call sounded at 4:30 and we awoke to find ice in our drinking cups, and sleeping bags white and stiff with frost but across the valley was a fairy scene, long to be remembered, a most charmingly beautiful moonlight illumination of the mountains."

The party broke camp and descended to Tahoma Creek, which was crossed on a fallen log. From there they followed the switchback trail to St. Andrews Park. The packtrain was unable to reach the parkland that evening, however, and the hikers had to descend into timber to meet the horses.

Camp Four [3800] was made in the forest primeval and the softest of beds were found on the thick moss in the hollows between fallen trees. This was a two-night camp so that most of the party took the opportunity the following day to visit St. Andrews Park proper. The lower bench of this park is a beautiful meadow with deep grass, alpine firs, and a crystal stream. The upper bench is filled by a little lake which later in the day made a fine swimming pool. Its outlet is subterranean by way of a big hole under a log into which the discharging waters rush with a deep throaty roar. Climbing the great cleaver between the Tahoma and Puyallup glaciers, the stupendous west side view was before us, Tahoma and Glacier Island on the right, the Puyallup glacier with its spouting serpent's tongue tip hanging far down the cliff in the vast and rugged gorge to the left, and over all, that marvelous dome! It was a sight to make one gasp and gaze in silent awe and wonder. The might, the magnificence, the splendor, the titanic proportions of it all must be seen to be appreciated.

Aug. 6, Friday: A 14-mile hike from St. Andrews Park and nearby Klapatche Park, over recently completed trail, brought the party to Camp Five (5300) at Elbow Lake in Sunset Park:

From Klapatche Park.

From Sunset Park.

. . . a beautiful amphitheatre dotted with the usual tall conical fir trees and partly surrounded by a high forested rocky ridge—the lower portion of the cleaver separating the Puyallup and South Mowich glaciers. This was a fine camping ground with several small lakes. Here another two-night camp was made, and on Saturday a large party climbed the cleaver to its apex where the government bench mark, 6,965 feet, was found, but owing to a dense fog which prevailed no views were obtained. A roster of the climbers was cached here in a celluloid tooth brush holder, the only weather-proof receptacle found in the party, and the rest of the day after returning to camp was spent in loafing.

Aug. 8, Sunday: A strenuous 16-mile hike, involving losing and regaining several thousand feet, brought the party to Crater Lake (since renamed Mowich Lake) and Camp Six (4929).

Aug. 9, Monday: A short hike from Mowich Lake led past Spray Falls into the upper part of Spray Park, where Camp Seven was set up at about 5800 feet.

Here again small lakes provided opportunities for swimming, and after lunch one small party climbed Hessong Rock and another Echo and Observation rocks, but most of us loafed and did our washing. Messrs. Gorton and Hazlehurst left us here to go ahead and do some scouting for the big climb, the

From Spray Park.

time for which was approaching. From Spray Park on, for several days, we were glad to leave the trail to the pack train, while we took to the rocky steeps, the snow banks, and glaciers.

Aug. 10, *Tuesday:*

. . . took us across the great Carbon Glacier, with its monstrous load of rock and gravel dumped upon it by the frequent avalanches which plunge from Willis Wall, through Moraine Park, and down into the lovely little valley of Mystic Lake where we made Camp Eight [5700]. It was here we began to get on intimate terms with the festive and seductive huckleberry, which from that time on for the rest of our journey proved a serious obstacle to anything like steady and soldierly marching. Here Mr. Gorton returned and reported that Mr. Nelson and Mr. Albertson had come into Glacier Basin and would make the preliminary climb the next day with Mr. Hazlehurst.

Aug. 11, *Wednesday:*

A second day was spent at Mystic Lake but no trips could be made on account of dense cloud. Boots and packs were made ready for the summit climb and the whole camp began to take on a certain tenseness of atmosphere in anticipation of the coming ascent. This was increased in the evening when Hazlehurst, Nelson, and Albertson came down from the heights and reported all sunshine above so that they had been able to scout a good route to the saddle, 13,500 feet. Above that it had not been necessary to go because the rest of the way is almost bare ground.

Aug. 12, Thursday: The day dawned dark and threatening, so no summit attempt was made. Instead, the party broke camp and crossed the Winthrop Glacier and St. Elmo Pass, then descended to Glacier Basin and Camp Nine (5900).

Aug. 13, Friday: The climbing party, numbering 57, loaded packs after lunch and climbed Inter Glacier to Camp Curtis, a barren rock ridge at 9000 feet overlooking the Emmons Glacier.

Soon a strange spectacle presented itself, the women were assigned quarters on the lower part of the ridge and the men higher up, and forthwith every mother's son and daughter was working like a beaver, literally scratching gravel to find a soft spot to sleep on. Dug down to a reasonably fine grade of gravel, the areas were leveled and buttressed and surrounded with boulder walls to keep out the keen wind that blew over the ridge from the glaciers close by, and in the course of an hour one might have thought he stood in the midst of an ancient cliff dweller's settlement. Apartments, single, double, and multiple, sprang up like magic, and some of the more enterprising builders began to advertise apartments for rent. Meanwhile Tom and company had built and covered a kitchen, and presently announced supper, which consisted of a cup of hot soup, made on a diminutive oil stove, one spoonful of beans immersed in the soup, and two pieces of hardtack . . .

From Moraine Park

After supper a half grown goat wandered up to the edge of the camp and secured a good deal of attention, especially from the photographers. Good views were obtained at about one hundred feet, and then the pretty creature scampered over the rocks and disappeared across the glacier. Taps was sounded at seven, and every one having donned all the clothing he had with him, crawled into his sleeping bag and rested as well as he could on his stony mattress.

Aug. 14, Saturday: The party was up at 4 o'clock and after a cup of hot tea and a bite of swieback began the ascent of the Emmons Glacier. The climbers did not rope together and utilized a line only for a handhold on the steeper stretches. The summit was reached without trouble at 2:40 p.m. After posing for group photographs they signed the register book, which was then placed in a metal box and chained to a stake driven into the gravel slope of the crater. Owing to the lateness of the hour, and knowing the Emmons Glacier would be in shadow soon, they began the descent after only 20 minutes on top. Shortcuts were taken enroute and camp was reached in 3 hours. They returned to their main camp at Glacier Basin after a brief pause for soup.

On upper Emmons Glacier.

From Summerland.

Aug. 15, Sunday: From Glacier Basin the party crossed the Emmons and Fryingpan Glaciers and pitched Camp Ten (5900) at Summerland. An extra day was taken for rest. Two climbing parties started on short trips but were caught in a thunderstorm, the only one of the entire outing.

Aug. 17, Tuesday: The route to the next campsite in Ohanapecosh Park led across a part of the Fryingpan Glacier. Since the pack train accompanied them they were forced to build a section of trail on a steep sidehill alongside the glacier; the pack horses successfully completed the climb and crossed the ice and snowfields above.

Camp Eleven [5100] was made in an imposing setting, deep in a valley surrounded by cliff, glacier, and forested ridge, torrents leaping from each side and joining to swell the wild boisterous Ohanapecosh River with its picturesque falls, Wauhaukaupauken, and the convenient rock bath tub a short distance below camp. And oh, the huckleberries!

Many agreed that Ohanapecosh Park was the most attractive camp site on the trip, and the vote was practically unanimous that the extra day our time schedule allowed be taken here instead of in Paradise Park. This allowed a side trip up the south wall of the valley and over into the Cowlitz country where magnificent views of the Cowlitz Glacier and part of its basaltic side walls were obtained from the ridge above. Adams, St. Helens, the

From Cowlitz Park.

Tatoosh, and Gibraltar were reminders that we had nearly completed our circuit of the mountain. The same day two of the men made the difficult climb of Cowlitz Chimneys.

Aug. 19, Thursday: From Ohanapecosh Park an old, deeply worn, Indian trail led the party southward along the ridge of Cowlitz Divide to where they joined the newly built trail down to Nickel Creek. Camp Twelve (3300) was set up in somber forest similar to that of their camp below St. Andrews Park 15 days earlier.

Aug. 20, Friday: The party crossed the Cowlitz Box Canyon, the deep and narrow gorge through which the muddy river "turns on its edge." The trail then took them along the hot and dusty burnt sides of Stevens Canyon, past Lake Louise and to the top of Mazama Ridge near Sluiskin Falls. Camp Thirteen (6100) here nearly completed the circuit; Paradise was only a short distance below.

Aug. 21, Saturday: The party hiked down to Longmire along the Paradise and Nisqually Rivers, then continued to Tahoma Creek and Camp Fourteen (2150):

. . . once more in a Robin Hood forest amid giant firs, and the next day we were whirled down to Ashford in the big autos, singing like mad to keep our spirits up, thence by a commonplace, prosaic old railroad trail to Tacoma and Seattle, where we were promptly swallowed up in the surging crowds of ordinary mortals who know not the mountain, the glaciers, the big forests, the roaring cataracts, the thrilling climb, the soul-expanding view, and who never lived for three glorious weeks above the clouds.

FIRST MORNING IN TOWN

There still are rushing rivers in my dreams;
There still are grinding boulders in the streams;
    There still is mountain madness,
    Thund'ring down in reckless gladness
—Tho I'm safely in my bed in town, it seems.

There is still a shining world of ice and snow;
There still are steps to slog and miles to go;
    There still are fragile bridges,
    And windy fearsome ridges,
—Tho the city sounds about me all say "No . . ."

There is still a threat'ning avalanche to round;
There still are blinding fog banks, summit bound;
    I can find no safe belay
    Yet the sun says "Do not stay" . . .
—Then I wake to find I'm home on level ground.

I'll be toiling up sublime eternal heights,
I'll be threading huge seracs by candle lights,
    I will pause where none may pass
    By some bottomless crevasse . . .
—I'll be dreaming that I'm climbing . . . many nights.

CLARK SCHURMAN
The Mountaineer, 1937

From Mazama Ridge.

The Wonderland Trail, as it became known after The Mountaineers outing of 1915, encircles Mount Rainier in the forest-to-alpine zone, with a total elevation gain (and loss) of about 21,000 feet in 90 miles. The pathway is one of the most scenic in the entire National Park system. Bridging countless streams and passing from the rain forests of deep valleys upward to numerous high mountain lakes, fir-sprinkled alpine meadows, and summer snowfields, the trail ranges in altitude from 2300 feet in the thickly wooded valleys of Ipsut Creek and Carbon River to about 6800 feet on the windswept rocks of Panhandle Gap. The trail can be traveled in segments of a day or two, or can be completed in 4-5 days, but is more enjoyably done in a week to 10 days. Designated campsites are located at 6-10 mile intervals around the mountain. Road access to the Wonderland Trail is at the following points: Longmire, end of West Side Road (if road is open to the terminus), Mowich Lake Road, Ipsut Creek Campground, Sunrise, White River Campground, Fryingpan Creek, Stevens Canyon (at Box Canyon), Reflection Lakes, Paradise, and Christine Falls.

HIGH-LEVEL ORBIT: A SUMMARY OF MOUNT RAINIERING

Climbers seeking a different sort of Rainier challenge than that offered by the summit would do well to consider the above-snowline encirclement of the mountain, a trip that offers continuous and unrestricted views of both the peak above and the foothills below. Some groups have done the circuit in several one-day stages, while others have completed the entire journey in an easy 4 days.

Hal Foss made a number of single-day traverses of various segments of the trip in July–October 1964. After thus becoming well-acquainted with the routes across the glaciers, over a long 4th of July weekend of 1967 he led Lee Henkle, Lynn Buchanan, and Jim Carlson on the first round-the-mountain-above-7000-feet trek. The orbit proved such a success Hal planned a second trip the following summer. Knowing of my interest in the circuit, he invited me to join him, along with Chief Park Ranger Joseph "Bill" Orr, Ranger Jim Erskine, Lee Henkle, and Lee Nelson. The trip was to carry me across both unknown terrain and across parts of the mountain that held many memories.

White River to Ptarmigan Ridge

We left White River Campground at 7:30 in the evening of June 28, 1968, loaded under 45-50-pound sacks, and hiked the relatively level 3.2 miles to Glacier Basin in 2 hours. Several inches of new snow and a light fall of flakes from a leaden sky had us questioning the forecast for clearing weather. Only occasionally could the upper part of the mountain be seen through clouds, dimly lit by the sun's last rays. The air was nippy as we pitched tents beneath the protecting limbs of alpine firs— we were off to a wintry start.

We were up at 6 o'clock to find a nearly cloudless sky and the basin and mountain above glistening under fresh snowfall. Passing through Glacier Basin we brushed snow from small hummocks along the trail, uncovering clusters of yellow glacier lilies and western anemones temporarily thwarted in their proclamations of summer.

A hard-frozen surface below St. Elmo Pass required crampons. After crossing the pass and descending to the edge of the Winthrop Glacier, we paused briefly to study the crevasse pattern and rope up. As we started over, a cloud drifted in and for a short stretch gave us prob-

Route followed on high-level orbit of Mount Rainier, June 28–July 2, 1968. Triangles indicate campsites. From map by author.

On Carbon Glacier.

lems in picking a way among several long crevasses. The fog lifted and dissipated quickly, however, and we gained the other side in bright sun.

From the Winthrop Glacier we ascended easily to the broad crest of lower Curtis Ridge and by noon had traversed open snow slopes to the edge of the Carbon Glacier. We were now on the ridge just above the rock-rimmed tent platforms used nearly 2 months earlier by Lee Nelson and me when, with five others, we had embarked on our "winter-season" climb of Liberty Ridge. Now, however, the new snow made conditions even more wintry on the face rising high above the Carbon Glacier. Willis Wall was plastered white and showed traces of fresh snowslides glistening against the steep incline.

We found no obstacles to crossing the lower Carbon Glacier at about the 7200-foot level, the lowest point of our round-the-mountain traverse. A steep climb from the Carbon to the broad surface of the Russell Glacier was made between two small icefalls where scattered blocks of snow indicated recent avalanches. The crossing of the Russell Glacier required an ascent to about 8700 feet to outflank several long crevasses. As we trudged across the upper Russell Glacier my thoughts went back to that day in late August 1941 when Leon Brigham, Jr., 21-year-old son of former guide Leon Brigham, fell to an icy death in a crevasse here.

After a seemingly endless hike across softening new snow, we finally reached the crest of Ptarmigan Ridge at 5:10 in the afternoon. Enroute we crossed fresh tracks of climbers on their way to a higher camp on the ridge, seeking an ascent of the route first climbed in 1935. We also noted several heavily laden figures far below, moving up the snowfield and eventually crossing our tracks behind us. They probably wondered about the tracks made *au contour* across the flanks of the mountain. After exchanging a few shouts we continued on, and learned later of their first ascent of Liberty Wall, made the next day.

We established camp at about 8500 feet in a small snow basin adjacent to the ridge. While unshouldering my pack I noticed the upper cross bar on the aluminum packframe was becoming detached from the uprights. A repair job with nylon cord and filament tape appeared to suffice for the moment, but I had misgivings about the frame disintegrating in the center of the North Mowich Glacier, far from a ready exit to the nearest roadhead. This brought to us all the realization that problems on an orbit of the mountain cannot always be solved by heading directly for the nearest timberline. A party in trouble on a remote flank of the peak must be particularly independent of outside help.

The clouds that through the day had occasionally concealed the upper part of the mountain cleared away toward evening. However, they still swirled in the deep gulf of the North Mowich Glacier to the west of camp, preventing us from visually scouting the route for the next day's traverse. While supper was being prepared by Foss, I selected a vantage point from which I could contemplate the rugged scene and mentally wander into the past history of this great north side. The names of Grage, Trosper, Bauer, Hossack, Daiber, Campbell, and Borrow mingled with those of more recent vintage who followed on the old routes and who pioneered a new era of climbing on the rotten cirque walls.

A chill breeze whipping across the ridge brought my thoughts back to the present. An examination of the black snow-melt tarps we had spread on nearby slopes to replenish our water supply indicated the sun's rays had lost their warmth. We retired to the tents for an excellent supper prepared by Foss—chicken stew and boned chicken, mixed with macaroni and cheese and topped off with hot jello and pudding. After relying on stoves to melt snow for a canteen supply for the coming day, and filling a pot for soaking dried apples and peaches for breakfast, we retired to sleeping bags.

Ptarmigan Ridge to Puyallup Cleaver

June 30 dawned cold and clear, the foothill peaks far below and to the east rising from a peaceful sea of valley fog. A pink glow on the upper mountain gradually turned to orange, then amber, as the sun rose above eastern Washington. Partaking of applesauce, peaches, instant breakfast, and jello, we broke camp and by 7:30 headed for the long talus slope descending to the North Mowich Glacier. We had to hike down the ridge about ¼ mile to find a continuous slope without cliffs. The snow covering the talus was firm in the morning shadow and we reached the bottom of the slope in 45 minutes and rested in warm sunshine at the edge of the North Mowich Glacier. Until now, no running water had been observed during our circuit, but suddenly a sweet, splashing music reached our ears. Soon we spotted a small stream flowing across morainal debris and disappearing beneath the edge of the glacier and in a few minutes had filled canteens for the long day ahead.

Turning our gaze to the mountain high above, and to the steep ice couloir at 11,000 feet on Ptarmigan Ridge, we noted four minute figures inching up the slope. It was a beautiful day and conditions were right for such a climb: the winter snowpack was well consolidated on the upper part of the mountain and the sky was cloudless. From our vantage point the slope they were on appeared nearly vertical; only our own experiences on similar "70-degree" slopes told us the angle was probably no more than 45-50°.

Avalanche track 2 miles long, from upper Mowich Face onto North Mowich Glacier.

Our view from camp of the undulating surface of the North Mowich Glacier showed that several crevasse-free corridors offered a relatively simple S-shaped route between ice breakups to the narrow rock ridge that separates the North Mowich and Edmunds Glaciers. High above, the broad 2-mile expanse of the Mowich Face was back-lighted dramatically as we began our crossing. We descended first into a broad trough, the center of which was filled with a chaos of partly thawed and refrozen ice blocks. Our eyes traced the debris path upward in a long curve to the base of the face, above which hung the thick ice cap that was the source of the avalanche a few days earlier. From our considerably foreshortened viewpoint it was difficult to conceive of an avalanche on the face extending so great a distance across the intervening expanse of icefalls and undulations without coming to rest somewhere enroute. With such thoughts we moved quickly over the frozen cascade and soon were breathing more freely on smoother slopes.

We crossed the center of the glacier a short distance uphill from Needle Rock, the sharp spire of lava that juts 200–250 feet above the ice breakups surrounding it—a lonely ship bucking the frozen sea. On the skyline beyond, a long wall of rock supports a thick ice cap which reminded me of the Canadian Rockies, where such caps delineate the plateau crests of the range. We worked our way up the glacier, rounding several long crevasses whose northern extremities disappeared beneath the avalanche debris. The sun was warming us rapidly and soon we were traveling in shirt sleeves. The glare from snow and ice on all sides had us liberally "creaming up."

Among us were varying formulas for protection against sun and glare. I had learned that a most comfortable response to "glacier lassitude" is to shield the head beneath a dampened triangular bandage. The white cloth reflects the sun's rays while the moisture keeps the head cool. A white hard hat partly filled with snow also serves to keep the head comfortable. A white shirt or parka further reflects radiation.

About noon, at around 8400 feet, we reached the line of rocks that marks the divide between the North Mowich and Edmunds Glaciers. Here we paused for nourishment from foodbags and canteens and to examine at closer hand the Mowich Face. Between the mountain and our vantage point, an undulation in the glacier surface hid the base of the face from view—the upper skyline looked deceptively near, and the slope considerably foreshortened. Long slivers of blue ice glistened in the sun where recently fallen snow had slid away. I could clearly see the route of our 1966 party directly above and through the rock bands at the top of the wall. To the right, above the head of the Edmunds Glacier, rose the long open slope climbed first in 1957. To the left of my route I studied another possibility—a long slope rising to the base of the icecap that overhangs the north half of the face. Without my realizing it, a party in town already was making plans—the slope was to be climbed a few weeks later.

Foss and Henkle pointed out the line of their previous year's traverse, considerably higher on the glacier than our present route; it had involved problems in finding a path among several ice breakups, and they were less protected from, and much nearer to, possible avalanches off the face.

Turning our gaze to the other direction and downslope, we could see the lowlands of Puget Sound country only through breaks in the cloud blanket. Far beyond, dimly white on the northwestern horizon, was the line of peaks of the Olympic Peninsula, while to the north Mount Baker and Glacier Peak rose prominently above lesser summits. Immediately below, where visible through rifts in the clouds, the Park boundary was dramatically defined by a line of demarcation beyond which were brownish foothills where logging operations had given the terrain a character reminiscent of the barren hills of my boyhood Southern California.

The Edmunds Glacier presented no crevasses on our traverse and in 45 minutes we were relaxing among warm rocks on the 9300-foot divide separating the Edmunds and South Mowich Glaciers. From here we had a view up the lower part of the Sunset Ridge route. Beyond the bergschrund at the head of the South Mowich rose the steep snow couloir leading high above and out of sight among rocks of the ridge crest. Looking down the mountain, we noted we were gaining a view of more familiar peaks—the ragged crest of the Colonnade rose across the deep canyon of the South Mowich Glacier at our feet and far beyond the broad surface of the Puyallup Glacier was Tokaloo Spire.

Bill Orr, in radio contact with the various ranger districts under his jurisdiction as Chief Ranger, called in from this new zone on the orbit. We began to pick up more clearly the transmissions from the south side of the mountain, while our contacts with the Carbon River Ranger Station began to fade. We felt much like astronauts, circling our own sphere and initiating communications with new stations as we lost those passing beyond radio contact. This was Bill's first close-up acquaintance with many sides of the peak and he became increasingly impressed with its size and beauty.

At 2 p.m., as we started to descend the steep slope to the South Mowich Glacier, we noted the sun had softened the snow considerably and a layer of mushy snow was now overlying ice. After a careful traverse above an area of crevasses we reached the far side of the narrow glacier and came to the trace of a recent snowslide. In a sitting position we attempted to propel ourselves partway by rowing with axes and keeping the feet aloft, but the snow was so mushy we finally had to complete the descent on foot.

The narrow trough at the near side of the South Mowich Glacier we crossed by skirting a few crevasses; this was followed by a slow trudge to the Puyallup Cleaver beyond, which we reached at 4:40 in the afternoon. Our two tents (a four-man Logan and a two-man tent) were pitched on a flat area on the edge of the glacier at about 9200 feet. The sun-warmed and windless crest of the nearby ridge offered Foss a choice of flat stones on which to prepare dinner.

Once again we had a problem gathering water. Lee Nelson and I spent a large part of early evening periodically descending a small cliff to fill canteens and waterbags from a slow trickle of snowmelt.

It was a warm and windless evening as we relaxed and enjoyed the panoramic view of the Tahoma Glacier below and Success Cleaver beyond. Above us and to the left stood St. Andrews Rock (11,562), partly obscuring the lower cirque of the Sunset Amphitheater. The high, vari-colored upper wall of the amphitheater rose on the skyline, its hues deepening as the sun dropped toward the horizon.

Twenty years earlier I had made my first climb of the Tahoma Glacier. We had camped at this same spot, but without tents. We had leveled the ridge crest and spread our sleeping bags directly on the volcanic sand. I recall that evening as one of the most beautiful I've ever experienced at a Rainier high camp. It had been a warm and cloudless

On Puyallup Cleaver at 9200 feet.

day and as the sun fell below the Olympic Mountains the numerous waterways of Puget Sound and Hood Canal and lowland lakes began to glisten in the pink reflection of the western horizon. I had with me at that time a cumbersome but powerful pair of binoculars brought by my father from Holland in 1910. With the 8-power glasses I had picked out ferries on the Seattle-Bremerton run and, as it became darker, the lights of cars moving along the Lake Washington Floating Bridge. The color had grown more intense as the sun disappeared and the icy crust of the foreground snow added sparkle to the alpenglow. Behind and above, the warm display of fading light across the upper Tahoma Glacier and Sunset Amphitheater had etched the scene deep in my mind. Tonight, except for more haze and a few clouds, the scene was the same. The sun's final rays across the western flank of Rainier inspired me to do a small watercolor; when the paper refused to dry in the growing chill of evening it was time to retire to the tent.

Puyallup Cleaver to Wilson Glacier

July 1 dawned cloudless, but being in the morning shadow of the mountain we slept a bit late, not awakened by the sun against the tent. The sun's rays long before had touched the foothills below, which in the clear air sharply showed a quilt pattern of forest and logged areas.

On Puyallup Cleaver, Tahoma Glacier on right.

By 7 o'clock we began the steep climb of frozen snow slopes leading toward St. Andrews Rock. In an hour we were at 10,000 feet, the highest point of the entire trip. From here a slope of ice covered by a thin crust of snow dropped steeply to the edge of the Tahoma Glacier. A large bergschrund at the bottom of the incline suggested that we execute our descent very carefully. Foss and Henkle led off just as the sun's rays came over the summit dome high above, backlighting the ice. Foss kicked his cramponed feet into the slope and proceeded in a long descending traverse to the left as the other roped pairs followed. A switchback to the right brought relief as we right-handers were now more comfortably positioned to arrest any slip. After rounding the right end of the long schrund we moved out to gentler terrain of the glacier surface.

The slanting rays of the sun were now highlighting and giving shape to several nearby ice cascades. We moved between these without difficulty, crampons crunching firmly into the hard surface. After topping a small rise we were able to define a clear route to about 8400 feet on the rocky divide between the Tahoma and South Tahoma Glaciers. Although the ensuing traverse of the glacial bowl warmed us considerably, a cool breeze on the ridge crest dictated a short halt for donning parkas.

Several undulations in the center of the South Tahoma Glacier required our threading a route among crevasses and towering seracs. This is the area where in late July 1947, I was one of a small group of guides and rangers led by Bill Butler which had found the first pieces of wreckage of the C-46 Marine plane that had crashed into the mountain the previous winter. By 10 o'clock we were across the glacier and sitting at about 8200 feet on the snowy crest of Success Cleaver. We were now well along toward the south side of the mountain. Foss and Henkle remarked how easily we were passing from one glacier to the next; on their previous trek they had greater problems with crevasses. Although the winter snowfall had been less than normal at lower elevations, above 8000 feet the snow lay at greater depth than in 1967.

We hiked up the cleaver a few hundred feet before finding a long and steep slope of snow that led without a break to the Pyramid Glacier below. The morning sun had softened the snow and in roped pairs we peeled off in exhilarating sitting glissades which terminated in the vast bowl below. The half-mile traverse of the crevasse-free glacier took only 15 minutes and shortly after noon we were scrambling up loose morainal debris to the 8000-foot crest of the ridge overlooking the Kautz Glacier.

High above, the Kautz ice cliff formed a glistening 200-foot band of white against the deep blue sky. Below, the glacier continued to its

Point Success and Kautz Glacier from edge of Success Glacier, with Kautz Cleaver in center.

terminus in the deeply entrenched valley above the box canyon, the source of the 1947 Kautz Creek Mudflow. From our vantage point we could now see familiar summits of the small but picturesque Tatoosh Range—Unicorn, Pinnacle, and Eagle Peaks—and realized we were a little more than halfway around the mountain. For me, the next leg of the circuit would be across terrain which held many memories from years as a summit guide and ranger at Paradise Valley.

We dozed briefly in the sun, then had a bite to eat before again shouldering our packs for the descent and crossing of the Kautz Glacier. That our loads seemed to be getting lighter each day was largely illusory: although we were eating more as our appetites increased (the first day or two were devoted principally to quenching thirst) our food was mostly of the dehydrated and freeze-dried variety, hence was not the chief contributor to pack weight.

An easy descent with only a few crevasses to round led to the main part of the Kautz Glacier. We crossed at slightly above 8000 feet, keeping below a large icefall that dominated the eastern half of the bowl. Considerable avalanche debris lay at the foot of the ice cataract, the upper part of which formed a broken and ominous wall high above our line of travel. We moved rapidly below the icefall, pausing only long enough near a pile of rocks to fill waterbag and canteens from a small murky pool. The crest of the opposite moraine was gained by a delicate scramble up loose boulders which occasionally departed down the steep slope and across the ice.

We were now at about 8500 feet, with a view to the east across the numerous small snowfields that are collectively the Van Trump Glacier. The slopes have few if any crevasses until late in summer and offered an easy traverse across to the rocky ridge above the Wilson Glacier. Enroute we came across a large chunk of hard rubber carrying a line of aluminum rivets—a small fragment of the Air Force jet trainer which had exploded higher on the mountain earlier in the year, killing its occupants. This is one of countless pieces of aircraft debris scattered across Rainier's slopes over many years. The number of planes which have terminated their flights against the mountain will never be known —the vast and complex expanses of Mount Rainier and the Cascade Range hide their secrets well.

At 3:30 p.m. our last camp of the circuit was pitched atop a scenic overlook, a flat-topped buttress (about 8700 feet) just large enough to comfortably hold our party. Owing to the relative warmth and lack of wind, four of us chose to sleep out while the other two set up the small tent. After leveling the volcanic soil we spread our thin plastic tarps, ½-inch sponge pads, sleeping bags, and, on top, the 56- by 84-inch "space blankets" developed by the space program as insulation-reflection shields.

As late afternoon merged into evening the shadows lengthened across the ridges and valleys below. The sharp peaks of the Tatoosh Range provided a backdrop for Paradise Valley. The meadows immediately around the Paradise complex were relatively free of the snow cover that generally characterizes the area this early in the summer, but above Alta Vista the winter white still dominated. To the west we traced the course of the Nisqually River past Longmire—a silver strand in a narrow path of gray gravel and boulders which cut a swath through the dark forest green. Below the terminus of the Nisqually Glacier, the Longmire-Paradise road climbed the long grade from Glacier Bridge to Ricksecker Point.

As evening wore on the minute glow of headlights could be seen moving up the road toward Paradise. There, more lights gave the locations of Paradise Inn and the new Visitor Center, buildings of widely spaced generations representing the old and new in mountain architecture. My mind was drawn back nearly 30 years to my first years of guiding on the Kautz route, on the lower part of which we were now camped. Although there were these evolutions in building design, and the related recent landscaping of the Paradise parking area and asphalting of nearby tourist trails, and there certainly was an increase in the checkerboard pattern of logged area beyond the Tatoosh Range, the scene was in many ways the same as in 1940. Paradise still occupied only an insignificant part of the panorama now spread below us on this warm night of July 1, 1968.

Snowfields of the Goat Rocks, far beyond the end of the Tatoosh Range, were receiving their last touch of the sun, and soon they too fell under the lavender, then gray, mantle of evening. Nearly 50 miles to the south the symmetrical Fujiyama cone of St. Helens was next to fade, followed by Hood, 95 miles away in Oregon. The last to cling to warmth was 12,307-foot Adams, 45 miles distant and second to Rainier among the Northwest's mighty volcanoes.

With the fading of the sun in the west our eyes turned toward the evening star faintly blinking overhead. Before long other stars emerged and soon the entire sky was a sea of onyx sprinkled with jewels. The only impositions of man on the nocturnal scene were the lights of Paradise far below, and of the logging community of Packwood beyond a notch in the Tatoosh Range, and a faint glow over Portland that outlined the dark form of St. Helens on the southwestern horizon. Above and behind us, the dark bulk of the mountain loomed silently, save for the sound of falling ice occasionally coming from the direction of the Nisqually Icefall.

To persons standing alone on the hill during a clear night such as this, the roll of the world eastward is almost a palpable movement. The sensation may be caused by the panoramic glide of the stars past earthly objects, which is perceptible in a few minutes of stillness, or by the better outlook upon space that the hill affords, or by the wind, or by the solitude; but whatever its origin, the impression of riding along is vivid and abiding.

THOMAS HARDY

Wilson Glacier to White River

We were somewhat apprehensive about finding a clear route through breakups on the Nisqually Glacier, out of sight beyond the far edge of the Wilson Glacier and lower part of Wapowety Cleaver, and therefore planned an early start on July 2. We arose to a clear morning and after a hasty breakfast left the ridge at 5:30 for the crossing of the firm, well-frozen surface of the Wilson. Midway on the glacier we came across two more airplane fragments—pieces of aluminum, one small section bearing the complete star-and-bar insignia of the Air Force.

The Wilson crossing was simple; we then ascended steep snow to the crumbling crest of Wapowety Cleaver at a notch of some 9300 feet and were relieved to find the Nisqually Glacier providing several broad avenues to the Muir snowfield. A steep descent of the edge of the ice, and a leap downward across a small bergschrund, brought us onto the undulating surface of the Nisqually. The route took us easily over and around several small rolls and across the broad track of an avalanche from the Nisqually Icefall, which had a considerably foreshortened aspect from our viewpoint. After a brief pause to contemplate the ever-changing nature of the route through that jumbled chaos which I climbed with Bob Craig in 1948, we reached the smooth gentle slope

Traversing below Nisqually Icefall.

of the Muir snowfield by 7 o'clock, only 1½ hours after leaving camp. A broad track made by the innumerable footprints of hikers and mountaineers heading toward Camp Muir reminded us of our proximity to the heavy foot traffic above Paradise Valley.

Rays of the morning sun hit us as we traversed quickly around the slopes below Anvil Rock and onto the Cowlitz Glacier. Soon we were shedding clothing and applying cream to our faces. The glare from the bright sun and snow of the past 3 days was beginning to take its toll: our eyes were becoming bloodshot despite the use of dark goggles. Bill Orr in particular was suffering; his eyelids and lips were getting puffed and following the trip he required medical attention for a day or two. The rest of us ended up with the customary cracked lips and peeling noses.

The Cowlitz was crossed without trouble by a slightly descending traverse to a notch at 8800 feet on the lower part of Cathedral Rocks. From here we easily moved onto the Ingraham Glacier and wound through a small breakup—an awkward step across a crevasse to the opposite wall was the only delay. Soon we were plugging up the steep snow ramp leading to the prominent notch on the ridge separating the Ingraham and Whitman Glaciers. This notch is a well-remembered feature on the route toward Little Tahoma from Paradise; the struggle to gain it is cursed by all who make the ascent. An hour of delicate maneuvering under our heavy packs on the loose, shingly slabs was required to bring us all to the ridge crest.

We sprawled in the rocks to eat lunch. It probably was from here that Allison Brown and his Indian companions began their ascent of the Ingraham Glacier in 1885 or 1886. If similar conditions prevailed in those days, the horses presumably were left at about this point.

Radio contact now was made with the White River Ranger Station. Bill requested that a vehicle meet us at about 3 o'clock on the road at Fryingpan Creek, to take us back to our cars at the White River Campground. In their circuit of the mountain the previous year Hal Foss and Lee Henkle had completed the journey by way of Camp Muir and a crossing of the Emmons Glacier to Steamboat Prow. Because of their problems in 1967 with large crevasses and icefalls in the middle of the Emmons we had decided on the lower route around the back side of Little Tahoma.

About 10:45 a.m. we left the rocks for the slight upward traverse of Whitman Glacier and headed for the most obvious low point on Whitman Crest at the opposite side. At 11:15 we attained the crest at about 9200 feet and rested briefly to study an entirely new panorama of the region we had covered during the first leg of the circuit. In 4 days the landscape had changed from winter to summer. Instead of a terrain covered by fresh snow, the ridges rising above Glacier Basin were brown and clear. Also, after having spent the past 2 days high above lush valleys on the west side of the peak, we were struck by the comparative aridity of the eastern part of the Park. In place of uniform dark-green forests (albeit considerably scarred and gridded by logging operations) of the western slope, we now overlooked a tawny landscape of open ridges rising above partly treeless valleys. The plateaus and upper slopes of Burroughs Mountain, Sourdough Mountains, and Goat Island Mountain were either devoid of vegetation or contained only a matting and scattered stands of small trees. The lower slopes were more heavily forested, but even these were broken by long fingers and cones of talus and scree. The farther ranges faded in the mid-day haze, but the uplifts of the Stuart Range and the volcanic cone of Glacier Peak were sharp against the northeast horizon.

From Whitman Crest we dropped onto the broad surface of the Fryingpan Glacier and contoured eastward about 1½ miles before beginning the descent to rock cliffs overlooking Summerland. From here the way was entirely downhill, with a rapid run to Summerland via several stimulating glissades on steep snows of Meany Crest. Our entry into the vegetation zone was marked by the welcome scents of drying grass, alpine flowers, and fir, and the nearly forgotten music of rivulets across the meadows. Several more sitting glissades in scattered forest below the meadow brought us to the dry surface of the Wonderland Trail. At this point, its duties nearly completed after the repair job on Ptarmigan Ridge 3 days earlier, my pack frame began falling apart, the bag held on my back only by a few strands of nylon cord. We quickly covered the 4 miles of trail to the White River Road, arriving at the waiting car at 2:45 in the afternoon.

In summary, our circuit took us about 25 miles in 4 days. We crossed 16 glaciers and gained (and lost) about 11,000 feet. Our total time of actual travel was about 40 hours.

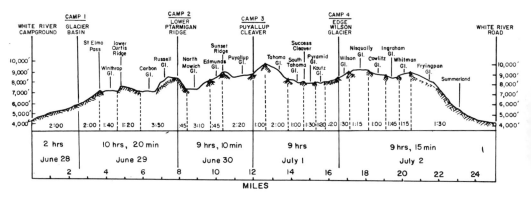

The ups and downs of high-level orbit of Mount Rainier, June 28–July 2, 1968. Traverse made counter-clockwise from White River Campground. Daily and point-to-point travel times are shown. Total gain (and loss) of altitude: 11,000 feet.

A few days later a seven-man party led by Bill Boulton of Spokane also circled the mountain above snowline, but in a clockwise direction starting from Paradise.

From the experience gained during these several high-level orbital traverses of Mount Rainier, members of both the Foss and Boulton parties agreed on the wisdom of advising Park authorities of the proposed itinerary before the trip. Such traverses so quickly move a party from one segment of the peak to another that, for early contact in case of emergencies, the various ranger districts around the mountain should be aware of the party's day-by-day locations and climbing plans.

20 *What's Next?*

In 1938 Don Woods declared Sunset Ridge to be one of the last routes left on Mount Rainier. About 20 years later my summary of ascents of the mountain (*American Alpine Journal*, 1957) implied that few major challenges remained—probably only half a dozen major ascents still enticed exploration. Yet, by the end of the 1972 climbing season more than 20 additional paths had been pioneered to the summit.

Despite periodic pronouncements that all worthwhile ridges, head-walls, glaciers, ice slopes, and snow fingers now have been climbed, it is apparent that new challenges will continue to crop up to stimulate those with a yen for adventure. There will be "mopping-up" operations: variations of old routes, combinations of two or more routes, first descents, traverses of the volcano at high level, and explorations of the tunnels and lakes in the summit craters. A greater freedom and minimized regulations which allow year-around climbing will stimulate winter mountaineering. However, the number of people reaching the top during the summer months may be reduced by regulations that now limit the number and sizes of parties on various routes. To many an oldtimer who recalls having the mountain to himself, this will mean a happy passing of the era of hundreds of climbers strung out in a deep trough delineating the way to the crater. Most certainly, it will encourage a wider distribution of climbers to more interesting routes that have been long neglected.

An increasing number of the fair sex are doing routes which 30 years ago were attempted only by a select group of male climbers. Already women have taken part in the arduous ascents of Ptarmigan and Liberty Ridges, Nisqually Icefall, and Success and Kautz Cleavers, and have shared in assaults on the icy, wind-blasted dome of mid-winter. Children too are learning the ways of mountaineering. Once thought damaging to young hearts, the strain of physical exertion at over 14,000 feet no longer causes great concern. A 7-year-old girl and at least three 9-year-old boys have been to Rainier's summit; a Park ranger's 5-year-old son has aspirations to return the honors to the male sex.

The reasons for climbing mountains perhaps have undergone a subtle change in recent years. To mountaineers of yesterday the sport's attraction was the basic simplicity and directness of purpose—its freedom from material restrictions, organizations, and legalities. They typically climbed with small parties of close friends and like-minded companions and found adventures that forged deeper friendships and provided greater esthetic rewards. Few sought publicity for their feats in the era when climbing was considered a foolish pastime, and many never recorded their discoveries except privately.

Today, after many decades of having to be explained and justified, climbing for its own sake has become accepted by the general public. As in the evolution of skiing from a pursuit by "Scandihoovians and nuts only," mountaineering has attained a high degree of respectability. And, like skiing, mountaineering has become a "what-to-wear" and "how-to-do-it-correctly" recreational activity.

A mere 30 years ago the mountain climber was decked out in wool clothing no longer suitable for any other purpose and selected primarily for durability. He had difficulty finding climbing boots, ice axes, crampons, and rope on the American market and was forced to send to Europe for such exotic items as tricouni and Swiss edge nails (many of the present generation have never heard of either). Immediately after World War II, the American-made (Ames) ice axes left by the mountain troops appeared in garden-tools sections of surplus stores.

Today the sport is the oyster of clothing and equipment manufacturers and retailers whose businesses are continuing to burgeon all over the country. Like fishermen, camera bugs, and auto buffs, mountaineers in an age of affluence are preoccupied with "things"—they are constantly alert for the latest developments in metal and plastic gadgetry, clothing and tentage, the more colorful the better. The breed of climbers coming out of World War II with baggy mountain pants, box-toed "bramani boots," and waterproof (but not sweatproof) tents of olive-drab rubberized nylon has been replaced by handsome young men and women, well-fed and highly proteined, clothed in colorful imports: wool knickers, turtleneck T-shirts and sweaters, double-lined boots, glistening hard hats, fluffy down parkas, and brilliant outer wind garments. The present generation is equipped with collapsible multipurpose axes and hammers with fiberglass shafts, nylon, perlon, and goldline ropes of varied and luminous hues, Jumar ascenders, rope clamps, snaplinks, pitons, and nuts of innumerable sizes and shapes, purposes, and prices—and of mysterious alloy combinations and exotic descriptions (blades, wedges, spoons, angles, rurps, bongs); these provide conversation at high camps that colorfully blossom with tents of ingenious design. A thorough knowledge of the latest in equipment and clothing has become, to some, a vital parameter of the sport, and no longer are climbing goals limited by a lack of proper tools for the job.

An ever-increasing knowledge of man's physical and mental makeup and of his capacity for endurance has been the subject of numerous studies and papers by physicians, psychologists, and sociologists—on the 1963 American Mount Everest Expedition a sociologist delved into the nature and effects of close living in cramped quarters at high alti-

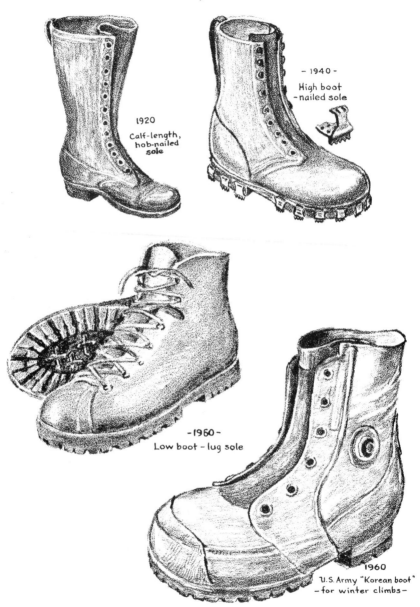

1920
Calf-length,
hob-nailed
sole

– 1940 –
High boot
–nailed sole

–1960–
Low boot – lug sole

1960
U.S. Army "Korean boot"
–for winter climbs–

Boot styles, 1920–60.

tudes. Mountaineering courses offer instruction that more rapidly orients the neophyte to the high world of ice and rock; 2 or 3 years of lectures, seminars, practice trips, and experience climbs have given sufficient background for many young climbers to move rapidly into expeditionary mountaineering of the highest order of difficulty. Many an oldtimer who seldom relished the thought of adding the cumbersome pitons of the 1940s to his already-heavy pack is amazed at the sophisticated hardware and acrobatics of today's young mountaineers.

The mountaineering literature of America also has changed from 30 years ago. Then, the available writings consisted chiefly of old classics covering Alpine explorations and climbs of the Victorian era, along with a few books on the Canadian Rockies and the few Himalayan expeditions of the 1920–30 period. Journals of mountaineering clubs generally described only the activities of members, which in most cases were limited to local climbs and outings; only occasionally did an account appear concerning a member's participation in a trip farther afield.

In 1951, Maurice Herzog's *Annapurna*, telling the story of the 1950 French expedition to the Himalayas, was the first mountaineering book to catch the imagination of the American public. This narrative of the nearly tragic first ascent of an 8000-meter peak became an overnight best-seller. The French team's achievement, followed in 1953 by the British conquest of Mount Everest and the Austrian-German climb of Nanga Parbat, marked the beginning of a new era. Today the shelves of American bookstores and libraries are lined with volumes on mountaineering explorations and ascents in ranges the world over. Books describing local climbing areas and climbing techniques are multiplying, as are pocket guides to local hikes, family backpack trips, and scenic auto viewpoints. Many of these publications have encouraged mass participation in outdoor recreation and have enlisted the support of the general public in the fight to preserve the nation's natural scenic attractions and wilderness areas.

Yet the increasing description of climbing routes and areas may someday reach the point of diluting the spirit of adventure which first drew men to the unknown heights. Then perhaps mountaineers will arrive at the point sought by young Delmar Fadden when he destroyed his compass and burned his map before heading into the wilds of the Olympic Peninsula. And, as aptly described by Dr. Richard Emerson, mountaineer-sociologist member of the 1963 American Mount Everest Expedition:

Every mountain climber *knows* that pleasure does not reside on the summit. Rather, it is found in the planning and in the execution of the plan. As every Englishman knows, the game is in the playing, not in the winning. By implication, the *fun* of play, the source of gratification or reinforcement, is distributed across the entire period of uncertainty, and the end point is often an anticlimax. A climber enjoys reaching the summit only if, like the Englishman, he can say of the mountain "good show." To a climber, the summit defines a problem, but pleasure is found in the *process of solving,* not in the solution . . . I predict a long future for this game. It will last as long as there are new walls. When climbers start to run out of new walls, then I predict that they will introduce a final rule: "Thou shalt not record or communicate route descriptions. Every man will be his own explorer on these walls."

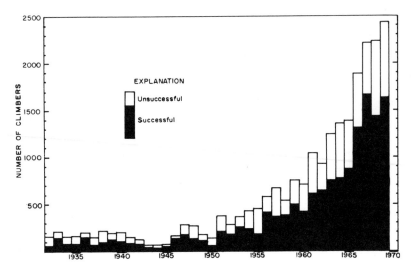

Summit climbing on Mount Rainier during period 1932–69.

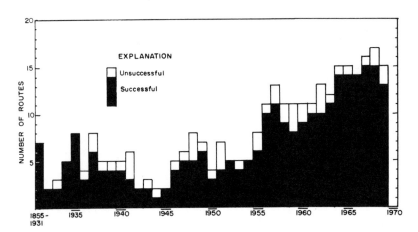

Summary of the number of routes climbed during the period 1855–1931, and of routes climbed and attempted each year thereafter through 1969.

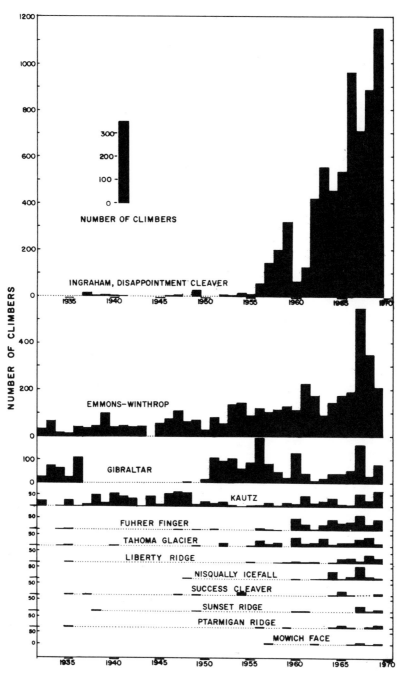

Number of climbers successful each year on the 12 most-used routes, for the period 1932–69. Data from Park Service records.

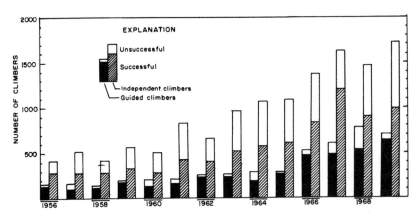

Comparison of guided and independent parties climbing on Mount Rainier during the period 1956–69. Data from Park Service records.

PART FOUR

MOUNTAIN
TRAGEDIES

21 A Long View

... We have been to the Pole and we shall die like gentlemen. I
regret only for the women we leave behind. . . . For my own sake I do
not regret this journey, which has shown that Englishmen can endure
hardships, help one another, and meet death with as great a fortitude
as ever in the past. We took risks, we knew we took them; things
have come out against us, and therefore we have no cause for
complaint. . . . Had we lived, I should have a tale to tell of the
hardihood, endurance, and courage of my companions which would
have stirred the heart of every Englishman. These rough notes and our
dead bodies must tell the tale. . . . For God's sake look after our
people. . . .

ROBERT FALCON SCOTT, 1912

During the 115 years from 1855 to 1970 the summit of Rainier was
visited by more than 20,000 climbers. In this time both experienced
mountaineers and neophyte hikers have wandered across the broken
icefields and up the rotten rocks. Individuals have made solitary ascents
in both winter and summer, many such episodes never officially reported—one man climbed the Emmons Glacier solo, using a sawed-off
garden hoe for an ice axe; others have made the climb in tennis shoes
and "hush-puppies." Parties numbering over a hundred climbers, of
varying ages and experiences, have plodded in tight lines along well-
beaten trails trenched in the more popular glacier routes, while on more
remote corners of the peak small parties of two or three have worked
their way up new lines of ascent, completely independent and cut off
from help under the ever-present threat of rock and ice fall, rapid
changes in weather, or a slip on steep ice. Yet in all these years and
under such conditions, treks to and from Rainier's summit have claimed
only 17 lives.

The remarkably high percentage of accident-free ascents may stem
both from the tight controls maintained on summit climbs of the past
by the Park Service and from the influence exerted over many years by
safety-conscious mountaineers of the Pacific Northwest. Unlike many
high peaks situated near large centers of population and easy of access
by well-beaten summer trails on snowless slopes, such as Mount Fuji
in Japan, Rainier has a terrain and summit generally attainable only by
people with some knowledge and experience in glacier travel. The
poorly informed and ill-equipped individuals out for an afternoon stroll
learn soon enough that the distance to the summit is deceptive and well
beyond a few hours' hike from the parking area. Most become dis-

couraged and turn back before becoming casualties; no dirt trail with switchbacks and railings entices the unwary toward the crater rim, and the atmosphere engendered at timberline visitor centers has been one of abiding respect for the peak.

For the past 50 years, until 1969, all those seeking to climb the mountain had first to register with the rangers and be cleared for the climb; this practice probably has dissuaded potential casualties from going far above timberline or has encouraged them to join professionally guided parties. As members of guide parties they have been given pre-climb instructions in the use of rope, crampons, and ice axe and in the techniques of self-rescue from a crevasse. By following the footsteps of the guide, and his experience in judging the conditions of snow and ice and weather, the ambitious neophyte has been able to realize his dreams without undue risk. Further, with the accelerated growth of mountaineering and the accompanying courses in climbing techniques and philosophy, the number of people safely completing the climb of the mountain has continued to increase.

Yet one should not become complacent over the statistics. The mountain always will be capable of taking full advantage of human error under the right combination of conditions—no amount of experience will guarantee a safe return from the heights.

22 Early Tragedies

The first fatal accident recorded on Rainier occurred during a descent of the mountain in July 1897, during the first climb of the peak by a large club-sponsored group, a party of 200 Mazamas. (A description of their travel to the mountain, arrival at Paradise, and ascent of the peak was given earlier.)

After the climb via the Gibraltar route on July 27, all but eight members of the party, who chose to remain on the summit overnight, returned to Camp Muir, which was reached at 9:30 p.m. At this point about half the climbers were given permission by guide Ed Curtis to continue down to Paradise that night. According to Miss Ella McBride (oral communication, 1963), it was a beautiful moonlit night. She was traveling with Professor McClure as they were scouting a route for those following. At a particular rocky point McClure told Miss McBride he was going to work his way down a short cliff. She turned away for a moment, then heard the sound of a fall. McClure apparently had slipped or caught his yard-long barometer on a projection which threw him off balance. He made no sound as he fell to his death on the rocks below.

Miss McBride had the impression McClure had fainted. She stated that, owing to his exertions in obtaining measurements on the summit earlier in the day, he had become extremely tired and during the descent had been continually thirsty, frequently asking for water from the canteen she carried.

The descent from Muir by the remainder of the party the following day almost cost two more lives when W. C. Ansley and Walter Rogers slid into a crevasse 200 feet above where McClure had met death. Although badly cut, Ansley worked his way from the crevasse and returned to Paradise where he reported the accident. Rogers was rescued by a relief party after midnight.

OTHER PRE-1929 TRAGEDIES

On August 14, 1909 T. V. Callaghan (50), Joseph W. Stevens (30), and L. M. Sterling left Reese's Camp at 4:20 a.m. for a one-day ascent of Rainier. They reached Camp Muir in about 2½ hours, then started up the Gibraltar route. They attained the top of Gibraltar at 11 a.m. The weather began deteriorating but the party kept moving upward, although Sterling, who was less experienced than the others, began dropping behind. At 13,000 feet he turned back while Callaghan and Stevens continued the climb. When Sterling arrived at Paradise he awaited the other two but they failed to return. The following day guide Joe Stampfler led a search party to the crater. There they found only the two alpenstocks of the climbers, who were never seen again (Aubrey L. Haines, Tacoma *Sunday Ledger-News Tribune*, September 11, 1955).

In early August 1911, a young man, Legh Osborn Garrett, disappeared during a solo ascent on Success Cleaver above the tent camp at Indian Henrys, where he was employed. His failure to return resulted in an exhaustive search on the upper part of the cleaver by a party that included guide Joe Stampfler, Rangers Sam Estes and Harry Greer, and three Army Engineers, Edgar Courtright, Alvah Boggs, and Clarence Parks. Heavy snowfall limited visibility during the 30-hour search and only a few tracks made by Garrett's canvas tennis shoes indicated the young man had reached the higher part of the ridge (Tacoma *News Tribune*, August 6, 1911).

On September 15, 1916 J. A. Fritsch, member of a seven-man summit party led by guide Jules Stampfler, stepped into a crevasse halfway between the summit and Gibraltar during the descent. He fell about 50 feet into the hole but was rescued and brought out only "dazed". He was rather weak but made it to the top of Gibraltar where Stampfler and another man remained with him through the night. The next morning he was partly carried back down the mountain. At Paradise he was examined by three doctors who declared he was not seriously injured, although somewhat dazed. He remained at Paradise Inn for 2 more days, then suddenly passed away in his room at 3:40 a.m., September 18.

On August 16, 1921 Jack Meredith of Portland was killed in a fall from Little Tahoma.

On August 25, 1924 Sidney W. Cole, a Stanford University student and athlete, suffered a basal skull fracture when hit by a bouncing boulder in the chute on the Gibraltar route. He had just pulled a younger climber out of the line of fire of the rock avalanche. He was in a party led by guide Hans Fuhrer which was making a descent from the summit. Cole died the next day.

23 Party Slides into Crevasse on Upper Ingraham: Wetzel and ·Greathouse, 1929

At 12:30 p.m. on July 2, 1929 a young apprentice guide, Harry Webster, arrived breathless at the Paradise Guide House with news of an accident high on the mountain. Webster had run down from Camp Muir after another guide, Bob Strobel, crippled and exhausted, had descended to Muir from the accident scene above Gibraltar.

Thus came the first report of the most highly publicized tragedy in Mount Rainier climbing history. Referred to since as "the Greathouse accident," the events that transpired over the 6-day period combined in a story of unbelievable suffering and heroism among members of the ill-fated party and the rescue team. One guide and a client were killed and the others in the six-man party were badly injured when the entire group fell into a deep crevasse following a long slide down the upper part of the mountain.

In the first summit attempt of the 1929 climbing season, the party was composed of the following men:

Leon H. Brigham, head guide, with 45 previous ascents of Rainier
Forrest G. Greathouse, apprentice guide, on his first climb of Rainier; football coach at Lincoln High School in Seattle and ex-teammate of Harold "Red" Grange at the University of Illinois
Robert Strobel, apprentice guide, with two previous ascents of the mountain
Yancy Bradshaw, Cambridge, Massachusetts
E. P. Weatherly, Jr., Kansas City, Missouri
Edwin A. Wetzel, Milwaukee, Wisconsin

According to a report supplied me by Harry B. Cunningham, chief guide on Rainier during the period 1925–32, the sequence of events is summarized as follows.

On July 1, 1929, apprentice guides Robert Strobel and Harry Webster left Paradise for Camp Muir at 9 o'clock in the morning, accompanied by a pack train carrying food and equipment for the summer operations. This advance party reached Muir at 1 p.m. The main climbing party left Paradise later in the day and arrived at Muir about 6 p.m.

At 1 a.m. on July 2 the summit party left Muir. The six men were

The party before climb. From left: Forrest Greathouse, Edwin Wetzel, E.P. Weatherly, Yancey Bradshaw, Leon Brigham.

tied together on one rope (as was customary in those days) in the following order: Brigham, Wetzel, Greathouse, Bradshaw, Weatherly, Strobel. None in the party wore crampons (not often used in those days). The climb progressed without undue difficulty past the Gibraltar ledges and to the top of Gibraltar Rock at Camp Comfort. Wetzel now appeared tired, but no more so than most people making the ascent. Because of the cold wind it was not deemed wise to leave him alone so the party proceeded upward after a brief rest, all expressing a desire to continue to the top.

Aside from a cloud cap atop the mountain and a few clouds below, the sky was clear. However, before they had ascended halfway to the summit the cloud cap dropped upon the climbers and they were enveloped in a strong blizzard, "the worst that I have ever experienced," according to Brigham, ". . . particles of ice swept into our faces and eyes. It was necessary to chop steps all the way up." Wetzel was becoming exhausted and it was necessary for Brigham to drag and half carry him to the anticipated protection of the crater rim, which by now was closer than the rocks they had left below. For the last 200 feet Wetzel was supported between Brigham and Strobel, who had untied from the lower end of the rope to assist. The wind was so fierce they all had to crouch low and crawl the remaining distance. The crater was reached at 7:40 a.m. Brigham signed their names in the book at Register Rock.

But the hoped-for protection inside the crater was not to be had. The raging wind was extremely cold and the climbers felt themselves growing numb. After only a 10-minute rest they started down in the following order: Brigham, Wetzel, Weatherly, Bradshaw, Greathouse, and Strobel. From the beginning of the descent, Wetzel seemed incapable of remaining on his feet and continually dropped to a sitting position—he wanted to sit down and slide, which was out of the question. Every time he sat down his action put a strain on those roped above him, throwing them off balance in the high winds that hit their backs. Because the snow surface was so solidly frozen the party found it impossible to get their axes in deep enough to employ the usual method of descending steep terrain—the two end men anchoring the rope with their axes while those between used it as a handline. Wetzel complained his hands were too numb to grasp the rope.

Brigham was forced to chop steps all the way down, which further slowed progress. Wetzel was unable to place his feet in the steps and had to be continually anchored by those above him. Then, according to Brigham's later report:

> Without warning the man at the end of the line slipped, lost his footing, and shot down the incline. The men had been cautioned to dig their stocks and axes in with every step in order to prevent being swept down. With the wind pushing us from the back and a fallen man pulling below, it was impossible for the next man to hold, and one by one we were all swept down. It all happened in the fraction of a second. The snow was so hard it was impossible to get our axes in deep enough to hold. We rushed down the steep incline with tremendous speed. Just when or how we hit the crevasse I do not know. The fog was so thick we could not see.

Strobel, at the rear of the line, was the man who slipped; he described it as follows:

> I am unable to say what caused me to lose my footing. I may have been blown over, jerked off my feet, or missed a step. What it was I do not know. As we went down the steep snow and ice I screamed. Greathouse tried to dig his axe in but in vain. In an instant we were all being swept down at a great speed. I got but one glimpse of the side of the crevasse as we went over and in. I welcomed the darkness and the shelter of unconsciousness. When I awakened my first thought was to get from under the individuals piled on top of me. Working through the snow, I managed to get from under and release myself from the rope.

Then, continuing Brigham's report:

> When I regained consciousness Strobel was the only one moving. As

soon as he was able to free himself of the rope I ordered him to try and find a way out and go for help. I never saw or heard from him again until I reached Muir some hours later. Greathouse was laying on his side and never moved. I rolled him partly over and worked on him without avail. Very slow and weak breathing was the only visible sign of life. I next cut Weatherly free from the ledge upon which he was pinned. As soon as I chipped the ice and snow away he was able to move a little. The rope was taut and I managed to cut it loose.

Bradshaw was able to move his hands and feet, though he seemed to be entirely out of his head, talking, mumbling, and groaning. Wetzel regained consciousness but was unable to stand. He said that he was entirely spent. Bradshaw and I crawled along a ledge until we saw light, and by cutting steps we managed to crawl along a narrow ledge above. Helping one another to work our way up to the opening with Weatherly following, I instructed Wetzel to keep moving his hands and feet, left all the food there, and told him to get Greathouse to moving his hands and feet should he regain consciousness.

. . . It is impossible to judge the exact time that we were in the crevasse. It was at least two hours. Nine hours were required to make the trip from the crevasse to Muir, and in crawling most of the way, Bradshaw and I were unconscious a good part of the time.

Strobel's departure from the accident scene and return to Camp Muir for help are narrated by him as follows:

We were all in a terrible daze and had to move very slowly. We realized that there was extreme danger of the great blocks of snow and ice coming in from overhead or the false floor that we were resting on caving through. All about us was porous, rotten snow and ice. Some seventy-five feet above and to the right I could see light, so I began working my way up over the grade to what was evidently a plug in the great crevasse. Finally I reached an opening on the lower side from which I could see Camp Comfort. I yelled to the others that I had found a way out, but I doubted if they could follow me as I had better use of my arms and legs than they. The wind was howling so that I doubt if they heard me. I had to cross two snow bridges and jump two other crevasses in order to get to Comfort. From there I worked my way down Gibraltar and on to Muir. When I was telling the men at Muir about our experiences I again lost consciousness.

Once the news of the accident had been carried by Harry Webster to Paradise, a rescue operation was quickly activated under the control of Chief Guide Cunningham and the Park Superintendent. Ranger Charlie Browne already was at Muir, having arrived late on the same day as the climbing party; he had gone up to make a check of the Park Service equipment and facilities. Immediately upon arrival of Strobel at Muir, Browne had hastened alone up the mountain, passing Brigham and Bradshaw on the Gibraltar ledge as they painfully made their way down for help.

Within an hour after Webster brought the news, a rescue party left on horses for Camp Muir. In the party were John Davis (Paradise District Ranger), guides Johnny Day, Jerrold Ballaine, and Nuls Widman and four others. This group was followed later by two small teams.

The first rescue group reached Muir at 5 p.m. and headed up with stretchers, ropes, and first-aid supplies. Above Muir they met Brigham and Bradshaw who, although both badly injured, urged the rescue group to hurry to the accident scene. At Camp Misery (start of Gibraltar ledge) they came across Weatherly, who had been helped down the ice chute at the upper end of Gibraltar by Ranger Browne.

Earlier on the tragic day, Charlie Browne had proceeded on his solitary rescue mission above Camp Muir. After passing Brigham and Bradshaw near Camp Misery, and assisting Weatherly down the chutes below Camp Comfort, Browne climbed through the storm to the crevasse to attempt to help the remaining two climbers, Greathouse and Wetzel. After hearing no signs of life in the deep hole, Browne noted tracks from the crevasse heading toward the Ingraham Glacier. Following these a half mile down the Ingraham, he found Wetzel unconscious, his clothing nearly torn from his body, and apparently breathing his last. Browne could not move Wetzel so he dug a trench in the snow and rolled him into the hole to keep him from falling farther down the steep glacier. Browne took 2 hours step-cutting to regain the top of Gibraltar Rock before returning to Camp Muir, and then to Paradise, which he reached at 9:30 p.m.

The rescue group that had arrived at Muir that night continued up the mountain in darkness. Lacking knowledge of which crevasse contained the remaining accident victims, they were forced to examine each one they crossed. After 3 hours of futile effort the party returned to Muir.

The search efforts were continued next day when Charlie Browne led another party to Muir. Besides Browne, the group included two guides, Ken Olson and Frank "Swede" Willard, and Orville Pound, Monty Snider, and Paul A. Williams (visiting Sierra Club climber). This group hoped to cross Cathedral Rocks to the Ingraham Glacier to recover Wetzel's body.

In the meantime the party led by Day returned to the upper slopes, found Wetzel's body and brought it down to Camp Muir. En route to Muir the body slipped from the grasp of the party and fell into another crevasse. It was retrieved by Willard, Day, and Ben Smith. Wetzel's remains were then carried to Paradise, reached at 10:30 p.m., July 3.

Several efforts were made in subsequent days to recover the body of Greathouse, still deep in the crevasse. Two guides requested further attempts be abandoned to prevent further loss of life.

However, on July 6, at 3 p.m., 4 days after the accident, Major

Tomlinson, Superintendent of Mount Rainier National Park, a large party of rangers, guides, and experienced Northwest mountaineers to the accident scene under the leadership of Charlie Browne.

On July 7 at 5:30 a.m. Browne's party, with W. T. Hukari of the Hood River Crag Rats, left Camp Muir and arrived at the crevasse at 8 a.m. They immediately saw the crevasse floor had caved in and Greathouse's body was now even more deeply buried by snow and ice. At considerable personal risk, Browne was lowered into the crevasse. At 8:40 a.m., about 80 feet down, he located the body and after 20 minutes of chopping away snow and ice was able to free the body and attach it to ropes lowered from above. The remains of guide Forrest G. Greathouse were brought back to Camp Muir, then to Paradise that evening. The notch between Cathedral Rocks and Gibraltar Rock, through which the bodies of Greathouse and Wetzel were evacuated, has since been grimly referred to as Cadaver Gap.

Injuries suffered by the survivors of the fall: Brigham—severance of two ribs, two scalp wounds, cuts on face, neck, and lower back, shock and exposure; Weatherly—cuts on chest and buttocks, sprain of lower back, shock; Bradshaw—broken left jawbone, cuts on face and chest, bruises, shock and exposure; Strobel—bruises and cuts.

For his leadership in the rescue operation and his part in recovery of the bodies Ranger Browne was awarded the first citation for heroism ever given by the Department of the Interior.

To learn the causes of the accident, an evaluation was made by all concerned, at the request of Superintendent Tomlinson. A major result of the tragic lesson was the requiring of caulked or nailed boots or crampons for both guides and clients on the summit ascents. The use of alpenstocks was still permitted, however, until after World War II.

Recovery of Greathouse's body from crevasse.

Ranger Charlie Browne.

24 A Slip on the Upper
Nisqually: Zinn, 1931

The Greathouse accident was still fresh in the memories of Northwest climbers when another tragedy occurred near the same place. The conditions that precipitated the two accidents were entirely different, however, and the 1931 tragedy involved an unroped two-man non-guided party.

The weekend of July 4 began with prospects for a large number of climbers trying for the summit from Camp Muir. To reserve enough bunk space in the cabins, Chief Guide Cunningham sent Henry Swanson ahead on the morning of the 4th. The guide party, led by Nulsen Widman, was small and composed of two guides and three clients. Upon their arrival at Muir at 6:30 they found both cabins filled, with three to four to a bunk, some on the floor and on the roof, and many sleeping in the protection of small rock windbreaks outside the cabins; in all about 80-85 people were at Muir that night. Guide Widman noted many were poorly equipped, some had boots without caulks, and some had rented what gear they had from the Guide House. A few climbers were wearing only shorts.

A strong northwest wind the next morning discouraged many from leaving Muir and only the guided party and four other parties of three, four, nine, and two each left for the summit. Widman's group started about 2 a.m., following the independent groups that had left at midnight or soon after. It was clear, cold, and windy above a cloud layer at about 8000 feet and Widman had to chop steps in places from Muir up.

The party of nine, mostly Mazamas led by Clem Blakeney, and the two-man party of Kenneth and Robert Zinn moved slowly and the guide party overtook them below Camp Misery; from there on the independent (non-guided) parties were able to follow the guide party close behind. The Mazamas were using a ¾-inch cotton rope, with three members not tied in, while the unroped Zinn brothers were following in the footsteps of the Mazamas. Only two in these parties wore crampons, three carried axes, and the rest had alpenstocks. As the three groups ascended the chutes a strong wind carried down small particles of rock and ice. One large stone struck guide Swanson and he fell unconscious for a few minutes with a small scalp wound. After a quick recovery he was able to proceed.

All went well until the guide party was about 800 feet from the summit crater. A sudden cry drew their attention to the two men below the Blakeney party sliding down the icy slopes. One of the men disappeared from view over the rolls of the summit dome, while the other came to a stop. Widman quickly unroped and hurried down 300 feet, arriving in time to help the fallen man, Kenneth Zinn, to his feet.

Zinn, of Portland, Oregon, said the other man was his brother Robert. Robert had been at the end of the line of climbers and apparently was too exhausted to continue, so requested he be allowed to return to camp alone. After being advised by Blakeney not to go down, but to remain at this point on the slope while the other parties continued to the summit, Robert Zinn sat down on the snow. Almost immediately he started sliding. Kenneth attempted to catch him and slid a short distance before coming to a stop. Robert's slide went unchecked and he gained momentum steadily. He slid from about 13,700 feet to about 12,000 feet in a linear distance of about 3400 feet. He struck the badly broken part of the Nisqually Glacier immediately above the ice cliff opposite the upper end of the Gibraltar ledge. What had happened to him was not readily apparent as the guide party, the Mazamas, and the other parties descended to search.

A part of Zinn's alpenstock was found first, in a crevasse 700 feet below where the slip started, then a pair of scissors from his first-aid kit. Clem Blakeney was lowered into one crevasse but could find no sign of the climber. In the belief that Zinn's body had bounced and fallen over the 200-foot ice cliff, the parties returned to Camp Misery. Guide Swanson hurried down to Paradise to report the accident, arriving there at 1:25 p.m.

A search party headed by District Ranger Charlie Browne (hero of the 1929 tragedy) left Paradise at 4:30 p.m. Included in the party were Chief Ranger John Davis, veteran guide Frank "Swede" Willard, the young second-year guide William J. "Bill" Butler, and two horse guides and a Park Company employee. The ensuing operation was to mark for Bill Butler the beginning of 30 years of heroic rescue efforts on Mount Rainier.

Browne's party left Camp Muir at 2 a.m., Monday, July 6 and traversed across to the broad area below the Nisqually ice cliff. They searched the entire cirque but could find no trace of the missing climber. They returned to Muir at 6:30 a.m.

On July 7 the search was resumed. Chief Ranger Davis and Ranger Browne became ill at Camp Misery and had to return to Muir; Browne placed Bill Butler in charge of operations above. Butler's party continued up to 13,000 feet, then descended along the approximate line of the fall, looking into every crevasse enroute. Butler was lowered into three or four crevasses and found articles in each—gloves, hat, toothbrush, first-aid kit, and glasses. Above the Nisqually ice cliff the imprint of a body was found in the snow surface, indicating the fall of the body into a nearby crevasse. About 75 feet above the edge of the cliff Willard noted a hand visible in a deep crevasse—tears filled the eyes of all as they came to the end of the long search. With a parka, Willard signalled up and down three times to H. B. Cunningham, watching through a telescope at Paradise. Cunningham responded with a mirror flash.

Butler and Willard were lowered into the crevasse. They found the body badly broken and frozen around an ice pinnacle. Considerable time was required to chop loose and bring up the 208-pound body of Zinn from the icy vault. It was left in the snow nearby for the night as the weary party returned to Muir. The following day Butler and Willard led a group of eight climbers upward, back to the body for further evacuation. While descending the upper Cowlitz Glacier below The Beehive and moving the body in pendulum swings across the slopes, a rope slipped loose at one point and the body slid down the glacier into a 125-foot crevasse. Again Butler was lowered into the hole for the recovery, refusing to allow others to take the risks. The body was then carried to McClure Rock where it was returned to Paradise by horse.

In describing the search later, Willard reported that "Bill Butler should be highly commended for his excellent leadership and work. He kept his head at all times and took the most dangerous jobs willingly." For their part in recovering Zinn's body, Willard and Butler received high commendation from the Secretary of the Interior.

The Park Service inquiry determined that both the Blakeney party and the Zinn brothers were poorly equipped and, although they had registered at the Paradise Ranger Station, no close examination had been made of their equipment; some of the climbers were observed by guide Widman putting caulks in their boots at Camp Muir the night before the climb. At that time the regulations required boots with caulks, hobnails, tricouni nails, or crampons, and an ice axe or alpenstock.

Information given to me by Portland photographer Ray Atkeson in April 1969 throws some light on the summit-climb registration in those early days, which seems to be similar to the recently revised system now in use. According to Atkeson, the ranger checkouts were strict and designed to keep track of who was on the mountain. Atkeson was in the three-man party that had been in the lead at the time of the accident. Following the tragic slip of Zinn down the mountain, Atkeson's group helped belay several of the unroped climbers down the ice chute near the top of Gibraltar Rock. Atkeson stated that, while being checked out for the climb the day before, no close observation was made by the rangers of the number of ropes in each party probably because they were preoccupied in observing through binoculars the movements of five climbers high on the summit dome—these climbers had not registered for the ascent. Upon meeting the group of five at Camp Muir later in the day, Atkeson noted they had no rope and only one alpenstock among them and that at least two wore tennis shoes. It had been a warm day and the climbers reported they had no trouble with cold feet high on the mountain.

In a semi-comical adventure only 2 weeks later, a soldier who was AWOL from Fort Lewis complained of a heart attack while climbing with a party above Camp Muir. After a rescue party carried him back to Paradise he was confronted by his commanding officer. The unsympathetic officer, apparently with an accurate insight of the young man's character, ordered him to walk from the Guide House to the Lodge, then returned him to Fort Lewis for KP duty.

25 Solo Winter Ascent: Fadden, 1936

Few mountain tragedies in the Pacific Northwest held the public attention so long as that which befell 22-year old Delmar Fadden during his solitary winter climb in late January of 1936. The story took 2 weeks to unfold to its climax as nation-wide news coverage kept the public informed of events high on the icy slopes.

At 5 p.m. on January 20, 1936 Chief Ranger John M. Davis received a radio message from a winter seasonal employee, Larry Jensen, at the White River Entrance Station. Jensen reported a young man, Donald Fadden, had visited the station, saying his twin brother Delmar had not returned from a week of solitary skiing at Glacier Basin. Upon this word of a possible missing person, Davis directed District Ranger Oscar A. Sedergren and Ranger Bill Butler to collect their gear for a trip to the basin. Also notified was White River District Ranger Charlie Browne, who was in Seattle on leave at the time.

Davis, Sedergren, and Butler left Longmire for White River early on January 21. There they met Donald Fadden, who said his brother had gone to Glacier Basin to ski, snowshoe, paint, and sketch, and that he might hike up to Steamboat Prow. He said Delmar had gone by the ranger station at 11 p.m. the week before in his solitary trek into the Park. With this information, and after a brief stop at the ranger station, Browne, Davis, Sedergren, and Butler continued on snowshoes to the White River Campground, which was reached at dark. From there they were able to maintain radio communication with Larry Jensen at the ranger station. They noted Fadden's tracks went past the patrol cabin without approaching it.

The next day, January 22, they continued on Fadden's tracks to Glacier Basin, noting where he had spent a night or two at an old mine cabin at Storbo Camp. Evidence of food and cooking suggested Fadden had left the cabin not later than January 19. The search party continued as far as the lower end of Inter Glacier, then returned to White River Campground. It was there they learned by radio from Jensen that Donald Fadden said his brother was carrying a supply of wands to mark the route up the mountain and might have gone for the summit.

Early on the morning of January 23 the group ascended to Steamboat Prow, finding two wands in the snow a little way above. It was bitter cold and they retreated, searching down the north edge of the Emmons Glacier to about 4800 feet before crossing over the ridge to

Glacier Basin and returning to the White River Campground long after dark. Radio contact with Longmire advised them another search party was enroute from Seattle, all men experienced on Rainier.

On January 24 Jack Hossack and Bob Buschman, a close climbing friend of Fadden, headed for Summerland to check the shelter for signs of the missing man; Ome Daiber and Joe Halwax set out for the White River Campground; Sedergren, Butler, and Browne climbed to Yakima Park. Browne remained at Yakima Park to observe the summit area with the powerful telescope mounted there, while the next day Butler and Sedergren hiked to Mystic Lake to check the shelter cabin. Hossack and Buschman found no signs of Fadden at Summerland, so proceeded up the mountain to Steamboat Prow by way of the lower Emmons Glacier. The journey was a long one and they spent a night on the glacier before meeting Daiber and Halwax at the Prow next morning.

On January 26 Butler and Sedergren returned from Mystic Lake, while Daiber, Buschman, Hossack, and Halwax climbed above Steamboat Prow. They found two more wands, then two snowshoes, separated. At 11,000 feet they began searching crevasses but an approaching storm drove them back to Glacier Basin. Next day all returned to Seattle except Butler, Davis, Browne, and Sedergren, who remained at the entrance station to await further word following a proposed flight over the mountain by Daiber.

On January 29, from a small plane piloted by Elliott Merrill, Ome Daiber and photographer Charles Laidlow spotted the body of Delmar Fadden lying on the upper slope of the Emmons Glacier at about 13,000 feet. The long search was over—now a difficult evacuation remained.

Sites of tragedies on upper slopes of Mount Rainier, 1929–57.

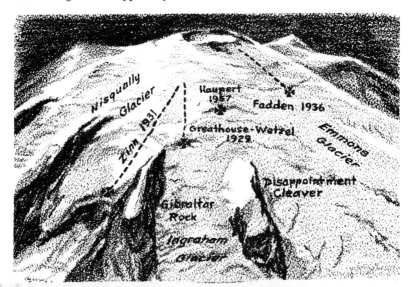

Delmar Fadden.
Fadden's body as found frozen on upper Emmons Glacier.

A large party including packers and climbers gathered the next day, and with long delays enroute, arrived at Glacier Basin about midnight. After a short rest the group headed up the mountain at 5:30 a.m. Skis took them a couple of miles, then hard snow necessitated the donning of crampons for the ascent to Steamboat Prow. At the Prow a recovery party was roped as follows: Daiber-Davis-Gilbreath; Butler-Buschman. The glacier surface was windpacked and easy traveling, but when the sun went behind the mountain the temperature dropped rapidly to 0°F and below. The body was reached by Daiber, Buschman, and Gilbreath (Davis had tired and re-roped with Butler) at 3:10 p.m.; Butler and Davis arrived a few minutes later.

Fadden was found face down, head downslope, solidly frozen. The crampon on his left foot was missing; his other crampon was partly off the toe of his soft-soled muckluck boot (an eskimo boot coming above the knee). His hands were bare, he had no axe, his mouth and nostrils were filled with snow. It was apparent he had suffered a fall, been knocked out, then froze to death without regaining consciousness.

The body was lashed into a canvas tarp and lowered by the five weary, cold men down the steep glacier. Great difficulty was encountered owing to the awkward weight, roughness of the surface, and very cold temperatures. The body was continually anchored during the descent to prevent it from slipping loose. A little moonlight helped after dark and the Prow was reached at 7:15 p.m. The body was left there for the night as the tired party returned to Glacier Basin, all badly frostbitten, Gilbreath so much so he continued hiking out even though near exhaustion. Wendell Trosper, who had come up to the Prow with Harland Eastwood to assist the evacuation, was also severely frostbitten and accompanied Gilbreath back to Seattle for treatment.[1]

On February 1 a support party returned to the Prow for the body, which was carried down on a toboggan. The following day marked the end of the long ordeal as Fadden's still solidly frozen remains were placed in a hearse waiting at the White River Ranger Station.

As an aftermath to the tragic affair, a roll of film found in Fadden's pocket was developed. It showed views across the summit crater and verified the belief he had made the top and met his death on the descent. The cloud and lighting conditions in the photos were compared with weather records of the previous 2 weeks and indicated he probably had reached the summit January 17. The summer after Fadden's death, Arnie Campbell and Jim Borrow followed the youth's trail markers to the summit and located his camp in the crater. According to Campbell (written communication, January 1969), the number of empty cans lying about gave evidence Fadden had spent several days on the summit.

Ranger Butler's part in the heroic search and evacuation operations was recognized by his being given permanent appointment as Park ranger by President Roosevelt. Several efforts were made by public-spirited citizens to reward those taking part in the lengthy search operation, but when one prominent businessman attempted to capitalize on the project the climbers withdrew from further participation.

In retrospect we might ask: what manner of man was Delmar Fadden? What sort of person would venture alone to the summit of

Photos from film found in Fadden's camera. Left: view down Emmons Glacier to Little Tahoma; right: view across crater.

[1]See footnote on p. 253

Rainier in the middle of winter? With these queries in mind after perusing Park records of the climb decades later, in 1969 I had the pleasure of a visit with Fadden's sister, Mrs. George Gilbert, and his older brother Gene; Delmar's twin brother Don was in Alaska at the time. I was provided full access to Delmar's photo albums and scrapbooks of the 1930s and gained an insight into the young man's character and aspirations.

From his early childhood in the Seahurst area of southwestern King County, Delmar displayed an unusually energetic interest in outdoor activities of all kinds, but particularly in mountaineering. He was a talented artist and writer and very popular at Highline High School. As a Boy Scout he had worked his way to Eagle rank. In 1930 and 1931, in company with two companions on each occasion, he made his first extended climbing trips into the Olympic Mountains. The notations in his photo album give itemized lists of food, equipment, and clothing used on each trip. The following summer, from July 31 to August 29, Fadden made a highly publicized solo trek across the Olympic Mountains.

Stating that he was going unarmed—"to see things, not shoot things"—Fadden started his hike from Lake Quinault under a 56-pound pack which held all he considered necessary, including a few fishhooks, and a camera "to get close-ups of a cougar and Mount Olympus in the moonlight." To spice the adventure, after his parents had driven to the lake and departed, Fadden deliberately destroyed his compass and a few days later burned his map ("I'm free! Whoopee!") He then crossed several passes and climbed a few peaks, including Mounts Tom and Olympus, the latter ascent timed for a night on the summit during full moon. At the end of the 30-day trip the youth arrived at the mouth of Big Quilcene River on Hood Canal, barely recognizable to his parents after losing 30 of his normal 160 pounds. To augment his food supply Fadden had stoned several grouse and during the final days he had survived on plant bulbs, frogs, and polliwogs. The journey had its rough moments of near-starvation and of rain and lightning storms, but Fadden's poetic bent was undismayed:

> It isn't raining rain to me,
> No pretty daffodils.
> It's just raining misery
> With pains and aches and chills.

Fadden first responded to the challenge of Rainier in 1931, when he hiked to Steamboat Prow from Sunrise via Burroughs Mountain. The following year on October 7–8 Fadden and a friend, Bert Kattron, repeated the climb to the Prow, where Kattron remained while Fadden continued alone to about 12,000 feet on the heavily crevassed glacier of early autumn. He turned back owing to lateness of the hour, but his photo album clearly shows the icy conditions; he made several explorations into shallow crevasses. A week later, following the first heavy snowfall of the season, Fadden returned to the route with Bob Buschman. Wintry conditions, and the fresh snow covering the crevasses that had been so widely exposed the previous week, stopped the two at the Prow. Near there they spent the night huddled in one sleeping bag at the bottom of a crevasse. Fadden's album notations read: "Slept at the bottom of this crevice—cold! Shoes froze (not oiled), took ½ hr. to get them on—had to warm them in bed; gloves like bent wire or steel clamped on ice pick just where I left them last night. 2 slept in one sleeping bag—broke side—wet, freezing, snow—What a night; can of half frozen beans for supper." Fadden's desire for exploration was not dampened, however. He added: "Bob tied rope to me and lowered me further down in to another ice cave where I snapped this picture. Only little light. Notice snow mound which sifted in from hole above."

Fadden came back to the mountain with Buschman December 26–27, 1932, this time via the south side. They climbed to Anvil Rock but were again rebuffed by bad weather. The following year, on September 1–2, 1933, Fadden finally realized his goal—a solo ascent to the summit via the Emmons Glacier. Because his film of the climb turned out blank, he returned the next weekend. Leaving Sunrise at midnight, he climbed to the Prow in 4 hours by way of Burroughs Mountain and Inter Glacier and reached Columbia Crest at 10 a.m., exactly 10 hours from the parking lot. After 2 hours on the summit, during which he took a photo of himself by means of a cord attached to the camera, he started down. He reached Sunrise at 6 p.m., completing an impressive, though unpublicized, 18-hour round trip of this very long route.

Though the weather was good on the summit, Fadden included notations in his album that describe the descent of the Emmons Glacier in fog:

Clouds obscure crevasses such as this one until immediately upon it. Fortunately I was following my footsteps—But to come upon such a scene further up the mt. is most confusing. You don't know which way to follow it. And as I found I chose the wrong direction back on the mt. and came near coming down the Emmons Glac. (too far to south). Bad business—traveling in fog. I got lost on Burroughs Mtn. and wandered around for 2½ hours.

In 1934 Fadden began his efforts to attain Rainier's summit in winter:

It has long been my determination to scale the mount & when I could get no one to try with me, I willingly went alone. Although unsuccessful because of weather, I am all the more confident of Future success . . . Dec. 27, hiked to Prow alone, deep snow, wearying trip, broke snowshoes, 60 lb pack, slept in snow, very cold. Began hike 10 PM, planned to reach Starbo at dawn, but deep snow prevented this . . . it seemed hopeless to continue; yet to turn back before I had actually begun was ugly to me . . . Reached Starbo on 3rd day after dark. Cleared up, continued to Prow for night there. Returned next day.

Delmar Fadden's life was cut short at its prime, but his soul doubtless would have had it no other way. Many lines in his scrapbook reveal his deep passion for the quiet beauty of dark forests, starry skies, winter storms, and icy heights. Perhaps he anticipated his manner of passing:

> If a dream
> Meant anything to me
> Would it seem
> A bold reality?
>
> If I knew
> My hand of fate,
> Would I do—
> Or hesitate?

Footnote to p. 250

Several well-known Northwest climbers and skiers played significant roles in the perilous midwinter evacuation of Fadden's remains from high on the mountain. Among those bringing the body down from Steamboat Prow to the White River Ranger Station were Harland Eastwood, a powerful, one-armed mountaineer who served as patrol ranger at the White River Campground during the early 1930s, and Ken Syverson, who ran the ski school at Paradise in those days. Along with The Mountaineers' Amos Hand, Tacoma, and the Park Service's Art Collins, Charles Drysdale, Don Loehrke, and Dan Pryde, they worked in temperatures reported by Wendell Trosper as "pushing the mercury to the bottom" of a thermometer that recorded to minus 25°F. (57 degrees below freezing).

It is interesting to note that during the summer of 1986 Harland Eastwood, 80, was back at his old stomping grounds in the Park, reoccupying the log patrol cabin of his youth at the White River Campground. There, with his wife Esther, he served as a volunteer-assistant in the Park Service's VIPS program (Volunteers in Parks) and he had a chance to relive some old memories. Doubtless, his venerable presence in the campground, along with his anecdotes of early-day search and rescue trips on the mountain, provided an added dimension to the campers' enjoyment of the Park.

26 Collapse of a Snowbridge: Haupert, 1957

It was to be the last guided climb of the summer of 1957. The weather was favorable over the Labor Day weekend and the guide route up the Ingraham Glacier above Camp Muir had been in good shape for the many parties that had used it during the previous 2½ months. Guide Gary Rose was to head the party, while I went along to assist him—I occasionally guided during weekends that summer.

Our group of 12 left Paradise about noon on Saturday, August 31, and reached Camp Muir in good time at about 5 p.m. Leaving Muir at 2:30 the following morning, we were tied into three ropes as follows: Gary Rose-Bill Haupert-Robert Burgess-Nadine Nuttley; Fred Tuttle-Kirk Stromberg-Don McLane-Bob West; me-Dr. J. H. Lehmann-Mrs. and Mr. Bob Michael. The night had been unusually warm; some had enjoyed sleeping outside on the cabin roof.

Although composed of two women and several inexperienced men, the group moved up the mountain rapidly. As the eastern sky pinkened and the sun rose there were indications it would be an unusually fine, warm day, even at the higher altitudes. Eventually we shed parkas and sweaters and young Bill Haupert stripped bare to the waist. Being well-tanned from a summer with the U.S. Forest Service in Idaho, it hardly seemed necessary for him to apply sun cream.

By about 8:30 a.m. we had climbed above Disappointment Cleaver and reached 13,000 feet, about 1½ hours below the crater rim. Several steep rolls in the summit ice dome were crossed as we followed the wide track well-marked from the many previous climbs of the summer. Gary Rose was leading the first rope up one of the rolls, the slope being about 50 feet high and at an angle of about 30°.

Suddenly the entire slope shuddered and we heard a dull thud. Glancing up, we saw the lower half of the steep roll breaking up and dropping into a broad chasm, Rose and Haupert disappearing amidst falling blocks of ice and snow. The rope tightened on Burgess and Miss Nuttley, who dug their axes into the snow. Our two lower rope teams quickly moved up to give support as the ice dust finally settled in the newly exposed crevasse. I unroped and hurried to the lower edge, calling for Gary and Bill. Gary's voice came back, saying he was alright but that Haupert was buried.

The hole revealed was about 100-150 feet long and 15 feet across,

254

with the upper wall of the crevasse about 15-20 feet above the lower lip. Fallen ice blocks filled the hole to within 8 feet of the lower lip. As I reached the crevasse Rose was free of the snow and was hurriedly digging with his hands at a block of ice that covered Haupert; only his arm was showing. In a few minutes we uncovered his head and upper body. He was bleeding slightly at the mouth but was conscious and said he had broken a couple of teeth. He also complained his neck hurt and asked us to support his neck and head. He had no feeling in his legs and asked that they be straightened out once he was freed from the debris.

Dr. J. H. Lehmann and two others also climbed into the crevasse. The doctor's examination indicated Bill had suffered a broken back or damaged spinal cord. Because the upper lip of the crevasse hung menacingly over us, we deemed it wise to remove Haupert to safer ground on the slope below. A packframe was placed beneath his back and four or five of the party carefully carried him from the crevasse and placed him in a shallow trough dug in the snow. Dr. Lehmann administered one capsule of morphine and soon Bill dozed off. It was 8:50 a.m., about 20 minutes after the accident.

Since it was apparent a stretcher evacuation was necessary and more manpower was needed, Tuttle and I hurried down to Camp Muir. Enroute we met other climbers who hastened up the mountain to render aid in the form of a tent, extra sleeping bags and clothing, a stove, and food. At Muir a radio message was sent to Park Headquarters at Longmire, requesting helicopter assistance if possible near the 13,000-foot level, or an airdrop of stretcher and food. Park Headquarters immediately telephoned Ome Daiber of the Mountain Rescue Council in Seattle, who in turn contacted the U.S. Coast Guard Air-Sea Rescue Unit for information on helicopters capable of attaining that altitude. Unfortunately none was in the Northwest at the time; planes then were assigned to airdrop the requested supplies.

In the meantime, while a ranger-guide group started up from Paradise, the party at the crevasse was joined by the other climbers and a tent was set up over Haupert. At 2:30, leaving Dr. Lehmann and one of the climbers from the other party with Haupert, Gary Rose led the remainder of his clients back to Muir. Enroute he rejoined me and members of an advance rescue team that had come up from Paradise (Chief Guide Dick McGowan, Jack Melill, Bob Barton, Bob Bodenburg, Bob Kennedy, Bob Rogers, Louis Kirk, Keith Miller, Doug Evans, and Jim Ellis). As we started back up the glacier we met two of a party of four Austrian climbers who said the other two had retrieved one of the stretchers dropped on the upper slopes by a circling U.S. Coast Guard plane. Soon after, we met the other two Austrians, who gave us the sad news that Bill Haupert had passed away a short time earlier, at 5:40 p.m.

The evacuation of Haupert's body to the crest of Disappointment Cleaver was made that night. The following day a large team of climbers lowered him down Disappointment Cleaver onto lower Ingraham Glacier and back to Camp Muir. From there the remains were carried by horse to Paradise.

In personal retrospection on the death of the handsome young man, I can see no way the sad event might have been averted. In the American Alpine Club's annual accident report a statement was made that perhaps Haupert's inexperience resulted in his being unable to skillfully avoid the falling ice blocks or to land more safely. However, in witnessing the accident from the slope below, I can testify that in no way would it have been possible for a climber to control his fall among the large fragments of ice. In anticipation of future such collapses of the ice underlying the steep undulations of the upper Emmons and Ingraham Glaciers, it might be well for a party to surmount them as near their ends as is feasible, particularly during abnormally warm days.

27 Triple Summit Tragedy: Bressler, Horn, and Carman, 1959

Near the end of the summer of 1959 a tragedy on the summit of Mount Rainier claimed the lives of a climber stricken with pulmonary edema and two flyers who attempted to drop oxygen to him at the summit camp. A week of storm followed the deaths and the evacuation of the climber's body required the efforts of several rescue teams at different times.

Dr. Calder T. "Tup" Bressler, geology professor at Western Washington State College in Bellingham, had a long record of climbs throughout the Cascade Range. In the 1930s Bressler was one of a close-knit group of friends who formed the Ptarmigan Climbing Club and made numerous explorations and first ascents in the North Cascades. Among their achievements that gained lasting fame was the first traverse along the Cascade Crest between Sulphur Creek and Cascade Pass, since labeled the "Ptarmigan Traverse."

In late August 1959 Bressler was invited by Dr. Maynard M. Miller, director of the study, "Project Crater," to visit the summit camp on Rainier. Bressler had been active during the summer and had no trouble reaching the top. The next afternoon, after a night at the tent camp on the rim of the west crater, he complained of feeling rather enervated. He went to bed early. At 4:30 a.m. Barry Prather noted Bressler was groaning.

A radio-telephone call to the project's physician, Dr. T. R. "Ted" Haley in Tacoma, resulted in diagnosis of possible pulmonary edema. Oxygen at camp was administered but by afternoon Bressler was in a coma.

Late in the evening of September 2, after early efforts to reach camp failed, pilot Harold L. Horn, who had been airdropping supplies to the camp during the summer, prepared to fly requested additional oxygen cylinders to the summit. With him as passenger was Charles R. Carman. Making a late start from the airport, they finally circled the summit of the peak near twilight. The accident was not observed by those at camp, but when the plane failed to make the drop and did not return to the airport, a message was radioed down the mountain. Possibly a sudden downdraft, coupled with fading visibility, caused the small plane to dive into the summit snowfield, where it was found a few days later immediately east of Point Success.

At dawn the following day Tup Bressler quietly passed away. Evacuation of the body soon began but a storm struck the party on the Ingraham Glacier and the body had to be left while the group descended to Camp Muir. For the next week the storm piled new snow on the peak, covering the downed aircraft and Bressler. During a brief clearing a party returned to the Ingraham Glacier and after considerable probing found the body beneath 4 feet of fresh snow. The remains were then transported to Paradise.

Nearly a week passed before the weather cleared sufficiently to allow a ground party to search for the plane. Finally it was spotted from the air, only a few inches of one tire showing above the flat surface of the summit snowfield a short distance east of Point Success. The ground party was led by Bill Butler and included Maynard Miller, Dave Mahre, Barry Prather, Don Jones, Nile Albright, Dave Potter, and me. We were guided to the site from the air and found the plane on its back, both occupants apparently having died on impact. Owing to the difficulty of evacuating the frozen remains from the plane, they were left at the crash site high on Rainier (*Harvard Mountaineering*, 1961).

28 Death Near Liberty Cap: Chamay, 1968

Until 1968 all tragic endings to summit climbs of Rainier had come on the well-traveled southern flanks, mostly on the Gibraltar route. The first tragedy to occur on a north-wall route was that on the upper part of Liberty Ridge which claimed the life of Seattle climber Pat Chamay. The following account of his death from high-altitude pulmonary edema is taken from a report to the Park Superintendent by Ray Smutek.

The climbing party, consisting of Chamay, Ian Wade, Dave Hambly, and Smutek, registered for the climb at the White River Entrance Station on Friday, June 21, 1968. The group's intended route was Liberty Ridge.

Because of rain the departure was delayed until Saturday morning. At about 8 a.m. they left Sunrise in foggy but calm weather, climbed over Burroughs Mountain and descended to St. Elmo Pass, and crossed the Winthrop Glacier. On the glacier they met another party also aiming for Liberty Ridge; the two groups remained in close contact during most of the climb. They traversed the lower slopes of Curtis Ridge, dropped onto the Carbon Glacier, and ascended to near the base of the ridge. The two parties climbed to the notch above Thumb Rock, where they camped at 10,500 feet. Everyone was tired but not unduly so.

At 7 o'clock on the morning of June 22, the Chamay party began the ascent of the upper part of the ridge about half an hour behind the other party. They traveled at a normal pace to about 12,000 feet, where Chamay began to slow down. By the time they reached 13,000 feet he was showing signs of extreme fatigue. At that point the other group began to pull away and eventually disappeared over the crest of Liberty Cap. Since the terrain was easing, the Chamay party continued upward. However, Chamay grew more exhausted and 3 hours were required to reach a flat area about 200 feet below Liberty Cap. The group rested in a small notch near rocks overlooking the Sunset Amphitheater. Chamay asked the party to camp there and await morning to climb over the top. He complained of cold feet and was concerned about frostbite.

There was no indication of anything more serious than fatigue so Smutek remained with Chamay while Wade and Hambly, to conserve food and fuel, went on to Liberty Cap and down the mountain to Camp Schurman, with instructions to expect Chamay and Smutek the following day. Smutek set up a tent, gave Chamay his heavy sleeping bag for additional warmth, cooked soup for dinner, and filled the water bottles. They retired for the night at about 8 o'clock, with everything apparently in order.

Early Monday morning, June 24, Chamay's heavy breathing awakened Smutek. As Smutek prepared breakfast he became aware Chamay was not responsive to his conversation and was falling into a comatose state. Chamay managed to drink a little sugar-water with assistance, but could do little else.

Smutek went outside and placed ground-to-air signals in the snow, then began a long wait. As morning progressed Chamay's breathing grew louder and at 11 a.m. became syrupy. By 1 p.m. he began to foam from the mouth and nose. Smutek realized his companion was suffering from pulmonary edema and could not survive long without being brought to a lower elevation or being administered oxygen.

At 3:30 p.m., while Smutek was preparing his pack for a descent to Camp Schurman to make radio contact and speed rescue efforts, Chamay stopped breathing. Smutek remained with him another half hour to make sure there were no signs of life; he could detect no pulse or respiration and eye reflexes were totally absent.

After seeing he could be of no further help, Smutek ended his sad vigil and descended to Camp Schurman. Running nearly all the way, and twice breaking through hidden crevasses, he reached the cabin in an hour. There he made radio contact with the ranger station.

Late that evening an Air Force helicopter from McChord Field flew to the mountain and landed near the tent at 14,000 feet. The evacuation of Chamay's body, which required only a few minutes, marked the first such mission to the icy crown of Liberty Cap.

Smutek's comments (written communication, December 1968) are worth noting:

> There is certainly a lesson to be learned from this tragic event. Pulmonary Edema is an insidious disease which may strike anyone. Prior exposure to high elevations is no guarantee of immunity. Pat had climbed Rainier many times. He had done Ptarmigan Ridge, Mowich Face, the Kautz, and the Nisqually during the years I knew him, and I believe he had several ascents before that. He had also been high on McKinley, but acclimatization problems stopped him there. The year before Liberty Ridge, Pat and I did the Nisqually, and he was very strong at the summit. Strangely, I was almost incapacitated by mountain sickness on that climb. Almost in the inverse of the Liberty Ridge situation. Was that a forewarning of pulmonary edema?

29 Rockfall on Curtis Ridge: Dockery, 1969

It was inevitable that sooner or later "the Nordwand" would claim lives among those seeking the toughest challenges on the great peak. The death of Pat Chamay in 1968 was followed early the next summer by the second tragedy on a north-side route.

On June 15, 1969 a nearly completed ascent of Curtis Ridge came to an abrupt end amid a shower of loose rock on a steep slope at 12,000 feet. Killed immediately was George "Tim" Dockery (37); injured were party leader Gary Frederickson (27) and Peter Sandstedt (22); escaping injury were Glen Frederickson (20) and Carl Moore (32). Although the accident occurred late on a clear and warm Sunday afternoon, news of the tragic consequences was not forthcoming until a Mountain Rescue unit made contact with the climbing party 48 hours later. Details of the accident provided later by Gary Frederickson (written communication, June 23, 1969) indicate the party was well-equipped and had made numerous climbs of Rainier by various routes. This particular ascent was in preparation for a planned expedition to the Andes later in the year.

The Frederickson party left the White River Campground Friday afternoon, June 13, and hiked through Glacier Basin and over St. Elmo Pass to camp on the moraine at the edge of the Winthrop Glacier. Here they experienced a spectacular electrical storm followed by heavy rain. Saturday morning the storm had cleared so they continued across the glacier and up Curtis Ridge to the rappel point off the gendarme at 10,400 feet. They noted fresh snow on the upper ridge, which they believed would help cement the loose rocks. After making the rappel they moved up the ridge crest to a bivouac site at 10,700 feet, which was reached at 2 p.m. They scouted the route ahead to the Aid Pitch, then retired to camp. The weather was warm and windless.

Sunday morning dawned clear but a strong cold wind delayed the departure until after 7:30. The Aid Pitch was climbed without difficulty; however, the prussiking was time-consuming and they didn't all complete the pitch until shortly after noon. No rockfall was noted as they continued working their way up the ridge. Then, as extracted from a report by Gary Frederickson (written communication, June 23, 1969):

By 3:30 P.M. we were in the midst of the maze of chutes and gullies leading to the summit snow-finger. At about 12,000′ . . . a route decision was called for, for on the east side of the buttress was a steep, icy gully which became an unknown quantity where it changed angle about 200'-300' above us; and on the west side of the buttress lay a concave, cirque-like bowl which appeared to offer an exit onto the top of the buttress by way of a ledge on the head of the cirque wall. Since we were climbing without crampons and since the latter route appeared to be very straight-forward we decided to try it first. At this point our fate was sealed . . .

As we advanced . . . over rocky, boulder-studded terrain that was becoming increasingly steeper, we were roped into two teams: I was leading the first team which had George in the middle and Pete on the end. Glen and Carl made up the second team which followed below and to one side. At about 4 P.M. and at an elevation of 12,200' I heard the sound of falling rock and twisted around to see two large rocks bounding down upon Pete. In an instant he had been overpowered by the rocks (or rock) and was being thrown backward down the slope.

Although my position didn't offer much protection, I grabbed what I could and hung on for the tug that I knew was coming. And come it did! The shock of the pull so overpowered me that I was pulled off my position as if shot from a slingshot. After the first few violent collisions with the slope and the ensuing bounces I was sure that death was imminent and only hoped that it would be swift and painless. Glen and Carl said that I rocketed by them 15' in the air as the three of us somersaulted down the slope toward the first of a series of terraced cliffs which eventually dropped onto lower Willis Wall and finally onto the Carbon Glacier many thousands of feet below us.

After being knocked nearly senseless, it all stopped, and I was aware of hanging over a shallow cliff. Miraculously we had stopped! After we had fallen nearly 200 vertical feet the rope had snagged around a small nubbin of rock and had held even though cut halfway through. I tested for broken bones and was amazed to find none. Later examination convinced me that my Bell Toptex hardhat had saved my life. I was soon conscious of a tugging at my waist and started to yell for slack. By this time too, I could hear Pete yelling to be lowered but I was concerned by the lack of sound from George's direction. Glen and Carl were soon down to where they could see me. Their matter-of-fact statement that George didn't look good registered without emotion in my dazed mind. After first checking to see that I was all right, they rushed off to secure George so that I could be helped up the cliff and so that they could begin the rather complicated manipulations which were required to lower Pete to the ledge below the cliff he was hanging over.

While securing George, Glen determined that he was dead. Death had likely been instantaneous. During this entire period Pete was yelling and pleading to be lowered. After helping me up the cliff Glen rejoined Carl and they began to help Pete. Although Pete had become incoherent at times, they learned that he had little, if any, use of his arms and decided that the two of them wouldn't be able to raise him up the cliff without assistance. Their only course then was to lower him to the ledge at the foot of the cliff, about 50' below their position. Following this they returned to the rock nubbin where I had been waiting and we held a council of war to determine our next moves.

Frederickson's account then describes the loss of two packs, breakage of their one stove, and an inventory of what clothing, equipment, and food remained. Knowing they would be spending at least one night before their absence was noted and Mountain Rescue personnel would begin the search, they prepared for a long stay on the steep slope. Food and water were lowered to Sandstedt, stranded on the ledge 75 feet below and unable to move his arms. He was out of sight and communication was difficult. To alleviate his solitary ordeal, the others never told him Dockery was dead; this he was not to learn until 2 days later, after he had been rescued.

The Frederickson brothers and Moore dug a small platform on the nose of the ridge, the site protected from rockfall by the nubbin above. The two-man bivouac sack was anchored to the platform and the three crowded inside, tied independent of the shelter to other ropes anchored to rocks above. A fitful night followed, but fortunately it was clear and mild.

The next day (Monday) they spread two pieces of colored material in an "X"—the ground-to-air signal of "unable to proceed." By afternoon the continuing warm weather that had blessed them in the night and provided thirst-quenching snowmelt through the day began loosening rocks, endangering movements about the slope and toward the cliff overlooking Sandstedt.

At 4 p.m. a plane circled, flew toward them a couple times, then winged off without any signals. The climbers learned later only four of them had been spotted—Dockery's dark clothing blended into the rocks. Toward evening they noted helicopter activity around Steamboat Prow but knew it was too late for a daring twilight rescue. The following day (Tuesday) the sky was quiet all morning, causing some concern about progress of rescue efforts. Finally, in the afternoon, helicopters began flying overhead to the summit ice cap high above. About 4 p.m., 48 hours after the accident, they heard a shout from the ridge directly above.

The difficulty of the first rescue-evacuation from the upper rim of Willis Wall was fully envisioned when the climbing party was spotted by a Park ranger party in a plane piloted by Jim Beech of Ashford. Returning to Longmire, the rangers initiated rescue efforts by calling John Simac and arranging for assistance by the Tacoma Mountain Rescue unit. A four-man Park Service team meanwhile was airlifted to Camp Schurman to begin the ascent to the 13,600-foot saddle above Curtis Ridge, where they would be in position for a ground evacuation or to support a helicopter rescue.

Tuesday morning the Park Service team found tough going up the Emmons Glacier. The warm weather (40°F at 7 a.m.) had softened the snow to slush and the rescuers were exhausted when they reached

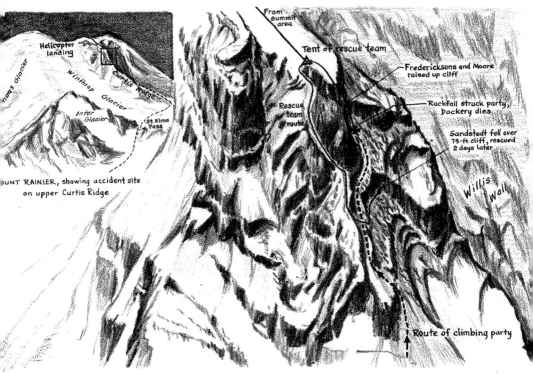

Labels on image:
- Helicopter landing
- Winthrop Glacier
- Curtis Ridge
- Inter Glacier
- St. Elmo Pass
- ...ous Glacier
- ...UNT RAINIER, showing accident site on upper Curtis Ridge
- From summit area
- Tent of rescue team
- Fredericksons and Moore raised up cliff
- Rockfall struck party, Dockery dies
- Sandstedt fell over 75-ft. cliff, rescued 2 days later
- Rescue team route
- Willis Wall
- Route of climbing party

Upper Curtis Ridge detail, showing site of Dockery tragedy.

the summit area about noon. A number of the top climbers in the Northwest were now assembling at Sunrise, awaiting favorable conditions for the helicopters to function at high altitudes in the warm air. Finally, at 2 p.m. Lee Nelson was the first man lifted to the high saddle, followed soon after by Jim Mitchell and Dan Davis. Lee Nelson describes ensuing events:

Jim and I roped up and began the descent to Curtis Ridge. A tent had been erected in the saddle, and a ranger informed me his people were very tired and would follow us later if we needed support. It was about 3 p.m. Jim and I climbed down until we were directly above the stranded climbers. We made voice contact with three sitting together on a small bench below a 150-foot cliff of rotten rock. The leader calmly told us that two of them were uninjured, two were injured but not in need of immediate medical aid, and one was dead . . . Jim Mitchell radioed this information to Sunrise, using the proper code word to report the fatality.

Jim and I unroped so we would not pull rocks loose to endanger the three men who were in the direct fall line below us, then we began a search for a safe route down. The time was 4:30 p.m. I climbed down a steep ice gully to the west of the cliff but unfortunately it terminated at a 50-foot vertical cliff of rotten rock, with no apparent route to the three. As I climbed back I heard a rockslide on the 150-foot cliff. Mitchell said a 50-pound rock narrowly missed the three men. I then requested that a helicopter with a 200-foot cable and "horse collar" be sent in to pick up the climbers below and transport them to a snowfield on the lower Curtis Ridge. A chopper was sent up without the gear to check hovering conditions. The pilot thought the air was too turbulent for a horse-collar pickup.

At this time Dave Mahre and Dan Davis arrived on the scene. Dave, Dan, and I explored the rock ridge to the east of the cliff. This rock was sounder and Dave suggested a rope be lowered from this point to the three below. Other men arrived from above at about 6 p.m. Dave and I roped up and began a search down the east side [Russell Cliff] for a route to Pete Sandstedt, the injured man stranded alone on the lower ledge. We descended via a steep snow traverse onto a ridge, then, protected by one rock piton, we went down a steep ice gully that ran out onto a short nearly vertical rock pitch. Then, after descending a snow finger too far, we backtracked up to the piton pitch where we made voice contact with Sandstedt . . . as it was growing late, another night in his grotto didn't appeal to him.

Dave and I radioed up to Mitchell to check the progress of the evacuation of the upper three men. It was going nicely above; they had hauled one man up and estimated they would have the other two in about 20 minutes. We held our position on the ridge so as not to be clobbered by rockfall from the activity above us. At about 9 p.m. Mitchell radioed down that the upper three climbers had been hauled up and the route above was clear for us to begin our evacuation of Sandstedt. Dave led down the steep gully belayed by me, then I climbed down to Dave where he belayed me as I traversed to the left (west) on a downsloping ledge of loose dry mud and boulders. There was a good view down Willis Wall to the upper Carbon Glacier. I found a large boulder that seemed fairly secure in the dry mud, and belayed Dave over to me. He then belayed while I climbed into the grotto. Pete was happy to see us.

I climbed to within 15 feet of Pete only to be stopped by downsloping boulders and mud covered by 2-6 inches of slippery ice from water dripping from the overhang above. On the third attempt I reached Pete, tied him into the middle of the rope, put gloves on his hands and started him across the traverse with a tight rope from Dave to me. Pete had no ice axe or crampons, could not see well, and had a dislocated right arm, but in the waning light he climbed slowly and beautifully along the ledge to the gully. When we reached a small shelf at the base of the gully, we heard shouts from Jim Wickwire and Lou Whittaker who had just completed anchoring the route above. We stopped for a moment to dig out headlamps and to give food and water to Sandstedt, then tied him into the end of the line tossed down from above. With Jim and Lou pulling from above and Dave pushing from below, Sandstedt climbed the difficult piton pitch. From that point it was just a matter of time to the bivouac camp that had been set up at the lower end of the snow slope that capped the upper part of Curtis Ridge. We arrived there at about 1:30 a.m. Wednesday, stuffed Sandstedt into Chuck Crenchaw's tent, fed him hot chocolate and soup, watched the stars for a few hours, then climbed up to the saddle for the helicopter pickup early in the morning; Dockery's body also was airlifted from the accident site.

The foregoing dramatic accounts make little mention of the logistical and cost problems involved in the rescue and evacuation. According to a detailed report of the rescue operation prepared by Gene Fear, base operations leader for the Tacoma unit of the Mountain Rescue Council, about 60 men were used at various points for a period of 46 hours—a total of 2760 man-hours; four helicopters were used to varying extents depending on their altitude capabilities, with a total of 36 flights in 26 flight-hours lifting men on and off the peak. At $200 per hour, the cost was about $5200. The total cost of the rescue, counting helicopters and their pilots and personnel, and figuring wages of both Park Service and volunteer personnel very conservatively, was calculated to be some $11,700.

Had no helicopters been available—and there were times during the early phases of the rescue it was doubted they could be obtained—and if the operation had had to be carried out entirely on foot, the cost in manpower would have been near $15,000.

On the other hand, had high-altitude helicopters been available through a federal or state agency and had these choppers been equipped with cables for a lowering-and-raising system, the rescue time would have been shortened about 20 hours. Only Park Service personnel would have been required beside the helicopter crews and the total cost would have been less than $1000.

The above comparisons do not consider numerous other factors: the dangers involved in rockfall and darkness, flight conditions at such high altitudes and at the high temperature that prevailed during the 2-day operation; families of those involved; those indirectly affected such as employers of the men; personal equipment lost; vehicles used for transportation; long-distance phone calls for assistance; and food and gasoline. The costs of these are unknown but are estimated to be large, if calculable. It is apparent that any savings in time and manpower resulting from the ready availability of suitable aircraft and equipment would bring a comparable saving in these factors as well.

30 A Slip on Hard Ice of the Winthrop: Kupperberg and Stevens, 1969

On July 13, 1969, less than a month after the tragedy on Curtis Ridge, two Mountaineers, David Stevens and Mark Kupperberg, were killed when their rope team failed to arrest a slip on hard ice on the upper Winthrop Glacier and slid approximately 2000 feet before falling into a deep crevasse. The third member of the team, Chris Marshall, survived with serious but not permanent injuries. This was the first fatal accident on The Mountaineers' organized Rainier climbs in the 35 years of their Climbing Course.

The following account is based on the official report prepared by a special committee of The Mountaineers.

On Friday evening of July 11 most of the party, led by Herman Gross, arrived at White River Campground and registered at the guard station. By 8 p.m. nearly all the climbers had departed for an overnight camp in Glacier Basin.

Shortly after 7 a.m. Saturday the 16 Mountaineers started for Steamboat Prow. The weather was not promising—rain mixed with wet snow was falling intermittently. The party arrived at Camp Schurman on the Prow a little after 3 p.m. The weather had cleared and most of the trek was in excellent weather. From the Prow the Seattle group saw 11 climbers from the Tacoma branch of The Mountaineers toiling up the mountain with overnight packs. The Tacoma climbers had spent Friday night in the hut at Camp Schurman and planned to camp overnight on the glacier at about 12,500 feet. The group was led by Bruce Becker and was composed of nine men and two women.

The Seattle party settled down in the hut and Gross made rope team assignments. The four rope leaders beside Gross—Mark Kupperberg, Lester Harms, Gary Griffith, and Lowell Ericsson—were graduates of the Basic Climbing Course and students of the Intermediate Climbing Course. Four teams were equipped with the standard 120-foot $\frac{7}{16}$-inch manila rope provided by the club; one team had a 150-foot length of $\frac{7}{16}$-inch goldline rope.

At about 5 p.m. another group arrived at Steamboat Prow—nine climbers, mostly from the Bremerton area, led by Jack Newman.

On Sunday, July 13, the Seattle party was roped up and moving out at 1:30 a.m. The Bremerton party left about 15 minutes later. At the time of departure the sky was clear, there was no wind, and the snow was frozen hard. Herman Gross set a slow, deliberate pace designed to keep the party close together and rotated rope teams to the lead position so all might gain experience.

The Bremerton party followed. The Tacoma group left high camp on the Winthrop Glacier at 5:45 a.m. and returned to the normal climbing route.

Conditions were clear and cold. The temperature was 16°F and winds were light to moderate. The snow was firmly crusted and the crust was too deep to break through with an ice-axe spike unless an extra thrust was made. The snow was interspersed with patches of ice and in places the Tacoma party cut steps to facilitate progress of the two women. At about 13,000 feet a Tacoma climber slipped but arrested himself before any pull was felt by his ropemates. The party cut steps more frequently thereafter. The leader, Bruce Becker, conferred with Jim Sanford (chairman of the Climbing Committee of the Tacoma branch) about turning back if ice conditions did not improve. They decided to go on, feeling the afternoon probably would soften the glacier and that a descent of the icy slope at this time of morning would be particularly hazardous.

The Bremerton party also experienced a fall at about 13,000 feet. The leader of the last team slipped, lost grip on his axe, and slid about 75 feet before being arrested by his ropemates. Fortunately for the fallen man, his axe stuck in the snow and was easily recovered. Shortly after, the last man on Newman's rope lost a crampon and immediately fell, pulling the middle man a few feet down the slope. Newman stopped the fall without being nudged from his arrest position.

Snow conditions above 13,400 feet allowed much easier travel, despite occasional breakthroughs of the crust. The wind had increased steadily, however—liquid in canteens froze and a number of climbers donned face protectors. By the time the crater rim was reached, a little after 11 a.m., the wind velocity was estimated to be between 40 and 60 miles per hour. About an hour was spent on the summit, then the parties began descending.

At about 13,400 feet, Kupperberg slipped. His ropemates, Stevens and Marshall, went into self-arrest. The party proceeded down a little farther. Near a serac, Kupperberg slipped again, although no one witnessed this second fall. Another climber, Richard Rigg, stated that pick scratches on the surface indicated one person slid about 30 feet before stopping and breaking up the crust. The final fall came a few hundred feet from this point, about 10 minutes later.

As is usual among several eye-witness accounts, there is some disparity in descriptions of the final and tragic fall. Since apparently nobody was actually watching the team until the cry "Falling!" attracted attention, the beginning is in doubt. Witnesses closest to the scene agree that continuous attempts to stop the slide by self-arrest were made, and that in fact the team seemed to slow down and almost have the fall controlled at least once, but that the person nearly stopped each time was pulled from his position by others on the team who were at that moment out of control.

After sliding some distance the team hurtled a small crevasse, struck the lower lip, and lost any semblance of control. One witness believes he saw an ice axe fly in the air at this point. The team continued accelerating and in another 50 feet or so slid over a broad snow bridge covering a huge crevasse about 30 feet wide. (Later, near here, an axe was found sticking in the snow in arrest position.) The team then shot over a steep ice cliff, estimated to be 30–40 feet high, and out of sight of higher teams. The beginning of the fall was at about 12,500 feet; the final crevasse was at about 11,200 feet—a slope distance of some 2000 feet.

The two Seattle rope teams farther down the mountain did not witness the beginning of the fall. Les Harms saw the team, with all three persons in the air, flying over a large crevasse and then sliding down the slope out of his view. Lowell Ericsson, who was lower, saw the team hurtling two crevasses. One of the younger, less-experienced climbers remarked they were glissading—before he realized he was watching an uncontrolled fall.

Everyone who witnessed the accident was momentarily stunned. Herman Gross got his team started from a rest spot on a small serac and moved down immediately, following the fall line marked by scratches in the snow. He shouted to the rest of the party to halt teams that were unaware of what had happened. Gross' team continued down, finding the axe stuck in the snow and then noting the final path of the slide, a trough 15 inches wide leading to a crevasse.

Gross sent part of the group down to Camp Schurman to radio for help while his team and several others of the three parties, now united in the emergency, reached the crevasse where the skid marks terminated at the upper lip. The parties converged at the lower lip. Gross peered in but could not see the bottom. Then he heard a call; someone was alive.

Chris Marshall was the one who had shouted, having heard voices above. He said his companions were nowhere in sight and apparently buried. He was worried about ice falling from above and requested that a hard hat be lowered. The climbers began preparing for his rescue.

Richard Rigg, with extensive prior experience in caving (a sport which uses rappelling techniques), volunteered to descend into the crevasse. Belayed from above for the first 20 feet, and using a double-brake bar, Rigg rappelled on a 150-foot synthetic rope. At 40 feet down he passed a snow ledge 6 feet thick which the falling climbers had struck and plunged through, leaving a hole about 10 feet wide. He continued to the bottom, about 125 feet down, and there found Marshall, who was standing up, leaning against the crevasse wall.

Marshall does not remember losing consciousness after falling into the crevasse but may have done so. He had landed face down with his feet slightly lower than his head. His Cruiser-style rigid-frame pack probably cushioned the fall, but also wedged in on top of him, making disentanglement difficult. Fortunately he had been tied into the climbing rope by a carabiner and thus could unsnap it; it would have been difficult if not impossible to untie a knot, since the rope was taut and buried in the snow beneath him. Marshall's right wrist was broken, his ankle was sprained, and he complained of a sore neck. He had put on a parka he had found lying near him and was able to keep relatively warm without digging into his own pack.

Rigg used a webbing to fashion a diaper sling for Marshall, then secured him to the rappel rope with this and a chest sling. He was ready for evacuation when a signal from the people above indicated they were ready to raise the injured man. A Z-system of pulleys and ropes brought Marshall to the surface, where a platform had been cut for him to be laid comfortably amidst donations of sleeping bags, extra parkas, and ensolite pads. First aid, rendered by two physicians in the party, Dr. Roger Barrett and Dr. Arthur Radcliffe, included treatment for shock and exposure and splinting of his ankle.

Meanwhile, in the crevasse, Rigg, who now was unroped, requested ice screws for anchors while he explored further for the other

Those who gave their lives.
Edgar McClure, Delmar Fadden, Bill Haupert.

victims. Rigg did not wear a parka but managed to keep warm by moving about. He was standing on a platform of snow that had been knocked loose by the falling climbers. He probed this area and a few feet down uncovered a foot, then a hand—completely lifeless, blue and cold. He knew neither of the two had survived.

In view of Marshall's injuries it was determined that evacuation without a stretcher would be extremely dangerous. As the party could not rely on arrival of a helicopter before dark, they began preparing a camp in which Marshall could survive the night. Platforms had been cut in the hard snow with Gross' "survival saw" and preparations were being made to set up two tents when a helicopter passed over several times in efforts to find a suitable landing site. The chopper slid off the steep icy surface on its first attempt, then landed successfully 400 feet uphill from the crevasse at about 8:20 p.m.

Park Rangers Cleve Pinnix and John Dalle-Molle emerged from the helicopter, which was piloted by Ray Hauseman of Alpine Helicopters. Carrying a stretcher, they descended on foot to the crevasse, where they assumed command of the operation. After an appraisal, Pinnix radioed a request to have two more rangers flown to the scene. The chopper then brought Rangers Don Meredith and Tim Hall. Evacuating Marshall was a slow, difficult, hazardous procedure, moving across hard steep ice immediately above another crevasse—those lifting the stretcher had to be secured by belays wherever possible. The helicopter's landing site was reached just about dark. The stretcher could not be loaded inside the cabin so Marshall was strapped securely to one side and a ranger clung to the other side to balance the weight. The helicopter landed at the Sunrise parking lot after dark, aided by the headlights of lined-up cars. Marshall was transported by Park Service vehicle to a hospital in Enumclaw.

Calder Bressler, Pat Chamay, George Dockery.

The climbing parties and remaining three rangers descended to Schurman hut for the night. On Monday, July 14, while some climbers left the mountain, the others returned with the rangers to the crevasse. Ranger Dalle-Molle descended into the crevasse while Pinnix directed operations above. The bodies of Kupperberg and Stevens were found, hauled to the surface by 1:30 p.m., and transported to Camp Schurman at about 5:30 p.m. A support party of 22 men, led by Ranger Lee Henkle, assisted in the evacuation of the bodies around Steamboat Prow and down Inter Glacier to the trail at Glacier Basin. There a wheeled litter brought the accident victims to the White River Campground late that night.

The tragic consequences of the slip high on the mountain, on what normally is considered the "dog route" of Mount Rainier, point out that conditions can be extremely hazardous when steep snow surfaces become a sheet of hard ice. Although not difficult to ascend with normal use of crampons, axe, and rope, such terrain becomes a trap for weary climbers on the descent.

In recent years, several skiers, snowboarders, and snowshoers have become lost while traveling to and from Camp Muir, usually after becoming separated from their party in poor visbility or initially traveling alone. Some are never found.

31 Tragedies on Lower Slopes and Peaks

The higher slopes of Rainier have no monopoly on tragedy; indeed, more people have perished on the lower slopes and lesser peaks of the Park. A summary of the deaths at lower elevations is presented here for the lessons they carry. The information and analyses have come from Park Service files, the American Alpine Club's annual accident and safety reports, and reports of the Seattle and Tacoma Mountain Rescue units.

On August 12, 1912, while descending from the top of Pinnacle Peak with a party of Y.M.C.A. youths (10 girls and 4 boys) led by guides H. R. Carter and Frank Walton, Charlotte Hunt, a Seattle schoolteacher, was killed in a fall. She apparently suffered dizziness and lost her footing on a seemingly secure stance.

On September 1, 1915 C. W. Ferguson was killed instantly by a block of ice he poked loose from the ceiling of an ice cave in the Paradise Glacier. He was in a party of 17 guided by Harry Greer. Apparently against the instructions of Greer, Ferguson with his wife and two boys went ahead and entered a tunnel under the ice.

On August 14, 1917 Dorothy Haskell fell into a crevasse on the Paradise Glacier while hiking unroped with her father and mother and a Mr. Palmer. Her body was located on a shelf 25 feet down, covered by 5-6 feet of snow. Use of a rope on crevassed areas had not yet become common.

On August 22, 1924 guide Paul Moser was killed in a fall from Unicorn Peak in the Tatoosh Range while climbing with another guide, Joe Griggs. Apparently the men were not roped at the time and Moser had extended himself to a precarious position in leading above Griggs. Recovery of the badly broken body from slopes far below required a large crew of Park Service and Park Company employees from Paradise.

On April 13, 1940 skier Sigurd Hall was killed instantly when he crashed into fog-shrouded rocks during the annual Silver Skis Race from Camp Muir to Paradise. An inquiry into the accident brought out conflicting reports on the degree of visibility on the course. Apparently fog drifted in and out during the race. The tragedy, along with our entry into World War II, resulted in cessation of the annual event for several years.

In 1941 Leon Brigham, who had suffered so during the Greathouse-Wetzel accident of 1929, experienced a still greater tragedy. On August 10 Brigham's 21-year-old son Leon, Jr., an end on the University of Washington football team and an ardent mountaineer, died in a crevasse on the Russell Glacier. Young Brigham, with companions Richard Ruoff, Richard Berner, Harrison Holland, and William Stromberg, were on a one-day exploring trip on the lower slopes of the mountain's north side. After climbing one or two small peaks (possibly Observation and Echo Rocks) the youths headed back down the glacier. Although they had a rope with them and used it occasionally while photographing each other being lowered into crevasses, they were not roped during the descent. At times they tested snow bridges, anchoring each other only by grasping the shaft of an axe held by companions. Then, as Brigham was testing one such snow bridge, holding onto Holland's axe, the snow collapsed and Brigham dropped from sight, his hands letting go of the axe. A brief muffled groan was followed by silence. Receiving no response to calls, Ruoff was lowered into the crevasse about 10 feet but could see nothing. The grief-stricken boys then split up, Ruoff and Stromberg remaining at the scene while Berner and Holland headed down to the Carbon River Ranger Station, which they reached about 4:30 p.m. A rescue team composed of Rangers Bill Butler, Gordon Patterson, Bob Sutermeister, and Park Company employees Frank Perrin and K Molenaar headed up the mountain late that night, accompanied by Leon Brigham, Sr. and his younger son Charles (age 15). Charles remained at Mowich Lake while the remainder of the party pushed on past Spray Park to the Russell Glacier, reached early the next morning. Butler and Patterson were lowered into the crevasse and after an hour and a half of digging found the body buried beneath 8 feet of snow. It was lifted from the chasm and carried back to the waiting pack horse in Spray Park, then to Mowich Lake and a ranger patrol vehicle for the sad trip to Seattle (Seattle Post-Intelligencer, August 11–22, 1941).

On August 11, 1954 Clare Combat was killed by a fall into rocks at the bottom of a long snow slope down which she slid after losing her footing and her ice axe. She was a member of a large party of Mountaineers hiking to Meany Crest above Summerland. On descending, the leader had given the group permission to glissade the slope in his tracks. The victim apparently was unsure as she began her glissade and lost her footing soon after.

On November 30, 1957, while snowshoeing toward Anvil Rock with a companion, Lowell Linn decided to turn back alone. He disappeared during the hike down to Paradise. Fog and snow prevented an adequate search for several days and Linn has never been found. He was not properly clothed or equipped and had no food for bivouac.

On June 15, 1967, during the return from a family hike to the

Paradise Glacier ice caves, Phyllis Louden (mother) and daughters Kelly (5) and Karen (4) were killed by a slide into a stream under the snow. The father, Melvin Louden, and son Mark (6) had earlier fallen into a cave nearby but made their way back to Paradise, unaware the others had also slid down the same snow slope into the many-chambered hole. The bodies of Mrs. Louden and one daughter were found and recovered the next day; the third body was recovered by a SCUBA diver 2 days after the tragedy. Apparently the family had attempted a short-cut to the road below by way of the gully of snow which had become hardened and icy after the sun left it. They also failed to note, before they started sliding, the hole at the bottom of the gully.

On September 10, 1967 Elmer Post (39) and David Post (19) died after a fall into a crevasse on the upper Paradise Glacier, just off the normal route to Camp Muir. Another member of the party, James Bartram (19), survived the stormy night in the crevasse, crawled out next morning, and was seen and saved by a Park Ranger search team. The party had been hiking to Camp Muir but decided to descend when the weather deteriorated to freezing rain and snow. Poor visibility caused them to wander off the route and onto the glacier, where Bartram, the rear man on the rope, broke through the snow into the crevasse. Elmer Post fell in while attempting to help Bartram out of the hole; David Post then climbed into the crevasse, where all three decided to wait out the storm. An unroped companion meanwhile found his way back to Paradise, nearly in a state of shock and unable to tell rangers clearly the whereabouts of the accident. Back in the crevasse, Bartram descended to the floor, finding room there to move about and keep warm. Although he urged the Posts to join him, they remained where they were and died of exposure about 3 hours after the accident. The main cause of this tragedy was clothing inadequate even for the weather encountered at the start of the trip. They had no waterproof clothing and very little wool clothing.

On February 17–18, 1968, enroute back from an exploratory trip to the Paradise ice caves, Edith Anderson died of exposure following a night in an improvised snow cave. Mrs. Anderson, her husband Charles, and David Mischke had hiked to the ice caves to continue an exploration and photography program initiated earlier in the winter. Starting the hike in unseasonally balmy weather, they were dressed mainly in cotton clothing and were not equipped for winter conditions. As they left the ice caves for the return trip in midafternoon, the weather deteriorated and soon they were wandering in a blizzard white-out, unable to find their way either to Paradise or back to the ice cave. Using a pan they carried, they dug a cave into a snow cornice and crawled in for the night, the woman between the two men for warmth, since she was the coldest. That night and next morning, after being alerted by friends of the missing persons, Park rangers made several unsuccessful efforts to reach the ice caves and to search the terrain enroute. Visibility was so poor in the severe storm that at times searchers could not see the lights of the Thiokol snow vehicle 50 feet away. Conditions prevented their contacting the missing trio until the second morning, after Mischke had found his way to Paradise to give directions. Upon arrival at the 2-foot-square, 6-foot-deep hole, the rangers found Anderson in a mild state of shock, but easily evacuated. Mrs. Anderson was apparently not breathing and had no perceptible pulse or pupillary reaction. Upon arrival at Paradise Ranger Station she was pronounced dead.

On June 14–16, 1968 Dr. James M. Reddick died in a snow cave dug into the surface of the snowfield below Camp Muir during a prolonged storm. With Dr. Reddick were his two children, Sharon (12) and David (11), who survived 2 days in the shallow trench. The tragedy began to develop when Reddick's party of five started for Camp Muir in fair weather, but with forecasts for storm. When it began raining and blowing the party split up just below 9000 feet—one father and daughter turning back. Although not feeling well, Reddick, an experienced mountaineer, urged himself and his children on toward Camp Muir, asking, "Would Whittaker turn back?" The storm increased in severity and eventually Reddick dug a shallow trench in the snowfield about 500 feet below Anvil Rock. An ensolite (sponge) pad was placed in the bottom of the hole and the children got into their sleeping bags topped by a poncho. The zipper on Dr. Reddick's bag jammed so he was forced to lie on top of it rather than inside. Although soaked by rain and sleet, the children managed to maintain body heat for the 2 days inside their bags, but Dr. Reddick died after the first night, possibly from a combination of exposure and pulmonary edema. Search efforts were hampered by the bad weather. Luckily, on the second day, through a break in the driving fog and rain, Ranger Jim Valder spotted a small part of a pack sticking from the snow near the shelter. The children were found and quickly transferred to a tent erected nearby, warmed up, fed, and brought to Paradise by akja (plastic rescue sled).

On September 12, 1968, Milton Armstrong (54), a retired Navy man, hiked to Camp Muir after signing out at the Alta Vista register above the Paradise Ranger Station. Because he failed to give his car license number, rangers were unable to verify whether he had not returned until the 16th. In the meantime, a severe storm hit the area on the 13th and continued several days. Rangers found Armstrong's pack at Camp Muir with a note indicating he was going for a short hike. Rangers and Mountain Rescue Council members attempted to search for several days in extremely bad weather, but could find no trace of the missing man. Exactly 2 years later, on September 12, 1970, Armstrong's body was found in a snowdrift near the top of the Cowlitz Glacier, below Camp Misery.

On August 29, 1968 Lieutenant (j.g.) Martin J. Quinn of the *U.S.S. Enterprise* (anchored at Bremerton) fell 300 feet to his death down a rock chute while climbing unroped with a companion on the lower slopes of Mother Mountain near Ipsut Creek Campground.

On March 9, 1969 John Aigars, while skiing alone above Paradise, was caught by an avalanche below Panorama Point and died of suffocation. His body was located 2 days later by a German police dog of a Pierce County dog search-and-rescue group. The trained dog's sense of smell enabled him to find the body within 30 minutes after release in the search area. Over many years a number of skiers and climbers have been caught here in slides off Panorama Point, fortunately none of serious consequence until Aigars' death. The tragedy might have been averted had Aigars been accompanied by another person.

FATALITIES DURING CLIMBS
ON MOUNT RAINIER, 1897-1999

*Data Sources are National Park Service, Mountain
Rescue Association, and The American Alpine Club*

YEAR	DATE	NAME(S)	PARTY NO.	PROF. GUIDED	CAUSE
1897	7/27	Prof. Edgar McClure	large		Fall from rock during night
1909	8/14	T.V. Callaghan Joseph W. Stevens	3		Disappeared at summit in storm
1911	8/-	Legh O. Garrett	1		Disappeared in storm near top
1916	9/18	J. A. Fritsch	x		Died three days after surviving fall in Crevasse
1921	8/16	Jack Meredith	7		Fall from Little Tahoma
1929	7/2	Forrest G. Greathouse Edwin A. Wetzel	6		Slide into crevasse at 12,000 ft.
1931	7/5	Robert Zinn	2		Slide into crevasse
1936	1/-	Delmar Fadden	1		Fall, then frozen in descent of Emmons Glacier
1941	8/10	Leon Brigham, Jr.	5		Fall into crevasse, Russell Gl.
1957	9/1	William Haupert	12	x	Crushed during collapse of snow bridge
1957	11/30	Lowell Linn	1		Disappeared in snowstorm
1959	9/2	Calder T. Bressler	large		Pulmonary edema at summit
1967	9/10	Elmer and David Post	3		Slide into crevasse, died of exposure
1968	6/15	Dr. James M. Reddick	3		In cave during snowstorm, exposure
1968	6/23	Patrick Chamay	4		Pulmonary edema on upper Liberty Ridge
1968	9/12	Milton J. Armstrong	1		Probably exposure; body later found above Camp Muir
1969	6/15	George T. Dockery	5		Rockfall on Curtis Ridge
1969	7/13	Mark Kupperberg David Stevens	large		Slide into crevasse on Winthrop Glacier
1971	8/1	Michael Ferry	5		Fall into crevasse on Ingraham Glacier
1974	11/18	David Taylor	2		Snow avalanche on Success Cleaver
1975	8/14	Mark Jackson	3		Rockfall on Mowich Face
1977	2/16	Jack Wilkins	4		Uncontrolled glissade off Success Cleaver
1977	7/6	Dean Klapper	5		Into crevasse during sitting glissade on Emmons Glacier
1977	9/7	Mary Gnehm	11		Slide of roped party on upper Ingraham Glacier
1978	5/31	Todd Davis	3		Avalanche down Fuhrer Finger
1978	9/8	Shirley Voight Guillermo Mendoza	2		Climb into storm on Ingraham Glacier
1979	3/4	Willi Unsoeld Janie Diepenbrock	21		Slab avalanche on upper Cowlitz Glacier

Fatalities During Climbs
on Mount Rainier, 1897-1999

Continued

Year	Date	Name(s)	Party No.	Prof. Guided	Cause
1979	9/1	Dale Click	?		Fall into crevasse on Inter Glacier, exposure
1981	5/24	Doug Fowler	2		Fall from Liberty Ridge
1981	6/21	10 clients, 1 guide (worst accident in mountain's history)	29	x	Ice avalanche off Disappointment Cleaver
1983	5/7	Doug Vercoe	3		Fall from cornice, Anvil Rock
1983	5/29	Christopher Blight	6		Crevasse on Emmons Glacier, while assisting in rescue of another from crevasse
1983	9/5	Patrick Hill Douglas Velder	2		Inexperienced, fall from Disappointment Cleaver
1985	1/-	Fuat Dikman	1		Fall from Liberty Ridge, body found in May
1987	5/26-6/2	John Weis John Witterberger	2		From stove and lamp fumes, suffocated on Liberty Ridge
1987	6/18	Kurt Fengler	?		Crevasse fall, Emmons Glacier
1988	5/12	Craig S. Adkison, David Kellowkowski, Greg Remmick	3		Fall from Liberty Ridge
1989	3/18	William Saul	1		Plane crash into Willis Wall
1989	5/10	Richard Mooney Peter Derdowski	2		Exposure at Liberty Cap Fall from Liberty Ridge while going for help for Mooney
1990	1/20	Randall Bates	2		Plane crash at crater rim
1990	7/2	Harry Card, David Bowen Mike Curran, Randy Dierdan, David Smith	5		Plane crash, upper Kautz Glacier
1990	10/28	James F. Kampe	4		Lost during ski climb to Camp Muir
1991	1/3	Mark Fogerty	3		Fall while skiing down west edge of Muir Snowfield
1991	5/17	James Tuttle	2		Died in crevasse, Ingraham Glacier
1991	9/1	Karl Feichmeier	2		Ditto
1991	9/2	Ken Seifert	1		Ditto (climbed without registering)
1992	2/29	Greg Terry, Jeff Vallee	2		Possible avalanche, Fuhrer Finger
1992	6/21	Michael Price	2		Crevasse in Emmons Glacier, after climb of Liberty Ridge
1995	8/12	Phillip Otis, Sean Ryan	2		Park rangers fell 1200 feet from 12,000-ft. level on Emmons Glacier
1995	8/20	Karl Ahrends, Scott Porter			Fell 2400 ft. from 12,000-ft. level on Emmons Glacier (ascending)
1996	7/12	Jeremy C. Zaccardi			Asthma attack at 12,500-ft level on Emmons Glacier

Fatalities During Climbs on Mount Rainier, 1897-1999

Continued

Year	Date	Name(s)	Party No.	Prof. Guided	Cause
1997	7/29	Don McIntyre	2		Companion slipped into victim while removing snow from crampons and both fell into crevasse; companion survived
1998	6/11	Patrick Nestler	30?	x	Snow avalanche on Disappointment Cleaver, two rope teams hit, Nestler died of injuries and hypothermia while dangling from rope in freezing water
1999	5/24	David Perrson	2		After solo ascent to summit, unroped skier fell from Liberty Ridge to Carbon Glacier
1999	10/24	Nicholas Giromini	2		Fall and hypothermia on Cowlitz Glacier above Camp Muir

NOTE: Since 1999, when tabulating summit-climb fatalities, the National Park Service has limited information to the date, cause, and location of the fatalities.

Year	Date	Cause
2002	9/23	Struck by falling rock during descent of Disappointment Cleaver
	6/6	Two climbers fell during descent of Ingraham Glacier
2004	5/15	Blunt head injury on "Black Pyramid"
	5/29	Two climbers fell from above 13,000-ft level of Liberty Ridge
	5/29	One climber found in shallow depression on Liberty Ridge
	6/3	200-ft fall at 11,300 ft on Liberty Ridge
	6/12	Two climbers in short falls at 9000 ft on Liberty Ridge
	10/24	Avalanche swept climber into crevasse on Ingraham Glacier

TOTAL: 93 SUMMIT-CLIMB FATALITIES THROUGH 2004

PART FIVE

THE GUIDES

WARNING
HIDDEN CREVASSES
"ROPE UP"
RECOMMENDED
BEYOND HERE

32 Of Mountain Men

Guides are no foolhardy adventurers: they live, they do their job.
Every day in the summer they get up very early to question the sky and
the wind. The day before, perhaps, they were uneasy, for long clouds
scarred the western horizon. They feared a night of worsening
weather; the Milky Way shone too brightly, the cold delayed its
coming. But now, if the north wind won the upper hand, the weather
is good, the guide can rouse his client and set out. Then the rope will
join together two beings who now live as one. During these hours
the guide is linked with a stranger who will become a friend. When
two men share the good and the bad, then they are no longer strangers.

GASTON REBUFFAT
Starlight and Storm, 1957

The men who since the late 1800s have led tourists and visiting climbers to the icy crown of Mount Rainier have come from diverse back-
grounds and have gone on to a variety of professions. The character of
the eras in which they were born and raised probably determined to a
great extent the type of men who guided on the mountain, where they
went after their summers on the peak, and what opportunities were
afforded them through guiding.

Most of the guides of the pre-1940 era, before outdoor recreation
and mountaineering became the big businesses they are today, came to
the mountain as much to earn money for continuance of college educa-
tions as to further their climbing experiences. Many went into businesses and professions totally unrelated to mountaineering and some
retained little interest in climbing after their summers in the Park. To a
few the mountain was just a meal ticket during the tourist season or a
retreat from the congestion of city life—reportedly one man began a
4-year stint as a guide only after escaping into the Park to evade legal
proceedings in town.

Since World War II, with the increasing orientation of mountain
climbing to specialized equipment and techniques, some guides have
graduated into recreational-equipment businesses and teaching positions utilizing their climbing experience. Others have parlayed their
knowledge gained on the rock, snow, and ice of Rainier into scientific
endeavors in geology and glaciology. Many postwar guides have taken
advantage of growing opportunities and affluence to join expeditions
to Alaska, the Andes, and the Himalayas. Conversely, in recent years
several guides have been employed at Paradise as a result of prestige
gained in other climbing areas and as members of major expeditions.

Leading tourists to Rainier's crater by the most direct path has never demanded the highly technical skills required among the top alpine climbers of today. From the beginning the professional guide service based at Paradise has used the route best suited for taking large parties up the peak. Except for the early 1900s, when a guide service operated from a tent camp at Indian Henrys Hunting Ground on Rainier's west side, only the Gibraltar, Kautz, and Ingraham routes on the Paradise side have been used by the guides. Most of those who pay for guides desire merely to climb the mountain by the most assured line of ascent, and only rarely has a climber-client shown any interest in a more challenging route. Hence the guides are fully occupied during busy summers in leading a "dog route," and only through their ice-climbing classes and Camp Muir seminars do they get a chance to sharpen the technical skills needed on more difficult routes.

But even on the relatively direct glacier climbs the guides must learn how to cope with problems of leading neophytes of unknown physical and mental reserves into a world where altitude, storms, and deep snow often combine to make Rainier as tough as any Himalayan giant. Those who do a number of climbs up the peak invariably become well-acquainted with storms of arctic severity. Such experiences test the stamina and fortitude of the most-skilled guide, and few survive summit storms on Rainier without gaining a humble respect for the mountain. The added responsibility of being in charge of a large group of clients whose reactions to stress situations are not known doubles the need for sagacity. I fully concur with the statement by Frank "Swede" Willard, a well-known guide of the 1930s, that it is often a considerably greater challenge to haul a party of neophytes up a simple route than to tackle unknown terrain with a small group of highly experienced companions.

THE INDIANS

The very early ascents of the mountain by white men were made without mountain guides as such but usually the party was accompanied either by an Indian who preferred to remain near timberline (except for Wapowety in 1857) or by members of local pioneer families. Among the Indian "guides" who led the early explorers into the Park area was Saluskin of the Yakima Indians. Interviews with the chief in 1917 by historian Lucallus V. McWhorter (Haines, 1962) elicited a story of the Indian's contact as a youth with climbers in 1855 when he led two men, one apparently a Mexican, to the Mystic Lake area. The men were surveyors working on the boundaries of the Yakima Indian Reservation.

The next Indian to enter the picture was Wapowety, who in 1857 accompanied Lieutenant Kautz and his small party in the nearly complete climb to the summit from the south. Wapowety apparently did not share his tribesmen's fear of the peak. Wapowety Cleaver is named for him.

The part played by Sluiskin in the climb by Stevens and Van Trump in 1870 was described earlier; his name has been given to Sluiskin Falls and Sluiskin Peak. The Indian had little use for mountaineering, however, although as a hunter he apparently was well-acquainted with the timbered foothills and lower meadows.

The vaguely recorded climb via the Ingraham Glacier in 1885 or 1886 by a white hunter named Allison L. Brown was made in company with a party of Yakima Indians. This is the first report of Indians as a group climbing high on Rainier's slopes, although tribal legends and Sluiskin's account of his grandfather's climb to the crater strongly suggest they visited the summit area long before the coming of the "King George man" and "Boston man."

The next Indian to guide newcomers to the mountain was So-to-lick, more commonly known as Indian Henry. In 1883 Henry accompanied P. B. Van Trump, George B. Bayley, and James Longmire to above snowline. He had been hired because he stated he could take packhorses to snowline, which he did admirably by reaching nearly to Cowlitz Cleaver (about Camp Muir) with the animals (Van Trump, *The Mountaineer*, 1915).

THE LONGMIRE ERA

James Longmire, who with pack animals led Stevens and Van Trump to the base of the mountain near Bear Prairie in 1870, climbed the peak in 1883 with Van Trump. On this trip he discovered the warm mineral springs where a year later he constructed the first cabin inside what is now the National Park. With his sons he then constructed a trail and built a hotel at the present site of Longmire.

Len Longmire, grandson of James Longmire and son of Elcaine Longmire, was the first self-proclaimed guide on Rainier. In 1890 Len climbed to the summit with a party that included Miss Fay Fuller, the climb that marked the first recorded ascent by a woman. For 20 years after his ascent Longmire scaled the mountain frequently, taking tourists to the summit from Camp Muir at a charge of $1 each. In August 1962 it was my pleasure to visit Len Longmire (age 93) at a rest home in McKenna, near Yelm, birthplace of many of the Longmire clan. Although his mind was vague on more recent events, Len clearly recalled the many details of those climbs of 70 years before.

Len's brother Ben, although never a summit guide, figured prominently in early activities in the new National Park. In 1915 he was asked by Dr. Edmond S. Meany, President of The Mountaineers, to submit an account of some of his memorable experiences on the mountain. The following excerpts provide interesting observations of his days in the area:

My first trip to the mountain was in 1887 and I have been on top of every little hill around the mountain hunting for cougars, wild cats, and game of all kinds. In 1911 Edward S. Hall, the Park Supervisor, put me in as Park hunter. Perhaps he was afraid I might kill something that was branded U.S. and took that way to protect the game. In 1912 I was made a ranger and filled that position the best I could.

Mount Ararat I named because I found there some long slabs of wood that had turned to stone and I thought they might have been part of old Noah's boat. I also found a stump with a ring around it as if his rope might have been tied there. It was all stone. I named Martha Falls after my mother. I never named anything after a girl. Bill Stafford named some Falls, Sylvia Falls, after his sweetheart and she has not spoken to him since . . .

Ben Longmire, with a string of pack burros, served as a supply line between foothill communities and the Park for many years. He brought his animals to Camp Muir loaded with cement and lumber and was instrumental in construction of the stone shelter cabins there in 1916 and 1921.

THE EARLY 1900S

In 1903 John Reese, who operated "Camp of the Clouds" at Paradise, started the first guide concession there. Beside leading ascents himself, Reese employed several guides, the most famous being Joe Stampfler. "Little Joe" began his career on the mountain after being invited as a boy of 14 in 1888 to live with the Longmires. He accompanied and led many parties to the top from Paradise and also from a tent camp at Indian Henrys Hunting Ground, both before and after 1900. His younger brother, Jules, also guided from Paradise during part of this period and later (1914, 1918–19). Both men were to meet tragic deaths years later. In September 1926 Joe Stampfler (age 54) was found drowned off a dock in Tacoma (Tacoma *News Tribune*, September 28, 1926); in February 1944 Jules Stampfler (age 67) was struck and killed by a train near Sunset Beach, Tacoma (Seattle *Times*, February 21, 1944).

In 1911, following recommendations by Francois Matthes of the U.S. Geological Survey after two men perished in a storm on Rainier, Park Superintendent Edward S. Hall instituted an "Official Guide System" patterned after that of the Swiss. Of this system Hall stated,

"While the present guiding system in the Park is crude compared with that of the Swiss Alps, the number and class of tourists attempting the summit does not warrant, at this time, a system of regulations that would add greatly to the expense of making these ascents, but the number in each party should be limited to eight persons. Four persons were authorized to act as guides in the Park during the season of 1911, one of whom was not permitted to guide to the summit nor across any glacier. Those authorized to guide to the summit are mountaineers of known ability, and no accidents of a serious nature have occurred where parties have been accompanied by these official guides."

In 1912 seven guides were authorized by the Park Superintendent to take parties to the summit of Rainier. In 1914 authorization was given the following four guides and their rates of pay per summit trip: Harry Greer, $25; Jules Stampfler, $25; F. H. Tuell, $25; and H. A. Loss (assistant guide), $15.

33 Rainier National Park Company Era (1916–42)

In 1916 the newly formed Rainier National Park Company took over complete operation of all concessionaire facilities in the Park, including the guide service at Paradise Valley. For the next 26 years the Company ran the guide concession through a chief guide selected from the ranks of well-known Northwest leaders in outdoor recreation and Scouting activities. The chief guides generally picked their staff from among local mountaineers and young college athletes, many of the latter taking their first climbing steps on Rainier. In the 1920s the guide staff was provided colorful augmentation by professional guides from the Alps, notable among these being the Swiss brothers, Hans and Heinie Fuhrer.

Leading tourists up the mountain in that era generally involved only a strong determination and patience but, by present-day standards, only a meager knowledge of the use of ice axe and rope. A dozen or more tourists would be tied together on one rope, sometimes only by an arm loop, or else they merely maintained a strong grasp on the rope at the more precarious pitches on the climb. Generally, during the descent of the steeper parts of the slope, the climbing rope was anchored at each end by an axe or alpenstock in the hands of the guide and the tourists then used this as a handline. Crampons were unknown, or considered a dangerous nuisance, among even the guides. The climbers' boots generally were fitted with metal caulks screwed into the leather soles, or in a few cases by more sophisticated Swiss edge nails imported from Europe. These served for traction on the ice of the steep upper slopes, where the axe of the guide also frequently came into play by chopping steps on the longer stretches.

The first chief guide to serve the Park Company was Asahel Curtis, a member of The Mountaineers and a man who contributed to early explorations and ascents in the Cascades and Olympics. Curtis operated the guide service only in 1917 and later gained more lasting fame in the Pacific Northwest as a professional scenic photographer.

Otis B. Sperlin, also a member of The Mountaineers, succeeded Curtis and served as chief guide in 1918. He was followed in 1919 by Joseph T. Hazard, a widely-traveled climber, educator, and writer whose articles and books brought early attention to the high volcanoes of the Northwest.

In those early years women occasionally were hired as guides to lead tourists to the nearby glaciers and to assist in few summit ascents.

Joe Hazard, Asahel Curtis.

Among them was Alma Wagen, teacher from Tacoma's Stadium High School. In 1918 Miss Wagen guided under Otis B. Sperlin, also of Stadium High, and also under Joe Hazard's leadership in 1919–20. Of Miss Wagen, Chief Guide Hazard wrote: "The career of Alma Wagen as a mountain guide is striking . . . she led the John D. Rockefeller, Jr. party like a master." Another woman, Emma Vaughan, was a member of the 1923 guide staff.

Among the accounts of guiding in the early 1920s is that provided by Wesley Langlow, who served from 1919–26. Excerpts from a letter to me by Langlow (1969) follow:

Alma D. Wagen . . . was unique at the time, dressed colorfully and was most competent on the glacier tours of that day. Jake Shidell shared summit guide trips with Hans Fuhrer in 1919 . . . Jake was a short stocky frontier style person with an ice axe as tall as he was. I was with the hotel staff part of 1917 and 1918, "graduated" to the guide staff for 1919 as a sort of errand boy and general helper with assignments as assistant guide as occasion demanded . . . [in 1926] we had a somewhat expanded group . . . no "summit" guides as such, but with each taking a turn at that more lucrative field. In those days the monthly wage was around $90, room and board, with $50 for each summit trip as chief, and $20 for each assistant per trip.

Roughly one guide was to handle summit trips up to ten persons (minimum was 5 people unless the $50 fee was paid by fewer) with an asst. guide for each additional ten persons. I believe the "hey-day" of guided trips was 1924–25–26 as we had day and half day "tours" well patronized and many summit parties of 30 and even 50 people. Can you imagine taking on up to 50 assorted individuals based on appearance alone, without previous experience, getting them into rented outfits with a box lunch tied around their middle with some string and heading for the summit with just a hope for good weather. Next, picture Muir with just the old cabin and a pile of beaten-down mattresses and well used blankets with 20 or 30 persons waiting for the hot tea or suffering nausea and scouting around for a pumice slope out of the wind in which to put some blankets. The old cabin held mighty few and I preferred the fresh air even tho we were caught out in sudden snow storms more than once. Old Muir held 6 or 8 laid side by side & sleep was out of the question. I am thinking of this experience, not from the standpoint of a climber or camper, but of hotel guests used to the best in travel services of the time getting into the primitive conditions involved in climbing via Muir in the 1920's. Of course we had way stations for depositing the sick & the weak but despite ineffective screening of summit candidates our rate of failure was not excessive. Our accident rate was next to nothing. But Gibraltar and the Chutes were always a serious problem and getting 20 or 30 people up and back down safely was more fortune than skill. I believe the Mountaineer Annual had a short story on our abortive use of World War I steel helmets to avoid Gibraltar rock fall.

Our equipment was non-technical. We had manila [hemp] rope—heavy and not too long & we did not "tie" in the party. That would have been disastrous under the circumstances. The rope slid loosely thru the palm of the hand. It was meant to keep the party together and in the track. The front guide alone tied into the rope. On the descent the rear guide would attempt to belay by means of the ice axe. Our shoes were heavily caulked— half-inch protruding spikes—great on ice, tough on rocks. I never saw a pair of crampons inside the guide house in my day. The Swiss guides used the heavy Swiss nails for the first time.

There was no formal training of guides. We learned by observation and experience. Some had exposure as members of The Mountaineers . . . There was no rescue training. Even the Swiss guides just climbed and we observed. Rock work was confined to Unicorn, Pinnacle and the Tatoosh peaks. We used a fixed rope in the Chutes whenever possible to anchor it. For some years we packed a wooden ladder above Camp Comfort [at upper end of Gibraltar Rock] to stand upright to reach the upper edge of the vast summit crevasses. We had no knowledge of pitons or other hardware for rocks. Artificial aids were not thought "proper" mountaineering at that time. In the early (3 a.m.) starts from Muir, the head guide carried an old fashioned farm lantern to spot the "trail" & everyone else stumbled along behind. We never thought about flashlites (dawn came soon anyway). The alpine stock was adequate for the parties. It gave support going up and down and was soon mastered whereas the ice axe would have been a dangerous instrument. Even Hans [Fuhrer] was impaled by his axe on Mt. Hood. Only along the Gibraltar overhang was the alpine stock in the way. Canteens were rarely used so pieces of ice were liquid plus keeping a prune pit to suck on.

Very few new routes were tried by the guides as their time was well occupied . . . I escorted members of the Prairie Club of Chicago from Paradise to White River camp via Williwakas, Cowlitz, Whitman & Fryingpan Glaciers—all new territory to me at the time.

Doubtless the first Rainier guide also to achieve distinction in other climbing areas was Hans Fuhrer. Born near Grindelwald, Switzer-

land in 1888, Hans learned the ways of climbing early under the tute-
lage of his father and grandfather, who were Alpine guides. In 1912
Hans came to America and Oregon. He was the first truly licensed guide
to begin service in the Pacific Northwest and from 1915 through 1918
led over 100 parties to the summit of Mount Hood. His fame spread
rapidly and in 1919 he was asked by Joe Hazard to join the guide staff
of the Rainier National Park Company. In 5 years Hans and his younger
brother Heinie, who joined him a year later, guided over 3500 people
to the summit via the Gibraltar route, often with 40-50 people in one
party. (During this time, their father was still guiding on the Matterhorn.) Each of the brothers is reported to have made over 150 ascents
of the mountain. Hans' guiding and pioneering of new routes on Hood
and Rainier were only the beginning of a long period of exploration of
mountains of the Pacific Northwest and Canadian Rockies. From 1925
to 1932 Hans guided for Canadian National Railways and for another
7 years he guided independently, leading many of America's top climbers of the day to numerous previously untrodden summits of the Canadian Rockies. Notable among his climbs are several routes on Mount
Robson, including a 1938 first ascent of the broad northeast ridge from
Helmet Col—Hans was 51 at the time. In 1927 Alfred J. Ostheimer
III, an eastern scientist-mountaineer, enlisted Hans' services for a summer of exploration and mapping in the Columbia and Clemenceau Icefields. Spending 63 days in the field, they climbed 35 peaks over 10,000
feet, 28 of these being first ascents. In 1935 Hans was invited to join
the Wood Yukon Expedition. During the course of the summer's mapping of previously unexplored mountain and glacier country, Hans led
the party in the first ascent of 16,644-foot Mount Steele (*American
Alpine Journal*, 1936).

Tommy Hermans, Heinie Fuhrer, Alma Wagen, Hans Fuhrer.

In 1925, the summer after Hans Führer left Rainier and the last summer of his brother Heinie's service there, the guide concession came under the leadership of Harry B. Cunningham, prominent Seattle educator, Scout executive, and youth counselor. "H.B." operated the guide service until 1932 and during this time trained many young men to lead ascents. It was his sad experience to be chief guide during the tragic summers of 1929 and 1931, when several lives were lost. Cunningham's guides were both victims and heroes of the dramas played high on Rainier's slopes.

Harry Cunningham's service on Rainier spanned those years marked by a change in attitude toward the use of ice axe and crampons. Cunningham's own earlier experiences with such equipment and with general climbing techniques during the pre-1930 era are described below (excerpts from letter, December 1968):

My own first climb was with a party of nine led by a man named Reese who operated a camp near Alta Vista. This was in 1911. Ice axes and crampons were unknown. Mr. Reese carried a hand axe to cut steps in the ice. As I recall this timber cruiser 24" handled axe was the same one used to cut kindling for his camp cook stove.

In 1912 Maj. E. S. Ingraham led a party of seven up the north side from the White River Gold Camp. Two Swede miners who spoke no English joined us at the camp. Prior to starting the climb the Swedes put another sole on our boots (made from a worn out leather belt formerly used on the mine's stamping mill). Into the combined three-quarter inch soles they inserted wood screws, then filed the heads to a point. These men heated a mattock in the mine forge and shaped it into a crude and heavy ice axe. Our life line was a ¾" manila rope. We left the mine at 10 p.m. and climbed by moonlight until 3 a.m. We crouched behind a snow ridge with only a canvas tarp and two double blankets. Sleep was impossible so we started on at 4:30. About 6:30 Major Ingraham gave out (he was at least 62 years old—perhaps older).

After a meal of hard tack, prunes and lime candy, he (Ingraham) with two of the climbers returned to our 3 a.m. camp. The remaining six climbers continued the climb until 11 a.m. We estimated that we were within 750-1,000 feet of the top, when out of nowhere a cloud cap formed on top of the mountain and the wind rose to gale force. We started back down the mountain, but were soon enveloped in clouds and driven snow.

The Swedes had chewed tobacco or "snoose" all during the trip up—spitting tobacco juice every few feet. The tobacco stains left on the snow and ice proved to be excellent trail markers as we worked our way back to camp and the mine.

Of his later experiences with equipment while operating the guide service, Cunningham wrote:

There were no crampons available locally in 1925. In the middle of my first season, I purchased a poorly made eight-prong pair from Abercrombie-Fitch. They were too heavy and laced to the foot with heavy raw-hide thongs. Heinie Fuhrer refused to use them as did the other summit guides. Tricouni plate and edge nails replaced screw calks in 1926. In 1927 I imported three pairs of ten point crampons from the Attenhofer Co. of Zurich, Switzerland. These were locked up in the store room at Camp Muir. They were used by the lead guide only two or three times before thieves used broken bunk irons to pry the lock off the door. Every item including the crampons and blankets stored at Camp Muir were stolen or destroyed.

A new supply of crampons was ordered in 1928. Thereafter they were required equipment for the lead guide on all summit climbs. Brigham had crampons on that fatal climb in 1929, Greathouse did not.

(During my interview with Leon Brigham in 1969, he stated that his crampons had been borrowed and were not returned; hence he did not have them during this climb.) Cunningham continues:

It was the first trip for Greathouse and it was felt that without any previous experience on ice crampons would be a handicap and dangerous until such time as he had gained some experience. After that accident both guide and anchor man were required to wear crampons.

The great Depression, paved roads and introduction of mass airplane travel . . . all combined to make overnight stay in the park less desirable and not necessary. Fewer guided tours and more in-out trips the same day greatly curtailed the guide business and number of guides.

Among the most active on Cunningham's guide staff was Leon Brigham, who served from 1925 to 1929. The injuries he suffered in the 1929 accident which claimed the life of fellow guide Forrest Great-house brought an end to Brigham's summers on the mountain. He had come to the Northwest upon completing his studies at Iowa State University. After guiding on the mountain he entered physical education work in Seattle. For many years he served as football coach at Garfield

Harry "H.B." Cunningham, Leon Brigham, Ben Thompson.

High School, then became Director of Athletics for the Seattle school system, from which position he retired a few years ago.

In 1933 Ben Thompson served as chief guide. Thompson had been a guide on Mount Baker and later became co-partner in the Anderson and Thompson ski-manufacturing business in Seattle. He left the company many years ago and is now living in the East, where he is a cartoonist for several national magazines.

Following Thompson as chief guide during the 1930s were Frank "Swede" Willard (1934–35), J. Wendell Trosper (1936), and Gene Jack (1937–38). Willard had guided during the period 1925–33, under both the regimes of Cunningham and Thompson. During his 8 years on the mountain he was active in the search operations following both the Greathouse-Wetzel and Zinn tragedies. Swede provided me with the following interesting comments:

My first introduction to mountaineering was with Joe Hazard. He gave me lots of good sound advice on techniques, etc. I started as a guide by getting into rescue trips when I was a dishwasher in the kitchen of Paradise Inn. That was about 1925 . . . I have climbed Rainier about 100 times. I know of one summer when times were so tough I did all the climbing to the summit by myself with Darroch Crooks as assistant. We were hitting them every three days all summer. We lost about 20 lbs that year. Counting turn backs at Camp Comfort and out of the crater, putting up ropes, rescue trips, it would go over a 100.—I made more money climbing in the summer than teaching school in Yakima County. . . . I could write a book on all of this . . . just on the Rainier guides alone. Great fellows. Hundreds of stories. Of course one of the best was Bill Butler . . . the stories we could tell together. His first ascent as an assistant, a green kid from Chattanooga, Tenn. . . the first accident he helped out with, etc. . .

I have started out with 70 to the summit with one assistant. Then one year I took a man to the top who was 70 years of age. Another time I took a young boy who was 9. I have been trapped overnight twice in the crater, with a party. Had tourists get hit with rocks, they slipped off the 2″ rope in the chutes. Had one woman try 3 times (at $62.00 a clip) to get to the top. Two of us finally took her up alone and carried her the last 100 feet unconscious.

I have had 30 below zero on that hill with a 60 mile wind. Another time we almost burned up on the hill because the sun was so bright. Was snow blind for two weeks once, because I broke my glasses. One year I had a party of 4 and we had to lose a thousand feet [of altitude] because a snow bridge went out while we were coming down.

I remember having loggers caulks for my shoes and that was all. We chopped steps from Camp Comfort [top of Gibraltar Rock] all the way up and down . . . I must have been one of the first to wear crampons on any mountain in the West. The tourists didn't get to use them because they were too dangerous . . . I can remember the entire roof of the big stone cabin being blown off by terrific winds. We carried stuff on our backs . . . and practically rebuilt the thing . . . H. B. Cunningham was such a great guy . . . like a father to us . . . really a great man to lead young guys.

Mt. climbing makes or breaks you . . . I look at that great mountain and can't help being excited that I had been a part of it . . . Strange I never had one kind of accident . . . It really wasn't that I was a skilled climber or guide. We were so lucky. We didn't have equipment—great strategy and a lot of guts and pride that we could beat the hill . . . Actually we knew little about climbing techniques . . . When you're young, strong, and cocky nothing stops you.

Of his days as chief guide (1933–34), Willard states:

Actually being Chief Guide then wasn't much. Not like in Cunningham's day. I really was a climber and not a valley boy . . . In those days (at least when I was Chief Guide) no one led a party until he had 10 summit trips as an assistant . . . Actually when I hired [Les] Yansen, [Gene] Jack, [Dick] Klinge, [Ariel] Edmiston, etc., not many had climbed except Trosper. Trosper had been around a little . . . was an old dependable plugger who got up and down the hill without any problems . . . There were only a handful of guys who actually were Summit Guides. Course lots of us climbed the mountain many times before we ever entered the Guide Dept. I had climbed the Kautz route with old man Hazard when I was 14 years old.

Guiding as you know isn't climbing. I had climbed with many Europeans but very few guys have the patience, the guts, etc. to take a bunch of tourists and baby them up that hill . . . being a guide is one thing [but] climbing on your own roped in to guys who are as good as you or better is something else.

I used to love taking a bunch of guides up the hill to put in the ropes in the chutes, placing wooden ladders in places above. What a ball it was . . . not to have to analyze every guy step-by-step, put their crampons on, put their feet into a hole . . . put them to bed, get them up, feed them. That guiding . . . get them to the top no matter what. *But* the big thing in your mind was you gotta get them back, *you got to get them back.* You turn around a thousand feet from the top because a cap has covered the crater. You hurry your party back, stop at Muir, look around and the mountain is clear as a bell. Everybody has that look in their eyes, even your assistant—of what a lousy guide you are, "We could have made it."

As you get older every summer, how many times you say: "What am I doing here? I must be crazy."

Some guides continued their mountaineering activities on Rainier as Park rangers either on seasonal or permanent status; only a few made the Park Service their career. The most notable among these is William Jackson "Bill" Butler, whose climbing and search and rescue exploits over more than 30 years have become legendary and the subject of much publicity, which runs against his unassuming nature.

Bill Butler's first acquaintance with Rainier came during the summer of 1929, at the time of the Wetzel-Greathouse tragedy. While in Tacoma, enroute from Tennessee to Alaska on a homestead-seeking trip, Butler heard of the drama in progress on the mountain looming high on the southeastern horizon. He immediately changed his plans and headed for Rainier—on foot. Too bashful to thumb a ride, he walked all the way to near Ashford, where he finally was offered a lift into the Park. Until his retirement from the Park Service in 1963, Butler spent the ensuing years as a permanent fixture on the mountain. The remainder of the summer and fall of 1929 he worked on a road construction crew in the Park and during the following two summers served as a guide on H. B. Cunningham's staff. In 1933 he began his Park Service career as a ranger, his appointment being on a conditional basis. His leading role in subsequent year-around search and rescue operations earned him permanent status, by proclamation of President Roosevelt in 1936. Later he became Paradise District Ranger and Assistant Chief Ranger of the Park.

Although several times offered more lucrative assignments and opportunities for transfer to other areas in the National Park system, Bill Butler chose to remain on the mountain and in the Park he knew so well. During his long period of climbing on Rainier he never sought fame as a mountaineer, nor participation in a major expedition for which he would have been so well-suited; instead, he quietly and happily pursued his life on the mountain with his vivacious wife Marthie, whom he had met when she worked as a waitress in the Park.

Perhaps the most eloquent testimonial to Bill Butler's career in public service was that given him during one of his last years in the Park. In October 1960, under the impression he was being sent to Los Angeles on official business, Bill suddenly found himself "on stage" as the honored subject of the TV program "This is Your Life." Butler's normally ruddy face turned several hues deeper from embarrassment.

Bill Butler and Frank "Swede" Willard. Bill Butler and wife Marthie.

Wendell Trosper, Fred Thieme.

The only thing that prevented his darting out of the auditorium was the moral support and presence on the program of many Rainier friends.

Most of those who served as summit guides on Rainier in the era preceding World War II seldom ventured on other but the well-worn "guide route" and many knew little about other sides of the great peak. Among the few exceptions was J. Wendell "Wendy" Trosper, who guided 1933–37. Wendy was one of the first to explore Ptarmigan Ridge, reaching about 12,000 feet in 1933, and to pioneer new lines of ascent on Sunset Amphitheater and Sunset Ridge. He made over 90 ascents of the peak and was the first to climb Rainier by 10 different routes. Trosper made a ski descent from near the summit of Little Tahoma in April 1933 and was among the top competitors in the world-famous Silver Skis Race at Paradise in the mid-1930s.

Wendy Trosper's close climbing companion on many explorations of the peak was Fred Thieme, who later became vice-president of the University of Washington and then president of the University of Colorado.

Clark E. Schurman served as chief guide from 1939 through 1942. A widower most of his life, Schurman devoted his abundant energy and talent to Scout activities and to developing mountaineering techniques and a philosophy oriented to safety. An intense, brusk little man with the military way and mustache of General Pershing, he had a soul highly sensitive to the beauties of the mountain and to the dreams of youth—it was Clark Schurman who significantly altered my life when he suggested I give up milking cows, enroll in college, and guide during the summers.

Visitors to the small musty auditorium in the basement of the Guide House long remembered Schurman's evening program of tinted

Gene Jack, Fritz Weissner (visiting climber of international fame), Clark Schurman, Dick Klinge.

lantern slides (and the first Kodachrome slides) which revealed the beauties of the mountain and its surrounding parklands. Schurman's poetic interpretations of the great natural forces at work helped bring the mountain close to the hearts of his guests.

During my period of service in Schurman's highly disciplined regime, characterized by a "by-the-numbers" operation of the Guide House, seven to nine men were on the staff. We were paid $85 a month, from which $30 was taken for room and board—for summit trips we received an extra $25 as lead guide and $15 as assistant. We did not compete for tips with bus-boys, waitresses, and room clerks, as The Chief frowned upon such demeaning activity among the prestigious green-shirted guide personnel. Yet, we occasionally augmented our monthly income by solicitous handling of Cooks Tour-ist customers on the Paradise ice-cave trips.

Our duties were many and varied: we caught the large red buses of the RNPCo as they rounded the last bend below Paradise Inn, jumping onto the running board and welcoming the tours with an exuberant speech about the doings in the valley, the horse trips, and the hikes with foot guides to the ice caves and "tin-pants nature-coasting" down adjacent snow slopes. One of my chores was to operate the slide projector for Schurman's nightly talks. We then outfitted the eager customers for the next morning's hikes. Following the return from the twice-daily 4-hour hikes, we scrubbed boots and hung them in the drying room. To top off the evening the guides were expected to head for Paradise Inn and mingle with visiting dowagers, dance with them, and talk them into joining our next day's ice-cave trip—and we had to keep smiling through it all. Small wonder most of us were disappointed whenever a summit trip left without us.

Even on the big climb, however, we were not completely cut off from contact with the Guide House. By means of an effective Schurmanism, each of our clients was identified by an initial on his rented pack and by a Morse Code signal which could be used in the flashlight communication from Camp Hazard (on the Kautz route). The Chief then was able to identify members of the team in case of emergencies. Or, by signals we could request the next summit party to bring up another gallon of white gas or an extra sleeping bag or more efficient stove. The pre-arranged 9 p.m. signalling between the large searchlight on the upper porch of the Guide House and the small flashes emanating from 11,000 feet on the dark bulk of the mountain always created a big stir in the valley. Then, when we reached the crater rim, we were obliged to send flashes down with the large mirror cached there. Invariably all the signalling from the peak brought a rash of flashlight and mirror operations from all parts of the valley below.

Guides of 1940. From left: Clark Schurman, Bob Hoxsey, Worth McClure, Jr., Ken Spangenberg, Bob Sutermeister, Dee Molenaar, Les Yansen.

After his 4-year period of running the guide service, Schurman helped plan and direct Camp Long, a city park in West Seattle designed for use by Scout groups and mountaineering clubs. There Schurman created a concrete "glacier," complete with crevasses and steps fashioned into the steep "ice face," for use in climbing instruction. He is best known at Camp Long for his design and construction of Monitor Rock (after his death re-named Schurman Rock). A 20-foot-high "spire" made of native stone and concrete, the rock incorporates in its various sides the features that characterize a typical rock climb: ledges, chimneys, laybacks, overhangs, chockstones, friction pitches. For over 20 years the rock has served as the in-town training ground for mountaineering classes. Each year hundreds of neophyte climbers, students in the numerous climbing courses being conducted each spring throughout the Puget Sound area, gather at Camp Long for a day of learning the moves of rock climbing and steep glacier travel.

Not until several years after his death in 1955 did Clark Schurman's long-expressed dream materialize in the construction of a shelter cabin at 9500-foot Steamboat Prow. Named Camp Schurman in memory of "The Chief," the cabin was constructed by volunteer labor, with material purchased by donations from numerous former Scouts, guides, and outdoor lovers who knew him over many years, and by money raised from a sale of oil paintings done by Schurman in his later years.

The author in 1940, in the days of the ice-axe loop, downless parka, and nailed boots.

34 Post-World War II Guides

During the war years 1943–45 there was little climbing activity on Rainier and the Park Company gave up its operation of the guide concession. In 1946 the guide service was revived as an independent concession under the direction of Ed Kennedy as chief guide. Kennedy was a well-rounded Northwest climber who during the pre-war period had made numerous first ascents and explorations in the Cascades. He suffered a broken back in a fall from The Tooth, a peak near Snoqualmie Pass, but recovered sufficiently to serve during the war in the 10th Mountain Division. Wounded and hospitalized in the Italian campaign, Kennedy arrived at Rainier "well wired together." His fellow guides included fellow ex-Mountain Troopers Gordie Butterfield and Jim Nussbaum and international ski racer and climber Bil Dunaway.

Dunaway continued the guide service in 1947 with Bob Parker (also from the 10th Mountain Division), Chuck Welsh, and me. I found it good to be back on the mountain, and on the Kautz route, after 4 years in the Coast Guard. In 1948 I began serving as a seasonal ranger, Parker and Dunaway went to Europe, and the guide service was up for grabs, but no qualified candidates were available. Two men from Chicago showed up, claiming extensive climbing experience, particularly in the Tetons, and desiring to take over the concession. However, upon a demonstration of their snow-climbing techniques during a day with the rangers on the Nisqually Glacier, they were rejected—they were unable to make a self-arrest on snow even after being given instructions.

The summer of 1949 found Chuck Welsh back in the guide service, along with fellow Seattle climbers-skiers Bob Craig and Bob Kuss (Ross). In 1950 two French mountaineers and skiers, Roby Albuoy and Ollie Chiseaux, ran the concession—the first time in Rainier's history that local climbers were not guiding on the peak.

Bil Dunaway returned from a year in Europe to take the guide service again in 1951. With him, for their first of many summers on the mountain, were the young twins from West Seattle, Jim and Louie Whittaker. The Whittakers operated the guide concession together in 1952, then served a hitch in the Army's Mountain and Cold Weather Training Command in Colorado before returning to the guide service in 1954. During their absence in 1953 the concession was operated by Dr. Paul Gerstmann and Dick Krizman.

During 1938–42, and after the war until 1951, guided parties chiefly used the Kautz route. When the Whittakers began guiding in 1951

Jim Whittaker, Bil Dunaway, and Lou Whittaker, in 1951.

they concentrated on developing routes that could again utilize the cabins at Camp Muir. The twins reopened Gibraltar as a guide route in 1951 and thus virtually ended use of the Kautz by the guide staff.

The Whittakers were the first of the postwar generation of climbers to guide on the mountain. Many young mountaineers followed in subsequent years, both as guides and future participants in major expeditions to all parts of the world. Besides the Whittakers, this marked the beginning of the era of Dick McGowan, Gary Rose, Gil Blinn, Lute Jerstad, Herb Staley, the Ullin brothers, and many other excellent young climbers. Several achieved fame on the remote peaks of Alaska, Yukon Territory, the Andes, Antarctica, and the Himalayas. Doubtless the most widely heralded has been Jim Whittaker, who in 1963 was the first American to plant Old Glory on the summit of Mount Everest.

The Whittakers continued guiding during the summers after their return from the Army, then went into the outdoor and recreational equipment business. Eventually Jim became general manager for Recreational Equipment, Inc. in Seattle while Louie opened Whittaker's Chalet, an outdoor-equipment store chain in Tacoma. Both men continue to climb Rainier and Louie currently (1970) serves during the summer as chief guide. Jim Whittaker's unique position of being first American atop Everest has opened new horizons and opportunities with their attendant obligations, and his mountaineering has been somewhat curtailed in recent years. However, in 1965 he joined Senator Robert F. Kennedy, George Senner, Barry Prather, Bill Prater, Jim Craig, Bill Allard, and me in the first ascent of the Yukon's Mount Kennedy, the peak named by the Canadian government in honor of the late President John F. Kennedy (whom Jim had met at a White House reception following the return of the American Everest Expedition). Jim and Senator Bob Kennedy subsequently formed a close friendship that was tragically terminated by an assassin's bullet in Los Angeles in June 1968.

Jim Whittaker speaks of his personal feelings for the mountain on his skyline (written communication, February 1969):

Mt. Rainier has all the features of Mt. Everest except the lack of oxygen that goes with higher elevations. As far as glaciers, icefalls, rock ridges, and a true summit are concerned, Mt. Rainier has them all. The weather on Rainier can reach a severity equal to that of the highest mountain in the world . . . the thing that makes the climb such a reward are the difficulties encountered along the way. Without these, Rainier would not be the enriching influence that it is for people in the Northwest.

Dick McGowan served as chief guide during the period 1956–65 and during his regime instituted the 5-day climbing seminars held throughout the summers at Camp Muir. McGowan's experience on several Alaskan and two major Himalayan expeditions (Lhotse in 1955 and Masherbrum in 1960) provided the background for the success and continuing popularity of the seminars. In Seattle during this time McGowan opened his Alpine Hut, the first in a chain of mountaineering equipment stores.

The Camp Muir seminars conducted by McGowan's staff included leading Northwest mountaineers as guest lecturers. The open-air, high-altitude classes covered techniques of high-angle snow and ice climbing

and glacier travel, crevasse rescue, mountaineering medicine and first aid, routefinding, mountain weather, expeditionary mountaineering and philosophy, climbing equipment, clothing and food, geology, and mountaineering history. After 4 days of instruction and rigorous exercise on the rugged glacier terrain around Camp Muir, the visiting climbers generally were in top shape and well-acclimatized for the summit trip the final day of the seminar—if the weather hadn't deteriorated by then.

On McGowan's staff during 1960–62 was Luther G. Jerstad, a young man whose accomplishments on the basketball court at Pacific Lutheran University in Tacoma later were overshadowed by his attainment of the summit of Mount Everest. Jerstad's gaining a berth on the Everest team came in the final days of selection by expedition leader Norman Dyhrenfurth, but all who endorsed Lute's membership were confident he would carry his share of the load. During the ensuing 4-month expedition, Jerstad climbed to the 26,200-foot South Col twice in support of Whittaker's successful assault on the summit, and once again during his and Barry Bishop's climb to Everest's crown 3 weeks later.

Jerstad offers the following observations on his experiences on Rainier:

The value of Mt. Rainier to one who goes on to expedition climbing and to larger peaks is both psychological and physical. Ascents of Rainier require that a man learns to carry heavy loads, sometimes through deep snow for ten to fifteen hours at a time. Under such loads, often carried during storms that arise suddenly, a man must persevere and calmly accept the biting winds and blasting ice particles hurled at him. He must be in control of himself at all times or he might well perish. Emergencies and illness must be expected, and fatigue and mental irritation be anticipated. Maturity and

Bob Craig and author in 1949, planning a climb.   *Chuck Welsh.*

selflessness become imperative. Without these qualities, a man will not be a strong expedition climber. Rainier provides a training and testing ground where a future expedition climber can come to know himself, his strengths, his weaknesses, his sense of humor, and his concept of responsibility to his comrades.

In 1966–67 the concession was operated by Jack Melill, a Seattle schoolteacher who for the previous 10 summers had served as seasonal ranger at Paradise. Melill continued the seminars as part of his summer operations. In 1966 his staff led 477 climbers to the summit, nearly doubling the previous year's total of 261 clients. The rapid increase was to continue in succeeding summers.

A change in management in 1968 brought Lou Whittaker back to head the guide service. Lou was helped by a number of competent climbers and in 1969 he brought to his staff Phursumba Sherpa, brilliant young (26) Nepalese climber and brother-in-law of Nawang Gombu, who in 1963 had stood on Everest's summit with Jim Whittaker. Phursumba had been a member of the 1965 all-Indian expedition to Mount Everest. He personally reached about 27,000 feet during the successful assault on the summit by three separate parties. He later gained experience as an instructor in Tenzing Norgay's Himalayan Mountaineering Institute at Darjeeling, India. Phursumba speaks fluent English and he has made a ready transition to climbing guide and instructor at Paradise. Also with Whittaker's staff in 1969 was the Austrian climber, Adolf "Adi" Weissensteiner, who came to Rainier with a background of fine climbs in the Alps and as a member of the 1967 Austrian expedition to the Pamir Mountains of the Soviet Union.

Many veteran Northwest mountaineers are seeing their sons carry on the family tradition. Among the guides in recent years have been

"K" Molenaar, George Senner.

Twins Jim and Lou Whittaker with Hans Fuhrer (guide of 1920s), at Paradise in 1952.

Gary, Jay, and Jim Ullin, sons of old-time Bremerton climber-guide Chet Ullin; George Heuston, son of "vintage climber" Frank Heuston of Shelton; Bruce Davis, son of John Davis, former president of The Mountaineers, and Carl Whittaker, son of "Big Jim," and his friend Joe Kennedy, son of Ethel and the late Senator Robert F. Kennedy. These and many other young men, most of whom have gained the rudiments of mountaineering early in life and who have absorbed the increasing sophistication of climbing techniques in their 'teens—and the attractive young women who have served both as cooks at Camp Muir and as assistants on summit climbs—will continue to insure a steady flow of competent glacier and summit guides to Mount Rainier.

Gary Rose. Dick McGowan and Gil Blinn.

Fred Beckey
Pete Schoening

Herb Staley
Dan Davis

 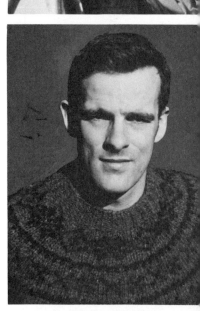

Chuck Crenchaw
Lee Nelson

Gene Prater
Bill Prater

Members of Sherpa Climbing Club of eastern Washington.

Dave Mahre
Jim Wickwire

Fred Dunham
Fred Stanley

Jay and Gary Ullin

Judy Waller, first woman to climb
Ptarmigan and Liberty Ridges.

Phursumba Sherpa

Jim Whittaker
Lute Jerstad

Rainier climbers and guides who were members of
1963 American Mount Everest Expedition.

Willi Unsoeld
Tom Hornbein

Maynard Miller
Barry Prather

35 In Retrospect

Together we have known apprehension, uncertainty and fear; but of what importance is all that? For it was only there that we discovered many things of which we had previously known nothing: a joy that was new to us, happiness that was doubled because it was shared, a wordless friendship which was no mere superficial impulse.

GASTON REBUFFAT
Starlight and Storm

As the shadows lengthen in Life's afternoon, we cling all the more fondly to the friends of our youth.

JOHN MUIR

In my 30 years on and about Mount Rainier—since I first appeared at the Guide House in 1939 wearing blue jeans and knee-length "rattle-snake boots" and equipped with an "ice axe" fashioned from a garden tool—I have been privileged to share experiences with climbers of several eras of mountaineering. The mountain has become for me a source of contemplation not only for its overwhelming physical dominance but also for its rich human associations. Rainier has become a personality evolved from the personalities of those I've met on its slopes —the mountaineers who have given the best of themselves to learn the secrets hidden among the high cirques and ridges and across vast snowfields.

As I recall treks on the peak, each slope stirs memories which in total have given to me a lasting impression of the mountain's character. As I thumb through my mountaineering diary, or spend a winter evening "sorting slides," I am compelled to pause in retrospection of climbs and expeditions, of slopes and summits, and of the close friendships I've gained in the high barren world of ice and rock. Notations on weather and snow and ice conditions, on times required for an ascent, and on misadventures enroute, all bring back to life the spice of many happy days spent in the mountains.

Mount Rainier is many things to many people. It forever is changing in mood and aspect, as directed by sometimes dramatic, sometimes subtle, changes in weather, cloud cover, and play of light and shadow across ridges and snowfields. The peak casts an everchanging spell by morning, afternoon, and evening—and by moonlight. Often in the direct, unshadowed light of high noon in midsummer, the mountain is the least enchanting, a bland mass of brown rock and white snow.

Conversely, under its full ermine wrap of winter, and in pink twilight, the mountain is the most feminine—in contrast to the harsh dusty lines of late summer. Rarely does one find Mount Rainier completely as remembered from a previous visit.

Memories often are most strongly revived by sounds and smells. As one moves from the lowlands and up the mountain, what happy thoughts are conjured by the springtime pungency of alder buds bursting forth from thickets still bottomed in snow; the smell of freshly dampened trails and the whispering of fir boughs or the far-off muffled roar of a waterfall; the scent of wood smoke and crackle of the forest campfire; the smell of leather and creak of the pack; the fragrance of lupine and soft gurgle of a heather-trenched brook; the sudden, high-pitched whistle of the marmot; the deep throaty echoes coming from deep within the ice where surface meltwater cascades into a glacier *moulin*; the smell of white gas or butane and the hiss of the mountain stove at high camp; the otherwise prosaic aroma of Chap-Stik, Sno-Seal, and sun cream; the crunch of crampons sinking into frozen early-morning snow; the ozone-gunpowder pungency of metal striking rock; and the flapping of fabric of parka or tent as gusts of wind remind one of the vagaries of high-mountain weather—these and many more ingredients form the Rainier climbing atmosphere.

The physical movements of climbing are no less a part of the esthetic enjoyment of mountaineering. Even though climbing movements lack the nostalgia-inducing elements of sight, sound, and smell, there are definite joys in being physically in tune with the high-mountain environment. But only one in the top condition of a guide, or of an expedition climber, can appreciate most fully the pure pleasure derivable from prolonged physical exertion.

Generally, the casual climber returns home a mixture of elation and exhaustion—mostly the latter—and a day or two later is stiff and sore in joints and muscles. Skinned knuckles and scratches not noticed during the climb become stiffened by healing tissue, sun-baked lips and noses become cracked and blistered, and deep aches penetrate where pack straps have dug into shoulders and back—not to mention the usual blisters on toes and heels. Yet in a week or two the climber is ready to go again, pack made up anew, and including another package of band-aids.

On the other hand, the mountain guide and expedition climber learn the full pleasures of being in physical harmony with his mountains. The aches and pains of early season are obliterated by time and distance, sore throats have been long removed from the germ centers of town, and the climber rapidly swings into a routine of performing tough chores. Lungs enlarge to unsuspected capacity and a deep breath is like an injection of vitamins into the blood stream; the town-stagnant step gains new strength, agility, and quickness, and the climber feels a rebirth of the youthful exuberance for running and leaping.

Even the drudgery of slogging in deep snow under heavy packs can have its pleasures. In the gradual adaptation of a steady pace of breathing and moving upward, one can become entranced by the natural rhythm possible between the slow lunging step and a breathing that can become melodious—as an old tune is whistled between the teeth. Even perspiration—under healthy steady exertion—becomes as a lubricant. In all the moves of the conditioned mountaineer there are such expressions of harmony and rhythm—swinging the axe against ice or the hammer against the piton, stomping crampons into ice or frozen snow, lunging across a chasm or leaping a crevasse, or simply taking in or paying out the belay rope.

I have been asked whether I ever get tired of climbing Mount Rainier. Many times I have preempted such a question by strongly commenting that "this was my last climb of that old snow hump." Such feelings generally come after a climb up a "dog route" with which I've become too familiar and which was made on a clear and warm—and crowded—weekend on the mountain.

With others like myself, guides and rangers who had become weary of continually repeating a common route in order to satisfy requests of neophyte friends to take them up Rainier, it has been easy to become blasé about further ascents of the mountain, and to ponder why we keep going back. Perhaps the most convincing testimony of our feelings after one summer of "over-climbing" the peak was demonstrated by fellow-ranger Elvin "Bob" Johnson late in the summer of 1950. With four companions (K Molenaar, George Senner, Hank Daub, and Aubrey Haines) Bob left the ranger station, heavily laden as usual. About 15 minutes later Bob was back, alone. He had gotten as far as Alta Vista, a few hundred feet above the parking area. There he had stopped to adjust his pack, then taken a long, hard look at the mountain. Suddenly he wheeled back down the trail with an emphatic, "Aw, to hell with it!"

Sometimes it is the pre-climb, in-the-sack apprehensions that, for a few climbers, eventually turn the pure joy of the sport into grim tenacity. After one has been personally involved in a mountain accident or tragedy and has allowed himself to dwell too long on the event, he is particularly prone—when fighting for restful oblivion in his sleeping bag—to be trapped by a mind that conjures up all the possibilities for disaster on the forthcoming climb. Perhaps he feels he's been lucky so far but that his number is about up. The deaths of former climbing companions, and near misses to himself, loom in the mind as he blinks from the bag at the surrounding tent wall or star-studded sky. As he squirms for comfort and rest, the faint tinkling of a falling ice fragment is forebodingly magnified to a crash and the rustle of the tent fabric becomes an approaching blizzard. At such times of accentuated supine inactivity one's adrenalin becomes aroused in mental efforts to resolve a physical situation that hasn't happened and in all probability will not happen. Through this, the greatest irritant is that of believing one's companions are sleeping soundly.

Thus it always is a welcome relief to finally leave the bag and become busy again, in preparing breakfast and getting roped up. Then the climber again is a reciprocating part of the surrounding physical world which in pre-dawn fantasy was so filled with apprehension—and he is glad he didn't mention his fears to his more complacent buddies (who in fact may have experienced the same mental anguish). Once again he moves with the terrain, skirting a crevasse or icefall here, dodging a falling pebble there—the apprehensions vanish and are forgotten as action takes over. Once again the climber is master of his fate and a freely moving agent, able and desirous of being involved in the physical elements of mountaineering.

Some climbers never repeat a climb they've once made. A few (as Fred Beckey) will seldom make a climb unless it's a pioneering effort—a first ascent; to these mountaineers the main basis for climbing obviously is the challenge of the unknown and untried, the virgin summit or wall. Conversely, there are those who care only to trod the beaten trail; perhaps their interest is guided by a sentiment for traveling terrain with an historic past, or to compare notes with those of earlier climbers—or to be assured a better chance at success. Still others care little whether or not a route has been climbed before so long as it provides them personally with a new experience. The knowledge that a previous party has proven the route "will go" doubtless gives a psychological boost, but the personal challenge still remains.

Many persons who've been indoctrinated to climbing through classes conducted by mountaineering clubs have found enjoyment in the sociability of large-party trips. Some seldom make non-club ascents and continue most of their activity as members or leaders of club-sponsored climbs. Obviously, to derive continued pleasure from traveling in groups of 10 to 100 or more people, one must have a well-developed social nature; generally these people have little in common with those individualists who find pleasure in solo climbing.

There also are those mountaineers whose climbing activities over several years have gradually become absorbed in the demands of mountain search and rescue operations—some MRC personnel seldom climb "for fun" anymore. Although often carrying out a thankless task, these individuals have found in their Good Samaritan work the incentive to develop special skills and equipment that have later been beneficial to pure mountaineering. Certainly, the requirements of maneuvering an injured climber or a fatality across extremely difficult terrain, and under weather conditions that would normally keep them home, have provided a highly sophisticated form of challenge.

In the final analysis, the full enjoyment of mountain climbing includes a basic joy in experiencing and being in contact with the natural world of rock and ice, a love of physical exertion and of good companionship, and a challenging objective. Once a climber no longer enjoys the adventurous and physically demanding aspects of the sport, and no longer is able to fully commit himself to a common struggle with others toward a distant summit, he becomes a liability to the party. It then behooves him to retire to the slippered ease of the hearthside, there to smoke his pipe and live in the past.

For most mountaineers the main ingredient for a happy climb is good companionship. The joy of mountaineering cannot be far removed from the joy of having chance acquaintances in the hills become, under fire, fast and lasting friends. As one's climbing extends into the middle years he becomes all the more aware of the camaraderie developed among friends who've shared numerous ascents on many peaks. Whereas in the neophyte years a climber's youthful exuberance often requires only that the peak challenges his physical potential, in later years the mellowing process takes over and the aging mountaineer dwells more on the enjoyment of companions and shared experiences.

I will let my good friend George Senner have the last few words, which summarize the feelings of many of our contemporaries:

Mount Rainier has been and continues to be to me the "standard" for the "good life". Over the last 30 years I have found peace, health, happiness, comradeship, humility, and patience in scrambling over its ridges and glaciers and climbing to its crest. In contrast to the asphalt and concrete of man's cities, this pile of lava and ice has satisfied and stimulated all my senses. The experiences and memories founded on this mountain are endless.

I met "the love of my life" on the slopes of the mountain—my closest friends have shared with me the beautiful days, the storms, the alpine meadows, and the high lovely camps. I hold no spot on earth in higher esteem. Though I have also enjoyed memorable trips in the high Alps and in the Alaskan and Yukon wilderness, my thoughts always come back to this peak.

Anyone can benefit from the influence of the mountain. After a few days high on the rock and snow, all of one's faculties are sharpened. The meadows are so green, the flowers so colorful and the flowing streams so sweet as one descends from the barren world above. There is no room left here for petty worries, depression, or negative thoughts—one is re-oriented. Man is as he should be.

Last campfires never die. And you and I
On separate ways to Life's December,
Will always dream by this last fire
And have this mountain to remember.

CLARK E. SCHURMAN

PART SIX ADDENDUM

Noteworthy Mountaineering

Summary of New Routes Climbed Since 1972. (See table on p. 152–153.)

Mount Rainier:

1973, July 8: Russell Cliff climbed via central rock-cliff bands, by Dean Bentley (age 15, "youngest first ascenter"), Jim Springer (18, "oldest leader of a first ascent"), John Thompson.

1974, June: Russell Cliff, via steep snow/ice face on left, by Chris Mahre, Dave Mahre, Gene Prater.

1974, July 4–6: Nisqually Glacier, entire length from terminus to crater rim, by Dave Briggs, Laurie Briggs, Fred Hart, Dan Luchtel, Ken Luedeke; camps at 6100 and 9800 feet.

1978, March 20: Willis Wall, via western couloir to 12,500 feet, then descent via Liberty Ridge, by Steve Doty, Jerome Eberharter, Jon Olson; 7 hours up couloir of water, ice and loose rock.

1978, June 30–July 4: Mowich Face, via ascent of rock band below ice cap, traverse left at base of ice cliff, then up steep ice slope to upper Ptarmigan Ridge; bivouac, then to Liberty Cap. By Dave Gordon, Howard Weaver, and Scott———(last name not known).

1982, May 24: South Tahoma Headwall, via climb diagonally left up broad steep snow slope below rock bands near crest of Tahoma Cleaver, then up several ice slopes and rock bands to Point Success, by Sean Meehan and Tod Woolridge.

Little Tahoma:

1979, January 7–8: North Face, first winter ascent, via hike from Paradise. Face well-covered by ice and snow, and crampons used entirely on five-hour climb. By George Dunn and Eric Simonson.

1980–81, December 30–January 1: West Ridge from base at separation of Ingraham and Emmons Glaciers; partially on north side of ridge in lower parts and south side on upper part, with bivouac halfway. By Matt Christensen and Paul Cook.

ASCENT BY SOVIET MOUNTAINEERS

In early September 1975 a group of six climbers from the Soviet Union visited various climbing areas of the United States, as part of a U.S.-U.S.S.R. climbers exchange program sponsored by The American Alpine Club. The Soviets were led by 69-year-old Vitaly Abalakov, famed "Father of Soviet Mountaineering." Excepting Abalakov, all made an ascent of Rainier via the Kautz Glacier ice-chute route. According to other climbers on the mountain that day, the Soviets displayed unusual dexterity and confidence in rapidly scaling and descending the steep chute, utilizing only their crampons without chopping steps in the ice. Among the group was Sergei Bershov, 27, four times speed-climbing champion of the Soviet Union; a few years later (in 1982) Bershov was in the first party of eleven Soviets to ascend a difficult new route on Mount Everest's southwest face.

ASCENT BY SENIOR CITIZEN: JULIUS BOEHM

During July 28–31, 1978, in a climb that took four days round trip from Paradise, 80-year-old Julius Boehm ascended the Ingraham Glacier-Disappointment Cleaver route. The popular Swiss-born candymaker of Issaquah, Washington, who had previously climbed the mountain at age 70 via the Emmons–Winthrop Glacier route, was in a seven-man party that was led by Rainier veterans George Senner, Charles "Bud" Robinson, and Dick Wahlstrom, and included Dr. Julian Ansell, Dr. James Tupper, and *Seattle Times* Foreign Affairs writer Svein Gilje.

Dr. Ansell provides the following information on the medical aspects of the trip with Julius:

> In preparation for the climb with Julius I consulted with Dr. Tom Hornbein, Everest climber, physiologist, and anesthesiologist, along with Seattle cardiologists Len Cobb and Steve Yarnell. Hornbein said there was no precedent for an 80-year-old climbing Rainier, but suggested we carry oxygen. Cobb made the astute observation that "his legs, not his heart" would be the problem, and Yarnell arranged for a lightweight continuous electrocardiographic tracing through Medical Communications System Associates of Seattle.
>
> Of most importance was that we climbed the mountain with strong people with great knowledge of Rainier—George Senner, Dick Wahlstrom, and Bud Robinson. Dr. James Tupper, who had personally treated Julius for orthopedic problems, was great support for any medical problems.
>
> The usual two-day marathon of Rainier was lengthened to four, and Julius stayed at Paradise the night before to increase his opportunity to acclimatize. He predicted correctly that he "never had trouble with altitude and wouldn't this time." Perhaps camping the first night at 8900 feet and the second night at 11,000 feet en route to the summit was helpful. Certainly the more deliberate pace gave him the opportunity to recuperate from each day's effort.

Julius is by any standard a remarkable 80-year-old. He does not wear glasses and could easily spot climbers on the glaciers a mile away. He is slight and appears closer to 65 than 80. He climbed the Matterhorn and Rainier at age 70. His resting pulse is 80 (the same as mine). His maximum heart rate recorded on the climb was 120. On the summit after signing the register his pulse was 90 (same as mine). The electrocardiogram he wore showed only two ectopic (extra) beats during a 12-hour recording. Julius's skin always felt warm to the touch and he was the last in the party to put on extra clothing when the evening chill came. When asked how he felt he had two answers. One was a Viennese-accented "Perrr . . . fect"; the other was "pretty good." He had some difficulty while wearing sun goggles locating steps kicked ahead of him. This tendency was exaggerated when he wore crampons but he negotiated a tricky little ice ledge over a crevasse at 13,500 feet without difficulty. His tolerance was basically 3000 vertical feet per day. When he lost energy his legs became weak. He recuperated completely after a few hours' rest. Even though he sometimes called out, "slower please," he tenaciously kept moving to complete the climb. At no time was the available oxygen required.

By sunrise of the day following the summit climb Julius was again "perrr . . . fect" and moved with long skating strides down the lower snowfields. Shortly after the trip I was asked if I would recommend that other 80-year-olds climb Rainier. My answer was that I would recommend the climb to anyone of any age in good physical shape with the desire and proper support.

Julius Boehm

CIRCLING THE MOUNTAIN ON SKIS

The first (and unexpectedly adventurous) ski encirclement of Mount Rainier—on nordic touring skis—was made May 24–30, 1986, by N. L. Kirkland, 40; Terry Pritchards, 31; Dana Rush, 34, and Dr. Roy Walters, 43. Though made during a spell of clear weather, the seven-day clockwise journey from Paradise passed through very cold temperatures and high winds, as well as icefalls and dangerous crevasse conditions. While crossing the South Mowich Glacier, Kirkland survived a plunge into a deep crevasse, nearly suffocating when his face was pressed into the crevasse wall. Later, on the Emmons Glacier, the party was forced to detour upward to 13,000 feet to find a way through and down the Ingraham Glacier icefall, en route back to Paradise.

ASCENTS BY THE HANDICAPPED

Perhaps the ultimate challenge to be met in the ascent of Rainier's steep icy slopes is that imposed by various physical handicaps, and in recent years the mountain has provided such a testing ground.

On July 28, 1978, Jack Graves, a one-legged amputee, skied solo from the summit via the Ingraham Glacier. Graves, owner of Seattle Prosthetics, Inc., utilized an artificial leg he designed especially for skiing and climbing. The trip was made in excellent weather conditions, but during the descent Graves slipped and slid a short distance before he stopped by using the sharp edges of a ski—the one on his artificial leg. Graves was later fined $50 by the Park Service because he had failed to obtain a permit for the solo climb: he lacked the climbing experience necessary for solo attempts on the mountain. (From article by Svein Gilje. *Seattle Times*, August 6, 1978)

In early July 1981 a large party of handicapped people ("Project Pelion") succeeded in placing nine of its eleven members on the summit, in an ascent via the Disappointment Cleaver route, with the other two members stopping above the 11,800-foot level. Organized by project leader Phil Bartow, the climb was led by Jim Whittaker with the help of fourteen others, including Whittaker's wife Dianne Roberts, two doctors (Dr. Roy Fitzgerald, Dr. Piro Kramer), climber/cinematographer Rick Ridgeway, and newsman Svein Gilje. The handicapped group included seven blind members (Kirk Adams, 19; Raymond Keith, 41; Justin McDevitt, 29; Fred Noesner, 34; Sheila Holzworth, 19; Doug Wakefield, 40, and Dr. Judith Oehler, 34), two deaf members (Alec Naiman, 27, and Paul Stefurak, 35—also a mute), an epileptic (Richard Rose, 36), and a one-legged Viet-Nam War veteran (Charles L. O'Brien, 34, who in 1973 had climbed Rainier with a prosthetic leg).

Other ascents by one-legged climbers include those via the Emmons Glacier by Don Bennett on July 17, 1982, and Sarah Doherty on August 3, 1984. Bennett, who lost his right leg in a boating accident in 1972, had been turned back by a storm just below the crater rim on a previous attempt in 1981. On his successful climb, made in the company of five others, Bennett was aided by special crutches fitted with large ski baskets and sharp spikes. Doherty, 24, who had lost her right leg at age 13 in an auto-bicycle accident, was accompanied by several others and was aided by special ski-pole crutches. A year later, in 1985, Doherty became the first amputee to attain the summit of 20,300-foot Mount McKinley in Alaska.

SPEED CLIMBS

Rapid, one-day roundtrips to Rainier's summit have been recorded earlier: Ranger Bill Butler's time of 11 hours, 20 minutes on Fuhrer Finger in the 1930s (p. 80); Delmar Fadden's 18-hour trip via Emmons Glacier from Sunrise, in September 1933 (p. 252); and the two fast climbs via the Gibraltar and Cadaver Gap routes during the summer of 1959 (p. 71–72). However, there were few efforts to better the latter record of 6 hours, 41 minutes until more recent years. Record-breaking was not to be ignored by a younger generation, and since the early 1980s climbers have taken the challenge of Rainier to new extremes in efforts to better each other's times on the mountain.

The trip from Paradise to Camp Muir has become a popular test, and climbers in running shoes and shorts, carrying only ski poles, routinely make the trip in less than 1½ hours. The fastest trip to date was accomplished by NPS Ranger Bundy Phillips and U. S. Biathalon competitor Josh Thompson. Thompson reached Muir in 1 hour 4 minutes and was followed a minute later by Phillips. According to Phillips, Thompson was barely breathing hard.

The summit climb has also become the focus of determined efforts at record-setting. Whereas the efforts in 1959 were via the Gibraltar ledges and Cadaver Gap routes, recent speed climbs have utilized the guide route on Disappointment Cleaver, despite its greater length. Initially, the climbs were made in late summer, when the route had been well-established and climbers were usually in the best of shape. A good knowledge of the route also has enabled some to climb solo (with NPS permission), although several parties have elected to make the climb in pairs.

The first of the rapid roundtrips was made by Rainier guide Craig Van Hoy on September 7, 1981, when he did the Disappointment Cleaver route in 5 hours, 25 minutes; he made it to the top in 3 hours, 40 minutes, and signed the register book there. The second fast trip was made by Van Hoy with fellow guide John Smolich in September 1983. With full standard climbing attire, including plastic boots, crampons, and ice axes. Van Hoy and Smolich reached Columbia Crest in 3 hours, 50 minutes. After signing the register, they descended, with Van Hoy reaching Paradise in the roundtrip time of 5 hours, 20 minutes, and Smolich following five minutes later. This time stood against several subsequent attempts until it was bettered in July 1985 by Ken Evans, 39, of White Pass, Wash., with a time of 5 hours, 9 minutes. Travelling light—with ski poles and running shoes all the way—Evans and a companion, Matt Christensen of Yakima, reached Columbia Crest in 3 hours, 44 minutes. However, the team did not use up valuable time in signing the summit register, as done by predecessors. (It should be noted that the Park Service does not recognize such speed-climb records as "official.")

Another aspect of speed climbing has been the growing popularity of the one-day roundtrip ascents of various climbing routes, mostly by guides on their days off. Three guides in particular—Craig Van Hoy, Jason Edwards, and John Smolich—were in the forefront of such efforts, having made fast roundtrip (car-to-car) climbs of Success Cleaver (13 hours), Sunset Ridge (14 hours), Nisqually Icefall (16 hours), Central Mowich Face (19 hours), Liberty Ridge (21 hours), and Ptarmigan Ridge (22 hours).

The encirclement of the Wonderland Trail has also had its rapid-journey devotees. Normally requiring 10 to 14 days for an enjoyable hike, the trip has been done in considerably less time. In September 1984, Ken Evans (see above) ran the up-and-down Wonderland Trail in 29 hours, 10 minutes, carrying a flashlight during the period of darkness.

A new speed climb recognized by the Park Service is that established on August 9, 2004, by Chad Kellogg of Seattle, a roundtrip from Paradise to Columbia Crest in 4 hours, 59 minutes, and 1 second.

AGE RECORDS

New age records have been established for climbing the mountain. For men it is now 81 by Jack Borgenicht, and for women 77 by Bronka Sundstrom of Ashford. Bronka's is more than an age record, however, as on August 31, 2002, with guides Jason Edwards and Ryan Stephens, the diminutive (less than 5 feet tall) Polish-born woman made her first-ever climb of the mountain, and in the incredible roundtrip time from the Paradise trailhead of 19 hours.

Climbing Trends and Statistics

Summit-climbing statistics obtained from the National Park Service for the period since 1969 show a steady increase in the number of people reaching the top annually, from 1647 persons in 1969 to 4008 in 1985, with a highest summit visitation of 4856 people in 1982. These data show a great contrast to that for the period of 1930-early 1940s, when a mere 50 to 100 people attained the summit each summer. The accompanying graph illustrates the accelerated increase in ascents of Rainier, with the most marked increase occurring following the American ascent of Mount Everest in 1963.

The number of routes attempted and climbed each year, as shown on the graph, also has increased, indicating that more people are responding to the greater challenges—or greater privacy—of the peak's lesser known ridges and faces. The accompanying table presents a comparison of the numbers of people successfully climbing the 28 definable routes for which data are recorded by the Park Service in its annual mountaineering summaries.

Among the notable increases in ascents via the less-popular, non-guided routes since 1965 have been those on Liberty Ridge (1131 during the 20-year period 1965–1985, compared to a total of 30 during the previous 30 years—a 38-fold increase). Much of the increased popularity of this steep but direct route up Rainier's north flank has doubtless been due to its being publicized in the book *Fifty Classic Climbs of North America* (Roper and Steck, 1979). Other routes that once were considered "impossible" or "suicidal," and which today are receiving notably increasing climbing activity, are the Nisqually Icefall, Sunset and Ptarmigan Ridges, and the Mowich Face. Even such previously seldom-climbed routes as the Nisqually-Gibraltar Chute, Kautz Cleaver, Nisqually Ice Cliff, Wilson Headwall, Willis Wall, and Curtis Ridge are being attempted and climbed with increasing regularity.

The increasing number of ascents of the mountain virtually every month of the year has almost eliminated the need to differentiate between summer- and winter-season climbs. In the past, the "winter season" was defined as covering the period from the weekend after Labor Day to the weekend before Memorial Day, but the increase in springtime ascents has almost made the definition meaningless. For Park Service tabulations today, the winter climbing season coincides with the calendar winter—December 21 through March 21.

Number of Climbers
To Summit by Various Routes
(1855 through 1999)

Number of people making the ascents for various periods and totals for the period 1855-1999, as interpreted from NPS records.

Routes (clockwise from above Camp Muir, with year of first ascent) (Number of years)	1855-1964 (110)	1965-1985 (21)	1985-1999 (14)	Total (145)
Disappointment Cleaver (1950s?)	2,469	40,247	43,172	85,888
Ingraham Glacier Direct (1885?)	-?-	3,431	34,308	37,739
Gibralter Ledges (1870)	1,273	1,306	1.060	3,639
Nisqually-Gibralter Chute (1946)	5	93	27	125
Nisqually Ice Cliff (1962)	2	56	12	70
Nisqually Cleaver (1967)	0	14	0	14
Nisqually Icefall (1948)	31	277	110	418
Fuhrer Finger (1920)	174	1,589	929	2,692
Fuhrer Thumb (1972)	0	13	13	26
Wilson Headwall (1957)	2	53	52	107
Kautz Glacier (1857)	784	2,325	3,980	7,089
Kautz Headwall (1963)	3	30	25	58
Kautz Cleaver (1957)	2	83	74	159
Success Glacier Couloir (1960)	2	0	–	2
Success Cleaver (1905)	53	137	163	353
South Tahoma Headwall (1963)	2	6	0	8
Tahoma Cleaver (1959)	7	2	5	14
Tahoma Glacier (1891)	386	787	406	1,579
Puyallup Cleaver (poorly defined route)	–	–	31	31?
Sunset Amphitheater (1937)	14	15	0	29
Sunset Ridge (1938)	10	208	55	273
Mowich Face (w/variations; 1957)	15	170	29	214
Ptarmigan Ridge (w/variations; 1935)	9	161	56	226
Liberty Wall (1968)	0	3	4	7
Liberty Ridge (1935)	30	1,131	1,578	2,739
Willis Wall (w/variations; 1961)	11	41	4	56
Curtis Ridge (1957)	9	37	12	58
Russell Cliff (w/variations; 1960)	4	17	2	23
Emmons-Winthrop Glacier (1855?)	2,608	9,280	14,749	26,637
Totals	7,905	61,512	100,856	170,273

NUMBER OF CLIMBERS
TO SUMMIT SINCE 1932

NOTE: The National Park Service began maintaining annual mountaineering summaries in 1955. However, because these have varied in content and format between years, a consistent numerical record has been difficult to achieve between the related accompanying tabulations.

Period	Number	Average per year
1932-1950	1822	96
1951-1965	6863	458
1966-1985	60,693	3032
1986-1996	50,769	4615
1997-1999	20,073	6691
Total	140,220	

Note: In recent years, the closure of the West Side Road by frequent mudflows has decreased attempts on routes on the west side of the mountain. However, a few climbers have utilized mountain bikes to reach former trailheads.

Note: Since 1999, the Park Service information on climbing statistics has been limited to general summaries, rather than more complete information on the number of attempts and successes on each of some 25 climbing routes.

TOTAL SUMMIT CLIMBERS
(Both guided and independent)

GUIDED CLIMBERS

(Americans climb Everest)

(First ascent of Mount Everest)

(NOTE: Historic records show that approximately 170,300 people have reached the summit of Mount Rainier during the years 1855 through 1999.)

NUMBER OF CLIMBERS

Total number of climbers reaching the summit by all routes, 1932-1999, and number of guided climbers reaching the summit, 1955-1999. Data from National Park Service records.

The Guides

The professional guiding of clients to Rainier's summit has been established as a franchise operation under periodic review and approval by the National Park Service. Since 1968 the franchise has been held by Rainier Mountaineering, Inc. (RMI), under the direction of Lou Whittaker and Jerry Lynch. The guide service has changed its complexion from the relatively modest, summers-only operation of decades past and now includes a staff of fulltime professionals who lead climbs year-round, on Rainier (mostly during the summer season) and, during the fall-through-spring "off season," in other ranges of the world.

Whittaker first guided on Rainier in 1951 and has since climbed the mountain nearly 200 times by many routes, besides leading expeditions to McKinley, K2, and Everest; on the latter, he led the 1982 and successful 1984 expeditions on the North Face-Great Couloir. A charter member (1948) of Seattle's Mountain Rescue Council, Whittaker has taken part in numerous search and rescue operations on Rainier and elsewhere in the Cascade Range and Olympic Mountains. Lynch, a Tacoma attorney, has made many ascents of Rainier by several routes and taken part in expeditions to McKinley, the Mexican volcanoes, and peaks of South America.

The guide staff has included such world-renowned climbers as Nawang Gombu, nephew of Tenzing Norgay (with Edmund Hillary the first to ascend Everest) and the first person to climb Everest twice. Gombu directs the Himalayan Mountaineering Institute in Darjeeling, India, but frequently travels abroad to lead climbs of McKinley in the spring and work at Rainier during the summer.

The guide staff has also included several women in recent years. Among these was Marty Hoey, who had acquired sufficient expertise on Rainier and McKinley to gain participation in several major expeditions, including the American trips to the Soviet Union's Pamirs in 1974 and to Nanda Devi in the Garwhal Himalaya in 1975. Tragically, in May 1982, Hoey fell to her death from about 25,000 feet in the Great Couloir on Mount Everest's North Face, in an expedition led by Lou Whittaker and composed principally of members of the RMI guide staff.

Among the senior members of the guide staff, who've led more than 100 ascents of Rainier, are the following:

Joe Horiskey has guided since 1968 and logged more than 150 ascents of the mountain. During the spring-early summer seasons since 1975, Horiskey has guided a number of Mount McKinley expeditions, personally leading more than a dozen parties to the top of "Denali." He was also a member of the 1982 China-Everest Expedition led by Lou Whittaker.

Phil Ershler has guided on the mountain since 1971 and is the first person to have made more than 250 ascents of Rainier. During the off season Ershler is in charge of guided climbs in Mexico and South America and has also led numerous trips up Mount McKinley. Ershler was a member of expeditions to Mount Everest in 1982, 1983, and 1984; on the 1984 China-Everest Expedition, he became the first American to climb Everest by way of the northern approaches through Tibet/China. On October 20, 1984, in a solo effort on the final 1500 feet, he climbed to the summit via the Northeast Face and Great Couloir.

Since 1973, Eric Simonson has led more than 100 ascents of Rainier and over a dozen trips to McKinley. He was on the 1982 China-Everest Expedition and has led New Zealand and Himalayan climbs during the off season. He has made yearly climbs since 1979 of such peaks as Annapurna I, Hiunchuli, Fluted Peak, Nun in the Himalaya, and Peak Communism in the Soviet Union.

George Dunn since 1975 has become the second person to lead more than 200 ascents of Rainier; these include 30 in one season. Dunn has been twice to Mount Everest, and made several climbs of Mount McKinley in Alaska and of peaks in South America.

Peter Whittaker has been carrying on the tradition of his father, Lou, on Mount Rainier since 1975. He has over 100 ascents of the mountain and several of McKinley, and in 1984 he joined his father on the China-Everest Expedition. During the winters Whittaker serves as a helicopter-skiing guide at Snowbird, Utah.

Larry Nielson has guided on Rainier periodically for more than 15 years and also is a member of the "Century Club" with over 100 ascents, doing these by more than 25 routes on the mountain. Nielson has made his mark as one of the Northwest's most persistent climbers, doing many of the most difficult climbs in the Cascades. He reached about 27,500 feet on the 1982 China-Everest Expedition; and in 1983, as a member of an international group making the attempt via the South Col route, Nielson succeeded in being the first American to climb Everest without the use of supplemental oxygen.

Tracy Roberts, with more than 200 ascents of Rainier, has also led climbs in Alaska, the Alps, and South America, and he was on the 1982 China-Everest Expedition.

Andy Politz has made his mark with over 100 ascents of Rainier since 1975, several climbs of McKinley, trips to Nepal, New Zealand, and the Himalaya. In 1984 he made the first ascent of the South Face of Mount St. Elias in Alaska; in 1985 and 1986 he was a member of the two American ex-

Some of the widely travelled Rainier guides of the 1970s and 1980s . . .

Lou Whittaker

Jerry Lynch

Joe Horiskey

Marty Hoey

Nawang Gombu

Phil Ershler

Eric Simonson

Larry Nielson

George Dunn

Peter Whittaker

Dan Boyd

Tracy Roberts

Andy Politz

Gary Isaacs

John Smolich

Greg Wilson

Jason Edwards

Craig Van Hoy

peditions to the West Ridge of Everest, and was also on K2 in 1986.

Other guides with over 100 ascents of Rainier and who've also led climbs of McKinley and the Mexican volcanoes (and some with ascents in the Andes) include "Everesters" Dan Boyd, Gary Isaacs, John Smolich, and Greg Wilson; and Jason Edwards, Jeff Fong, Drew Kacmarcik, Chris Kerrebrock, Robert Link, Randy Sackett, Mike Targett, Dan Tobin, Craig Van Hoy, Ed Viesturs, and Ken Williams. (Kerrebrock died in a McKinley crevasse in 1981, and Smolich was killed by an avalanche on K2 in 1986.)

In eight recent summer seasons two women guides — Cate Casson and Heather MacDonald — have each made more than 100 trips to the Summit of the mountain.

The guiding of untried clients up the glaciered slopes of Mount Rainier has often required training sessions on the mountain prior to the summit assaults. For this, the guide service conducts day-long trips on snow slopes above Paradise and onto the nearby Nisqually Glacier, along with five-day seminars at Camp Muir. There, prospective summit clients are indoctrinated in the basic concepts of mountaineering, through sessions involving roped glacier travel and crevasse-rescue techniques. They also are led in discussions covering expeditionary mountaineering and climbing philosophy, mountaineering medicine and first aid, mountain weather and climate, geography and geology, local climbing history, and other pertinent topics. Statistics have shown the benefit of the seminar program—and the days of acclimatization at 10,000-foot Camp Muir—as the percentage of successful summit ascents is highest for these clients.

Another activity of the guides is to provide training to Park Service personnel in mountaineering and rescue techniques, and, when called upon, to assist in and lead rescue missions on the mountain. It should be noted, however, that the Park Service staff includes experienced climbers; among these in recent years have been Garry Olson and Bundy Phillips, who have made numerous ascents of the peak (including search and rescue missions) by many routes.

Mountain Tragedies Since 1969

As increasing numbers of people travel the mountainous backcountry of the Park, fatalities resulting from hiking and climbing accidents have continued to add to Park Service statistics. Most of the tragedies result from "human error" in judgment of one's ability and experience, and from being improperly clothed and equipped for prevailing weather and terrain conditions; in hindsight, most of the accidents were preventable.

In order of the number of incidents leading to the climbing tragedies, most have occurred as a result of falls from rock cliffs and on steep snow and ice terrain, followed by falls into crevasses, being lost in storms and perishing from exposure (hypothermia), snow avalanches, being struck by falling rocks, uncontrolled glissades ending in falls into rocks or over cliffs, high-altitude pulmonary edema (HAPE), and ice avalanches (this latter being a single incident that buried 11 climbers). Many accidents befall hikers scrambling on the lower peaks within the Park and usually result from inexperience or lack of adequate clothing and equipment. However, to the general public, the more dramatic tragedies are those occurring during ascents or descents of Mount Rainier.

The accompanying tabulation lists all summit-climb fatalities during the period 1970–1985, while two of the most highly publicized tragedies are described in more detail below and in the following pages.

SLAB AVALANCHE ON UPPER COWLITZ GLACIER:
WILLI UNSOELD AND JANIE DIEPENBROCK

On March 4, 1979, a slab avalanche on the steep slope below Cadaver Gap, near the head of Cowlitz Glacier, took the lives of Willi Unsoeld and Janie Diepenbrock. Unsoeld—52-year-old professor at The Evergreen State College (TESC) in Olympia and one of America's most famed and beloved mountaineers—and the 21-year-old student were members of a 21-person party that was descending to Camp Muir after an unsuccessful summit attempt. The group was in TESC's Outdoor Education Program and was part of a team of students participating in field trips during the week of the solar eclipse that occurred on February 26.

Unsoeld's party had taken four days to reach Camp Muir from Paradise, ascending cautiously during a period of avalanche hazard. En route to Muir they camped in tents a short distance above Paradise the first night and in snow caves above Panorama Point for two nights. This was Unsoeld's third climb since surgery the preceding summer to place metal "ball and socket" joints in his hips; he was still testing his self-proclaimed "bionic" approach to climbing.

On Thursday, March 1—the morning after the party's arrival at

Camp Muir—the weather was clear and beautiful, and the avalanche hazards appeared to have subsided to the extent that the daily forecasts by the U.S. Forest Service had ceased. Unsoeld and several others scouted the route across the upper Cowlitz Glacier to the base of the slope below Cadaver Gap. They found the snow firm for walking without snowshoes and observed no signs of avalanche activity. The following morning, while one student (Lloyd Johnson) stayed at Muir, the remaining party of 21 crossed the glacier and ascended through Cadaver Gap to the Ingraham Glacier, enjoying good weather and visibility; they left their snowshoes at Muir. They ascended near the center of the Ingraham, sinking in to their knees in places, then worked left to where they pitched their six tents at about 11,800 feet, next to the vertical wall of Gibraltar Rock. After camp was established, Unsoeld and students Ian Yolles, Bob Dash, Rolland Zoller, and Jeff Casebolt scouted the route above, to about 12,800 feet; good weather and visibility persisted through the day. Looking down from above, the party noted several large crevasses on the Ingraham Glacier adjacent to Cadaver Gap.

On Saturday, March 3, the party left camp at 5:30 a.m., with the intention of climbing to the summit. However, the weather was deteriorating, and three members of the party turned back at about 12,500 feet. Unsoeld moved slowly with the main party to about 13,000 feet before increasing wind and snow forced them to retreat as well, and they arrived back at camp about 10 a.m. With their Park Service radio they heard the 3-day forecast for increasing snowfall and high winds. Unsoeld announced that they would descend on Sunday, by way of the normal route down the Ingraham Glacier and around Cathedral Gap (farther down the ridge from Cadaver Gap). The snow continued to fall through the night and by morning they reported 3 to 4 feet of new snow covering camp, causing some tents to tear and partially collapse.

The party broke camp and began the descent about 10 a.m., with Unsoeld leading the first rope team. Visibility continued poor and they lost sight of the wands marking the route. They descended close to Gibraltar Rock instead of following their ascent route down the center of the glacier. Some rope teams had difficulty following the tracks of those ahead, but they tried to maintain visual contact through the blowing snow. Unsoeld's rope team reached Cadaver Gap and waited until all others had arrived. The wind had increased and was coming directly up and through the Gap at about 60 mph, bringing extreme cold.

Some of the other rope teams had been so slow in reaching the Gap that Unsoeld decided to descend directly down the Gap, rather than take the longer, unwanded route through the crevasses and seracs adjacent to the Gap onto the Ingraham Glacier and then on down to Cathedral Gap. He feared that the slowness of the party—some students were

SUMMARY OF FATALITIES DURING CLIMBS
OF MOUNT RAINIER, 1971–1985.

1971 8/1: Michael Ferry, 24, in party of five descending upper Ingraham Glacier at 13,500 ft without crampons, pulled off belay by another man, slid and fell into 65-ft crevasse.

1974 11/18: David Taylor, 24, in party of two caught by storm at 13,000 ft on Success Cleaver, started fresh-snow avalanche and carried over rock cliffs below; body never found.

1975 8/14: Mark Jackson, 17, in three-man party, killed at 11,800 ft by rockfall from upper Mowich Face

1977 2/16: Jack Wilkins, 55, in four-man party at 8300 ft on Success Cleaver, fell over 150-ft rock cliffs after uncontrolled sitting glissade down snow slope with icy patches.

1977 7/6: Dean Klapper, 33, in party of five descending upper Emmons Glacier unroped and not wearing crampons, slipped during sitting glissade, slid 1000 ft into crevasse.

1977 9/7: Mary Gnehm, 47, in guide party of 11, killed when her five-person rope team slid 1500 ft down upper Ingraham Glacier, after one man slipped on icy slope and made no effort to stop.

1978 5/31: Todd Davis, 24, in three-man party ascending Fuhrer Finger in switchbacking maneuver on soft steep snow, causing avalanche to break slope at 11,200 ft, all carried 2000 ft down; Davis buried and found dead.

1978 9/8: Shirli Voigt, 30, and Guillermo Mendoza, 28, climbed into storm on Ingraham Glacier in spite of advice by descending guide parties; evidently Mendoza injured by his crampons during slip, then both froze to death at 13,300 ft after Voigt tried to protect injured companion by digging trench and covering him with her body.

1979 3/4: Willi Unsoeld, 52, and Janie Diepenbrock, 21, in 21-person college group, battered at camp at 11,800 ft on Ingraham Glacier, then during descent their four-person rope team caught in deep, fresh-snow avalanche on upper Cowlitz Glacier, below Cadaver Gap. (See details.)

1979 9/1: Dale Click, died from exposure after falling into crevasse on Inter Glacier.

1981 5/24: Doug Fowler, 21, and Bruce Mooney, 20, fell from Liberty Ridge.

1981 6/21: Eleven members of a guide party buried by massive ice and snow avalanche on Ingraham Glacier that hurtled victims into deep crevasse; bodies never found. (See details.)

1981 7/16–18: Peter Brooks, fall from Liberty Ridge.

1983 5/7: Doug Vercoe, 34, in party of three climbing to Camp Muir in fog, fell over cornice above Anvil Rock and into deep crevasse below; body never found.

1983 5/29: Christopher Blight, 25, in party of six Mountaineers descending Emmons Glacier, fell to death in deep crevasse after unroping to assist in evacuation of another member of party who had fallen into same crevasse.

1983 9/5: Patrick Hill and Douglas Velder, fell 800 ft from Disappointment Cleaver, tied together with 25-ft rope, wearing blue jeans, tennis shoes inside rubber overboots with crampons strapped on loosely; had not registered for the climb.

1985 1/——: Fuat Dikman, fell from Liberty Ridge during solo climb; body found in May.

very tired and cold after the difficult night in the snow-battered tents—
would result in further delays and possibly another night out (with
the risk of hypothermia) if the longer, unmarked route was followed.
Also, the wind appeared to have improved snow conditions approaching
the Gap; the surface was firmer than during the ascent. Although Unsoeld remarked on the possibility of slab avalanche conditions, he felt
that this faster route provided the more favorable option under the
prevailing circumstances.

At 12:40 p.m. Unsoeld's rope of four (Unsoeld, Janie Diepenbrock,
Peter Miller, Frank Kaplan) started the descent from Cadaver Gap, after
he had requested that the others all maintain a 100-foot spacing between
rope teams. With the wind and snow blowing into their faces, Unsoeld
led, first working over the small ledge atop the initial rock hump on the
east side of the Gap, then west and onto the main snow slope. About
300 feet below the Gap, because visual contact was sporadic, Miller exchanged yells with Ian Yolles, who was leading the second rope down.
Then, at about 1:10 p.m., Miller thought Diepenbrock fell, so he immediately went into an arrest position, as did Kaplan above. However,
Janie's "fall" was the beginning of being pulled over a 2-to-3-foot slab
fracture line as the entire slope gave way. Miller and Kaplan were engulfed in the snow and were carried down with no chance of controlling
their descent. Miller came to a stop and had time only to make an air
space over his mouth and nose and thrust one hand upward through
the snow surface—an act that doubtless saved his life. The slide had
carried the rope team about 500 feet down the slope.

Kaplan had been able to shed his pack during the fall and made
attempts to keep himself near the surface by a swimming motion; he
was able to extricate himself from the snow in about 10 seconds. He saw
Miller's hand protruding from the snow farther down, so he quickly
descended and started digging with his hands, then found his pack nearby
and got out a shovel to resume digging. He got Miller's face clear of
snow, and Miller fainted. Kaplan continued digging.

In the meantime, the second rope team (Ian Yolles, Bruce Clifton,
Wanda Schroeder, David Ridley) was descending the snow slope, still
unaware that a slide had occurred. Ian Yolles, in the lead, fell over the
slab fracture line in the poor visibility and, recognizing it as a slab avalanche, quickly brought his team across the slope to the rocks on the
opposite side. They continued down and saw Kaplan digging and yelling
below; it was then that Yolles realized the first team had been caught in
the avalanche. The second team arrived at the scene about 1:25 p.m.
Schroeder and Clifton helped Kaplan dig out Miller and soon got him
free, while Yolles and Ridley traced the rope down through the avalanche
debris. Diepenbrock was found beneath 2 feet of snow, face down,

hands away from her face, cyanotic, and apparently dead. With some difficulty due to the position of her body, they rolled her over and Yolles began artificial resuscitation at about 1:40 p.m., while Ridley continued to trace the rope down toward Unsoeld. The rope was in and out of the snow and followed a circuitous course that made it difficult to trace and dig up, in places being caught beneath slab blocks. Finally, Unsoeld was found beneath 3 feet of compacted snow, face down and body across the slope, his face a bluish-gray color. Clifton began immediate resuscitation, then Yolles took over as he had more experience at it; it had been about 45 minutes since the avalanche occurred. Blowing and sloughing snow made it difficult to keep the hole open as they dug down. The third rope team (Jeff Casebolt, Penny Dempsey, Sean Downey) had arrived at the scene and, with the aid of more shovels, they dug him out enough to cut off his pack and remove the Park Service radio. Miller, who had by then recovered, contacted Park Service personnel to tell of the accident and the efforts in progress to revive Unsoeld and Diepenbrock.

By the time the fourth rope team (Bruce Ostermann, Doug White, Marjorie Butler, Sheri Gerson) arrived at the scene, attempts at resuscitation had ceased—neither victim had shown any signs of life. Diepenbrock's body had been freed completely and placed inside a sleeping bag. Another bag was placed partly beneath and over Unsoeld, who remained buried at the bottom of the pit. Wands were driven into the snow around the bodies to mark the spot. The fifth rope team (Rhea Dodd, Mary Ellen Fitzgerald, Eric Kessler) arrived on the scene after resuscitation had been discontinued, and the sixth team (Rolland Zoller, Bob Dash, Paul Fitch) arrived as the site was being abandoned.

Some of the group had lost mittens and wool caps during the rescue efforts, and fears of further slides were now expressed. Yolles assumed leadership of the party and initiated preparations for the 19 survivors to descend to Camp Muir. He asked Casebolt and Ostermann to lead out and Kessler to bring up the rear. They all emphasized the importance of keeping the party together and in visual contact, as the route was not well known and they were unable to find the wands placed during the ascent. They feared the possibility of missing Camp Muir and getting into a crevasse field on the Cowlitz Glacier.

Still roped together, the party left the avalanche site about 3 p.m. Some of the weaker members dropped their packs en route to allow faster progress against the high winds and snow that continued to blow into their faces. Sheri Gerson recalls fainting and being helped onward by others. Another avalanche path—hard, slippery ice—had to be crossed (none were wearing crampons at the time) but at about 4:30 p.m. the weary party came out at Camp Muir, the stronger students helping the weaker; Ostermann and Casebolt were credited by the others for bringing them safely to Muir. Even there they had problems getting into the cabin because the door had been barricaded shut from the inside by Lloyd Johnson, who had remained there since Friday.

Ian Yolles made radio contact with Paradise and reported the party safely back at Muir and the two victims still at the accident site. The ranger informed them that no rescue efforts could be made until the weather improved. A helicopter had made an attempt to reach the scene that afternoon but had been turned back by bad weather.

The following morning (Monday, March 5) initial efforts of a Park Service ground party to reach Camp Muir were thwarted by high avalanche danger and further deterioration of the weather. At the camp the students had a brief view of the avalanche area and noted that new avalanche debris appeared to have crossed the accident site.

On Tuesday, March 6, a ground party composed of personnel from the Park Service (led by Ranger de St. Croix) and Rainier Mountaineering (led by Lou Whittaker) finally reached Camp Muir and returned to Paradise with 18 of the survivors; Casebolt and Ostermann remained at Muir to aid in subsequent location of the bodies. On Wednesday, rangers and the two students searched for the bodies but noted that at least four additional avalanches had covered the site. The two students returned to Paradise and Olympia that afternoon.

Saturday, March 10, was a beautifully clear day, and a 21-person search party led by Chief Park Ranger Bob Dunnagan assembled at Camp Muir to continue the search for the bodies. The group consisted of six rangers, one avalanche expert from the State Department of Transportation, Forest Service snow ranger Ken White and 13 volunteers from Seattle, Tacoma, and Olympic (Bremerton) Mountain Rescue units. White brought a 75mm recoilless rifle to shoot the avalanche-prone slopes still endangering the accident site. Fifteen rounds were fired at the slopes of the upper Cowlitz Glacier, but only a few small slides resulted, and the snow surface was considered safe for ground search. In the meantime the snow had blown clear or settled in the area, uncovering some wands that allowed a narrowing of the search area. The use of 18-foot probes located the body of Willi Unsoeld at 11:30 a.m. and that of Janie Diepenbrock about 30 minutes later. The remains were evacuated to Paradise by sleds.

Willi Unsoeld and Janie Diepenbrock, though years apart in age, shared common ground in living closely to nature's beauties and challenges and striving toward the perfect union of man and wilderness. Janie had developed a love of the outdoor world early in life, and it was natural for her, after attending the National Outdoor Leadership School in Colorado, to be attracted to the Outdoor Education Program developed by

Willi Unsoeld *Janie Diepenbrock*

Unsoeld at The Evergreen State College. There a kinship developed between the two as she joined Evergreen's "guru" on several wilderness trips and climbs; her fellow students observed that she had developed an uncommon understanding of the relationship between man and nature and had achieved a deep personal happiness.

Unsoeld's death was felt deeply by the American mountaineering community and by the many whose lives he had touched—whether on a weekend trek into the Cascade and Olympic mountains of the Northwest, on a Teton climb or Himalayan expedition, or in an audience attending one of his numerous stimulating treatises on the joys of the mountain world and the attendant responsibilities of protecting and furthering the concept of the wilderness ethic. Unsoeld never sought the slippered ease of the hearthside, but continued to lead young people into the hills and to share his way of life.

ICE AVALANCHE ON INGRAHAM GLACIER:
DEATH TOLL OF ELEVEN WORST IN U.S. CLIMBING HISTORY

The month of June 1981 had been generally cool and wet, with much deep, new snow and poor weather high on the mountain. The ratio of success per summit party had been low, and the guides had had no opportunity to stomp in the usual entrenched track across the steep snow "nose" of lower Disappointment Cleaver.

On June 21 a party of 23 clients and six guides (John Day, leader; Chris Lynch, Tom O'Brien, Mike Targett, Peter Whittaker, and Greg Wilson) left Camp Muir at 4:00 a.m. At 5:30 a rope team of four led by Lynch turned back to Muir after three clients preferred not to proceed farther. Upon reaching the start of the traverse on the Ingraham Glacier toward the base of Disappointment Cleaver, most of the party halted while guides Day, Targett, and Whittaker scouted the route ahead on the steep snow traverse of the lower part of the cleaver. Finding the slope both too exposed and unprotectable against possible slips among the relatively inexperienced clients, and with the weather deteriorating, the guides decided it was unwise to continue the climb and began their return to the resting party.

Suddenly, high above on the margin of the Ingraham Glacier, a large serac toppled and fell, breaking into ice blocks that crashed down the slope, causing a large avalanche of ice and snow. The group below tried to outrun the slide, but it fanned out beyond the recognized hazard area and engulfed the entire party except the advance group of three guides. After the debris had settled, eleven climbers were missing, including guide O'Brien and clients David Boulton, Mark Ernlund, Ronald Farrell, Gordon Heneage, David Kidd, Jonathon Laitone, Ira Liedman, Henry Matthews, Craig Tippie, and Michael Watts. They had either been hurtled into a huge crevasse below or were buried by the thick avalanche debris. After an hour's search, all that was found were a pack, ice axe, and headlamp.

With poor visibility and worsening weather and snowfall, all survivors eventually returned to Camp Muir. Recovery efforts over the next two days (by personnel from the Park Service, guide service, and local Mountain Rescue units) were hampered by bad weather, and the search operations were called off on June 23rd, with no hope of ever recovering the bodies.

As further evidence of the unusually deep snowfall high on Northwest mountains in early summer 1981, the tragic loss of eleven on Rainier occurred on the same day as the death of five climbers on Mount Hood. There, a large party triggered an avalanche of deep snow high on the Cooper Spur (Northeast Ridge).

Incredible Survivals

On July 12, 1976, during Rainier Mountaineering's expedition seminar and planned ascent of the Kautz route, the large party was camped at about 11,300 feet on the rock ridge above the Turtle, the long and steep snowfield above the upper west margin of the Wilson Glacier. One of the guides' clients, Dr. Frederick Hamly, was cooking in a small pot when a sudden breeze blew off the lid; instinctively, Hamly lunged for it across the adjacent snow slope. Wearing only smooth-soled down booties on his feet, he slipped on the frozen snow surface and started a slide that he was unable to arrest, as he was not carrying an ice axe at the time. He rapidly gained speed on the steep slope and slid its entire 2000-foot length, then over the 75-foot ice cliff at the bottom. He came to rest in a mass of broken ice blocks on the upper Wilson Glacier, conscious but badly injured, with multiple fractures and internal injuries and a punctured lung.

The horrified guides descended the slope and reached the injured man in about 20 minutes. While some remained with him administering first aid and protection against the night's cold, others continued down the mountain for help, reaching the Paradise Ranger Station at midnight. The rangers requested Army helicopter assistance at dawn, then left immediately for the accident site, which they reached in about 3 hours—a remarkably fast climb. A MAST helicopter evacuated Hamly at 7:30 a.m.

Dr. Hamly spent a couple of weeks in the hospital recovering from his many injuries before returning to his home in San Diego. He made plans to return to Mount Rainier in 1979 to complete his unfinished climb.

The accident pointed out clearly the hazard in the common practice of wearing down booties around campsites, particularly where adjacent to steep snow slopes.

SEVEN-DAY STORM AT SUMMIT: JOHN AND ROD HOMINDA

When 39-year-old John Hominda of Tacoma and his teenage son Rod began their ascent of Rainier on August 29, 1978, they recognized the uncertainty of the weather and accordingly planned for winter climbing conditions, with plenty of clothing, food, fuel, and a strong tent. When they reached the summit the following afternoon they pitched their tent with the intention of camping two nights in the crater. Later that afternoon a severe thunderstorm enveloped the top of the mountain, blasting the tent with high winds and heavy snowfall. When the storm continued into the next day, the two climbers prepared for a long stay by securely anchoring the tent with extra nylon cord and their ice axes.

Realizing that such storms could last many days without relief, the pair concentrated on staying warm and dry while conserving their energy, food, and fuel. They spent most of their time sleeping and talking within the tent, with occasional periods of exercise to avoid apathy and to ensure good heat production and blood circulation. Activities such as snow removal, which required leaving the tent's protection, were carefully planned to minimize exposure to the wind and cold. After each venture outside, they removed ice and snow from their clothing prior to reentering the tent.

After seven days and nights of continued storm—and six feet of new snow—the two awoke to clear weather on September 6 and decided to break camp and descend. By 4 p.m. they had reentered the clouds at the 12,700-foot level and, recognizing that the new snow was extremely unstable and that further travel was unwise, they decided to stay where they were. They dug a snow cave to reduce exposure to the avalanching that could be heard in the vicinity. The entrance to the cave was covered by their bright yellow tent to facilitate spotting the shelter from the air.

Shortly after dusk a search helicopter took advantage of a break in the weather and located the stranded party. The two were plucked from the mountain and, except for minor frostbite and some weight loss, they survived in good spirits.

Prior physical conditioning, proper equipment, clothing, food, and fuel, coupled with good judgment, caution, and experience aided in the successful survival efforts of the father and son.

PLANE CRASH NEAR SUMMIT: ROBERT LEE AND DAVID SHINEN

At 3:30 p.m. on January 29, 1979, pilot Bob Lee (29) of Tacoma and student pilot Dave Shinen (21) of Seattle left the Tacoma Industrial Airport for a flight to Mount Rainier. They flew in Lee's 1947 two-seater Cessna 140 and, after reaching the mountain, they decided to fly over the summit area. They climbed to near the small plane's 15,000-foot altitude ceiling and flew northwesterly across the crater, moving at about 90 miles an hour with the estimated 20–30 mph wind. They crossed the main (east) crater and summit and then the west crater, reportedly only about 20–30 feet above the crater snows. When they reached the northwestern edge of the crater a downdraft caused the plane to suddenly lose altitude, and it hit the snow at or near the crater rim. The plane bounced twice down the steep outer slope of the crater, flipping over on the second bounce and then sliding about 500 feet before coming to rest at the bottom of the steep slope, upside down. It was about 5 p.m. The sunlight was fading, and the temperature was probably 20–25 degrees below zero.

Lee and Shinen were not injured, and during the slide down the slope each was asking how the other felt. The men had no water, food, matches, extra clothing, or flashlight. Shinen was wearing jeans, a wool shirt, corduroy work jacket, and Alaskan bushpack boots. Lee was wearing corduroy pants, a cotton shirt, an Eddie Bauer down parka, and smooth-soled work boots.

When they released their seat belts they dropped headfirst onto the ceiling of the overturned craft. They tried to transmit "Mayday" on their radio, but the transmitting antenna was broken; however, they could hear the Tacoma Industrial Airport with the receiving antenna. Shinen then climbed to the crater rim with the plane's emergency locator transmitter (ELT) in the hope of getting a better signal even though the battery was nearly two years old. He noticed steam coming from parts of the crater and recalled having heard or read about the summit steam caves as refuges for benighted climbers. The two men found a small cave on the western (outer) slope of the west crater, above the plane, and huddled together in the damp opening, wedged between the rock floor and icy ceiling. Shinen tried to sleep on a seat back he had taken from the plane while Lee tried to find comfort sitting on a foam pillow, to protect him from the hot steam vent beneath him. However, he still suffered slightly scalded buttocks. During the night Shinen managed to doze for about 20 minutes, but Lee got no sleep. Parts of their bodies were too hot from the steam while other parts were too cold from the low temperatures outside.

In the morning, with their clothing soaked from the steam, they risked hypothermia when they ventured outside about 8:30 a.m. The temperature was well below zero and the wind was increasing; with the windchill factor, the temperature probably was equivalent to 60–70 degrees below zero. When they returned to the plane, Lee's fingers were so numb he was unable to help Shinen in their initial efforts to fashion the receiving antenna into a transmitting antenna. Eventually, holding together the battery cables that had broken loose, they started broadcasting "Mayday" at about 9 a.m. In about 10 minutes a plane flew over.

Civil Air Patrol pilots had heard the signal and indicated they had also heard their ELT before the Mayday call. Within minutes, several other planes appeared and began making airdrops. A plastic jar was dropped with a note saying a helicopter would arrive in about two hours. Later a plastic tube tent and aluminum "space blanket" were dropped to the shivering men, who wrapped up in them.

About three hours later a Chinook helicopter arrived from Fort Lewis and landed for a pickup of the two men from the 13,500-foot saddle between the crater and Liberty Cap. They were carried first to the Paradise Ranger Station, then to St. Joseph's Hospital in Tacoma for examination. Shinen was released in about 45 minutes and Lee soon after, following treatment of his burns.

TWO DAYS IN A CREVASSE: RICK KIRSCHNER AND JOHN LOEHR

On July 25, 1974, rangers Rick Kirschner (27) and John Loehr (24) made a climb of Fuhrer Finger. At about 13,600 feet on the upper Nisqually Glacier, Kirschner broke through the snow cover and plunged 80 feet into a crevasse, pulling in Loehr behind him. Kirschner landed on his feet on a snow plug, unhurt, but Loehr fell deeper, about 120 feet, and suffered a fractured pelvis. Despite the injury, Loehr was able to climb up to Kirschner, who then erected a tent on the small platform. During the fall the outer pocket of Loehr's pack was ripped off and their stove was lost, eliminating their only source of heat for melting snow and cooking. They also lost their ice axes, one remaining stuck upright in the snow at the glacier surface. Kirschner made several efforts to climb the crevasse wall, using a sharpened spoon for a pick, but was unable to ascend the upper overhanging section of 15 feet.

The next day (July 26) rangers Dick Martin and Pat Harrison made an ascent by the same route and found the ice axe near the crevasse. However, they were unable to find any tracks or sign of trouble and could not see the bottom of the crevasse, so they continued to the summit and descended to Paradise. Upon their return they mentioned finding the axe, in time to forestall a planned ranger search of the lower Nisqually Glacier.

On July 27, more than 50 hours after the accident, a Hughes 500 helicopter was flown to the site, and rangers aboard spotted the two men in the crevasse. They were brought to the surface and to a tent camp established nearby for the night. The next morning a MAST helicopter evacuated them from the mountain; this marked the beginning of a week-long storm on the peak.

Noteworthy Mountaineering: 1980 through 1996

LENGTHY SKI DESCENT FROM SUMMIT

During May 3-4, 1980, a complete ski descent of the mountain was made from the summit to the Nisqually Bridge, via Fuhrer Finger. Accompanied during the climb by several others, the descending skiers included Dan Davis (skied from actual summit), Tom Janisch (from crater rim), and Jeff Haley (from 14,000 feet). En route down, they made an overnight stop at 10,000 feet, near the base of Fuhrer Finger.

THE BEAR WENT OVER THE MOUNTAIN

On August 17, 1990, at about 9:00 A.M., RMI guide Curtis Fawley took this photo of a small black bear descending the Kautz Ice Chute, at 12,000

Black bear descending the Kautz Ice Chute.

feet on Mount Rainier's upper southwest flank. At dawn—a few hours earlier—the bear was spotted by another party traversing the upper Emmons Glacier, on the northeast side of the mountain. At one point, Fawley's party observed the bear backing into a crevasse, then climbing out via the opposite vertical wall. Apparently some animals "know the mountain" and might even enjoy an occasional climb—or shortcut over the summit to some favored berry patch.

NEW RECORD ON WONDERLAND TRAIL

In September 1991, seasonal park ranger Dan Oswtrowski ran the Wonderland Trail around the mountain in 27 hours, 56 minutes, bettering Ken Evans' 1984 time of 29 hours, 10 minutes (see page 322).

81-YEAR-OLD CLIMBS THE MOUNTAIN

On August 30, 1992, Jack Borgenicht (81) completed a 3-day round-trip climb of Mount Rainier via the Disappointment Cleaver Route in an RMI-guided party led by Alex Van Steen. This eclipses the previous record of Julius Boehm, age 80^1/2. (See pp. 318-319.)

OLDER WOMAN'S RECORD CLIMB

On August 31, 2002, 5-foot tall, 77-year-old Bronka Sundstrom of Ashford, in company with RMI guides Jason Edwards and Ryan Stephens, left Paradise at 9 a.m., reached the summit in late afternoon and was back at Paradise at 4 a.m. the next morning, an incredible 19 hours roundtrip by the oldest woman to climb the mountain.

SKI DESCENT OF MOWICH FACE

On July 19, 1997, Armond Dubuque, Doug Ingersoll, and Andrew McClain climbed the 45-degree ice on mile-high, 2-mile-wide Mowich Face, then descended the face on skis—another example of challenges on the big mountain that are being met by the younger generation.

VICE PRESIDENT GORE CLIMBS RAINIER

In August 1999, Vice President Albert Gore and his 15-year-old son Albert III reached the summit of Mount Rainier in a severe windstorm that included hail and lightning. The climb was led by Seattle attorney and mountaineer Jim Frush, president of The American Alpine Club. Under the harsh weather conditions, most other members of the party (including Secret Service men) turned back below the summit.

PARAPLEGIC REACHES SUMMIT

On June 18, 2000, paraplegic climber Pete Rieke, a 45-year-old research chemist from Pasco, Wash., achieved Rainier's summit after two previously failed attempts. With some 40 supporters in several teams, including his wife Wreatha, Rieke's 10-day climb—slowed by high winds and subfreezing temperatures—was made via the steep Kautz Ice Chute Route. Sitting upright in the 65-lb, tracked "snow-pod" he had partly designed and built, he hand-cranked the bicycle-snowmobile hybrid to the top. He previously "cranked" Mount Hood.

Rieke lost the use of his legs in 1994 in a rock-climbing accident.

NOTE; See pages 278-79 for a complete summary of tragedies, 1897 through 1996.

Erline (Anderson) Reber, first woman to ski from the summit (Photo: Yakima Herald)

Bronka Sundstrom, oldest and fastest round-trip by a woman (Photo: Tacoma News-Tribune)

NUMBERS OF CLIMBERS
TO SUMMIT, 1986-1999

Based on author's interpretation of National Park Service records, which vary in format between years. Excluded are routes listed in previous summaries but not attempted during this period. No attempts or no data for route indicated by "–"; attempts without success indicated by "0"

Route	1986-93	1994	1995	1996	1997	1998	1999
Disappointment Cleaver	22,148	3,603	3,738	3,431	2,822	3,706	3,724
Ingraham Glacier Direct	3,478	73	13	181	316	79	154
Gibraltar Ledges	350	36	53	31	229	229	132
Nisqually-Gibraltar Chute	14	0	0	0	1	11	1
Nisqually Ice Cliff	12	0	0	0	0	0	0
Nisqually Icefall	79	0	3	0	11	13	4
Fuhrer Finger	499	59	65	31	139	66	70
Fuhrer Thumb	13	0	0	–	–	–	–
Wilson Headwall	27	0	2	10	3	3	7
Kautz Glacier (cliff/ice chute)	1,678	142	288	146	629	651	446
Kautz Headwall	21	4	0	0	0	0	0
Kautz Cleaver	26	8	0	11	8	21	0
Success Cleaver	51	14	13	17	22	29	17
Tahoma Cleaver	–	–	–	1	4	0	0
Tahoma Glacier	162	11	27	2	64	72	68
Sunset Amphitheater	–	–	0	0	–	–	–
Sunset Ridge	22	0	6	0	16	7	4
Mowich Face (w/variations)	14	5	2	0	4	0	4
Ptarmigan Ridge	19	8	4	0	11	3	11
Liberty Wall	4	–	0	0	0	0	0
Liberty Ridge	589	88	121	132	158	253	237
Willis Wall (w/variations)	4	0	0	0	0	0	0
Curtis Ridge	10	–	0	0	0	2	0
Russell Cliff	0	0	0	0	2	0	2
Emmons-Winthrop Glacier	6,107	1,063	841	1,128	1,460	2,163	1,987
Guided	13,275	1,899	1,962	2,077	3,184	3,778	3,801
Totals (including guided)	35,348	5,120	5,180	5,121	5,899	7,306	6,868
Little Tahoma	47	36	29	37	104	91	89

(See page 324 for comparison with pre-1986 data.)

Bibliography

REFERENCES CITED

Alpine Roamers: mimeographed annuals of the Alpine Roamers, Wenatchee.

American Alpine Club, 1960, A Climber's Guide to the Cascade and Olympic Mountains of Washington: by a committee of the Cascade Section of the AAC, and based on Fred Beckey's 1949 edition, New York.

——, annually published reports, Accidents in North American Mountaineering: by Safety Committee of AAC, New York.

American Alpine Journal, annually published journals of American Alpine Club, New York.

Bishop, B.C., 1963, Mount Rainier: Testing Ground for Everest: *in* National Geographic Magazine, May, 1963: National Geographic Society, Washington, D.C.

Brockman, C.F., 1952, The Story of Mount Rainier National Park: Mount Rainier Natural History Association, Longmire.

Cascadian (Cascadians, Cascadian Journal), mimeographed annuals of The Cascadians, Yakima.

Coombs, H.A., 1936, The Geology of Mount Rainier National Park: Univ. of Washington Publ. in Geology. v. 3, no. 2.

Crandell, D.R., 1969, The Geologic Story of Mount Rainier: U.S. Geol. Survey Bull. 1292.

——, 1969, Surficial Geology of Mount Rainier National Park, Washington: U.S. Geol. Survey, Bull. 1288.

——, 1971, Postglacial Lahars from Mount Rainier, Washington: U.S. Geol. Survey Prof. Paper 677.

Crandell, D.R., and Waldron, H.H., 1956, A Recent Volcanic Mudflow of Exceptional Dimensions from Mount Rainier, Washington: Am. Jour. Science, v. 254, no. 6, pp. 349–362.

Crandell, D.R., and Fahnestock, R.K., 1965, Rockfalls and Avalanches from Little Tahoma Peak on Mount Rainier, Washington: U.S. Geol. Survey Bull. 1221–A.

Crandell, D.R., and Mullineaux, D.R., 1967, Volcanic Hazards at Mount Rainier, Washington: U.S. Geol. Survey Bull. 1238.

Emmons, S.F., 1879, The Volcanoes of the Pacific Coast of the United States, *in* Jour. Amer. Geog. Society, vol. 9, pp. 45–65.

Fisk, R.S., Hopson, C.A., and Waters, A.C., 1963, Geology of Mount Rainier National Park, Washington: U.S. Geol. Survey Prof. Paper 444.

Haines, A.L., 1962, Mountain Fever: Oregon Historical Society, Portland.

Harvard Mountaineering: annually published journals of the Harvard Mountaineering Club, Cambridge.

Hopson, C.A., Waters, A.C., Bender, V.R., and Rubin, Meyer, 1962, The Latest Eruptions from Mount Rainier Volcano: Jour. Geology, v. 70, no. 6, pp. 635–647.

Ingraham, E.S., 1895, The Pacific Forest Reserve and Mt. Rainier—A Souvenir: privately published in limited number, Seattle.

Kautz, A.V., 1875, Ascent of Mount Rainier: Overland Monthly, v. 14, May, 1875, pp. 393–403.

Mazama: annually published journals of the Mazamas, Portland.

Meany, E.S., 1916, Mount Rainier: A Record of Exploration: Binfords and Mort, Portland.

Meier, M.F., 1966, Some Glaciological Interpretations of Remapping Programs on South Cascade, Nisqually, and Klawatti Glaciers, Washington: *in* Canadian Journal of Earth Sciences, v. 3, no. 6, paper 9, pp. 811–818.

Mountaineer, The: annually published journal of The Mountaineers, Seattle.

Moxham, R.M., 1970, Thermal Surveillance of Volcanoes, in Prediction of Volcanic Eruptions, T. Minikami, editor: UNESCO, Paris.

Mullineaux, D.R., Sigafoos, R.S., and Hendricks, E.L., 1969, A Historic Eruption of Mount Rainier, Washington: U.S. Geol. Survey Prof. Paper 650–D, pp. D15–D18.

Rebuffat, Gaston, 1957, Starlight and Storm: E.P. Dutton and Co., Inc., New York.

Rescue Rucksack: mimeographed newsletters of Tacoma Unit, Mountain Rescue Council, a member of Mountain Rescue Association.

Richardson, Donald, 1968, Glacier Outburst Floods in the Pacific Northwest: U.S. Geol. Survey Prof. Paper 600–D, pp. D79–D86.

Russell, I.C., 1898, Glaciers of Mount Rainier: U.S. Geol. Survey 18th Annual Report, 1896–97, part 2, pp. 349–415.

Scaylea, Josef, 1968, Moods of the Mountain: Superior Publishing Co., Seattle.

Scott, R.F., 1913, Scott's Last Expedition, The Journals of Captain R.F. Scott: Beacon Press, Boston.

Sierra Club Bulletin: annually published journals of the Sierra Club, San Francisco.

Summit: internationally distributed mountaineering magazine, generally 10 issues per year, Big Bear Lake, Calif.

Vancouver, George, 1801, A Voyage of Discovery to the North Pacific and 'Round the World: vol. 2, London.

Veatch, F.M., 1969, Analysis of a 24-Year Photographic Record of Nisqually Glacier, Mount Rainier National Park, Washington: U.S. Geol. Survey Prof. Paper 631.

Williams, J.H., 1911, The Mountain That Was God: G.P. Putnam's Sons, New York; John H. Williams, Tacoma.

Willis, Bailey, 1883, Canyons and Glaciers—A Journey to the Ice-Fields of Mount Tacoma: in The Northwesterner, vol. 1, no. 2, April 1883.

OTHER SUGGESTED READING

Beckey, Fred, 1986, Cascade Alpine Guide: Columbia River to Stevens Pass: The Mountaineers, Seattle.

——, 1969, Challenge of the North Cascades: The Mountaineers, Seattle.

Harrison, A.E., 1960, Exploring Glaciers with a Camera: Sierra Club, San Francisco.

Hazard, J.T., 1932, Snow Sentinels of the Pacific Northwest: Lowman and Hanford, Seattle.

Kirk, Ruth, 1968, Exploring Mount Rainier: Univ. of Washington Press, Seattle; maps by Dee Molenaar; flower drawings by Yoshi Nishihara.

Manning, Harvey, and Spring, Ira, second edition, 1978, 50 Hikes in Mount Rainier National Park: The Mountaineers, Seattle: photos by Bob and Ira Spring; maps by Marge Mueller.

Orlob, Helen, 1963, Mountain Rescues: Thomas Nelson and Sons, New York.

Peters, Ed (ed.), fourth edition, 1982, Mountaineering: The Freedom of the Hills: The Mountaineers, Seattle.

Prater, Gene, 1975, Snow Trails: The Mountaineers, Seattle.

Rusk, C.E., 1924, revised 1978, Tales of a Western Mountaineer: The Mountaineers, Seattle.

Schmoe, Floyd, 1925, Our Greatest Mountain: A Handbook for Mount Rainier National Park: G.P. Putnam's Sons, New York.

————, 1959, revised 1979, A Year in Paradise: The Mountaineers, Seattle.

Scott, J.D., 1969, We Climb High—A Thumbnail Chronology of the Mazamas, 1894–1964: The Mazamas, Portland.

Stagner, Howard, 1966, Behind the Scenery of Mount Rainier National Park: Mount Rainier Natural History Association, Longmire.

Sterling, E.M., third edition, 1983, Trips and Trails 2: The Mountaineers, Seattle; photos by Bob and Ira Spring; maps by Marge Mueller.

Weldon, Robert, and Potts, M.K., 1966, Guide to the Trails of Mount Rainier National Park: Mount Rainier Natural History Association, Longmire.

MAPS

Mount Rainier National Park, Washington: U.S. Geological Survey topographic quadrangle, scale 1 inch to mile, 100-foot contour intervals, first issued 1913, revised 1934 and 1955.

Mount Rainier National Park, Washington: painted oblique aerial view of the mountain and Park landscape, 24 by 34 inches, painted and published by Dee Molenaar, 1965 (P.O. Box 62, Burley, Washington, 98322).

PHOTO CREDITS

Photos are listed by page number for each photographer if known and/or donor. Where a page has more than one photo credit, photo numbers include letters, in sequence from left and top to bottom, beginning with "a."

Thomas J. Abercrombie (National Geographic Society staff) 310d; Wolf Bauer 124a; Charles Bell 144; Binfords and Mort, Publishers (E.S. Meany's *Mount Rainier—A Record of Exploration*) 40b, 41a, 46, 270a(?); Norman Bishop (National Park Service) 188, 189; Lucille Borrow 125c; Mrs. Calder T. Bressler 271a; William J. Butler 296b; C. Frank Brockman 41a; Arnie Campbell 125b; Chuck Crenchaw 271b; Harry B. Cunningham 293a; Asahel Curtis, Jr. 289b; Ome Daiber 249b; Dan Davis 307d; Doug Devin 180; Mrs. George T. Dockery 271c; Delmar Fadden 250; Mrs. George Gilbert 249a, 250, 270b; Ralph Guelfi 190; Dr. and Mrs. Raymond S. Haupert 270c; Mrs. Joseph T. (Margaret) Hazard 289a; Jack Hossack 124b; Gene Jack 298; Martha S. Kerr 41c; Jean Landry 155, 157; Cornelius "K" Molenaar 305b; Dee Molenaar 10, 173, 181a, 182a, 209, 282, 300, 302, 304b, 306a,b, 307a,b,c,e,f, 308a,b, 309a,c, 310a,c,e,f; The Mountaineers 125a, 196, 289a; National Park Service 32, 33a, 60, 91, 181b, 190, 242, 249b; Oregon Historical Society 40b; Austin S. Post (U.S. Geological Survey) 13, 69, 90, 99, 118, 145; George Purdy 182b, Rainier National Park Company 61, 70, 72, 238, 291, 293, 296a, 297, 299; Gary Rose 306c; George R. Senner 304a, 305a; Sierra Club 40a; Bob and Ira Spring 310b; Len and Judy Waller 309; Bradford Washburn 298; Bob Weber 300; Jim Wickwire 166, 307, 308c,d,e; Edith Maring Willey (watercolors by C.C. Maring) 56.

ADDENDUM CREDITS
Dee Molenaar 319; Ed LaChapelle 341a; Diepenbrock family 341b.
Modern guide photos provided by RMI guides.

Index

INDEX TO ADDENDUM